Formal Matters

Also by New Academia Publishing

Cinema

MOSCOW BELIEVES IN TEARS: Russians and Their Movies, by Louis Menashe

AMERICA REFLECTED: Language, Satire, Film, and the National Mind, by Peter C. Rollins

HERETICAL EMPIRICISM, by Pier Paolo Pasolini

PIER PAOLO PASOLINI: In Living Memory, edited by Ben Lawton and Maura Bergonzoni

EVERY STEP A STRUGGLE: Interviews with Seven Who Shaped the African-American Image in Movies, by Frank Manchel

IMAGING RUSSIA 2000: Film and Facts, by Anna Lawton

BEFORE THE FALL: Soviet Cinema in the Gorbachev Years, by Anna Lawton

Popular Culture/ Visual Culture

TERROR ON THE SCREEN: Witnesses and the Reanimation of Terrorism as Image Event, Popular Culture and Pornography, by Luke Howie

SCIENCE FICTION EXPERIENCE, by Angela Ndalianis

PASSION AND PERCEPTION: Essays on Russian Culture, by Richard Stites

SUPER/HEROES: From Hercules to Superman, edited by Wendy Haslem, Angela Ndalianis, and Chris Mackie

SHOPPING FOR JESUS: Faith in Marketing in the USA, Dominic Janes, ed.

REMEMBERING UTOPIA: The Culture of Everyday Life in Socialist Yugoslavia, edited by Breda Luthar and Maruša Pušnik

RUSSIAN FUTURISM: A History, by Vladimir Markov

WORDS IN REVOLUTION: Russian Futurist Manifestoes 1912-1928
A. Lawton and H. Eagle, eds., trs.

Read an excerpt at: www.newacademia.com

Formal Matters:

Studies in Film Adaptation and (Re)Evaluation

Bert Cardullo

Washington DC

Copyright © 2011 by Bert Cardullo

New Academia Publishing, 2011

All rights reserved. No part of this book may be reproduced or transmitted in any form or by any means, electronic or mechanical, including photocopying, recording, or by any information storage and retrieval system.

Printed in the United States of America

Library of Congress Control Number: 2011934733
ISBN 978-0-9836899-2-8 paperback (alk. paper)

New Academia Publishing
P.O. Box 27420, Washington, DC, 20038-7420
info@newacademia.com - www.newacademia.com

AUTHOR'S CONTACT INFORMATION:
email: robertcardullo@yahoo.com; robert.cardullo@ieu.edu.tr

Contents

Introduction: The Necessary Film, or Criticism Matters	vii
Part I. ADAPTATION STUDIES	1
Theatrical Melodrama, Dramatic Film, and the Rise of American Cinema: The Case of Griffith's *Way Down East*	3
Drama into Film and Filmic Drama: The Cases of *The Little Foxes*, *Betrayal*, *Edmond*, and *Henry V*	17
Pride and Prejudice, or Class and Character: *Room at the Top* Revisited	49
Fiction into Film: Tolstoy's *The Counterfeit Note* and Bresson's *L'Argent*; Dostoevsky's *A Gentle Spirit* and Bresson's *Une Femme douce*	63
High Infidelity: Sergei Bodrov's Film Adaptation of Tolstoy's "Prisoner of the Caucasus" (on *Prisoner of the Mountains*)	87
Literature Become Cinema: Notes on Three Emblematic Adaptations (*The Remains of the Day*, *The Dead*, and *Dangerous Liaisons*)	99
The Theater-of-Film of Hans-Jürgen Syberberg	121
Part II. CONTEMPORARY CINEMA IN (RE)VIEW	137
Suffer the Children (on Andrei Kravchuk's *The Italian* and Bahman Ghobadi's *Turtles Can Fly*)	139
Engendering Genre (on Lajos Koltai's *Fateless*, Hong Sang-soo's *Woman Is the Future of Man*, Carlos Reygadas's *Battle in Heaven*, and Julia Loktev's *Day Night Day Night*)	157
Westward Faux (on David Jacobson's *Down in the Valley*, John Hillcoat's *The Proposition*, and Ang Lee's *Brokeback Mountain*)	183
Odd Couples, or Unelected Affinities (on Bent Hamer's *Kitchen Stories*, Patrice Chéreau's *Son Frère* and *Gabrielle*, and Roger Michell's *Enduring Love*)	197

Serious Sex (on Ziad Doueiri's *Lila Says*, Pawel Pawlikowski's *My Summer of Love*, Laurent Cantet's *Heading South*, and Claude Chabrol's *The Bridesmaid*) ... 213

Windows on the World (on Mahamat-Saleh Haroun's *Abouna* and Ferzan Özpetek's *Facing Windows*) ... 233

A World on Film (on Hassan Yektapanah's *Djomeh*, Frieder Schlaich's *Otomo*, Tsai Ming-liang's *Goodbye Dragon Inn*, Pedro Almodóvar's *Bad Education*, and Catherine Breillat's *Sex Is Comedy*) ... 243

Part III. CLASSIC CINEMA (RE)CLASSIFIED ... 255

Without a Prayer: *Vengeance Is Mine* and the Cinema of Shohei Imamura ... 257

Modish Artifice versus Modern Art: Alain Resnais's *Last Year at Marienbad* in Light of Michelangelo Antonioni's *L'eclisse* ... 271

Re-reading the Rules: Jean Renoir's *La Règle du jeu* Reconsidered ... 285

All That Glitters: The Early Film Career of John Schlesinger (on *A Kind of Loving*, *Billy Liar*, and *Darling*) ... 299

Carl Dreyer's *Day of Wrath* and the Spirit of Tragedy ... 313

Same Time, Different Children (on Mrinal Sen's *The Case Is Closed* and Miguel Littin's *Alsino and the Condor*) ... 327

Mind over Medium (on Bo Widerberg's *Elvira Madigan*, Mike Nichols' *Carnal Knowledge*, Peter Bogdanovich's *The Last Picture Show*, Martin Scorsese's *Mean Streets*, John Hancock's *Bang the Drum Slowly*, Frank Perry's *Last Summer*, Robert Altman's *McCabe and Mrs. Miller*, Sydney Pollack's *They Shoot Horses, Don't They?*, Terrence Malick's *Badlands*, and George Roy Hill's *Slaughterhouse-Five*) ... 337

General Bibliography ... 375
Film Credits ... 381
Notes ... 405
Index ... 413

Introduction

The Necessary Film, or Criticism Matters

Film editing, or the instantaneous replacement of one moving visual field with another, was once not part of our daily experience. So nothing in 400 million years of vertebrate evolution prepared us for the visual assault of cinema. But amazingly enough, the process succeeded and we became accommodated to the idea of motion pictures. Even more, a mysterious extra meaning was gained from the juxtaposition of two images that was not present in either of the shots themselves. In short, we discovered that the human mind was predisposed to cinematic grammar as if it were an entirely natural, inborn language. Perhaps it is inborn, because we spend one-third of our lives in the nightly world of dreams. There, images are fragmented and different realities collide abruptly with what seems to have great meaning. In this way we can see film editing as, probably unwittingly, employing the power and means of dream.

For many millions of years, then, human beings were apparently carrying within them the ability to respond to film and were unconsciously awaiting its arrival in order to employ their dream-faculty more fully. Some of us have long believed that, through more recent centuries, theater artists and audiences themselves had also been longing for the film to be invented even without a clue that there could be such a medium. Many tricks of stagecraft in those centuries (particularly the nineteenth) were, without knowing it, attempting to be cross-cuts and superimpositions, or double exposures. Some dramatists even imagined their work in forms and perspectives that anticipated the birth of the cinema (most notably, and excitingly, Georg Büchner in *Danton's Death* [1835]). In his essay "Dickens, Griffith, and the Film Today," Sergei

Eisenstein shows how the novel itself—specifically, the novels of Charles Dickens—provided D. W. Griffith with a number of cinematic techniques, including equivalents to fades, dissolves, the breakdown into shots, and the concept of parallel editing. These novelistic and theatrical attempts at prognostication a few centuries earlier are puny stuff, though, because for millions of years homo sapiens had been subliminally prepared for the intricacies of film, had indeed been getting ready for them every night. Indeed, in a sense the last century, the mere centenary of film's existence, was the emotional and psychological goal of the ages—and continues to be into the twenty-first century.

When the first moving picture flashed onto a screen, the double life of all human beings thus became intensified. That double life consists, on the one hand, of actions and words and surfaces, and, on the other, of secrets and self-knowledges or self-ignorances, self-ignorings. That double life has been part of man's existence ever since art and religion were invented to make sure that he became aware of it. In the past 150 years or so, religion has receded further and further as revealer of that double life, and art has taken over more and more of the function; when film art came along, it made that revelation of doubleness inescapable, in fact more attractive. To wit: on the screen are facts, which at the same time are symbols; for this reason, they invoke doubleness at every moment, in every kind of picture. They stir up the concealments in our lives, both those concealments we like and those we don't like; they shake our histories, our hopes, and our heartbreaks into consciousness. Not completely, by any means. (Who could stand it?) And not more grandly or deeply than do the other arts. But more quickly and surely, because these facts, these symbols, do their stirring and shaking with visuals as well as with motion, serially and cumulatively.

Think of this process as applying to every frame of film and it is clear that when we sit before a screen, we run risks unprecedented in human history. A poem may or may not touch us; a play or novel may never get near us. But movies are inescapable. (In the case of poor films, we often have the sensation of fighting our way *out* of them.) When two screen lovers kiss, in any picture, that kiss has a minimum inescapability that is stronger than in other arts—both as an action before us and a metaphor for the "kissingness" in our own lives. Each of us is pinned privately to such a kiss in some degree of pleasure or pain or enlightenment. In romances or tragedies, in period films or modern dramas, in musical comedies or historical epics, in Westerns or farces, our beings—kissing or otherwise—are in some measure summoned up before us, in our own private visions. And I'd like to suggest that the fundamental way, conscious or not, in which we determine the quality of a film is by the degree to which the re-experiencing of ourselves coincides with our pride, our shames, our hopes, our honor.

Finally, it follows, distinctions among movies arise from the way they please or displease us with ourselves: not *whether* they please or displease but *how*. This is true, I believe, in every art today; it is not a cinema monopoly. But in the cinema it has become more true more swiftly and decisively because film has a much smaller heritage of received aesthetics to reassess; because film is bound more closely to the future than other arts seem to be (the reason is that, by its very episodic or "journeying" form, film reflects for viewers the belief that the world is a place in which man can leave the past behind and create his own future); and because film confronts us so immediately, so seductively, and so shockingly (especially on the larger-than-life screen) with at least some of the truth about what we have been doing with ourselves. To the extent that film exposes the viewer to this truth about himself, in his experience of the world or of fantasy, in his options for action or for privacy, to the extent that he can thus accept a film as worthy of himself or better than himself—to that extent a film is necessary to him. And it is that necessity, I am arguing, that ultimately sets its value.

Throughout history, two factors have formed people's taste in any art, their valuing of it, that is: knowledge of that art and knowledge of life. Obviously this is still true, but the function of taste seems to be altering. As formalist aesthetic canons have come to seem less and less tenable, standards in art and life have become more and more congruent, and as a result the function of taste is increasingly the selection and appraisal of the works that are most valuable—and most necessary—to the individual's very existence. So our means for evaluating films naturally become more and more involved with our means for evaluating experience; aesthetic standards don't become identical with standards in life but they are certainly related—and, one hopes, somewhat braver.

Of course the whole process means that human beings feed on themselves, on their own lives variously rearranged by art, as a source of values. But despite other prevalent beliefs about the past connected with theology and religion, we are coming to see that people have always been the source of their own values. In the century in which this responsibility, this liberation, became increasingly apparent—the twentieth—the intellect of man simultaneously provided a new art form, the film, to make the most of it.

That art form is obviously still with us, and now, in the twenty-first century, more than ever, it seems. And its critics proliferate in number, in part because of what I describe above: the "personal" element involved in the watching of any movie, and the ease nowadays with which, through the Internet, one can communicate that personal response to others. If, as Oscar Wilde once said, "Criticism is the highest form of autobiography"—because only by "intensifying his own personality" could the critic interpret the personality and work of others—then film criticism must be an even higher form.

What follows, in *Formal Matters: Studies in Film Adaptation and (Re)Evaluation*, is precisely such "autobiographical" criticism on my part, on what I consider to be some of the most necessary of necessary films—and film artists. The book is arranged thematically into three sections (with some inevitable overlap between those sections), from an investigation of the adaptation of both drama and fiction into film, to a consideration of some representative samples from the contemporary cinema, to a (re)classification of classics like *La Règle du jeu*, *L'eclisse*, and *Vengeance Is Mine*. Along the way, the reader will also find essays on such prominent French directors as Robert Bresson and Alain Resnais, as well as a meditation on the relationship among the cinema, memory, and criticism. All of these pieces are supplemented by a bibliography of related criticism, film credits, and a thoroughgoing index.

One purpose of *Formal Matters: Studies in Film Adaptation and (Re)Evaluation* is to stake out territory for a certain type of film critic, somewhere between a reviewer-journalist and a scholar-theorist. At a time when the movie review has degenerated into mere publicity for Hollywood pictures and film scholarship has become entangled in its own pseudo-scientific discourse, the author offers close readings of individual films, and film adaptations, that go beyond simple plot summaries and vague impressions about acting (the province of the newspaper review), on the one hand, yet that pull up short of oracular theoretical pronouncements on the state of the art (the province of the academic monograph), on the other hand. The essays contained in *Formal Matters* are thus acts of analysis and interpretation in the humanistic senses of those words, not gaseous musings or pedantic tracts. With elegance, clarity, and rigor, the author tries ever to demonstrate that the cinema *means* as well as shows, and his ultimate aim is to explain how moviemakers—be they adaptors, *auteurs*, or both—use the resources of the medium to pursue complex, significant human goals.

For this reason, *Formal Matters: Studies in Film Adaptation and (Re)Evaluation* is aimed at the educated or cultivated moviegoer as well as college students and professors. In addition to the general or common reader, students and teachers of university-level courses in movie criticism, media studies, international cinema, and independent film ought to find this book enlightening and helpful. It is *not* intended for the reader who is looking for a consumer guide to the movies, on the one hand; nor, on the other hand, is *Formal Matters* an erudite scholarly tome targeted only at a limited audience of specialists. Instead, it offers a refreshing, humanistic alternative to both the facile, stargazing monographs that one can find in any chain bookstore and the arcane academic publications that deal with phenomenology, historiography, the politics of gender, race, and class, and the cognitive dissection of film style and technique. The *film's* the thing, after all—the formal matter at hand.

From a glance at the table of contents in *Formal Matters*, the reader will quickly discover not only that a number of the films treated are European or Asian, but also that many of them—including the American ones—are "art films." I say "including the American ones" because by about 1920, long after American films had cornered the world market, a rough, debatable, but persistent generalization had come into being: America made entertainment movies (like Griffith's 1920 work *Way Down East*, treated here), while Europe (and later the rest of the world) made art films. Even back then some observers knew that there were great exceptions on both sides of that generalization, particularly the second part. (*Every* filmmaking country makes entertainment movies; they are the major portion of every nation's industry. But no country's entertainment movies have had the success of American pictures.) That generalization has become increasingly suspect as it has become increasingly plain that good entertainment films cannot be made by the ungifted; further, that some directors of alpine talent have spent their whole careers making works of entertainment.

Nonetheless, for compact purposes here, the terms "entertainment" and "art" can serve to distinguish between those films, however well made and aesthetically rewarding, whose original purpose was to pass the time; and those films, however poorly made and aesthetically pretentious, whose original purpose was the illumination of experience and the extension of consciousness. In this view, the generalization about American and European films has some validity—less than was assumed for decades, still some validity. And that validity has determined the make-up of the collection of pieces in *Formal Matters*. Which is to say that I write mainly about films made beyond American borders; and the relatively small number of American pictures I do write about, almost without exception, are art films.

To be sure, I wish there were more such American films, but the nature of movie production in the United States—which is almost totally commercial and unsubsidized—prevents their creation. There was some hope, during the late 1960s and early 1970s, that this situation would change due to the collapse of the Hollywood studio system, the increase in foreign-film importation (and therefore foreign influence), the soaring expense of moviemaking, and the rise of the independent, "personal" film (to satisfy, as it were, the increasing number of "personal" critics such as Pauline Kael, Andrew Sarris, and Dwight MacDonald). However, American filmmakers soon learned that "independent" means independent only of the old assembly line. Indeed, in some ways the new system is more harried, less self-confident, than the old studio procedure where picture-people knew precisely what they were doing, or thought they did, and for whom they were doing it.

Put another way, independent production now means that, for

each project, a producer not only needs to acquire a script and director and actors and facilities and distribution, he also has to acquire an audience—possibly a different audience for each film he produces, or at least not a relatively dependable general, homogeneous audience as in the past. No longer, then, is there any resemblance in the movie industry to a keeper throwing fish to trained seals. Making motion pictures is now much more like publishing books: each venture is a separate business enterprise, a separate risk and search. And the moment "personal" films don't make any money, they stop getting made in large numbers—as they have already done in comparison with the period of the late '60s and early '70s, when we saw such personal (and in some cases hugely moneymaking) pictures as *Easy Rider, The Hired Hand, Five Easy Pieces, Wanda, The Conversation, Badlands, Bonnie and Clyde, Alice's Restaurant, The Wild Bunch, The Rain People, The Graduate, Midnight Cowboy*, and many more.

The operative term at the start of the previous sentence is "money." The operative term in this book, by contrast, is "art." I have nothing against money (who really does?), but I like my art divorced from it, or divorced from dependence on it, as much as possible. I hope the reader will agree and read on with pleasure—as well as profit.

Bert Cardullo,
Izmir University of Economics, Turkey

Part I

ADAPTATION STUDIES

1

Theatrical Melodrama, Dramatic Film, and the Rise of American Cinema: The Case of Griffith's *Way Down East*

Among the films of D. W. Griffith (1875-1948), *The Birth of a Nation* (1915) and *Intolerance* (1916) are the most famous and, justly, the most praised. Lower in this group is the status of *Way Down East* (1920), but for me it is a picture of persistent strength and of exceptional interest in American cultural history. *Way Down East* was made from a highly successful stage play of the same name, written by Lottie Blair Parker, Joseph R. Grismer, and William A. Brady, which had its premiere at Newport, Rhode Island, on September 3, 1897, and was performed around the United States for more than twenty years. The Parker-Grismer-Brady play came at the end of a century in which the form of melodrama had dominated the American theater—so much so that it spawned several types, such as the rural melodrama of *Way Down East*.

What is a melodrama? The term has often been defined—it is one of the easier dramatic terms to define—but for my purposes I will try one more definition. Melodrama is a dramatic form using monochromatic characters and usually involving physical danger to the "good" protagonist, who is engaged in an external conflict with evil of one kind or another. The single essential ingredient in this recipe is earthly justice. A "straight" drama may merely imply justice or may end in irony at the absence of it; in tragedy, justice, if it comes at all, may come in the hereafter (if *it* comes at all). In melodrama, by contrast, justice may be slow but it is sure, and it is always seen to be done.

By implication, then, melodrama is an artistic strategy designed, *and desired*, to reconcile its audience to the way things are. In the nineteenth century its chief aim was to support the economic and moral system—a great deal was made in these plays of the "poor but honest" theme together with its companion, the "rich but exploitative" motif. (Today, melodrama supports different conventional ideas, as in the case of David Mamet's movie *House of Games* [1987] if not the much earlier film of Lillian Hellman's *The Little Foxes* [1941], which takes place at the same time as *Way Down East* but emphasizes almost exclusively the rapaciousness or acquisitiveness of the "haves.") Many thousands of farmers saw the play *Way Down East* in the years that it toured the country, and they must have known that this idyllic, Currier-and-Ives version of their lives was a long way from brute fact, but the fiction gave them two compensations: escape from the harshness and unpredictability of agricultural reality, and roles in which to imagine themselves outside the theater. As Eric Bentley once put it, "Melodrama is the naturalism of the dream life" (205).

Nowadays it may be necessary to explain the title of this play/film. "Down East" is an old phrase used to describe the farthest reaches of New England, particularly Maine, which at its tip is considerably east of Boston. The picture tells the entire story chronologically of innocent Anna Moore (including the portion that occurs before the play and is revealed there only through exposition), who lives with her mother "way down east" in the New England village of Belden. When they get into financial difficulties, the country girl goes, at her mother's request, to seek help from their rich and fashionable relatives in Boston, the Tremonts. Mrs. Tremont and her snobbish daughters treat her poorly, but Anna attracts the attention of an unscrupulous playboy named Lennox Sanderson. He has his way by tricking her into a false marriage, which he persuades her to keep secret on the ground that the revelation would anger his father (from whom he derives his support). Back home in her Maine village, Anna obeys until she becomes pregnant, at which time she asks to be publicly recognized as Mrs. Sanderson. The womanizer responds by telling her the truth and then leaving her to cope as best she can.

Some time later, Anna's mother dies, and Anna takes refuge in a rooming house in Belden, where her baby dies soon after its birth. Turned out by her censorious landlady, who suspects that she has no husband, Anna pitifully takes to the road with her few

Way Down East, dir. D. W. Griffith, 1920

possessions to look for work. She finds a position at the Bartlett farm, near Bartlett village, despite the reservations of Squire Bartlett about hiring someone whose past he and his family do not know. Anna proves her virtue through hard work (how else?), and the squire's son, David, falls in love with her. But when he declares himself, she tells him, without disclosing the reason, that nothing will ever be possible between them. As coincidence would have it (*has* to have it), the "reason"—Lennox Sanderson—lives nearby on a country estate. He soon discovers that Anna is on the Bartlett place and urges her to move on; she tries to obey what the society of her time would have perceived as a male superior, but the Bartletts, who know nothing of the Sanderson matter (though they know him), persuade their "hired girl" to remain.

The plot begins building to its crisis when, some months later, Maria Poole, the Belden landlady, visits Bartlett Village, sees Anna, and tells her story to the local gossip, Martha Perkins. After Martha relays the news to the squire, he goes to Belden to confirm it; when he learns that the story is true, he returns home that night and orders

Anna out of his house during a blinding snowstorm. She leaves, but not before denouncing Sanderson, who that very evening is an honored guest at the Bartlett house. Sanderson is thereupon attacked by David Bartlett and shown the door; then David goes out into the storm to find Anna. Hysterical and grief-stricken, she has collapsed on a frozen river just as the ice is beginning to break up in the spring thaw. When David finds her, Anna is being carried downstream on an ice cake toward the falls, yet he manages to follow her from floe to floe and complete his rescue right before she reaches the brink. Himself forgiving, the Squire now begs Anna's forgiveness as well, which she graciously grants; Sanderson offers to marry her authentically but is scornfully refused; and the film of *Way Down East* ends happily with the wedding of David and Anna.

Following Bernard Beckerman's lead (171) and distinguishing between "plot," which conventionally signifies the sequence of actions or events in a play, and "story," which designates all incidents and activities that occur before, after, *and* during the play—offstage as well as onstage—I should presently like to examine Griffith's adaptation of dramatic techniques to film and to consider his reasons for telling Anna Moore's story chronologically or episodically as opposed to climactically. The screenplay that Griffith used, the majority of which he himself wrote, is a model of the film adaptation of plays, in the sheerly technical sense. Much of the formal beauty of play design, as he surely knew, arises from limitation: the necessity to limit action and to arrange necessary combinations of characters on the stage. The skill with which these matters are handled can be a pleasure in itself, as well as positive enrichment of the drama. But this skill is not essential to the screenplay, which has infinitely greater freedom of physical and temporal movement, can unfold intertwined material into serial form, and can run virtually parallel actions. The contrast can easily be seen if the Parker-Grismer-Brady play script and the movie scenario by Griffith and Anthony Paul Kelly are placed alongside each other.

That movie scenario, it must be remembered, was written during the silent era. That is, even if the director had wanted simply to film the play as it stood, he would have been unable to do so without the heavy use of titles. This is because Anna's past is revealed through dialogue in the play, which has a late point of attack and therefore begins when she arrives at Bartlett Village in Maine looking for work—after her baby has died and she has been evicted from Maria Poole's rooming house. It is Lennox Sanderson's discovery of Anna on Squire Bartlett's farm, then, that provokes the drama of the Parker-Grismer-Brady play. Griffith, however, must tell Anna's story long before this occurrence: through pictures (and the discreet use of titles), and beginning with this country girl's visit to Boston.

Beyond the merely descriptive or illustrative images of his narrative, Griffith uses nature to evoke characters' inner states where a drama would use, for instance, the soliloquy; he also uses nature as a silent but expressive character. An example of the latter "use" occurs when Anna is thrown out by her landlady, after her baby's death: there is a lovely long shot of Anna starting down a country road, her few possessions in a box under her arm, and this shot bitterly contrasts the beauty of the countryside with this young woman's sorry state. Indeed, the environment underlines Anna's desolation by seeming to overwhelm her—a tiny figure by contrast who becomes even smaller as she walks away from the camera. Shots of nature are used differently, to endorse a character's feelings, in at least two instances in *Way Down East*. In one, Anna meets with David Bartlett near a waterfall that pours into a gleaming, tranquil river, which reflects the couple's contentment even as the cascade represents the passion surging inside them. Similarly, during the storm sequence there is a powerful congruence between the raging blizzard and Anna's turbulent feelings as she wanders all alone at night.

There is plenty of suspense by the time we get to the snowstorm, but what about early in the film? The sources of tension in the play *Way Down East* are the gradual revelation of Anna's certain secret and the definition of her relationship with Lennox Sanderson. But these tensions disappear in the movie because we follow Anna from her very first meeting with Sanderson, after she has arrived in Boston from rural Maine to visit her wealthy aunt. (One big advantage of the film's method, though, is that Griffith can give Anna the experience of betrayal and loss of her child "onstage," thus making her a differently seen, more sympathetic character by the time she reaches the point of what was her first entrance in the play.) Perhaps believing that an equivalent of dramatic suspense would be necessary to hold the audience's interest in his chronological tale of Anna's ordeal, Griffith creates tension in the first half of the film, before his heroine leaves Boston, through *visual* means in addition to creating literal visual tension.

The first type is produced when, several times, a scene from life on Squire Bartlett's farm is inserted into or intercut with the action in Boston. Griffith knew he had the problem of establishing the Bartlett home and his male romantic lead before Anna reaches them—about half an hour into the story. (In the play of *Way Down East*, the reverse is true: Anna does not arrive at the Bartlett farm until fairly late in the first act, most of which is spent introducing David Bartlett and his parents as well as some local types.) So he solved the problem with a device deliberately borrowed from the Dickensian novel: he inserts the title "Chapter Two . . . Bartlett Village" and proceeds to give us glimpses of the place and its most prominent family. We do not know that this is where Anna will eventually seek refuge and find salvation through David, but we assume that the director is showing us these scenes for a purpose that will become clear. In fact, the lack of clarity is itself an enticement, and we eagerly anticipate an explanation of the presence of the Bartletts and their farm in the movie.

Literal visual tension is created in the film of *Way Down East* in two ways. Life in the sophisticated city, in Boston, is filled with verticals—tall doorways, spiral staircases, high ceilings—whereas life in simple, bucolic Maine, in the inserted country scenes, is composed mainly of horizontals—the long porch of the Bartlett family house, the flat land, the background action that crosses the screen from right to left (as when the sheriff drives his horse-drawn wagon up to the farm's gated entrance). In addition to this horizontal-vertical juxtaposition, there is the larger, even more striking one of outdoors against indoors. Almost all the shots of the country in the first half of *Way Down East* take place outside, in the fresh air and sunlight. By contrast, all the shots of the city occur indoors, in darkened, smoke-filled rooms. The atmosphere in Boston is frenetic: there seemingly are round-the-clock parties. The inhabitants of Bartlett village, for their part, are so relaxed that some of them even fall asleep during the day. (This may explain the otherwise curious shot of David in bed on a sunny afternoon, starting suddenly from sleep only when Anna, as yet unknown to him, is entering into the bogus marriage with Sanderson miles away.)

With the aid of such visual tension, Griffith could film the whole of Anna's story, as opposed to solely the plot of the play, and doing that gave him one large advantage: he could make it appear less melodramatic, or, better, he could enhance the *realism* of the melodrama, of its settings and actions. Clearly, Anna is enmeshed in Manichean circumstances in the movie, but, just as clearly, she passes through them, and *we see her do so*. Although she is victimized by Sanderson on account of her rustic innocence, Anna struggles to make her own destiny: she endures the disgrace (at the time) of giving birth out of wedlock and the grief of her baby's death, then creates a new life for herself through hard work at Squire Bartlett's farm. Circumstance intervenes again in the persons of her erstwhile seducer and of her former landlady, who, with Martha Perkins' aid, betrays Anna's past to the squire. And again Anna fights against her victimization: she rightly accuses Sanderson of gross deception in front of his neighbors, then defiantly walks out of the farmhouse into the blizzard to end all blizzards.

Because we witnessed Anna's strength and bravery after she was deserted by Sanderson and were not simply told about them, we find those qualities in her here at the end more believable. Because we witnessed Anna's journey from the Maine countryside to Boston, then from there back to Maine and on to Squire Bartlett's farm, we are more willing to view her final foray into the snow as possible escape rather than probable death. In the play of *Way Down East*, we only hear of Anna's incredible rescue; in the film, we see it happen, seemingly without gimmick, and her rescue thus becomes credible. After this, her forgiveness by Squire Bartlett (because she was tricked into immorality) and marriage to David can be only anticlimax, whereas, in the play, they are meant to be epiphany.

I do not mean to imply that Griffith increases the literary value of the Parker-Grismer-Brady script by expanding it in time and space. *Way Down East* is still a melodrama. What he accomplishes, however, in adapting the play to the screen is to point up a significant difference between the two forms. Not the most obvious one—that theater is more verbal and cinema more visual—but the difference in artistic structure and philosophical assumption between drama and film. The paradigm of dramatic structure in the West up to Ibsen in the late nineteenth century, with the exception of Shakespeare and his coevals, had been intensive or Aristotelian—a form in which, philosophically speaking, the protagonist is caught in a highly contracted situation, his end foretold before the plot begins and his range of choice therefore increasingly reduced, for the plot in this case is enmeshed in the toils of a story with a long as well as a weighty past. Film form is by its very nature *extensive*, for the camera can easily extend itself over time and space as it covers the whole of the story, in this way militating against highly compressed circumstances and always leaving possibilities or alternatives open for the characters, insofar as action is concerned. (Shakespeare's plays are often called "cinematic" precisely because their own structure is extensive.)

In adapting *Way Down East* to film, Griffith essentially dropped the intensive structure in which Anna Moore had been trapped (only to be miraculously-cum-melodramatically rescued from it at the last minute by David Bartlett) into an extensive one, with favorable or liberating results for the melodrama as well as for the character of Anna. What Griffith was discovering, along with his audience, was that film not only satisfies a craving for the replication or redemption of physical reality, but also for freedom—from the restrictions of time and place, from the limitations of language, and *from the past*. Action in film is thus more of a journey in the present than a confrontation based on the past—the one filled with possibility or promise, the other with fatalism or foreboding. And if stage melodrama, in which villainy is punished and virtue rewarded, was a last-second escape from the past, melodramatic film is an extended departure from it.

Stage melodrama provided its audiences in the nineteenth century with momentary relief from a world in which man felt himself a prisoner of his past, possibly of his own origins, and where justice was most often *not* done. The myth of such melodrama was that of spiritual redemption by bourgeois standards. Hence Anna is a secular saint, truly good, suffering for the sins and blindness of her fellows, finally undergoing an agony that reveals her purity. She is betrayed in her trust, she goes through travail, she labors in humility, she declines the happiness of David's love because she is unworthy, and she shows that death holds no terror for her. At last she achieves heaven: on earth.

To extend the analogy, the God in the story is the Squire—the owner of the Eden. It is he who at first is about to expel Anna from the Garden, who finds the largesse in his heart to let her remain on trust, and who at last provides the crucial forgiveness—because when she sinned, she did not know it; she was tricked into immortality, though she thought she was behaving rightly. Not only is Anna forgiven, but when she marries David she wears white, her virginity restored by dispensation of the Squire. Here then, in capsule, is sainthood founded on respectability, which was possibly the chief criterion for social survival in the nineteenth century.

But not in the twentieth, and certainly not the twenty-first century. Yet Griffith had a sense of the continuing function of melodrama in a bourgeois, mock-egalitarian society. He also must have had some sense of the pluralistic nature of the public at any given time, the perception that new, even avant-garde, interests can coexist with old, traditional ones. (For instance, I don't think he would have been surprised that, during the 1969–1970 movie season, *Easy Rider* and *Airport* were successes simultaneously.) So in 1920, the same year that O'Neill wrote *Beyond the Horizon*, in which Stravinsky and Satie were already known composers, when Picasso and Matisse themselves were known painters, and two years after the end of a world war that had altered certain traditions and beliefs forever, Griffith paid around $175,000—much more than the entire cost of his *Birth of a Nation*—for the screen rights to a twenty-three-year-old rural melodrama.

Before making his first of many short films in 1908, Griffith himself had had plenty of experience in the theater, a theater that was full of plays like the one by Parker, Grismer, and Brady: he had begun acting in 1897 (the same year, to repeat, in which *Way Down East* was first produced on stage), at the age of twenty-two, with a stock company in his native Kentucky, had struggled in a number of other stock and road companies, then had written a melodrama that had been produced, unsuccessfully, in Washington, D.C., in 1907. Out of this experience, evidently, came the conviction that he knew how to make *Way Down East* "work" and that the postwar public had not shed all its old affinities. And, very clearly, he also understood how film was talking over the form and function of melodrama from the theater, expanding it in the directions toward which it had been moving.

One of those directions included the theater's wishful embrace of cinematic form, not only because of that form's photographic realism, but also because, by its very (expansive) nature, film reflected for melodramatically conditioned spectators in the early twentieth century the belief that the world was a place in which man could leave the past behind and create his own future, where earthly justice for past wrongs would become a moot point—to be left in the past. *Way Down East*, then, represents a landmark in the transition between two worlds: of an intensive play structure and an extensive cinematic one, of Aristotelian drama and Eisensteinian film, of nineteenth-century theater culture and twentieth-century movie magic. It is as if, in filming *Way Down East* after the seminally cinematic *Birth of a Nation* and *Intolerance* and late in the historical process that saw film make over theatrical melodrama, Griffith were going back to mark simultaneously his own beginnings on the nineteenth-century stage and his movement into film in 1908, when, out of theater work, he took a job with the Biograph Company of New York. The rest, to alter the phrase only slightly, is film history.

D. W. GRIFFITH: A CHRONOLOGY

1875: Born in La Grange, near Crestwood, Kentucky, to Jacob "Roaring Jake" Griffith and Mary Perkins Oglesby.

1882: Griffith's father dies.

1889: Moves to Louisville with his mother, who opens a boarding house. The venture soon fails.

1895: Begins appearing as an actor onstage in Louisville.

1906: Marries actress Linda Arvidsen.

1907: James K. Hackett produces Griffith's play *A Fool and a Girl*. It flops drastically.

Begins working as an actor for Edison Studios. His first role is in Edwin S. Porter's *Rescued from an Eagle's Nest*.

1908: Leaves Edison for the struggling Biograph studio for a salary of $5 a day.

Reluctantly directs his first film for Biograph, *The Adventures of Dollie*, after Wallace McCutcheon, the studio's principal director, falls ill. Arthur Marvin is the cameraman. The film premieres on July 14th.

1909: Griffith's *Pippa Passes* becomes the first film to be reviewed in the *New York Times*.

1910: Makes the first of regular visits to California with his film crew to shoot films.

1913: Makes his first feature film, *Judith of Bethulia*.

Leaves Biograph when the studio refuses to allow him to produce feature-length films. With their star director gone—and much of their stock company following him—Biograph immediately goes into decline.

1914: Forms Reliance-Majestic Studios with Harry Aitken and then enters into partnership with Mack Sennett and Thomas Ince in Triangle.

1915: The twelve-reel *Birth of a Nation* premieres in Los Angeles. The film is a sensation despite the controversy provoked by its racist content.

1916: *Intolerance*, Griffith's equally ambitious sequel to *Birth of a Nation*, fails to make a profit despite critical praise.

Issues a pamphlet, *The Rise and Fall of Free Speech in America*, denouncing censors who he claims are slowing the development of film as an art by censoring freedom of expression

1919: Founds United Artists with Mary Pickford, Douglas Fairbanks, and Charles Chaplin.

1921: Griffith's *Dream Street*, the first American feature film with a fully synchronized music-and-effects soundtrack.

1924: Leaves United Artists for Paramount following the failure of *Isn't Life Wonderful?*

1930: *Abraham Lincoln*, Griffith's first full-sound picture, is released.

1931: *The Struggle*, Griffith's final film, is released. It fails to win an audience and is pulled from cinemas after just one week

1936: Woody Van Dyke asks Griffith to help shoot the earthquake sequence for the film *San Francisco*, although he isn't credited for his work.

Divorces Linda Arvidsen twenty-five years after they separated to marry Evelyn Baldwin.

Receives a special Oscar from the Academy of Motion Picture Arts & Sciences for his contributions to film art.

1948: Dies of a cerebral hemorrhage in an ambulance after being discovered unconscious in his room at the Knickerbocker Hotel in Los Angeles.

1950: The Directors' Guild of America provides a stone and bronze monument for Griffith's gravesite at Mount Tabor Methodist Church Graveyard in Centerfield, Kentucky.

1953: The Directors' Guild of America introduces its highest honor, The D. W. Griffith Award.

1975: The U.S. Postal Service issues a ten-cent stamp honoring Griffith.

1980: It is revealed that all but 30 of Griffith's 534 films have been preserved.

1999: The Director's Guild of America President Jack Shea and the DGA National Board announce that the D. W. Griffith Award is to be renamed the DGA Lifetime Achievement Award because his film *Birth of a Nation* had "helped foster intolerable racial stereotypes."

2008: The Hollywood Heritage Museum screens a number of Griffith's earliest films to commemorate the centennial of his first work as a film director.

WORKS CITED and BIBLIOGRAPHY

Allen, Michael. *Family Secrets: The Feature Films of D. W. Griffith*. London: British Film Institute, 1999.

Beckerman, Bernard. *Dynamics of Drama: Theory and Method of Analysis*. 1970. New York: Drama Book Specialists, 1979.

Bentley, Eric. *The Life of the Drama*. New York: Atheneum, 1964.

Brewster, Ben, and Lea Jacobs. *Theatre to Cinema: Stage Pictorialism and the Early Feature Film*. New York: Oxford University Press, 1997.

Fischer, Lucy. "*Way Down East*: Melodrama, Metaphor, and the Maternal Body." In Fisher's *Cinematernity: Film, Motherhood, Genre*. Princeton, N.J.: Princeton University Press, 1996. 56-72.

Gerould, Daniel, ed. *Melodrama*. New York: New York Literary Forum, 1980.

Griffith, D. W. "Moving Pictures Can Get Nothing from the Stage" and "Some Prophecies: Film and Theatre." Excerpted from *The Theatre*, 19 (June 1914): 311-312, 314, 316, and *The Editor* (April 24, 1915): 407-410.

Grimsted, David. *Melodrama Unveiled: American Theater and Culture, 1800-1850*. Berkeley: University of California Press, 1987.

Gunning, Tom. "Filmed Narrative and the Theatrical Ideal: Griffith and the *film d'art*." In *Les premiers ans du cinéma français*. Ed. P. Guibbert. Perpignan, France: L'Institut Jean Vigo, 1985. 123-129.

_____. *D. W. Griffith and the Origins of American Narrative Film*. Urbana: University of Illinois Press, 1991.

Heilman, Robert B. *Tragedy and Melodrama: Versions of Experience*. Seattle: University of Washington Press, 1968.

Henderson, Robert M. *D. W. Griffith: His Life and Work*. New York: Oxford University Press, 1972.

Lennig, Arthur. "The Birth of *Way Down East*." *Quarterly Review of Film Studies*, 6.1 (Winter 1981): 105-116.

Mayer, David. *Stagestruck Filmmaker: D. W. Griffith and the American Theatre*. Iowa City: University of Iowa Press, 2009.

McDonnell, Patricia. *On the Edge of Your Seat: Popular Theater and Film in Early Twentieth-Century American Art*. New Haven, Conn.: Yale University Press, 2002.

Mercer, John, and Martin Shingler. *Melodrama: Genre, Style, Sensibility*. London: Wallflower, 2004.

Merritt, Russell. "Rescued from a Perilous Nest: D. W. Griffith's Escape from Theatre into Film." *Cinema Journal*, 21.1 (Fall 1981): 2-30.

Rahill, Frank. *The World of Melodrama*. University Park: Penn State University Press, 1967.

Schickel, Richard. *D. W. Griffith: An American Life*. New York: Simon and Schuster, 1984.

Simmon, Scott. *The Films of D. W. Griffith*. New York: Cambridge University Press, 1993.

Singer, Ben. *Melodrama and Modernity: Early Sensational Cinema and Its Contexts*. New York: Columbia University Press, 2001.

Smith, James L. *Melodrama*. London: Methuen, 1973.

Vardac, A. Nicholas. *Stage to Screen: Theatrical Method from Garrick to Griffith*. Cambridge, Mass.: Harvard University Press, 1949. Reprint, *Stage to Screen: Theatrical Origins of Early Film, David Garrick to D. W. Griffith*. New York: Benjamin Blom, 1968; New York: Da Capo, 1987.

Wexman, Virginia Wright. "Suffering and Suffrage: Birth, the Female Body, and Women's Choices in D. W. Griffith's *Way Down East*." *The Velvet Light Trap*, 29 (Spring 1992): 53-65.

2

Drama into Film and Filmic Drama:
The Cases of *The Little Foxes*, *Betrayal*, *Edmond*, and *Henry V*

I thought I'd start by saying something about the adaptation of drama to film, mainly because so little is understood about the process of adaptation by even the educated filmgoer. Many people still cling to the naïve belief that drama and film, for example, are two aspects of the same art, except that drama is "live" while movies are "recorded." Certainly there are undeniable similarities between the two forms. Most obviously, both employ action as a principal means of communication: that is, what people *do* is a major source of meaning. Live theater and movies are also collaborative enterprises, involving the coordination of writers, directors, actors, designers, and technicians. Drama and film are both social arts in that they are exhibited before groups of people and are therefore experienced publicly as well as individually. But films are not mere recordings of plays. The language systems of these two art forms are fundamentally different, and movies have a far broader range of techniques at their disposal.

The surest sign of the clichéd mind in filmmaking is a feeling of obligation to "open up" plays when they become films and a conviction that this process proves superiority, that a play really comes into its own when it is filmed. We can really go to Italy in Franco Zeffirelli's film of *Romeo and Juliet* (1968), so for some people this picture automatically supersedes stage-bound theatrical productions. We can dissolve and cross-fade more easily in the movie of *Death of a Salesman* (1951), therefore the theater proves yet again just a tryout place for later perfect consummation on screen—despite, in this case, the theater's superior ability to suggest the childishness of Willy's sons (by having the adult actors of Biff and Happy play their boyhood selves) and the momentousness of Willy's adultery (by having it occur, not on location in Boston, but on the forestage—right in the Lomans' living room, as it were). And we can go outside in Mike Nichols' film of *Who's Afraid of Virginia Woolf?* (1966), so once more the theater is shown up as cribbed or confined, if not superficially realistic, even though the claustrophobic nature of George and Martha's single-set living room on the stage is part of the point of this long night's journey into day.

The trouble here is a confusion in aesthetic logic, an assumption that we are comparing apples and apples when we are really comparing apple and pears. Fundamentally, film takes the audience to the event, shifting the audience continually; theater takes the event to the audience, shifting it never. Just as the beauty of poetry often lies in tensions between the free flight of language and the molding capacity of form, so the beauty of drama often lies in tensions between imagination and theatrical exigency. To assume that the cinema's extension of a play's action is automatically an improvement is to change the subject: from the way theater builds upwards, folding one event upon another in almost perceptible vertical form, to the way film progresses horizontally. Figuratively speaking, theater works predominantly by building higher and higher in one place; film, despite the literally vertical progress of planes in the image, works predominantly in a lateral series of places. In this way, action in the cinema is more of a journey in the present than a confrontation based on the past (the usual form of tragedy in drama): the one is filled with possibility or promise, the other with suspense or foreboding. By its very form, it can then be said, film reflects for spectators in the twenty-first century the belief that the world is a place in which a person can leave the past behind and create his or her own future—hence one of the reasons the cinema took such a foothold, so early, in the history of our relatively young nation.

"Opening up" a play can be successful when the filmmaker knows clearly what he is doing and treats his film as a new work from a common source, as Richard Lester does in his admirable film of Ann Jellicoe's *The Knack* (1965). But most adaptors seem to think that any banal set of film gimmicks constitutes a liberation for which the poor cramped play ought to be grateful. One film that respects its dramatic source almost completely and is nevertheless cinematic is William Wyler's *The Little Foxes* (1941). Lillian Hellman's play from 1939 has undergone nearly no adaptation: for instance, there are no exterior scenes of dramatic action in the film—precisely the kind of scene, I have been arguing, that most directors would have deemed necessary in order to introduce a little "cinema" into this intractable theatrical mass.

The majority of the action in Wyler's film takes place on the same, totally neutral set, the ground-floor living room of a huge colonial house. At the back, a staircase leads to the second-floor bedrooms of Regina and Horace Giddens, which adjoin each other. (Regina and Horace are played by Bette Davis and Herbert Marshall respectively, and I shall use the actors' names in my discussion of the film version.) Nothing picturesque adds to the realism of this somber place, which is as impersonal as the setting of classical tragedy. The characters have a credible, if conventional, reason for confronting one another in the living room, whether they come from the outdoors or from their bedrooms; they can also plausibly

The Little Foxes, dir. William Wyler, 1941

linger in the living room. The staircase at the back plays a role similar to the one it would in the theater: it is purely an element of dramatic architecture, which in this case will be used to set off the characters in the vertical space of the frame. Let's look at the central scene of the film, the death of Herbert Marshall, which happens to take place in the living room and on the staircase. An analysis of this scene will reveal that to be cinematic a film adaptation not only doesn't have to go outdoors, it also doesn't have to feature either a mobile camera or lots of cutting.

First let me summarize the action of *The Little Foxes* up to and just beyond this point, which occurs toward the end. We are in the South at the turn of the century, where and when middle-class capitalism-cum-materialism has more than begun to eclipse aristocratic feudalism-cum-agrarianism. Two brothers, Ben and Oscar Hubbard, believe they can make a fortune by establishing the first mill in their town, which is surrounded by cotton plantations. Lacking the $75,000 needed for the venture, they seek the partnership of their sister, Regina Giddens, who, eager to share in the profits, promises to get the money from her wealthy husband, Horace, president of the local bank. Having just been brought home from the hospital in Baltimore by his devoted daughter, Alexandra, Horace has only a short time to live and refuses to become involved. Therefore, to help his father, Oscar's son, Lee, a clerk in Horace's bank, steals $80,000 in bonds from Horace's safe-deposit box, on the assumption that his uncle will not check the box for six months; and Ben and Oscar complete their business deal. Horace discovers the theft but tells Regina that he will not prosecute her brothers. On the contrary, he will call the theft a loan and make a new will in which Regina will receive only $80,000 in bonds, the exact amount of the theft. Thus Regina will share neither in her husband's fortune nor in the fortune the mill will make. While the two quarrel, Horace suffers a heart attack, but Regina refuses to administer a reviving drug and coldbloodedly stands by as he dies. With her knowledge of the theft, she then blackmails her brothers into assigning her a 75% interest in the mill, lest she prosecute them. Our scene is the quarrel between Regina and Horace, or, to switch back to the actor's names, between Bette Davis and Herbert Marshall, who has revealed to her the theft of his bonds.

Bette Davis is sitting in the middle ground facing the viewer, her head at the center of the screen; the lighting enhances the brightness of her heavily made-up face. In the foreground Herbert Marshall sits in three-quarter profile. The ruthless exchanges between husband and wife take place without any cutting from one character to the other, since the very positions of Davis and Marshall emphasize their separation and antagonism. Then comes the husband's heart attack, during which he begs his wife to get him his medicine from upstairs. From this instant all the drama in this scene derives from the immobility of both Bette Davis and the camera. Marshall is forced to stand up and go get the medicine himself, and this effort will kill him as he climbs the first few steps of the staircase.

In the theater, this scene would most likely have been staged in the same manner. A spotlight could have been focused on Bette Davis, and the spectator would have felt the same horror at her criminal inaction, the same anguish at the sight of her staggering victim. Yet, despite appearances, William Wyler's directing makes as extensive use as possible of the means offered him by the camera and the frame. Bette Davis' position at the center of the screen endows her with privilege and power in the geometry of the dramatic space. The whole scene revolves around her, but her frightening immobility takes its full impact only from Marshall's double exit from the frame, first in the foreground on the right, then in the mid-background on the left. Instead of following him in this lateral movement, as any less intelligent director would have done, Wyler's camera remains imperturbably immobile. When Marshall finally enters the frame for a second time and begins to climb the stairs, the cinematographer, Gregg Toland, acting at Wyler's request, is careful not to bring into focus the full depth of the image, so that Marshall's fall on the staircase and his death will not be clearly visible to the viewer. This artificial blurring augments our feeling of anxiety: as if over the shoulder of the dominant Bette Davis, who faces us and has her back toward her husband, we have to discern in the distance the outcome of a drama whose protagonist is nearly escaping us.

This analysis of Marshall's death in *The Little Foxes* clearly reveals how Wyler can make a whole scene revolve around one actor.

Bette Davis at the center of the screen is paralyzed, like a hoot owl by a spotlight, and around her the staggering Marshall weaves as a second—this time mobile—pole, whose shift first out of the frame and then into the background, draws with it all the dramatic attention. In addition, this shift creates tremendous suspense because is consists of a double disappearance from the frame, and because the focus on the staircase at the back is imperfect. One can see here how Wyler uses depth of field: as I've indicated, the director elected to have Toland envelop the character of the dying Marshall in a certain haziness, to have his cinematographer, as it were, befog the back of the frame. This was done to create so much anxiety in the viewer that he should almost want to push the immobile Bette Davis aside to have a better look. The dramatic development of this scene does indeed follow that of the dialogue and of the action itself, but the scene's cinematic expression superimposes its own evolution upon the dramatic development: a second action, as it were, that is the very story of the scene from the moment Marshall gets up from his chair to his collapse on the staircase.

We can see here everything that the cinema adds to the means of the theater, and we can also see that, paradoxically, the highest level of cinematic art coincides with the lowest level of *mise-en-scène*. Nothing could better heighten the dramatic power of this scene than the absolute *immobility* of the camera. Its slightest movement, which is a less skillful director would have deemed the right "cinematic" element to introduce, would have decreased the dramatic tension. Furthermore, the camera does not follow the path of the average viewer's eyes by cutting from Bette Davis to the frantic Marshall; instead, it obstructs our vision merely by recording, without full depth of field, the same scene in one continuous take. It is the stationary camera itself, in other words, that organizes the action in terms of the frame and the ideal coordinates of its two-dimensional geometric space. By means of the cinema, William Wyler has mined the artistic depths of this scene at the same time that he has respected its theatrical appearances.

To the real looks the actors would direct at one another on stage, one must add here the virtual "look" of the camera with which our own identifies. Wyler excels in making us sensitive to his camera's gaze. In *Jezebel* (1938), for example, there is the low-angle shot that clearly points the lens directly at Bette Davis's eyes looking down at the white cane that Henry Fonda holds in his hand with the intention of using it. We thus follow the dramatic line between the character and the object much better than we would have if, by the rules of conventional cutting, the camera had shown us the cane from the point of view of Bette Davis herself.

A variation on the same principle: in *The Little Foxes*, in order to make us understand the thoughts of the character who notices the small steel box in which the stolen bonds were locked and whose absence from the box is going to indicate theft, Wyler placed it in the foreground with the camera being this time at eye-level and at the same distance from the box as the eyes of the character. Our eyes no longer meet the character's eyes directly through the beheld object, as in the above-mentioned scene from *Jezebel*, but as if through a mirror. The angle of incidence of our own view of the object is, as it were, equal to the angle of reflection of the character's view, which angle takes us to this person's eyes. In any case, Wyler commands our mental vision according to the rigorous laws of an invisible dramatic optics.

Paradoxically, insofar as Wyler has never attempted to hide the novelistic or theatrical nature of most of his scripts, he has made all the more apparent the cinematic phenomenon in its utmost purity. Not once has the *auteur of The Best Years of Our Lives* (1946), *Jezebel*, or *The Little Foxes* said to himself *a priori* that he had to have a "cinematic look"; still, nobody can tell a story in cinematic terms better than he. For him, the action is expressed first by the actor. Like a director in the theater, Wyler conceives of his job of enhancing the action as beginning with the actor. The set and the camera are there only to permit the actor to focus upon himself the maximum dramatic intensity; they are not there to create a meaning unto themselves. Even though Wyler's approach is also that of the theater director, the latter has at his disposal only the very limited means of the stage. He can manipulate his means, but no matter what he does, the text and the actor constitute the essence of theatrical production.

Film, then, is not at all magnified theater on screen, the stage viewed constantly through opera glasses. The size of the image or unity of time has nothing to do with the matter. Cinema begins when the frame of the screen and the placement of the camera are used to enhance the action and the actor. In *The Little Foxes*, Wyler has changed almost nothing of the dramatic text or even of the set: one could say that he limited himself to directing the play in the way that a theater director would have directed it; and, furthermore, that he used the frame of the screen to *conceal* certain parts of the set and used the camera to bring the viewer closer to the action. What actor would not dream of being able to play a scene, immobile on a chair, in front of 5,000 viewers who don't miss the slightest movement of an eye? What theater director would not want the spectator in the worst seat at the back of the house to be able to see clearly the movements of his actors, and to read with ease his intentions at any moment in the action? Wyler didn't choose to do anything other than realize on film the essence of a theatrical *mise-en-scène* that would not use the lights and the set merely to ornament the actor and the text. Nevertheless, there is probably not a single shot in *The Little Foxes* that isn't pure cinema. Indeed, there is a hundred times more cinema, and better cinema at that, in one fixed shot of *The Little Foxes* than in all the exterior traveling shots, in all the natural settings, in all the geographical exoticism, in all the shots of the reverse side of the set, by means of which up to now the screen has ingeniously attempted to make us forget the stage.

I'd now like to treat Harold Pinter's play *Betrayal* (1978) because, along with Pinter's *No Man's Land* (1975) and *Old Times* (1971) and quite unlike Hellman's *The Little Foxes*, it has often been described as "cinematic" in its use of time-jumping or time-eliding strategies more common to film. In this connection, the three plays exhibit some of the impact of Pinter's work as a screenwriter on his playwriting. In fact his movie career has included screen adaptations of some of his plays (*The Caretaker* [1964] and *The Homecoming* [1973]), as well as of such novels as Robin Maugham's *The Servant* (1963), Nicholas Mosley's *Accident* (1967), L. P. Hartley's *The Go-Between* (1970), John Fowles's *The French Lieutenant's Woman* (1981), and Ian McEwan's *The Comfort of Strangers* (1991). In the case of each of the novels, Pinter exploited the structural flexibility of film to make a more complex narrative out of a conventional one, or to find an equivalent in film for the book's narrative voice and deployment of time.

The playwright's foremost achievement in this regard is his adaptation of *A Remembrance of Things Past* (literally, and better, titled *In Search of Lost Time*), Marcel Proust's fictional reminiscence about childhood, love, and sexual awakening. Pinter did the adaptation between his writing of *Old Times* and *No Man's Land*, which, taken together with *Betrayal*, form a trilogy on the nature of memory and the play of time; and, where those works bear the imprint of the dramatist's experience as a film scenarist, so too does Pinter's interest in Proust's novel gain significance in light of his own memory plays, including *Landscape* (1968) and *Silence* (1969). Unfortunately, *The Proust Screenplay*, as it is known, was never filmed, although it was successfully adapted by Pinter for staging at London's National Theatre in 2000.

Among Pinter's screen adaptations, *Betrayal* (1983) is my primary subject, so let me begin with the play itself—a filmic drama that was turned into a dramatic film. *Betrayal* concerns three middle-aged people: Jerry, a London literary agent who is married and a father; Emma, his lover for seven years, an art dealer who is married and a mother; and Robert, Emma's husband and Jerry's best friend from university days, who is a publisher. The story begins at its conclusion, in 1977, and moves backward to its beginning, in 1968. But Pinter doesn't use the reverse-chronological method slavishly, for three of the play's (and the film's) nine scenes occur temporally *after* the scene immediately preceding.

Betrayal opens when Jerry and Emma meet for a drink—again, in 1977; this is the first time they have seen each other in the two years since their affair ended (an affair that included a rented flat for the couple's afternoon meetings). Emma tells Jerry that she and Robert are separating, that they had a long talk the night before, that Robert confessed to a number of affairs and she told him about the long-finished affair with Jerry. (Thus her affair could have no real bearing on the break-up of her marriage.) As the story "progresses" backward, Jerry learns, to his astonishment, that Emma actually had told Robert about the affair four years ago. Robert had thus known about it while continuing his friendship and publishing relationship with Jerry, while remaining married to Emma, and while he had also been busy with his own dalliance (apparently much more casual than his wife's). The last scene is a party in 1968;

Betrayal, dir. David Jones, 1983

Jerry, who had been best man at Emma and Robert's wedding, declares his love for her. And, in a long moment of quiet during which she considers the affair we know has occurred, the play ends—or begins.

For me, the chief interest of *Betrayal* is in imagining a question mark after the title. Jerry and Emma use the term "betray" in the first scene, but who is betrayed, even in the most conventional love-triangle manner? Robert knew of his wife's affair, but he did nothing about it, in part clearly because he was having affairs of his own. Jerry and Emma were faithful (or is it "faithful"?) to each other during their affair. The title *Betrayal* thus sounds oddly rigid in contrast with the play that follows it, in which extramarital affairs are practically *de rigueur* for everyone. The backward journey of the action does show us one thing, though: that the desire which precipitated an affair was bound to fade in time. And it is amoral *time* that is probably the play's true Pinteresque resonance—the poignancy of passing time, the humorous-melancholy immanence of mortality—not any suggestion that its characters are immorally betraying the very idea of marriage, honor, or self.

The film of *Betrayal*, because of the inherent flexibility of cinematic form, makes the overall temporal pattern of the play seem less of a stunt. Beyond this, Pinter found new possibilities for the play in its film adaptation (itself directed by David Jones, essentially a theater director who has done extensive television work for the BBC). This matter of genre is one of distinction, not hierarchy; the play has qualities that the movie could not have. For example, in the London–New York stage production, directed by Peter Hall and designed (scenery, lighting, *and* costumes) by John Bury, every scene began with the actors immobile in dim silhouette, with city sounds behind them, and they were brought to motion by the coming of light. Each of the London settings was done in spare line and color; the one Venice scene was executed in curves. These theatrical devices helped to distill the play's realism poetically.

Film could not accommodate those devices: they would have worked against both realism *and* poetry. The film of *Betrayal* needs rooms that are rooms, with life going on in them before and after the bits of life we see. In the theater, plaques of action were placed before us as in a three-dimensional mosaic; on screen, the camera just seems to arrive at opportune moments in these people's ongoing lives—opportune for us, that is. Growing out of such an approach, Pinter fills in material around the edges that eases the play into this second form and, without fuss, corroborates it as film. For instance, we glimpse Emma's daughter at different ages, which makes her a kind of calendar; we see Emma getting into her car after the breakup of the affair and sitting there for a moment, crying; we see her husband in his office, verified as a publisher; we even see the landlady who rents the lovers their rendezvous and, without rudeness, disbelieves everything they tell her. Pinter handles these additions so that they don't flatten suggestion into explicitness, as they would in many a movie derived from a play: here the supplements certify and expand.

Moreover, in his first feature film, David Jones makes it plain that he understands how to use a camera, how to look and choose and move. Look at the opening sequence, for one—possibly planned by Pinter but perfectly fulfilled by Jones—which takes place outside Robert and Emma's house in 1977 as they bid goodnight to departing guests. The pair shut their front door—a kind of cut without actually cutting. Then the camera comes closer to the house, moving along to the kitchen window through which we see the couple conversing, not calmly. They proceed to slap each other. All this occurs in one long take, which visually certifies the essential contiguousness or inextricability of this couple's social and personal lives—in part because the camera itself begins here as a public observer, only to become a private *voyeur*.

In the next scene, focusing on Jerry and Emma in a pub the following day, Jones begins the cat-and-mouse editing technique that fills the rest of the picture, and he is greatly aided in this regard by the work of John Bloom. Jones and Bloom craft the film like jewelers, right to the finish where Jerry persuades Emma to start the affair whose end we have already witnessed. Her hand slides down the length of his phallic arm to his hand, and the two entwined hands—a pretty wryness—are the last things (*things*) we see. For all such cinematic adroitness, however, the film of *Betrayal* doesn't finally "deepen" the play, though it does deepen an element or tone that was in the original.

That tonal element can also be found in Pinter's *No Man's Land*, as well as in many of the plays of lesser English dramatists like Tom Stoppard and Simon Gray. Such works delineate a radical change in the locus of English comedy. (And make no mistake: *Betrayal*, on stage and screen if not on the page, can breathe only in the rarefied air of such comedy.) From the Elizabethan age until well into the twentieth century, that is, high comedy was virtually the exclusive preserve of wealthy, aristocratic characters. One reason was that the plots of high comedy were possible only to people with time on their hands, people who didn't have to work for a living. Another reason was that these people—I mean these people in the real world, not the characters based on them by Congreve and Sheridan and Wilde—developed comedic skill in their otherwise idle lives, qualities that distinguished them from everyone else beneath their station: of arch and elegance, of tease and (brusque) politeness, of rapier skill in the drawing-room duel of words.

Increasingly through the twentieth century and beyond, as those upper classes dwindled proportionately against an educated, reasonably affluent middle class, the talent for high comedy in life has been acquired by the middle class. Of course, the action now has to be worked around office hours and carefully planned vacations and nannies for the children, but many members of the English middle class today conduct their lives and conversations in a style as smoothly cruel and tacitly affectionate as they can make it, based on upper-class paradigms—themselves perhaps impelled by a quite English imperative to maintain poise, to keep the social backbone arched.

Harold Pinter, preeminent among his contemporaries, has perceived this social shift and writes a kind of high comedy about these middle-class people who, as far as the dailiness of their lives will permit, try to live those lives with high-comedic panache. And the tonal change in *Betrayal* from stage to screen has as much to do with the "opening up" of the play as it does with the intensification of this high-comic style in middle-class London life—partly because such "opening up," or "breaking out," permits the stylistic intensification through the situating of *haute* bourgeois existence in as realistic, even mundane, a daily context as possible.

Speaking of stylistic intensification, another kind is on display in the film of David Mamet's *Edmond* (2005), which I want to take up here because of this work's association with expressionism— an artistic movement that, like *Edmond*, itself began in the theater and moved into the cinema. Originally produced as a long one-act play in 1982, *Edmond* is an underrated piece, having been written between Mamet's stellar (and original) screenplay for *The Verdict* (1982) and his best drama, *Glengarry Glen Ross* (1984; filmed 1992), and consequently having suffered in comparison with those two highly publicized works. But *Edmond* stands on its own two feet, in part because it points up—as none of Mamet's other plays do—an aspect of his writing style that, like this particular drama itself, has been neglected. I mean the fact that Mamet's staccato or minimalist dialogue, with its occasional explosions, is essentially expressionistic, even when the plays themselves are not thoroughgoing expressionist works.

Mamet's language thus underscores the paradox of verism-cum-abstraction that inheres in all his work (but is even more apparent in his films, where verism is expected to a far greater degree than it is in the drama). The general linguistic texture is naturalistic, nearly stenographic—the broken sentences, the repetitions, the litanies of the everyday; then, suddenly, with a telegraphic word or phrase, and especially with an entire quizzical or contorted sentence, the vernacular lifts into an arch. As in, "The path of some crazed lunatic sees you as an invasion of his personal domain" (*American Buffalo* [1975]). Or, "People used to say that there are numbers of such magnitude that multiplying them by two made no difference" (*Glengarry Glen Ross*). And, from *Edmond*: "[God] may love the weak, but he protects the strong." With a lesser writer, such lines might seem to be fissures in verism; but Mamet otherwise so thoroughly certifies the accuracy of his ear that in these instances we feel we are flying past the character's actual powers of expression into the thoughts in him that he isn't always able to express. In this way the real is lifted into the abstract—or what I am calling the expressionistic.

That *Edmond* appears more expressionistic than Mamet's other plays stems less from its disgorged or deracinated language, however, than from its episodic form. It's what the Germans call both a "station" drama and a *Wandlungsdrama*, a drama of transformation-cum-regeneration that is composed of a series of stations, or stages (twenty-three in *Edmond*'s case), through which a character progresses as he takes the moral, spiritual, and emotional journey of his life. (A product of European religious drama of the Middle Ages, the original station play consisted of stations that were sometimes literally Stations of the Cross.) *Edmond* has been compared to Georg Büchner's proto-expressionistic play *Woyzeck* (1836), but Mamet's drama has more in common with Georg Kaiser's lesser-known expressionistic work *From Morn to Midnight* (1912).

In this play, a bank cashier, whose humanity has been crushed beneath the social conventions, economic system, and political structure of Wilhelminian Germany, succumbs to sexual temptation and both robs his bank and leaves his wife—to embark on a pilgrimage (to a bordello for some sensual fulfillment, to a sports stadium for some passionate gambling, to the Salvation Army for some soulful religion) in search of something beyond the material, the profane, the mechanized, the quotidian. When he doesn't find what he's looking for, he kills himself rather than be imprisoned for his crime. David Mamet's own play covers more than the twelve or so hours of *From Morn to Midnight*, but it, too, is about a character in desperate search of some new intensity, truth, or meaning in his life.

Edmund Burke is a forty-seven-year-old New York stockbroker on his way home early from work after a meeting has been rescheduled. Low on spiritual fuel, he stops to see a clairvoyant. She reads tarot cards and fatefully tells him, "You are not where you belong." (Imagined tarot cards fleck his mind thereafter, until, near the end of the play and the film, Edmond utters a line that is nearly an exact quotation from *Hamlet*: "There is a destiny that shapes our ends . . . rough-hew them how we may.") The result of the clairvoyant's counsel comes that evening at home when, after some clipped dialogue about a broken lamp, Edmond gets up and bluntly tells his wife he is leaving:

> WIFE: Will you bring me back some cigarettes? . . .
> EDMOND: I'm not coming back.

This simple statement fractures the somnolence of his life. A quick quarrel then discloses that Edmond hasn't loved his wife for years and doesn't think she's attractive: she simply no longer interests him sexually *or* spiritually. (Mamet, who wrote this film adaptation, puts the wife in bra and panties on screen, as he did not on stage, in order to emphasize Edmond's lack of interest.) For her part, the wife (who is unnamed: more on this later) seems angered less by the bad news than by her husband's detached manner in delivering it. Edmond doesn't care: he just turns his back and walks out on her—and on his mechanical, workaday existence. *Edmond* thus takes place, as it were, after the romance of the archetypal romantic comedy is over—when, in the absence of idealized, romantic love, a desire for a different kind of union or devotion takes over.

In Edmond's case, at least initially, that desire is for sheer sex, primarily of the oral (if not oracular) kind. His first stop after leaving his wife is a bar, where he meets a gabby, suave basketball fan who infers that Edmond feels as if his "balls were cut off." The fan then casually offers some possible solutions to this problem: "money," "adventure," "pussy," "self-destruction." "Pussy" it is, so the

Edmond, dir. Stuart Gordon, 2005

man-in-the-bar gives Edmond a tip about a strip club where he can slake his sexual needs. When a pretty, amiable B-girl there tells him her fee for oral sex and also asks him to buy an exorbitantly priced drink, he becomes incensed. Soon Edmond's gotten himself tossed out—the start of a long round of explosive confrontations with hookers, grifters, and pimps in which he keeps heatedly complaining about the cost ("It's too much!"), naïvely trying to apply bourgeois standards to an inherently corrupt underworld into which he nevertheless keeps sinking deeper and deeper.

His odyssey through New York's seedy underbelly takes Edmond to a peep show next and then to a massage parlor, before he decides to try to get his satisfaction out of a hand of three-card monte. When, however, he accuses the dealer of running a crooked game, the dealer and his shills pull him into an alley, beat him up, and steal his money. So Edmond goes to a pawnshop to trade his wedding ring for some cash—and, with no such prior plan, comes out with a knife (unlike Woyzeck, who goes to a pawnshop expressly to buy a knife with which to kill his common-law wife). Thus armed, he first threatens a woman on a subway platform, then uses the knife (and the racial epithets "jungle bunny," "nigger," and "coon," as well) on a leering, gold-toothed pimp who promises to take him to a prostitute but tries to hold him up instead—and in return gets a "knife-whipping" from Edmond that leaves this black man half dead.

Invigorated by this act of violence and experiencing the delirious liberation of living in the moment for the first time in his life, Edmond goes on a manic jag during which he is unable to keep his mouth shut as he babbles first to this stranger, then to that. One of those strangers turns out to be Glenna, a twenty-three-year-old waitress in a coffeehouse, whom he successfully propositions and whom he tells (after bedding her at her place), in a highly racialized speech, how alive beating the pimp has made him feel. An aspiring actress, Glenna—the only named character besides Edmond because, apart from him and in contrast to the generic secondary characters of expressionistic drama in general, she is the most humanized—compares his feeling of almost Dionysian ecstasy to the one she gets when she is acting. She thus fits into, shares, or even becomes a projection of Edmond's narcissistic framework, but only for a time, since Glenna proves to have a slightly different frame of reference from his. To wit: she refuses to join him in "leaving normal" and renouncing the past.

This provokes Edmond's rage and he kills her with his knife, as the fever of his quest for a higher reality, which has been burning through everything he has been doing, propels him past the rational into the hierophantic, the exalted, the truth. The truth, that is, according to Edmond Burke, but a grotesque compound of his lifelong frustrations by any other name. After he leaves Glenna's apartment, Edmond goes (like the Cashier in *From Morn to Midnight* after his bordello-visit) to a religious mission (a black Baptist one, no less) to hear a minister preach another kind of truth: that every soul can be redeemed through faith. But before he gets a chance to make his testament in front of all those assembled, Edmond is identified by the woman he accosted in the subway and is arrested—at this point, presumably only for the assault of this woman and for the attempted murder of the black pimp. (The woman's coincidental appearance here jars as it would not, or would to a much lesser degree, in the less veristic or more make-believe world of the theater.) And after a short reunion with his wife, who serves him with divorce papers, he ends up in a prison cell.

A big black man is assigned to his cell, and Edmond expresses conciliatory feelings toward this African-American as well as blacks in general, musing that "when we fear something, I think we wish for it." Uninterested, his cellmate beats Edmond into granting him sexual favors. In the last scene, the two men are simply living together (perhaps for life), affectionately; and the film ends as Edmond says "good night," kisses the other man, then turns over and goes to sleep. He thus ends in an unforeseen domesticity, enforced but safe, yet a domesticity, paradoxically, through which he reaches his apotheosis—and finds the gateway to spiritual freedom, inner peace, and personal transcendence.

All of this as the prison sex slave of his hulking black cellmate, mind you, the emphasis here being not on crushing others in an outside world where every interaction, or transaction, is a struggle for power (the typical Mamet meme), but on the tender mercy of surrender in an inside or inner world of one's own willing. If Edmond's eventual contentment in captivity suggests a Jean Genêt allegory, however, Mamet's hard, syncopated dialogue couldn't be less similar to Genêt's flowery porno-poetry. Mamet never surrenders—or never lets his characters surrender—the armor of expressionist direct-diction, which is to say the prison-house of a kind of language that so strenuously asserts the diminished self as to seal it off insuperably in its own subjective consciousness.

Mamet's theme, then, is not that we all share Edmond Burke's particular frustrations and hungers, but that we all have them in one form or another and can be interested in a man who not only discovers his own, but does so in such a way as to set himself *apart* from us—by feeling nothing beyond his own suffering. In this he again resembles Kaiser's Cashier, who never wastes a thought on the feelings or troubles of the wife and family he abandons, the waiter he cheats, the whores he abuses, the stadium spectator whose death he engineers. Ironically, the Cashier indirectly compares himself to Christ with his last words, "Ecce homo" (the same as those uttered by Pilate, in John 19:5, immediately before Jesus's crucifixion), though *Ecce homo* was also the title of the 1888 book in which Nietzsche unfavorably contrasted Christian ideals with his own superior ideal of the Übermensch, or superman. A cashier, of course, is no superman, but he isn't (or hasn't behaved like) a Christian, either—which is precisely Kaiser's point in having him utter words that simultaneously call to mind the Bible and Friedrich Nietzsche.

The same goes for Edmond Burke: he's a slave by the end of *Edmond*, not a superman and not even a Christian slave, and he finds himself in a hell of his own, self-satisfied creation. (Late in his existential descent, after his visit to the Baptist mission, he can be heard openly to ask, "You think there's a hell? You think we're there?") If Edmond is a selfless martyr of a kind, moreover, he is a martyr, not for mankind, like Christ, but for men—specifically for American men of the 1980s, when the straight white male was reeling from his loss of potency at the hands of women, gays, and especially blacks in a climate of rigid political correctness as well as institutionalized affirmative action. So, after sacrificing a female waitress and an African-American pimp, Edmond sacrifices himself: to the woman who identified him as her (and the pimp's) assailant, to the wife who divorces him, and finally to the black who sodomizes him.

Mamet himself, however, has not sacrificed any of Edmond's dialogue (or any other character's, for that matter) from the play to the more visual medium of film. But he does do something that, for all the film's incisiveness—an incisiveness aided by mostly nighttime settings, which mirror its protagonist's long night of the soul—takes away from the form-conscious, almost abstract or removed, effect of the original drama. In the play of *Edmond*, that is, the twenty-three brief scenes follow one another like consecutive yet separate glimpses of a journey, a sort of mobile slide show that gives an ironclad logic to Edmond's fate, paradoxically, because of the very absence of such logic, reason, or causality from the drama's words and actions themselves. In the film, by contrast, Mamet uses connective "tissue" between the scenes or stages of Edmond's "progress," and this connectiveness takes away from the fragmented or desultory (yet nonetheless fated) quality of the play's episodes—a quality that could only be enhanced by shifting sets and characters who enter and exit from the wings, and one that is meant to mirror the fragmented or irrational perception of the protagonist himself as he manically searches out his destiny.

For example, when Edmond arrives in prison, he is dragged nude and shackled down a corridor of cells while other convicts jeer and yell at him: so we are visually told that this once prim Manhattan businessman has shed his pinstripe respectability, not so much for the prison stripes of an inmate as for the naked vulnerability of a jailhouse punk. In the *play*, Edmond's wife ends her visit to him in prison, the scene ends, and we then immediately find him in his cell with the black man: no transitional journey through a hostile cellblock here. The play is thus like a medieval morality, modernized: profane, stark, abbreviated, final. The film of *Edmond* is more of a narrative stream: equally profane but less abbreviated (even at eighty minutes or so), more explanatory if not exculpatory, and consequently both less stark and less final. After all, the camera-eye, if not the eye of God, is watching Edmond and telling his tale. The play of *Edmond*, in contradistinction, presents his drama without benefit of a guide or narrator; David Mamet may have written the words, but his presence is otherwise undetectable. Indeed, in medieval terms, he is a *deus absconditus*. And Edmond himself is what Mamet impishly-cum-impiously has left behind: naked, unaccommodated, alienated man.

Edmond was directed by Stuart Gordon, who made a name for himself in the horror-film genre by adapting several H. P. Lovecraft stories to the screen, among them *Re-Animator* (1985), *From Beyond* (1986), *Castle Freak* (1995), and *Dagon* (2001). Only one touch here, a spray of blood, belongs in a horror movie; otherwise, Gordon deals fittingly with a script that has its own horror—and, unlike most horror movies, its own alchemical reality (as opposed to science fiction)—about it. He serves *Edmond* raw, if you will, without padding (except for the aforementioned "connective tissue," which I attribute to Mamet the scenarist) and without any attempt to open the film up any more than, as a drama, it already was "open," or set in a number of different locations.

This "open" or episodic aspect of *Edmond* naturally helps it to escape the "filmed play" feeling—a feeling that, unfortunately, the movie versions of Mamet's single-set plays *Oleanna* (1992; filmed 1994) and *Lakeboat* (1970; filmed 2000) could not escape. Something else helps *Edmond* to escape the theatrical trap as well: Gordon's playing of Mamet's stylized dialogue against the ultra-realism of the film's horror-suspense-thriller context, as opposed to overplaying the linguistic stylization for its own incantatory sake (as Mamet-the-writer/director himself seemed to do in his film *House of Games* [1987]) and thereby drying up or (to switch metaphors) flattening out the picture.

Edmond is additionally aided, in its transition from the theater to the cinema, not only by the continuity provided courtesy of Bobby Johnston's breathy, jazz-funk trumpet on the soundtrack, but also by Denis Maloney's cinematography. I'm referring both to the film's "horror look"—its hard-edged lighting by night (making the dark "colorful") and shadow-filled imagery by day (making daylight nearly black-and-white)—and to *Edmond*'s subjective or dream-like quality, as if the whole picture, the whole world, were being seen only though Edmond's feverish eyes. This expressionistic quality in the script can be realized onstage, it's true, but only with difficulty or obtrusiveness, and only intermittently, through the use of a spotlight that "sees out" exclusively from Edmond's perspective. But the point-of-view, or first-person, shot is easy to achieve in so narrative a medium as film, and we see plenty of such camera placements in *Edmond*: most of the time we are right there with the protagonist, in the middle of things, without the "relief" of any sweeping boom shots. The editing (by Andy Horwitz) also emphasizes *Edmond*'s dreamlike or subjectively expressionist aspect: one second, for example, Edmond is looking at a tarot card, and the next he's looking down at a dinner plate—the very kind of abrupt transition that is utterly natural to the dreaming, fantasizing, or "projective" mind.

Edmond's transition from stage to screen is not aided, alas, by the performance of Mamet regular (and theater-trained) William H.

Macy in the leading role. The big-eared, wattle-faced Macy is not a *bad* actor; he's a *supporting* or character actor who does his best work out of the spotlight, or in the shadow of stars. (Though I have never seen him on the stage, witness his supporting performances in such films as *Boogie Nights* [1997], *Wag the Dog* [1997], *Fargo* [1996], and *House of Games*.) As the central character here, however, he is out of his depth, or, rather, we never sense any real depth of character in his Edmond. To be sure, Macy is as authentic as he can be in all the shades of the role; he never sets a foot wrong, but he never sets an especially right one, either. Thus we rarely sense the Edmond Burke in whom all these feelings—about his wife, about sex and sexuality, about race, religion, politics, and vocation—have been repressed for decades and who is now both maniacally gleeful and pitifully frightened by the bursting of his personal dam. The result is that Macy's Edmond at times appears to be an almost comic character. What the role calls for, and what Macy cannot quite provide, is the sense not of a simple robot unleashed but of a complex man who has been imprisoned for years by rote, and whose potency is only now breaking out in the only way it could at this late juncture, through physical force rather than force of character.

Macy notwithstanding, *Edmond* is forever available on film, in a lucid version, and I am glad for it. Whatever this version's flaws, Mamet's incantation works again. And *Edmond*, like *American Buffalo*, to name only Mamet's second-best drama (also filmed, in 1996), is above all a species of incantation: profane, yes, but so desperate in its profanity as to take on spiritual overtones. Edmond may not be as vacuous as Don and Teach in *American Buffalo*, but, even as they do, he tries to create through language some sense of autonomous being. The difference is that the middle-class Edmond is reaching for a higher or more authentic being—hence the more singular and expressionistic his search as well as his speech; whereas Don and Teach (and to a lesser extent young Bobby, the third character in *American Buffalo*) are trying to create through their dialogue only some sense of their lowly—and shared—being, a verbal environment in which that being can at least subsist. *American Buffalo*, then, is solely (if superbly) an instance of dramatic naturalism. *Edmond* begins in domestic naturalism but quickly extends beyond it, into a kind of super- or supra-naturalism that I am calling expressionism.

And through its very form, that of a morality or mystery play, this film invokes the spirit (if not religion itself), or the spiritual search for order, meaning, and harmony.

Thus, once again in the relatively brief history of this cinematic medium, we are indirectly reminded that the cinema began as a profane event and eventually came to include the sacred, by which it is edifyingly represented at least in part in the film of *Edmond*; while its ancient predecessor, the theater (ironically, where *Edmond* originated), began as a sacred event and eventually came to include the profane—by which it is now overwhelmingly represented on all the world's stages.

Not, however, in the case of Shakespeare. Hence I'd like, lastly, to consider perhaps the finest of the many Shakespearean adaptations made over the last twenty years or so: Kenneth Branagh's film of *Henry V* (1989). Although I believe, with James Agee, that "the creation of new dramatic poetry is more important than the re-creation of old," and that "for such new poetry, movies offer the richest opportunity since Shakespeare's time," some remarks are nonetheless in order about a film based on the work of so "cinematic" a dramatic poet. By "cinematic" in this case, I mean not only Shakespeare's episodic form, which like film can move easily through time and space, but also his creation of poetic word-pictures that lend themselves in some measure to screen transformation—into visual images or metaphors.

Let's begin with the play itself: depending on your understanding of history, *Henry V* (1599) is either Granville-Baker's sentimental appeal to patriotism fatally devoid "of some spiritually significant idea," or it is Yeats's tragically ironic treatment of an amiable egotist whose "gross vices" and "coarse nerves" render him capable, finally, of moral evil. To most of Shakespeare's contemporaries, Henry was a great national hero whose exploits of two centuries earlier (he was King of England from 1413 until his death in 1422), depicted onstage, could only fan the patriotic fervor of a generation that had seen the defeat of the Spanish Armada.

To Laurence Olivier, directing and starring in the first film version of the play in 1944, Henry was the same national hero leading an outnumbered, underequipped army in the service of a different cause: the rallying of patriotic spirit during England's fight for survival against Nazi Germany. To Kenneth Branagh, directing and starring in the second film version (and in his first film, after much theater work in Britain) in an era of post-empire and relative anti-militarism, Henry is "someone who at times captured a certain fineness of the human spirit, and at other times was a really ruthless bastard. I wanted to get all of that. Shakespeare doesn't apologize for this man—in fact, he is quite uncompromising in the way he presents him," at the same time as he depicts a Henry who led to victory an English army that seemingly had no chance, in a stage of despair and decay as it were, with its discipline ragged.

Branagh is right, and he includes in his film much of the unattractive side of Henry that Olivier understandably had omitted, despite an apparent attempt on Branagh's part to create a sympathetic analogy between Henry's army and the self-confessedly dispirited Britain of the late 1980s. Unlike Olivier, for example, Branagh does not dilute through comedy the early scene in which the young king seeks tortuous legal justification from two ecclesiastics for the extension of his royal power to certain French duchies and ultimately to the French crown. Olivier's Archbishop of Canterbury and Bishop of Ely are straight man and clown to Henry's good-natured, gutsy adventurer; Branagh's churchmen are astute politicians looking to protect Church monies and land from Henry's grasp, even as the King looks to carry out his dying father's advice that he "busy giddy minds with foreign quarrels" so as to quiet rebellion at home. One shot epitomizes the relationship between Henry and his prelates (the kind of shot which, if somehow translated to the stage, would seem unduly forced): just before deciding to invade France, he is at the center of a tight frame, with Canterbury and Ely in profile, crowding him on either side.

Another shot shortly thereafter visually underscores the inevitability of war, the fact that nothing will get in Henry's way: as he commands that "every man now task his thought, / That this fair action may on foot be brought," the King exits, followed by his lords, by walking directly at the camera. This impetuous movement carries over into Henry's next scene, during which he cunningly and somewhat pleasurably stalks and entraps—literally as well as figuratively—the three English noblemen (one of them his cousin, the Earl of Cambridge) who had taken French gold to assassinate him.

Oliver eliminates this scene (perhaps feeling that this material was inappropriate to wartime) in addition to three others included by Branagh: Henry's threats to Charles VI of France that "hungry war" will open its "vasty jaws" and leave nothing but "the widows' tears, the orphans' cries, / The dead men's blood, the privy maidens' groans"; the hanging of Bardolph for robbing a French church, an execution ordered by Henry (but only mentioned by Shakespeare); and Henry's vicious threats to the Governor of Harfleur to surrender or

> ... in a moment look to see
> The blind and bloody soldier with foul hand
> Defile the locks of your shrill-shriking daughters;
> Your fathers taken by the silver beards,
> And their most reverend heads dash'd to the walls;
> Your naked infants spitted upon pikes,
> ...

(Even Branagh, however, stops short of having Henry give his soldiers the strategic order during the Battle of Agincourt to cut their prisoners' throats—an order made all the more chilling by the fact that it *precedes* Henry's discovery of the killing of the boys [who maintain the English baggage train] by the French.)

So as to remove all taint from the character of his Henry V, Olivier goes as far as to delete the King's prayer on the eve of the decisive Battle of Agincourt (1415), in which he asks that God not make him pay this day for his father's usurpation of the crown from Richard II. (Henry's father, Bolingbroke, became King Henry IV.) But Branagh is right to keep this petition in his film, for it is key to an understanding of the play as Shakespeare wrote it and as it occupies the last slot in the cycle containing *Richard III, Henry IV, Part One*, and *Henry IV, Part Two*. In these plays, Shakespeare presents a society in transition from the medieval view of the world as a great chain of being, an utterly planned cosmos, under the direction of one God, to the Renaissance and even modern view of the world as a collection of self-serving individuals under the rule of secular—and therefore mutable—law. Divine law, in the form of Richard II's divine mandate, is ruptured when Richard gets deposed by Bolingbroke, and the rebellions that follow (predicted by Richard) in both parts of *Henry IV* can be seen as a natural consequence of the break in the venerable structure of authority.

Thus *secular* law reigns at the start of *Henry V*, twisted to the new king's aggressive purposes by divine, and divinely acquisitive, hands. And despite Henry's invocation of the Lord at strategic moments in the drama, indeed, his pairing of God's will with England's destiny, it is secularism that wins the day at Agincourt and continues to do so during the troubled reign of Henry VI, "Whose state so many had the managing, / That they lost France, and made his England bleed." (The infant Henry VI succeeded his father, who died not long after his triumph without ever having truly consolidated his gains in France.) Branagh, in contrast to Olivier, includes these deflating lines by the Chorus at the end of his film—a chorus that has, up to this point, discharged its role as a narrative bridge in confident tones—and his aim in this as well as in his depiction of a complex Henry V could only be to capture Shakespeare's play in all its ambivalence: as a patriotic, even jingoistic paean to King and country, on the one hand, and an ironic, even bitter denunciation of moral and political disorder, on the other. That disorder pervades the three *Henry VI* plays together with *Richard III*, in all of which England continues to suffer retribution for Henry Bolingbroke's overthrow and murder of a rightful monarch, Richard II. In Shakespeare's wishful, Providential scheme, only with the restitution of the legitimate successor at the end of *Richard III*—Henry VII, the first Tudor king—can England enjoy peace and greatness once again. There is but temporary peace at the end of *Henry V*, and the King's newfound greatness will be short-lived.

As a script, then, Branagh's version of *Henry V*—which is notably more complete than Olivier's—succeeds in capturing the essence of Shakespeare's play, of Henry's character, which is high praise for any film adaptation of a literary or dramatic source and particularly of Shakespeare (where judicious cutting of dialogue is necessary to avoid the duplication of information and ideas supplied or suggested by the visuals). Indeed the film even includes two flashbacks of tavern scenes from *Henry IV, Part Two* in order to suggest the profligacy Prince-Hal-become-King-Henry has left behind as well as the humanity, the fellow-feeling, he has retained from Falstaff's world. But why include these scenes and not others from *Henry IV, Part One* that are equally important to the formation of Henry's character? I'm thinking of those scenes that depict a loveless, morbid, impudent Hotspur obsessed with the achievement of individual glory on the battlefield, a man whose boldness so attracts his enemy, Prince Hal, that the latter is moved to pronounce a benediction over Hotspur's dead body—a benediction that includes the following ill-omened lines:

> Ill-weav'd ambition, how much art thou shrunk!
> When that this body did contain a spirit,
> A kingdom for it was too small a bound,
> But now two paces of the vilest earth
> Is room enough. . . .

Kenneth Branagh's performance as Henry certainly could have benefited from a few more parts ruthless Hotspur and a few less parts complaisant Falstaff—Branagh tries to project the former quality, especially in moments like the speech before Harfleur, but his doughboy face and woolly voice get in his way. *Selfish* charm is what Henry should exude, yet Branagh can't quite manage that and there was no room for it in Olivier's idealized conception of the character. Patrick Doyle's nearly continuous music does help Branagh with one aspect of his character but not this one, since it emphasizes his alternatively sentimental and majestic topside, never his dark underbelly. (The near continuousness of this music, by the way, highlights a difference between Branagh's film of *Henry V* and Olivier's where William Walton's score was good *theater* music—easily adaptable for use in a stage presentation of the play during the entrances, exits, battles, and so on.)

Kenneth Macmillan's cinematography, by contrast, simultaneously contains both sides of Henry's world: indoors, warm sepia tones over a palette mainly of browns and blacks and grays; outdoors, more or less, the same narrow range of color embraced by a softening mist, which becomes most prominent where it is most needed—at the brutal Battle of Agincourt, with its clashing swords, whistling arrows, falling horses, and flying bodies. How appropriate that in what would finally be a victory for secularism,

Henry V, dir. Kenneth Branagh, 1989

Macmillan should keep his camera low to the ground—to the muck of earthly reality as against the pomp of imperial-celestial circumstance—and in fairly close, at a few points even agonizingly extending earthly time by shooting in slow motion.

Branagh's Agincourt is an anti-heroic, grotesque ballet fought in the rain, whereas Olivier's was a glorious, decorative pageant that took place on a sunny day, with the heavens as a backdrop. (Branagh's Agincourt thus has more in common with the mud-soaked, fragmented, gruesomely powerful Battle of Shrewsbury in Orson Welles's *Chimes at Midnight* [a.k.a. *Falstaff,* 1966] than with Olivier's shining set piece.) Toward the end of this sequence in each film, a Te Deum can be heard on the soundtrack. But in Branagh's *Henry V* this choral hymn, beginning with the words "We praise thee, O God," takes on a grim irony less in light of the carnage we see (in a lengthy, diagonal tracking shot, the camera follows the victorious yet stunned Henry as he carries the dead York across the battlefield, only to leave him at last and look out in long shot over an entire corpse-strewn landscape) than of the convulsion we know has taken place in the body politic and the Providential design.

There are no scenes of battle-as-glory, then, in *Henry V*. War is as real as it can cinematically be made to appear in this film: savage, chaotic, claustrophobic; and what political glory may have derived from Henry's victory at Agincourt proved ultimately to be illusory. Branagh's *Henry V* is flawed, alas, but this nobly intended picture is worth seeing again and again, not least for its graphic battle sequences. Indeed, it may be the battle sequences of *Henry V* that in the end finally impress themselves most on our memories—as they never could on stage—since they alone are enough to remind us that, be the combatants English vs. French, German vs. American, or Asian vs. Caucasian, war makes equal, suffering, humble beasts of us all, no matter how glorious or ignoble the cause. For the royal Henry V, as for his plebeian men, the battlefield was ironically both the first and the last level field on which they would play. After battle, after life, would come the real judgment day—if not heaven's, then history's.

Henry V, dir. Laurence Olivier, 1944

As for the besetting trouble of Shakespeare on film—the conflict between a work that lives in its language and a medium that tries to do without language as much as it can—Kenneth Branagh's *Henry V* achieves, in its essentials, that difficult double feat that André Bazin once envisaged: it respects its theatrical original while also respecting its modern film idiom, and in such a way that, at its best, Branagh's vision and Shakespeare's coincide. Unlike Olivier, who used a theater-on-film or filmed-theater approach and whose *Henry V* thus becomes a genuine mixed-media event, Branagh opts as completely for the cinematic as the work will permit. But, despite his limitations as an heroic actor (modest voice, slight build, undistinguished face), he never subverts the size and majesty of the drama by trying to "modernize" it. He concentrates on trying to render that size and majesty in film terms; and, if we allow for a few constrictions along the way when the play seems to bump up against the microphone and the camera, Branagh does as well as anyone has ever done in making Shakespeare—not Shakespearean hash—filmic. (And he does better here, in my view, than in his subsequent *Much Ado about Nothing* [1993] and *Hamlet* [1996], both of which were marred by [American] lapses in casting, and the latter of which was updated to the second half of the nineteenth century for no discernible reason.)

Let me conclude with a comparison between the openings of Branagh's and Olivier's films of *Henry V*, which seem to me to epitomize the divergent ways in which drama and film proceed to their respective ends. Olivier began with a panoramic shot of Elizabethan London, after which he focused on the Globe Theater and its bustle. Then out on stage came the costumed Chorus (Leslie Banks). Branagh's Chorus (Derek Jacobi) throws a huge electrical switch and lights up an empty film studio as he moves through it. (In the whole picture he is the only one in modern dress.) Olivier began and continued with the metaphor of theater on film. Branagh, by contrast, makes us understand at once that his medium is film alone and that cinematic means, rather than transmutations of theater, will be his matter.

Olivier's own first entrance consisted of sliding his profile into place as the actor waited backstage at the Globe to go on. Branagh's first entrance is as king, not as actor. The great doors of the council chamber open, and the young monarch is revealed in silhouette against strong backlighting before he walks toward us. The camera deputizes for him, as if to suggest that in this production the camera will be king, courtiers bowing to it as it passes them. When Henry sits on his throne, we get the briefest glimpse of his face before we see the courtiers again; only then do we return for our first real look at him. This, I submit, is a purely cinematic entrance—of a singularly dramatic kind.

WORKS CITED

Agee, James. *Agee on Film: Reviews and Comments*. Boston: Beacon Press, 1958.
Hellman, Lillian. *The Little Foxes*. New York: Random House, 1939.
Mamet, David. *Edmund*. New York: Grove Press, 1983.
Pinter, Harold. *Betrayal*. New York: Grove Press, 1979.
Shakespeare, William. *Henry V*. In *The Norton Shakespeare*. Ed. Stephen Greenblatt et al. New York: W. W. Norton, 1997. 1454-1521.

3

Pride and Prejudice, or Class and Character:
Room at the Top Revisited

The working class has been a major subject of British art since the mid-1950s, when novelists such as John Braine and Alan Sillitoe, together with dramatists like John Osborne and Arnold Wesker, began treating anti-Establishment themes in a style that can be accurately characterized as "social realism." Soon social realism crossed over into film, where it became known as "New Cinema," a movement whose ethos or social commitment was borrowed from Italian neorealism; whose own techniques were modeled upon those of the French New Wave; and whose scripts were often adaptations of plays and novels by blue-collar writers. One thinks especially of Jack Clayton's *Room at the Top* (1958), based on the novel by Braine, Tony Richardson's *Look Back in Anger* (1959), from the play by Osborne, and Karel Reisz's *Saturday Night and Sunday Morning* (1960), a version of the Sillitoe novel.

Social-realist art in Britain was the product of the "Angry Young Men"—angry at a society that had educated them above their class origins yet had inevitably failed to provide sufficient opportunities for them in so small a country as England; and angry at a government that had improved the living and working conditions of the proletariat but had done nothing to remove class barriers, had in fact locked those barriers more firmly in place by giving the workers what they wanted, to a point. Witness, in addition to the works cited above, such films as Richardson's *The Loneliness of the Long Distance Runner* (1962), from a Sillitoe story, as well as his *A Taste of Honey* (1961), from the play by Shelagh Delaney; Lindsay Anderson's *This Sporting Life* (1963), from the novel by David Storey; and Guy Green's *The Angry Silence* (1960), from an original screenplay by Bryan Forbes.

The United States produced its own class of angry young men during the 1930s, led by Clifford Odets and represented by the workers' theatre movement, but American anger at the plight of the underclass (as opposed to the exclusively black underclass) has largely disappeared from art, primarily because, after World War II, America's white blue-collar workers became *de facto* members of the middle class as wages and standards of living rose. Even those workers who haven't benefited materially tend to identify with those who have. And American films reflect this state of affairs: with the possible exception of an occasional fiction film such as *Northern Lights* (1979) or *Matewan* (1987) and the documentaries of someone like Barbara Kopple, American workers tend to be featured in heroic, solidarity-promoting plots that will culminate in their common betterment (for example, Elia Kazan's *On the Waterfront* [1954] and Martin Ritt's *Norma Rae* [1979]); or they find themselves successfully struggling to become their own boss, to run their own business and thus shed the title of mere "worker," in such films as *An American Romance* (1944) and *Mac* (1992).

British workers, by contrast, continue to be the subject of unsentimental, unglorified tales that depict their hostility toward the ruling-class Establishment, their disillusionment with the Welfare State, and often their own narrow-minded, cynical resistance to change, which is as much the result of a misplaced pride as it is of a moral poverty bred of isolation, hopelessness, and improvidence. These workers persist in being the subject of narrative, dramatic, and cinematic art (by such filmmakers as Ken Loach, Mike Leigh, and Terence Davies) for two simple reasons: a blooded working class continues to subsist in England and, like the blooded aristocracy in that country, it tenaciously defines itself by accent, occupation, and attitude; and British artists' anger at the plight of the underclass—an anger that first expressed itself in Europe in the second half of the nineteenth century under the banner of naturalism—has not subsided.

When the plight of that underclass is depicted on film, something happens that will be vital to this discussion, and which happens in all films. To wit: by placing a working-class life on screen, the cinema automatically makes that life fascinating for having been so framed. By thus attracting our interest in a proletarian protagonist, film confers a kind of importance on him or her, on a lower-echelon person to whom we wouldn't normally give second thought in real life. (Film in this way holds a special, intriguing power over us: the power to engage simply by the act of isolating and framing, by embodying images.) Some novels attempt to do the same, of course, but one could argue that they are not as successful as films because in a book a working-class protagonist remains an abstraction, a composite of words. The pleasure we take in paying rapt attention to, and caring a lot about, such a person *on film* (or, to a slightly lesser extent, in the theater) is naturally as damning as it is astonishing.

The subject here is *Room at the Top*, partly because it was unique among British social-realist films not only in its depiction of upward mobility as opposed to social immobilization (see Hill, 157, and see also Palmer's critical attack on Clayton's film as a representative work of British social realism), but also in its choice of genre—a choice intimately related to the issue of a character's rise and fall. At least five critics have written that the film of *Room at the Top* leans toward popular melodrama, particularly from the moment the industrialist, Mr. Brown, offers the protagonist Joe Lampton his daughter, Susan, in marriage (Houston, 58; Manvell, 43-44; Garbicz and Klinowski, 402; Gaston, 10; Sinyard, 57). According to this view, the "evil," greedy Joe agrees to the marriage, which then causes his "good," abandoned lover, Alice, to get so drunk that she kills herself in a car accident. This essay shall go against such a reading of the film, and it will do so primarily through an investigation of Joe's behavior at several crucial moments in the action.

Only the film of *Room at the Top* will be considered in depth here, not John Braine's novel of the same title (1957) on which it is based, because the film version is probably better known and, in any event, is essentially true to its source. Neil Paterson's screenplay, of which Braine approved, strengthens the storyline of the novel through the rearrangement of some incidents, the cutting of others, and the development of still others and of certain characters. In other words, the film heightens the *drama*, the interaction and clash of character, in the story; it pares the plot down to the essentials while it keeps, and enhances, the detail and atmosphere of the novel's locations in England's industrial north simply by photographing them. *Room at the Top* has been described as a "male weepie," but this is truer of the novel than of its cinematic adaptation, because the film eschews the special pleading of Joe Lampton's first-person narrative in the book and gives more prominence to the characters of Alice Aisgill and Susan Brown than Braine does.

Before receiving Mr. Brown's offer of marriage to his daughter over lunch at the exclusive "Conservative Club" of Warnley, in Yorkshire, Joe Lampton had declared his love for Alice Aisgill during a weekend at the coast. She is a Frenchwoman (in the film—possibly because of the casting of Simone Signoret in the role—but not in the novel) of obscure origins, perhaps from a working-class background similar to Joe's (he reminds her, she says, of a boy she once knew), who is married to an upper-class Englishman; Alice is thus, like Joe, an outsider in Warnley. Upon returning home from the coast for work in the city's Treasury Department, Joe is confronted by her husband, George, with the latter's knowledge of the illicit affair. George tells him that he will not grant Alice a divorce and that Joe must never see her again. If he does not comply, George Aisgill declares that he will drag Joe into court—which will break him financially as well as expose him to scandal—in addition to withholding monetary support from his wife.

When Joe meets with Mr. Brown, therefore, he is in a somewhat desperate situation: he knows that he does not love Susan and that he loves Alice, but may not be able to remain with her. Mr. Brown at first offers to set Joe up in business and make him a rich man in exchange for leaving Susan alone. Mr. Brown is testing Joe here, but he also means what he says. Joe is presented, in other words, with a way out of his desperate situation: if he gives up Susan for good, her father will buy him his own accounting firm, the income from which will enable Joe to fight George Aisgill in court and take Alice (whom he holds onto out of spite, not love) away from him.

Out of pride, out of a desire not to be manipulated in such a way by a member of the moneyed class—*not* out of love for Susan—Joe refuses her father's first offer, despite Mr. Brown's threat to ruin him if he does not accept. Impressed with Joe's show of character and with what appears to be his love for Susan, Mr. Brown then offers him both his daughter in marriage and a top job in the Brown family business, provided that he never see Alice Aisgill

Pride and Prejudice   53

again. Tellingly, Mr. Brown also reveals that Susan is pregnant by Joe. Himself once a member of the working class, the father thus has been testing this working-class young man's suitability for marriage. Joe is now confronted with the choice, on the one hand, of a good job in the Brown firm and Susan as a wife, whom he cannot betray for Alice; and, on the other hand, he is confronted with the choice of remaining in his job as an accountant for the city and risking everything by continuing to see Alice in the face of George Aisgill's warnings not to do do.

Joe's pride, his belief in himself as the equal of his so-called "betters"—and his consequent desire to love, and be loved by, one of them, as well as to share, through marriage, the upper class's power and fortune—had in the first place caused him to seek Susan's favor upon his arrival in Warnley from his dreary hometown of Dufton, in Gloucestershire. Now Joe's pride has placed him in a terrible tragic dilemma, marked by strong internal division: either he weds Susan and lives comfortably, if miserably, or he refuses to

Room at the Top, dir. Jack Clayton, 1958

marry her and attempts against all odds to win Alice as his wife. And one can be certain that if Joe refuses Mr. Brown's second offer, the latter will ensure that George Aisgill succeeds in his attempts to ruin Joe and Alice. As Mr. Brown (who calls Alice an "old whore") says, he can fix just about anything. Joe knows all this and therefore, after downing a double Scotch, he chooses Susan and a job in the Brown business. Later he courageously decides to tell Alice of his decision in person rather than writing her a letter, as Susan suggests. That, during their meeting, Joe says to Alice over and over again, "*I'm going to marry Susan!*" seems to indicate, however, more that he is talking himself into this decision than that he is declaring his mind made up.

Far from veering toward popular melodrama at the end, then, the film of *Room at the Top* approaches high tragedy. Joe is no villain who gets what he wants at some poor woman's expense. His spiritual life, awakened by his love for Alice, began its descent once he gave up his love for her and is over the moment she dies in the automobile crash. The film suggests as much in the office scene at Town Hall and its aftermath. Amidst congratulations from the secretaries and his fellow workers on his impending marriage to Susan and his appointment to the Brown firm, Joe overhears a conversation in which Alice's death is reported. He then smashes his champagne-filled glass to the floor and hastily exits, winding up late that night at a working-class pub where he gets thoroughly drunk in the company of a local girl.

Her jealous boyfriend and some of his cronies subsequently give Joe a vicious beating. In the novel, Joe fights back, but here he is masochistically passive, as if tragically willing his own (deserved) punishment. We sense this partly because, as he is being beaten in the film, a train whistle can be heard in the distance, so shrill that Joe looks up: for this is a ghostly reminder of the painful farewell scene between him and Alice after their idyllic few days together at the coast, during which they both seemed to sense the end of their relationship. After the beating, Joe gets thrown into a dirty canal whose surface aptly reflects the neon sign of one of Mr. Brown's factories. Joe's descent is now complete—for the moment, physically as well as spiritually. His spirit will remain in the gutter, despite the place he will soon take at the top through marriage to Susan. Correctly, he blames himself for Alice's death; just as correctly, if you will, he has chosen unhappy marriage with Susan over bankruptcy and disgrace for himself and Alice at George Aisgill's hands. Hence Joe Lampton's tragedy, not quite proletarian and not up to the aristocratic but something in between and all the worse for it.

When *Room at the Top* was released in America, Robert Hatch wrote that "the film repeatedly suggests that there is something important about Joe Lampton, but what it is never comes clear" (395). Philip Hartung echoed Hatch with the line, "I'm not sure that Joe Lampton is worth all this attention" (22). Joe would argue, as he does in the film, that he is "working class and proud of it"; that is, that he is important by virtue of *his*, and by extension the film's, belief in his importance, in his own special humanity. His tragedy is that he remains working class at heart at the same time as he assumes the manners and dress of, first the middle class, then the upper class; he remains working class in his pride, one might say. Further, Joe's tragedy is that, not satisfied with his sense of self-importance as the son of working-class parents who gave their lives during the war, and as the subsequent ward of a loving aunt and uncle, he strives to become important to people like the Browns.

The great irony is that at the moment he becomes "important" through marriage into the Brown family, Joe has ceased to be of importance to us. At the moment he reaches the top, he has in fact reached the bottom. Braine's novel ends with Joe's expression of remorse that no one understands him, but Clayton's film goes one step further by depicting the marriage itself, Joe's accompanying "recognition, and the most ironic of happy endings. Joe hesitates a long time before uttering a tepid "I do" during the wedding ceremony that will formally admit him to the top, as if he is completely aware of the finality of the "sentence" he is imposing on himself and wants to extend his freedom just a few more moments before losing it. His hesitation here is the externalization of the hesitation he inwardly felt at his decision to wed Susan in the first place, and which he tried to dispel by affirming again and again, "*I'm going to marry Susan!*"

The tears Joe sheds in the car as he and his bride are driven away from the church are thus for himself as well as for Alice.

Susan thinks these are tears of joy and sentiment as she happily declares "Till death do us part" to her new huband. But "death" for Joe in this instance means the death sentence that is his marriage and the death of all that was once good in him. Alone in spirit if not in body, he is seemingly encapsulated in the limousine—the image of luxury that had triggered his ambition, and one of a number of status-related car images that appear in both the novel and the film of *Room at the Top*—as we watch the open road quickly disappear behind him through the rear window. The last shot of the film is of the Bentley itself as it disappears into the distance and heads to the "top"—Joe Lampton's ultimate goal, at last achieved—yet at the same time travels down what seems to be an overpoweringly deserted, lonely street.

Connected with the issue of tragedy versus melodrama in *Room at the Top*, Penelope Houston posed the following question, without answering it, at the time of the film's British release: "Is [Joe] the victim of his own character, or of a social system which has formed him and given him bitterness?" (57). Joe is the victim of his own character *and* of the English social system; his tragedy is at once of his and his society's making. The pride that makes it impossible for him to accept Mr. Brown's offer of an accounting firm, in return for leaving Susan alone, was born, not in a vacuum and not to every working-class man in England, but of the resentment Joe in particular felt as a member of the oppressed laboring class in his native Dufton as well as in the Royal Air Force (where, he reports, as an enlisted man who rose to the rank of Sergeant, commissioned officers bossed him about). In other words, *he* felt the resentment, even bitterness, and his society supplied the discrimination that made him feel it.

Indeed, it is precisely the inevitability of Joe's fall that stems in considerable part from the nature of his own character, formed as it was by his experience during the war as well as by his life of poverty and social humiliation in Dufton. The war gave Joe a taste of freedom, a kind of holiday from class restrictions, and it was this period-aspect of *Room at the Top*—not Joe Lampton's working-class origins—that attracted the director of the film, war-veteran Jack Clayton (who, like his fellow war veterans Neil Paterson and Freddie Francis [cinematography], was not born into the working class, as was John Braine, the novel's author). According to Clayton, "Holidays abroad for the English . . . prior to 1939 were basically for rich people. But in the war there was this enormous flowing population, going all over the world, having totally new experiences" (Gow, 13).

The war also fueled Joe's feelings of resentment toward the upper class, represented by his haughty, sneering superior officers in the Royal Air Force. He admits that he did not try to break out during his three years in a German prisoner-of-war camp, unlike Susan's suitor Jack Wales, an officer who was successful in his escape attempt. (In John Westbrook's performance, the snobbish Wales comes off as being a much more unpleasant character than in the novel, as do the characters of George Aisgill and Susan's mother in Allan Cuthbertson's and Ambrosine Phillpotts's performances. The reason may be that this is in fact how the Joe of the film sees them, in a compensatory bow to his role as the first-person narrator of the novel.) Joe's pride caused him to wait out the war in prison, for he preferred detainment in one place by the Nazis to a kind of subjugation all over Europe by British officers.

On account of his pride, in other words, Joe chose to "entrap" himself in a German jail. Similarly, after experiencing the freedom of a larger, more variegated town like Warnley, he traps himself in marriage to Susan as the result of his pride, after refusing Mr. Brown's first offer—to set him up in business in return for leaving Susan alone—during lunch at the Warnley "Conservative Club." Just as Joe did not want to be ordered about willfully and contemptuously by Royal Air Force officers, he does not wish to be pressured to do something, for a price, by the commanding Mr. Brown.

The inevitability of Joe's fall is even reflected in *Room at the Top*'s visual style, as composed by the cinematographer Freddie Francis and the art director Ralph Brinton. Even as he is ostensibly enjoying his relative economic and social freedom in classier, "cosmopolitan" Warnley, the camera is "trapping" Joe the whole time through tight framing in restrictive settings. He lives in very cramped quarters, just as he did in Dufton: when he visits his aunt and uncle there, the scene is confined to one dark, dreary room whose low-hanging ceiling presses down on the characters. When Joe gets on the bus for work in Warnley with his fellow employee and housemate Charles Soames and has to stand, not only does the camera cut him off just below the waist, but many other passengers crowd around as well, hemming him in.

The camera also presses in on Joe when he telephones Susan after his return from Dufton, only to be told by her mother that she is vacationing in the south of France. We get a close-up of his face here, less to emphasize his emotional state than to stress his confinement, in character if not ultimately in career, within the working-class world of his origins. Moreover, this close-up is harshly juxtaposed against the full-body shot of Mrs. Brown answering her telephone in a spacious living room. Ironically, Joe is exultant after this call, declaring to Charles that the Browns are falling into his trap, that by removing their daughter from his sight they are only increasing her fondness for him. Joe barely has space to express his happiness in this scene, since the low walls and angled ceiling of his attic room seem to be collapsing in on him.

The camera's tight framing of Joe Lampton continues during his love scenes with Alice Aisgill. Naturally, when they are so framed in bed, their intimacy is underlined. But when the lovers are photographed sometimes from the neck up, at other times from the waist up, as they walk about their trysting place (the tiny apartment of Alice's friend, Elspeth) during an argument, something other than intimacy is being indicated. The camera is cutting them off, limiting their already limited space, and thereby suggesting that the world is closing in on them. At issue here, significantly, is Joe's pride, which has flared up in response to Alice's revelation that she had once posed nude for a photographer. Just as he was too proud to be subjugated by Royal Air Force officers during the war and will later be too proud to capitulate to Mr. Brown by accepting his offer of an accounting firm in return for breaking off with Susan, Joe is too proud to submit, in a manner of speaking, to all the men who are "having" Alice (through nude photographs)—and "having" her younger, more voluptuous self at that—at the same time as he has her. So upset is Joe at Alice's revelation that he ends the affair, only to reunite with her after his conquest of Susan. It is after they get back together that they sojourn on the coast, where, after it stops raining and they can leave their small cottage, they still seem confined: as they walk on the beach in the middle distance, the piles of a pier frame them on either side in the foreground.

Let's be clear: *Room at the Top* does not argue that Joe Lampton should have stuck to his own people, as his uncle advises him to do; that he should have been happy to live among the working class of Dufton at the same time as his accountant's salary enabled him to live above them, so to speak. (At one point during the movie, in order to get Joe away from Susan, Mr. Brown arranges a very good job for him back in Dufton, which Joe refuses when he learns who is responsible for it.) *Room at the Top* is not reactionary, it is not a cautionary tale, and neither is it revolutionary. The film does not emphasize the class struggle, as Peter Cowie maintains (224). Nor does it give, in Thomas W. Bohn and Richard L.Stromgren's words, human form to social protest through the character of Joe Lampton (306).

Joe knows that he is any man's equal, if not his better. He comes to Warnley with the city accountant's job in hand, so "equal opportunity" is not an issue in the film. As Stanley Kauffmann has written, in his pursuit of Susan, Joe "yearns for power, not equality" (21), yearns to join the upper class, not dismantle it. Joe is out for himself, not for the class of his origin; he is out to avenge past wrongs done to *him*, to get what is coming to *him*. His alienation from the working class becomes clear when, back in Dufton for the job interview Mr. Brown has secretly set up, he returns to his boyhood home, which is now a bomb site. When he tries to be friendly to the mother of a little girl with whom he had been talking and tells the woman that he used to live next to her house, she dismisses him as a total stranger and slams the door in his face.

For better or worse, then, the social classes are in place in *Room at the Top* and on the evidence will remain in place, *have* remained so. The issue is not the proletarian revolution, on the one hand, or the preservation of the class system, on the other, but Joe Lampton's attempt to rise through the classes. The film is timeless, not timely; its subject is a complex human being, not an oversimplified sociopolitical cause. Paradoxically, Joe's working-class pride drove him to educate himself out of the working class, then compelled him to try to get a piece of the upper class. Tragically, the pride that enabled him to endure years of poverty and social humiliation is the same pride that undoes him spiritually in the end. In a sense, the class of his origin finally has its revenge on him for leaving it, while he proves that class is no barrier to someone with strength, ability, and determination.

Of course, Joe pays a great price in order to prove his point—he "wastes" Alice Aisgill. She may be the "tragic waste" of this story, but one could argue that in killing herself she has also "killed" Joe and thus had her revenge on him. This, however, is revenge of an especially spiritual kind, adumbrated by Polonius's famous line in *Hamlet*, which is quoted by Joe and Alice together during their cottage-idyll by the sea: "This above all: to thine own self be true." In his courtship of Susan, Joe had seemed quite consciously *untrue* to himself by playing the role of the abused and misunderstood lover, at one stage even going down on his knees to her and having Susan the schoolgirl romantic fall for it. It is in the scenes with Alice, though, that the tension between identity and ambition, self and performance, becomes uncomfortable for Joe. Significantly, he later cannot remember Polonius's words, and it is Alice who has to complete Shakespeare's line for him. Not cited in Braine's novel, this line from *Hamlet* emphasizes the insistent theme or motif of authenticity that runs throughout the film, and it contains the core of Alice's ultimate, vengeful rebuke of the man she loves: not that he has betrayed her, but that he has betrayed himself.

In short, far from cheapening its action by resolving it through melodrama, the film of *Room at the Top* enriches that action throughout by consistently suggesting its tragic underpinnings. There are no black-and-white characters in the film, no genuine heroes or thoroughgoing villains, no defeat of the guilty and reward of the innocent: each of the central characters wins, and each one loses. Put another way, that's life—or it's tragedy.

WORKS CITED

Bohn, Thomas W., and Richard L. Stromgren. *Light and Shadows: A History of Motion Pictures*. 2nd ed. Sherman Oaks, Calif.: Alfred Publishing Co., 1978.

Cowie, Peter. *Seventy Years of Cinema*. South Brunswick, New Jersey: A. S. Barnes, 1969.

Garbicz, Adam, and Jacek Klinowski. *Cinema, the Magic Vehicle: A Guide to Its Achievement*. Metuchen, New Jersey: Scarecrow Press, 1979.

Gaston, George M. A. *Jack Clayton: A Guide to References and Resources.* Boston: G. K. Hall, 1981.

Gow, Gordon. "The Way Things Are: Jack Clayton in an Interview." *Films and Filming*, 20.7 (April 1974): 10-14.

Hartung, Philip. "The Screen: All the Sad Young Men Are Angry." *Commonweal*, 3 April 1959.

Hatch, Robert. "Films." *The Nation*, 25 April 1959.

Hill, John. *Sex, Class, and Realism: British Cinema 1956-1963.* London: BFI Publishing, 1986.

Houston, Penelope. "Room at the Top?" *Sight and Sound*, 28.2 (Spring 1959).

Kauffmann, Stanley. "Angry Man on the Make." *The New Republic*, 13 April 1959.

Manvell, Roger. *New Cinema in Britain.* London: Studio Vista, 1969.

Palmer, R. Barton. "What Was New in the British New Wave?: Reviewing *Room at the Top.*" *Journal of Popular Film and Television,* 14.3 (Fall 1986): 125-135.

Sinyard, Neil. *Jack Clayton.* Manchester, U.K.: Manchester University Press, 2000.

4

Fiction into Film:
Tolstoy's *The Counterfeit Note* and Bresson's *L'Argent*; Dostoevsky's *A Gentle Spirit* and Bresson's *Une Femme douce*

All of Robert Bresson's feature films after *Les Anges du péché* (1943) have literary antecedents of one form or another. Two are from Dostoevsky (*Une Femme douce* [1969], *Quatre nuits d'un rêveur* [1971]), two from Bernanos (*Mouchette* [1967], *Journal d'un curé de campagne* [1951]), one from Tolstoy (*L'Argent* [1983]), and one from Diderot (*Les Dames du Bois de Boulogne* [1945]), while *Un Condamné à mort s'est échappé* (1956) and *Le Procès de Jeanne d'Arc* (1962) are based on written accounts of true events. In addition, *Pickpocket* (1959) is clearly influenced by Dostoevsky's *Crime and Punishment* and *Au hasard, Balthazar* (1966) has a premise similar to *The Idiot*. *Lancelot du Lac* (1974), for its part, is derived from Sir Thomas Malory's Arthurian legends, while *Le Diable probablement* (1977) was inspired by a newspaper report, as stated at the start of the film. Even a longstanding, unrealized film project of Bresson's was to come from a literary source—in this case, the Book of Genesis (*Genèse*).

By the time he completed the adaptation of *L'Argent* (*Money*) in 1983, Bresson (1901-1999) was probably the oldest active director in the world. But his evolution had been in striking contrast to that of his contemporaries. Even if we do not take into account those filmmakers whose declines had been conspicuous, most of the senior statesmen of the cinema showed in their later phases a serenity of style, an autumnal detachment from reality, which compares with that of elder artists in other genres such as the drama, the novel, and poetry. Not so with Bresson. *L'Argent*, his thirteenth and final film (freely adapted from Tolstoy's 1905 novella *The Counterfeit Note*), was made in essentially the same strict, tense, controlled style—here used in the depiction of extraordinary violence—that he used in *Les Anges du péché* (*Angels of the Streets*) in 1943.

Hence Buffon was mistaken: style is not the man himself, it's the universe as seen by the man. (Many a disorderly person has been an artist with an orderly style.) But neither is style a separable system into which an artist feeds material. Van Gogh didn't look at the night sky and decide that it would be pretty to paint the constellations as whirls. And Joyce didn't decide it would be clever to describe that same sky as "the heaventree of stars hung with humid nightblue fruit." Neither artist had, in a sense, much choice. His style, of course, was refined through a lifetime and first drafts were not often final drafts, but the temper and vision of that style were given from the start.

Thus it's impossible to imagine Bresson *deciding* to make *L'Argent* as he did. On the basis of his career, we can assume that, at some time after he had read Tolstoy's story, his mind and imagination shaped the structure and look of his film in ways that his mind and imagination had long been doing. It's a kind of fatalism, I believe. Not all fine artists work in the same way all their lives: the Japanese director Yasujiro Ozu is one who did not. But some, like Bresson, do.

Consequently you know, if you're familiar with Bresson's *oeuvre*, that *L'Argent* was made with non-actors. He rarely used professionals, and he called his untrained non-professionals "models," whom he instructed to speak their lines and move their bodies without conscious interpretation or motivation, in a determined attempt on this director's part to keep them from psychologizing their characters. Bresson hated acting and often said so. He chose people instead who had what he considered the right personal qualities for their roles, and he said that he never used people twice because the second time they would try to give him what he wanted in place of what they were. It's as if he were guided by Kleist's line that "Grace appears most purely in that human form which either has no consciousness or has an infinite consciousness: that is, in the puppet or in the god." Since Bresson couldn't employ gods, he got as close as possible to puppets—with non-actors. They enact the story of *L'Argent*, as of Bresson's other films, much as medieval townsfolk might have enacted a mystery or morality play, with little skill and much conviction.

Apart from the acting—or non-acting—you also know, if you've seen Bresson's films, that if the subject was contemporary (as it is in *L'Argent*), the sounds of metropolitan life were probably heard under the credits, as if to adumbrate the role that such sound, *any* sound, would play in the film to follow. You recall that the story was told with almost Trappist austerity and emotional economy, in such an elliptical, fragmentary, even lacunary way that only in its interstices can be found its poetry—indeed, much of its meaning. You recall as well that Bresson's camera fixed on places a moment before characters entered and remained a moment after they left, not only to include environment as a character but also to signify that humans are transient in the world; and you are aware that, in any one of his films, probably a chain of consequences would begin with an event seemingly unrelated to the conclusion.

In our time, when we are saturated more than ever with images of the most superficially realistic kind, particularly on television, Bresson thus tried to wash our eyes and lead us to see differently— to bathe our vision, as it were, in an alternative reality. Moreover, his distrust of words—Bresson's laconic dialogue is almost as characteristic of his work as the neutral tone of its delivery—often made him choose characters (like Mouchette in the film of the same name, or like the truck driver of *L'Argent*) who have little or no ability to speak, and who therefore suffer their oppression in silence. And often we see as little of them as we hear of their dialogue, for Bresson liked to focus his camera on a door through which a person passed or on a "headless" body approaching a door, turning the knob, and passing through. (His rare moving shots were usually reserved for that kind of traversal.)

When it isn't doorknobs in *L'Argent*, it's cell doors—in prisons that are so clean and well-run, so intensely physical as well as aural, so much a part of society's organization, that they freeze the marrow. (The suggestion, of course, is that humanity itself, inside or outside prison, is trapped behind four walls. Possibly prisons figure so often in Bresson's films—in addition to *L'Argent*, they can be found in *A Man Escaped, Pickpocket, The Trial of Joan of Arc*, and as early as *Les Anges du péché*—and are the most emblematic of his décors, because he himself spent eighteen months in a German P.O.W. camp during World War II.) Bresson thus put places, things, and people on virtually the same plane of importance. Other directors do this, too—Antonioni, for instance. But with Antonioni, it's to show that the physical world is inescapable, almost a person itself; Bresson, by contrast, wanted to show that the world and the things in it are as much a part of God's mind as the people in the world.

Let me address the world of *L'Argent* in a bit more detail, because its pattern is simple yet common in the work of Bresson: a pebble is moved, and the eventual result is an avalanche. A teenaged Parisian from a wealthy home asks his father for extra money, besides his weekly allowance, to repay a debt. The money is refused. The teenager then consults a friend of his age and station, who has counterfeit banknotes (no explanation of the source) and knows where to pass them (no explanation of the knowledge). The youths pass off a false note to a woman in a camera shop. When her husband discovers the fraud, he passes off the note to the driver of an oil-delivery truck. The truck driver is subsequently framed as a passer of counterfeit money and the ensuing scandal causes him to lose his job. In order to continue supporting his family, he tries driving a getaway car for some criminals, but their heist doesn't go so well and he is sent to prison for three years. While incarcerated,

L'Argent, dir. Robert Bresson, 1983

his child dies of diphtheria and his wife leaves him. Crazed upon release from jail, the former husband and father turns to theft, violent crime, and eventually cold-blooded murder before turning himself in to the police—for good, as it were.

This seemingly random and ultimately sensationalistic story holds because, as in all of Bresson, the focus is not on the story, it's on matters of which we get only some visible-audible evidence. That is to say, to the devoutly Catholic Bresson, evil is as much a part of life as good, and what happens here en route to God's judgment is not to be taken as proof or disproof of God's being. Though the sentimentalist in Tolstoy (on display in *The Counterfeit Note*) would disagree, God does not prove, does not want to prove, his existence by making the good prosper and the wicked suffer, by aiding the morally weak or rescuing the ethically misled. (The most religious person in the film becomes a murder victim.) This world is, after all, only this world, says *L'Argent*; God alone knows everything, the suffering of the faithful and also the suffering of the sinner.

Bresson's world-view is well conveyed here by his two cinematographers, Emmanuel Machuel and Pasqualino de Santis (who had worked for Bresson before). All the colors look pre-Raphaelite, conveying the innocent idea of blue or red or any other color. And this fits Bresson's "innocent" method: violence runs through *L'Argent* but is never seen. When the truckdriver commits a double murder, for instance, all we see of it is the tap water that runs red in a basin for a few moments as he washes his hands. When he commits ax killings, the only stroke we see occurs when he hits a lamp. This "innocence" extends to the last sequence of the film. The driver, who has killed off a family in an isolated country house, goes to an inn, where he sits and has a cognac. It is then that he turns himself in: by calmly walking over to some policemen standing at the bar and confessing his crimes. In the next shot we are with the crowd outside the inn door. As they watch, the police come out, taking the driver away. We never see him again; instead, the camera places us with the innocent bystanders, who continue to watch the door, watching for more police, more prisoners. But there will be no more, and the film ends on the image of the crowd, waiting and watching—the constant disposition of every moviegoer as well, to be sure, but, even more so, the habitual stance of the audience of any Bresson film, where the emphasis falls on the watching (and the hearing) *while* you're waiting.

The other remarkable aspect of Bresson's *oeuvre*, aside from the consistency of his style, can be deduced from the content of *L'Argent* as summarized above: to wit, forty years after his real beginning in 1943 with *Les Anges du péché*, his films still had the power to create scandal. (The director disowned his first feature, a surrealist comedy called *Les Affaires publiques* [1934], which was once thought to be lost but was found again in 1988 at the Cinémathèque française in Paris and publicly re-screened there for the first time.) Even as *Pickpocket* was rejected by many at the time of its release (but hailed by New Wave filmmakers like François Truffaut, Jean-Luc Godard, and Louis Malle, then making their first films, as a landmark in modern cinema), *L'Argent* was booed by the audience at Cannes in 1983 despite the fact that it won the Grand Prize for creative cinema (together with Andrei Tarkovsky's *Nostalgia*).

The director himself faced a violent reaction when he received the award from Orson Welles—himself no stranger to rejection and scandal. The irony in this instance was that Bresson, the avowed Catholic and a political conservative, was attacked by all the right-wing newspapers in France that in the past had defended his films. At the core of this attack, one can detect an exasperation with, even a hostility toward, an artist whose lack of commercial success had nonetheless never made him sacrifice one iota of his integrity, and who always maintained his rigorous artistic standards.

It is sometimes forgotten that part of Bresson's integrity—his moral or ethical rigor, if you will—was his insistence on treating his share of socially as well as linguistically marginalized characters, in such films as *Pickpocket*, *Au hasard, Balthazar*, and *Mouchette*. Yet no one would ever have called him a working-class naturalist like Luc and Jean-Pierre Dardenne, whose pictures, even though they sometimes have an implicit Christian component (especially *Rosetta* [1999] and *The Son* [2002]), are closer in subject to the social-problem play tradition of the European naturalistic theater. Bresson, by contrast, was a transcendental stylist (to use Paul Schrader's term) concerned to unite the spiritualism of religious cinema with realism's redemption of the physical world in its organic wholeness

Fiction into Film   69

if not otherness, its inviolable mystery, and its eternal primacy or self-evidence.

I would like now to reconsider what I believe to be Bresson's most underrated film from a literary source: *Une Femme douce*, or *A Gentle Creature*.[1] This was his first work in color and his ninth film, after the 1876 novella *A Gentle Spirit* by Dostoevsky, which, like a number of Dostoevsky's earlier works (and like Bresson's own *Le Diable probablement*), was inspired not by a literary source but by a news report about the suicide of a seamstress who threw herself out a window clutching an icon in her hands. (Though not inspired by a literary source, *A Gentle Spirit* does feature extensive literary illusions to writers such as Gogol, Hugo, Mill, Herzen, Lermontov, Lesage, Kraevsky, Pushkin, and Shakespeare.) Bresson regarded Dostoevsky as the world's greatest novelist, doubtless for his spiritual strain—an almost existential one, in contrast with the sentimental religiosity of Tolstoy—because Bresson avoids Dostoevsky's preoccupation with truth and his probing of human psychology or motivation. Put another way, this most Catholic of filmmakers (French or otherwise) always forbids the surface as well as the depths of naturalism from distracting us from the mystical moments in his films, which cannot be explicated or revealed in any positivistic manner.

Those moments, to be sure, involve cinematic characters, but Bresson makes us focus, not on the story in the human beings on screen, but on the human beings in the story and their sometimes complete lack of connection to or understanding of what happens to them. Bresson almost disconnects character from story in this way. His is an extreme reaction to decades of "dramatic" pictures, where character is action and action character; "action" movies, in which the characters are designed to fit the exciting plot; and films "of character," where the plot is designed to present interesting characters—those with a "story," that is. To the oversimplifications of character of the cinema before him, Bresson responds by not simplifying anything, by explaining almost nothing. To the self-obsession of the Hollywood star system, the "dream factory," Bresson responds in the extreme by calling for complete self-denial on the part of his actors. (Hence his designation of them as "models."[2])

Let us begin simply with the plot of *Une Femme douce*, so that we can instructively compare what Bresson and Dostoevsky do with more or less the same series of events. A contemporary young woman in her early twenties, unnamed and of uncertain background as well as insufficient means, for no apparent reason marries a pawnbroker, also unnamed, whom she meets in his shop. She tells this man that she does not love him, and she makes it very clear that she disdains his, and all, money; if she is marrying to escape her origins, it remains unclear exactly what those origins were and why she is choosing to escape them in this particular way. The woman (as she is called in the credits, like "the man") and her husband go through periods of much unhappiness—we even see her with another man at one point, but we cannot be sure that she has been unfaithful—and some calm. Then she nearly shoots her spouse to death in his sleep. Later she becomes quite ill, and, once she recovers, matters appear to be righting themselves between her and her husband. Nonetheless, she proceeds to jump to her death from the balcony of their Paris apartment.

Une Femme douce, dir. Robert Bresson, 1969

The plot, as well as the urban setting, of Dostoevsky's novella *A Gentle Spirit* is substantially similar to this one, allowing for differences in time (mid-to-late nineteenth century) and age (the wife is sixteen years old), with a few major exceptions. The first is that the backgrounds of the young woman and the pawnbroker are filled in—as they as not in *Une Femme douce*:

> Her father and mother were dead, they had died three years before, and she had been left with two disreputable aunts: though it is saying too little to call them disreputable. One aunt was a widow with a large family (six children, one smaller than another), the other a horrid old maid. Both were horrid. Her father was in the service, but only as a copying clerk, and was only a gentleman by courtesy; in fact, everything was in my favour. I came as though from a higher world; I was anyway a retired lieutenant of a brilliant regiment, a gentleman by birth, independent and all the rest of it, and as for my pawnbroker's shop, her aunts could only have looked on that with respect. She had been living in slavery at her aunts' for these three years . . . She taught her aunt's children; she made their clothes; and towards the end not only washed the clothes, but . . . even scrubbed the floors. (Constance Garnett translation)

Moreover, Dostoevsky's pawnbroker goes so far as to analyze his own behavior, stating that he is "not particularly talented, not particularly intelligent, not particularly good-natured," calling himself a "cheap egoist," and declaring that, in taking up the pawnbroking business, he was revenging himself on society. His past behavior is even investigated—by his wife. She learns from a military officer named Efinovitch that her husband had been dismissed from the armed services on account of his cowardice in refusing to fight a duel, and that for three years afterwards he wandered the streets of Petersburg like a tramp, begging for coins and spending his nights in pool halls. But the wife does not use this information against her husband, choosing instead to remain loyal to him—in part because she seems to understand, as the pawnbroker himself confesses in chapter seven (the first one in Part II of the novella), that the "gloomy past" and his "ruined reputation" have troubled him "every day, every hour," and that, in marrying, he was bringing a much needed "friend" into his home.

The final big difference between the plots of the novella and the film is that the young wife in Dostoevsky's narrative is at first very loving toward her husband, whose offer of marriage she chooses over that of a shopkeeper, with the result that the main turns of the plot, as described in my summary of *Une Femme douce*, are easily explained. The husband in the novella—he is the narrator both of the novella and of Bresson's film—distrusts, out of his own perverse obsession with verifiable as opposed to intuited truth, his wife's love for him ("She loved me . . . she wanted to love . . . she was trying to love"), so he decides to test it. He is cold toward her and, despite his own dishonorable discharge from the military and resulting penury, holds over her head the fact that he has rescued her from her poor beginnings. For these reasons, she eventually comes to hate her husband and almost to commit adultery. By chapter six, the last one in Part I of the novella (whose second part contains four chapters), she is even ready to shoot him. With his wife's gun at his temple one morning, the man awakens from his sleep but does not move. Yet she cannot fire.

That same day she contracts "brain fever," from which she slowly recovers as a result of medical care paid for by her husband. So complete is her recovery that she even begins to sing in his presence, an act that prompts him to kiss her feet, promise to be a changed man, and offer his wife a trip to Boulogne-sur-Mer in France. Nonetheless, a short time later the wife—a religious woman who has continued to feel great remorse for her near murder of her husband—atones for her "sin" by leaping to her death while clutching a Christian icon. The wife in fact is lying on her bier at the beginning of the novella with her husband at her side, reviewing his marriage in an attempt to understand why she committed suicide.

What the husband winds up understanding is that his own contrariness is the cause of all his unhappiness, a contrariness suggested by his brooding not only over the certainty of his wife's love for him, but also over the certainty of God's very existence. (Witness such declarations of his, in chapters seven and ten respectively, as "What is the use of praying—it's only a sin!" and "Everything is dead and . . . men are alone—around them is silence—that is earth!") The pawnbroker concludes that all men live in unbreachable solitude, a solitude, in his case—just as in the cases of the alienated, embittered pawnbrokers or moneylenders in much of Dostoevsky's fiction, especially *Crime and Punishment* and *The Idiot*—that is the result of *kosnost*, or the spiritual stagnation which results from material pursuits.[3]

Any such explanations, like those above,[4] of what happens in *Une Femme douce* pale beside the facts, however, and the facts are almost all Bresson gives us in this eighty-eight-minute film (as elsewhere in his *oeuvre*) and all that we should consider if we are to be able to interpret the work justly. One fact that critics have inexplicably ignored, and that I take to be the foundation of any sound interpretation of *Une Femme douce*, is the young woman's declaration in the beginning that she does not love the man she intends to marry. Put another way, it is not at all clear *why* she marries him, and certainly the sum of the evidence points to the conclusion that they are so different from each other as to be nearly exact opposites. (No, the "opposites attract" theory of romance doesn't work here, for nothing the young woman does indicates that she is even attracted to the pawnbroker, let alone in love with him.)

The pawnbroker, for his part, although he may wish to marry this woman, does not make known why, after so many years of bachelorhood, he suddenly wants to wed someone *about whom he knows so little*. (To emphasize the pawnbroker's hitherto confirmed bachelorhood, Bresson creates the on-screen character of a live-in maid, whom, significantly, he does not dismiss after his marriage.) Certainly he gets little or no response from his fiancée, however much he may think he loves her, and they could hardly be said to carry on anything resembling a courtship.

In a word, these two are simply not meant for each other, and I am maintaining that Bresson makes sure we know this right from the start. Bresson's subject is thus not the rise and fall of a modern marriage, say, on account of financial problems or sexual infidelity. (This *is* Germaine Dulac's subject in *La souriante Madame Beudet* [1922], a kind of early feminist film that deals with the problem of a husband's economic domination of his wife, and to which, in letter but not in spirit, *Une Femme douce* bears some resemblance.) The couple in *Une Femme douce* don't even fall out in direct conflict with each other over a genuine issue that is raised in the film, and which derives from Dostoevsky's novella: the spiritually transcendent way of life over the materially driven one. These two are fallen out, as it were, when they first meet.

What Bresson does in *Une Femme douce*, then, is the reverse of what Dostoevsky does in *A Gentle Spirit*. The latter has the husband test the love of his wife and conclude that all human beings live in unbreachable solitude. Bresson has the husband and wife living in unbreachable solitude from the start and tests the duty, if not the love, toward them of the maid Anna, the character whom Bresson adds and purposefully names so that she will stand in for us, the audience. There is no such character "present" in the novella, which presented Dostoevsky with a conundrum that he addressed in his foreword to the work, for his narrator tells the whole tale to himself (*not* to his servant, Lukeria) yet somehow communicates it to us as readers. Dostoevsky solved the problem by positing the presence of an imaginary stenographer as the agency of narrative communication, and it is this convention or conceit that led him to give *A Gentle Spirit* the subtitle "A Fantastic Story."

Although Bresson could just as easily have had the husband narrate the story of his marriage alone and unseen, in intermittent voiceover, he has us watch the husband tell it to Anna in the same room where his wife's corpse lies on their marital bed; like the wife's body lying in the street after she jumps to her death, which we see at the *start* of the film, this is another telling image—the dead woman juxtaposed against the (re)union of man and maid—of the end-of-the marriage-in-its-beginning. In other words, Bresson's film, like Dostoevsky's novella, has a fatalistic, late point of attack in which, as the Russian formalists put it, the "plot" (*syuzhet* or *discours*)—the sequence of events in the present—is subsumed by the "story" (*fabula* or *histoire*)—the series of events that begins in the past, before the plot begins, and that not only includes the present but in fact determines it.[5] Dostoevsky deploys such a point of attack for ironic purposes, to undermine the pawnbroker's sense of his own autonomy and rationality, while Bresson uses the same point of attack to reflect his Jansenist belief in predestination and the absence or illusion of free will.

Whereas Dostoevsky had used the spiritual to express, or critique, the nihilistic, Bresson thus uses the nihilistic to express, or confirm, the spiritual.[6] Let me go into some detail as to how he does this, chiefly by concentrating on the contrast between the figures of the man and the woman. Since most of what we learn about her is designed solely to establish how different from the pawnbroker she is, she does not add up to a unified character of depth and originality, or "color," with whom we can readily identify. She walks into the pawnbroker's shop, and immediately the otherwise beautiful Dominique Sanda, in her first screen role (and giving more of a "performance" here than Bresson usually allowed his "models"), is unsympathetic: her clothing is drab, her hair is disheveled, she makes very little eye-contact with anyone, and her walk has about it at the same time a timidity and an urgency that make it unnerving.

The pawnbroker, by contrast, is meticulous in appearance, sparing in gesture, and steady in his walk; he looks directly at all whom he encounters (whereas his customers avert their gaze), but with eyes that one cannot look into and a face that, eerily, is neither handsome nor plain. This is clearly a man (as "modeled" by Guy Frangin) who "understands" the world and how to get along in it, not be "had" by it. A pawnbroker to the core, he is someone to whom money is everything, and what can't be seen, touched, and stored is not worth talking about—which is one of the reasons, as he himself says, that he is unable to pray. He accumulates item after item in his pawnshop, yet, unlike his counterpart in *A Gentle Spirit*, he never sells anything: he likes his money, but apparently he likes his "things," too. His wife, on the other hand, gives away his money for worthless objects when she is working in the pawnshop (in the novella, she just "price[s] things above their worth"); before she was married, she pawned her own last possessions in order to get a few more books to read. Her husband, for his part, has shelves of books, not one of which we ever see him take down to read, unlike Dostoevsky's pawnbroker, who is able to quote Goethe.

The husband likes books for their "thingness," yet he will not read them so as to rise above the world of things. The woman longs to do so, but realizes that, as a human being, she can only achieve her goal to a limited extent. She indirectly reveals this knowledge when, early in *Une Femme douce*, she declares, "We're all—men and animals—composed of the same matter, the same raw materials." Later we have this truism visually confirmed when the young woman and her husband visit a museum of natural history, where she goes on to ask, "Do birds learn to sing from their parents, or is the ability to sing present in them at birth?" (This question may have been suggested by the title of one of the two theater productions Dostoevsky's heroine is permitted by her husband to attend: *Songbirds*.) The wife yearns beyond a universe in which all is such nature, nurture, *matter*, and where human beings themselves frequently seem to behave in a preconditioned manner: preconditioned to beautify the self, to marry, to reproduce, to gather wealth and possessions, to enter society—in a word, to pursue happiness. (The ironically titled *Pursuit of Happiness* is the second theatrical production that the wife attends in *A Gentle Spirit*.)

Throughout the film the suggestion is that, obsessed with possessing matter (including his wife, or her body), the husband responds to situations in a preconditioned or "correct" manner, whereas his wife responds in the most unforeseen, and sometimes bizarre, of ways. Indeed, almost all her behavior in *Une Femme douce* is choreographed according to this ideal of the unexpected or the gratuitous. When she and her husband enter their bedroom on their wedding night, for example, the young woman quickly turns on the television set but does not watch it. The man does, but what he sees could be called the image of his own dead-end behavior pattern: cars racing in a circle. (He drives an automobile, she doesn't.) Later the husband will watch *horses* racing around a track on the same television, then World War II fighter planes flying round in endless circles as they try to out-maneuver one another in dogfights.

Meanwhile, incongruously, the wife nearly runs about the room in preparation for bed, wrapped in a towel that dislodges itself by accident as opposed to being dislodged in an act of sexual enticement. At one point she carelessly tosses her nightgown onto the bed, in much the same way she will leave underclothes strewn about it during the day and scatters her books everywhere, showing no respect for the material, for objects or possessions. At another point, this young woman takes a bath but doesn't drain the dirty water

Fiction into Film 77

and even leaves the faucet running, which her husband then turns off. Moreover, she spurns money yet likes to eat fancy pastries; she enjoys jazz but plays Bach and Purcell, too. The wife wants a bouquet so much she goes as far as to pick sunflowers alongside a road, then quickly tosses them away when she sees that, nearby, some couples are gathering their own bouquets of sunflowers.

This woman is different even in dying. (Her suicide ends as well as begins the film.) We do not get her point of view of the street before she leaps from the balcony, nor do we await her fall from below, from the position where she will soon find herself. As the wife jumps in daylight, we "innocently" see a potted plant fall off the small table from which she leaped, we watch the table topple over, and we are given a slow-motion shot of her shawl floating discursively to the ground after her—as if it were both her surviving soul or spirit and a final reminder of the unpredictability of her human nature—to be followed by a series of shadows and feet that flutter toward her dead body. (She placed a white shawl around her shoulders before jumping, even as she fingered the Christ figure retained from the gold crucifix she had pawned at her future husband's shop.) Off-camera during her fall, the young woman lands in the street, cars screech to a halt, and we await her husband's discovery of her death.

If, even in suicide, the wife's behavior has not been categorizable, has once again been somewhere "in between"—we can never predict quite where, we do not know quite why—then Bresson's camera itself is always literally somewhere in between, except when it is teasing us with a subjective camera-placement or point-of-view shot. (As when, in a bit of intertextuality comparable to the richly literary intertextuality that permeates *A Gentle Spirit*, the man and woman attend a French movie called *Benjamin* [1968]—a costume drama trading on the wiles of love—and a production of *Hamlet*, i.e., the kinds of narratives or dramas, unlike *Une Femme douce*, we are accustomed to seeing and hearing, in which we are more or less easily able to identify with the characters, their worlds, their experiences.) There are many shots of doors, of empty stairways, of the objects filling the pawnbroker's shop and his apartment.

The camera is also "in between" in its representation of people: we get hands and arms cut off bodies, bodies cut off from heads, just torsos, just feet. As usual in his work, Bresson thus makes "matter" of the human body. Moreover, he films the material world, the literal distance between the husband and the wife, to emphasize the fact that these two people live in unbreachable solitude, on either side of a great chasm. The last shot of *Une Femme douce* is of the lid to the woman's coffin being screwed tight, as the material world—the actual coffin lid, the world of things which she has at last transcended—continues to separate her, in death, from her husband, just as it did in life.

If these two characters are so permanently "separated" or irreconcilably different, one might ask, why did they choose to get married? I don't know; I don't think that they know (if they do, they do not tell us); and Bresson doesn't care because, as I have more than suggested, this couple's "psychology" is not the focus of *Une Femme douce* as it is of Dostoevsky's *A Gentle Spirit*. Perhaps the man and the woman get together out of their own perversity, but the film does not contain this idea: it just doesn't contradict it. Likewise, the film doesn't contradict the possibility that the young woman marries the pawnbroker only because it is the unexpected thing to do. For Bresson, then, their marriage is not a relationship to be explored, but instead a device to be used.

To wit: marriage is universally perceived to be the most intimate state in which two people can live, and Bresson counterpoints this perception of ours with the almost total lack of intimacy that exists between the husband and the wife in his film. In other words, the director does not allow us to identify with the marriage of the pawnbroker and the young woman, to see ourselves in them, because he doesn't indicate that they marry for the reasons *we* usually associate with marrying: love, money, convenience, convention, children. They wed, they are unhappy, they reach a fragile understanding, then she kills herself. The husband, in his narration—it is not narration in the proper sense, but more on this later—attempts to discover why his wife committed suicide, but he cannot find an answer. He doesn't know why she killed herself, nor do we, and neither does Bresson.

My point is not that every human action in *Une Femme douce* is without explanation, without cause or motive—for instance, the wife's near murder of her husband after he discovers her

Fiction into Film 79

with another man *can* be accounted for—but that these individual explanations become beside the point when one considers that there is no explanation in the film, as there is in Dostoevsky's novella, as to why the pawnbroker and the young woman got married in the first place. What becomes important, therefore, is not so much their relationship with each other as our relationship with each of them, and Anna's with the pawnbroker. This is why the camera shifts periodically from *its* illustration of past events to the husband pacing back and forth in the bedroom in the present, telling *his* story of the marriage: not only to point up that *neither* narrative account provides the "answers," but also to emphasize that this man, as character or person apart from his story, is the proper focus of our concerns. So too is his wife, literally apart from her story in death, lying in the road at the beginning of the film even as she lies there at its conclusion.

Clearly, then, unlike Dostoevsky, Bresson wants more from us than our "understanding" of the husband and wife's relationship, our feeling sorry for them for their frailties and obsessions, because ultimately this is only feeling sorry for ourselves; or it is making these characters do the work of our living, which is too easy. The remarkable aspect of this film is that we do much of the feeling and querying for the actors, not in identification with them as they do it, but *in their place*: we feel and query for them as we imagine they would. And this has the effect of making us think absolutely about their situation, instead of about theirs plus our own. Bresson, in this way, wants us to feel for and care about characters whom we do not "recognize," who reveal as little that is "like us" as possible, namely, the heights and depths of strong emotion: love, hate, anger, regret, happiness, sadness.

To this end, Bresson forces his actors to deny themselves in the portrayal of their characters. He denies *himself* in his shooting of these characters: for the most part, the camera is held steady in the middle distance, there is no panning or tracking, and there are no high- and low-angle shots—objectivity or distance that Bresson can afford because of the very lack of appeal of his main characters. The director asks us in turn to deny ourselves in our perception of these characters and their actions. He demands that we pay attention to the husband and wife for themselves, no matter how uninviting or inexpressive they may appear, no matter how their story resembles little more than a skimpy newspaper report.

The fact that, as in the case of *Une Femme douce*, Bresson almost always made his films from preexisting texts should be a signal that he was not interested in the creation of original character for its own sake, or even in the re-creation of traditionally arresting and appealing character. (This is one reason he never gives names to the husband and wife, who are unnamed in *A Gentle Spirit*, as well, but where their anonymity does not have the same effect since we are privy to the pawnbroker-narrator's innermost thoughts about himself and his wife.) The fact that he frequently began his films by telling us what would happen at the end should be a signal, as well: that he was not primarily concerned to tell stories for the suspense they could create. That suspense was not Bresson's main concern is further indicated by the film's doubling of its action, as it were. The effect of having the husband narrate parts of the story to Anna—the enactment of which we then see in flashback—is less to show us discrepancies in the husband's version as compared with "what really happened" than to obliterate the newness or freshness of story, the interest in it *per se*. It is precisely through the filming of both the husband's narration and its subsequent repetition in action instead of words that Bresson accomplishes this.

Bresson asks us, not to fully fathom this "double-narrative," to decipher the how and why of the whole story, but simply to believe that it occurred and to take witness if not pity. His is a nearly perverse demand, which is to say a kind of religious one. If we can comply and perform the requisite act of faith, of utter selflessness, together with a leap of the imagination, *Une Femme douce* becomes for us something resembling a religious or spiritual experience. It becomes an experience, furthermore, that also teaches an important aesthetic lesson: that we must acknowledge the existence of the inexplicable in, as well as beyond, art. For it need not be art's job to make people and the world more intelligible than they are, but instead to re-present their mystery or ineffableness, their integrity or irreducibility, if you will, their connection to something irretrievably their own or some other's—like God himself.[7] All may not be grace for the young woman at the end of *Une Femme douce*, then, as it was for the *curé* of Ambricourt at the conclusion of Bresson's *Jour-*

nal d'un curé de campagne, who utters these words of spiritual certitude ("All is grace") as he is dying. But all is not nothingness, either.

Anna the maid seems to have learned the lesson of inexplicability or irreducibility from life rather than art, for she knows as little as we do about the motives for, and causes of, the husband's and the wife's behavior, yet she utters not one querying or querulous word to either of them in the course of the picture. Indeed, Anna utters only a few lines through all of *Une Femme douce*. (By contrast, it is Lukeria, the servant in Dostoevsky's *A Gentle Spirit*, who not only provides the details of the wife's past to the pawnbroker at the start of their relationship, but also later gives the description of her suicide—which Lukeria helplessly witnesses—that the widower himself recounts in his narration.) Yes, she is the couple's maid, but her silence and impassivity (especially as she is played by Jane Lobré) here appear to go beyond the call of a servant's duty. Before the end of the film, Anna leaves the room in which she has quietly listened to the husband's narrative of his and his wife's relationship; but she will not leave him, as Dostoevsky's Lukeria threatened to leave the pawnbroker's service directly after the burial of his wife. She will remain with him during and after the funeral of the young woman because, as the husband himself admits, *he will need her*.

Bresson, by implication, asks the same of us: that, figuratively speaking, we do not desert this man in his time of need, that we recognize his humanity despite the fact we cannot comprehend his, or his marriage's deepest secrets. If there is anyone in *Une Femme douce* with whom we should "identify," then, it is Anna. And if we can be said to identify with the husband and wife at all, it is in the sense, as I have implied, that they seem as puzzled by what is happening to them as we are. This is not only character almost disconnected from story, it is character nearly disconnected from *self*. Thus are we disconnected from *our* selves, our certain egos, and made to look, not for the moral or balance in the story, the symmetry of feeling and form, of ideas and execution, but simply and inescapably for the only remaining tie that binds us to the characters depicted on screen: the human one, or the only one that cannot be explained away.

As one may deduce from my concentration above on *Une Femme douce*'s method, Bresson's films, unlike Dostoevsky's fictions, are even more distinguished for their method or their style than for their individual subject matter. That is because Bresson's subjects pale beside his treatment of them, so much so that it is almost as if the director were making the same movie time after time. How ironic, or perhaps appropriate, that he filmed number nine in color (though elegantly understated or "innocent" color it is, as photographed by Ghislain Cloquet) because, as he later wrote in *Notes on Cinematography* (1975), he felt color was more true to life.[8] Like the theorist André Bazin's true filmmaker, Bresson thus attained his power through his method, which is less a thing literally to be described or expressed (as in such terms as color, deep focus, handheld camerawork, and long takes) than an inner orientation enabling an outward quest. That quest, in Bresson's case—but doubtless not in the case of the spiritually conflicted Dostoevsky—is to honor God's universe by using his art to render the reality of that universe, and, through its reality, both the miracle of its creation and the mystery of its being.

From first to last, then, Bresson's films trace one of the most disciplined, intricate, and satisfying artistic achievements in the history of the medium. No less than D. W. Griffith and Sergei Eisenstein, Robert Bresson sought to advance the art of the cinema, to create a purely filmic narrative form through a progressive refinement of this young art's tools and strategies—through the mastery, in his words, of "cinematography" over the "cinema." Like a dutiful student of Rudolf Arnheim and the theory that called for film to free itself from the established arts and discover its "inherent" nature, Bresson discarded, film by film, the inherited conventions—not only the actor but the dramatic structure of scenes in favor of a series of neutral sequences, often using sound to avoid visual redundancy. For Bresson, getting to the essence of each film narrative was synonymous with getting to the essence of the medium.

To be sure, not everyone agrees about Bresson's stature and importance: he did, and does, have his dissenters, certainly among members of the popular press but also among serious critics like Vernon Young, Stanley Kauffmann, and John Simon. You can understand the dissent against Bresson when you consider some critics' comparison of Bresson's style to that of such modernist atonal composers as Arnold Schoenberg, Anton Weber, or

Olivier Messiaen, at the same time as they point out that, unlike conventional filmmakers, Bresson was working in an intellectual, reflective manner rather than an unreflective, visceral one. Similarly, these critics sometimes pair Bresson and Mark Rothko, whose paintings, with their large canvases of strong color and a minimum of variation, are known for the spareness if not poverty of their expression—like Bresson's films. To fully understand the dissent against Bresson, however, you also have to remember that his Catholicism, nay, his religiosity itself, was out of step in the existentialist-dominated intellectual climate of 1950s France, even as it was unfashionable in the materialist-obsessed, know-nothing culture of 1980s America.

Still, to see Bresson's films—to see only *L'Argent* and *Une Femme douce*, the pictures under consideration here—is to marvel that other directors have had the ingenuity to evolve such elaborate styles and yet restrict them to superficial messages. It might even be said that watching a Bresson film is to risk conversion *away* from the cinema. His meaning is so clearly inspirational, and his treatment so remorselessly interior, that he shames the extrinsic glamour and extravagance of so many movies. Shame on them, and God bless him.

BIBLIOGRAPHY

Andersen, Zsuzsanna Bjørn. "The Concepts of Domination and Powerlessness in F. M. Dostoevsky's *A Gentle Spirit.*" *Dostoevsky Studies*, n.s. 4 (2000): 53-60.

Armes, Roy. "Innovators and Independents: Robert Bresson." In *Great Film Directors: A Critical Anthology*. Ed. Leo Braudy and Morris Dickstein. New York: Oxford University Press, 1978.

Atwell, Lee. "*Une Femme douce.*" *Film Quarterly*, 23.4 (Summer 1970): 54-56.

Ayfre, Amédée, et al. *The Films of Robert Bresson*. New York: Praeger, 1970.

Belknap, Robert L. "*The Gentle Creature* as the Climax of a Work of Art That Almost Exists." *Dostoevsky Studies*, n.s. 4 (2000): 35-42.

Ben-Gad, Schmuel. "*L'Argent.*" *Film Quarterly*, 54.2 (Winter 2000-2001): 57-58.

Bresson, Robert. *Notes on Cinematography*. New York: Urizen Books, 1977.

Catteau, Jacques. *Dostoevsky and the Process of Literary Creation.* Trans. Audrey Littlewood. New York: Cambridge University Press, 1989.

Cunneen, Joseph E. *Robert Bresson: A Spiritual Style in Film.* New York: Continuum, 2003.

Dostoevsky, Fyodor. *A Gentle Spirit: A Fantastic Story.* Trans. Constance Garnett. New York: Minton, Balch and Company, 1931.

Fanger, Joseph. *Dostoevsky and Romantic Realism.* Chicago: University of Chicago Press, 1967.

Hanlon, Lindley. *Fragments: Bresson's Film Style.* Rutherford, N.J.: Fairleigh Dickinson University Press, 1986.

Hayward, Susan. "Cohesive Relations and Texture in Bresson's Film *L'Argent.*" *SubStance*, 15.3 (1986): 52-68.

Jackson, Robert Louis. *The Art of Dostoevsky: Delirium and Nocturnes.* Princeton, N.J.: Princeton University Press, 1981.

Johnson, William. "*L'Argent.*" *Film Quarterly*, 37.4 (Summer 1984): 18-21.

Jones, Kent. *L'Argent.* London: BFI Publishing, 1999.

Miller, R. F., ed. *Critical Essays on Dostoevsky.* Boston: G. K. Hall, 1986.

Milne, Tom. "Angels and Ministers: The Career of Robert Bresson." *Sight and Sound*, 56.4 (Autumn 1987): 285-287.

O'Toole, L. M. "Structure and Style in the Short Story: Dostoevsky's *A Gentle Spirit.*" *Tijdschrift voor Slavische Taal-en Letterkunde*, 1 (1972): 81-116.

Pipolo, Tony. *Robert Bresson: A Passion for Film.* New York: Oxford University Press, 2010.

Polhemus, Helen M. "Matter and Spirit in the Films of Robert Bresson." *Film Heritage*, 9.3 (Spring 1974): 12-16.

Prokosch, Mike. "Bresson's Stylistics Revisited." *Film Quarterly*, 25.2 (Winter 1971-1972): 30-32.

Quandt, James, ed. *Robert Bresson.* Toronto: Cinémathèque Ontario, 1998.

Reader, Keith. *Robert Bresson.* Manchester, U.K.: Manchester University Press, 2000.

Rhode, Eric. "Dostoevsky and Bresson." *Sight and Sound*, Spring 1970.

"Robert Bresson, 1901-1999" (special section). *Artforum International*, 38.8 (April 2000): 120-125, 161.

Sloan, Jane. *Robert Bresson: A Guide to References and Resources.* Boston: G. K. Hall, 1983.

Sontag, Susan. "Spiritual Style in the Films of Robert Bresson." *Seventh Art*, Summer 1964. Reprinted in Sontag's *Against Interpretation.* New York: Farrar, Straus & Giroux, 1966. 177-195.

"Special Section on Robert Bresson." *Film Comment*, 35.3 (May-June 1999).

"Special Section on Robert Bresson." *Film Comment*, 35.4 (July-August 1999).

Stadler, Eva M. "Bresson, Dostoevsky, Bakhtin: Adaptation as Intertextual Dialogue." *Quarterly Review of Film and Video*, 20.1 (January-March 2003).

Tomlinson, Doug. "Performance in the Films of Robert Bresson: The Aesthetics of Denial." In *More than a Method: Trends and Traditions in Contemporary Film Performance*. Ed. Cynthia Baron, Diane Carson, and Frank P. Tomasulo. Detroit, Michigan: Wayne State University Press, 2004.

Vaux, Sara Anson. "Divine Skepticism: The Films of Robert Bresson." *Christianity and Literature*, 53.4 (Summer 2004): 521-537.

Wasiolek, Edward. *Dostoevsky. The Major Fiction*. Cambridge, Mass.: Harvard University Press, 1964.

Westerbeck, Colin L. "Robert Bresson's Austere Vision." *Artforum*, 15 (November 1976): 52-57.

5

High Infidelity:
Sergei Bodrov's Film Adaptation of Tolstoy's "Prisoner of the Caucasus"

Prisoner of the Mountains (1996), by the Russian director Sergei Bodrov, is about cultural clash and the moral enlightenment as well as emotional awakening that, under the right circumstances, can come of it. Ironically, the "right circumstances," in this instance, are those of war and captivity. This was not exactly a new subject when the film was released in 1996—the attempt to reveal a human bond between characters who are otherwise military enemies, political opponents, religious rivals, or racial opposites—but it need *not* have been in the hands of a sensitive writer-director like Bodrov, interested in something other than sentimentality, hyperbole, and oversimplification.

Indeed, in Bodrov's case, he is a better *auteur* than the original author of the story on which *Prisoner of the Mountains* is based: Leo Tolstoy, the action of whose "Prisoner of the Caucasus" (1870) the Russian director, along with his co-scenarists Arif Aliyev and Boris Giller, transposed from the Chechnya of some 140 years ago (where and when Tolstoy did a portion of his military service) to the same general area today, on the northern slopes of the Caucasus mountains. In this area the Russian army is simultaneously governing and fighting the Muslim population—prior to that army's withdrawal in August 1996 as the result of a treaty signed between Chechnyan rebels and the Russian government, which had ordered a full-scale invasion of the former republic in December 1994.

The real-life Russian encounter with the Muslim world over the past thirty years, let alone the last century-and-a-half, has often been characterized by the violence of war rather than by attempts at understanding: in addition to the Chechnyan struggle (which erupted into war again in 2000) and a number of smaller engagements along the former Soviet border, there was the Afghan war of the early 1980s. Despite these conflicts, the Caucasus region has long fascinated Russians as the nearest manifestation of the inscrutable Orient, and nineteenth-century literature abounds with encounters between young Russians—frequently army officers—and this Muslim portion of their empire. To wit: the Russian title of Bodrov's film, whose literal translation is *Prisoner of the Caucasus*, was used not only in the short story by Tolstoy, but also in poems by Pushkin (1822) and Lermontov (1828) as well as in an 1883 opera by César Cui based on Pushkin's poem.

Moreover, *Prisoner of the Mountains* is not the first Russian movie to feature the Caucasus in the wake of the Chechnyan wars. Vladimir Khotinenko's *The Muslim* (1995) told the tale of a young Russian soldier who returns to his native village after having embraced the Islamic faith during his stint as a prisoner of war, only to be met by family and friends with incomprehension and violence; while Aleksei Balabanov's *Brother* (1997) followed Bodrov's film with the story of a Chechnyan war veteran who turns into a Petersburg killer. Subsequent to *Prisoner of the Mountains*, as well—and a bit like it—Alexander Rogozhkin's *The Checkpoint* (1999) offered a sympathetic portrayal of a group of Russian soldiers manning an isolated outpost, who nonetheless remain alien occupiers in the strange, nearly incomprehensible region of the Caucasus, despised by the locals and exploited by their own commanders for personal prestige and gain; while Alexander Sokurov's anti-war film *Alexandra* (2007) told the tale of a grandmother visiting her son on the front-line during the Second Chechnyan War

Prisoner of the Mountains is distinctive, however, in being entirely set among the Muslim rebels, many of them played by local people who had never acted before. (Such a setting can also be found in subsequent Russian films like Andrei Konchalovsky's *House of Fools* [2002] and Mariya Saakyan's *The Lighthouse* [2006], each of which takes place in Chechnya and foregrounds Chechnyan characters.) Yet from these locals Sergei Bodrov coaxed natural, unforced performances, even as he had done from non-professional actors in three of his six features prior to *Prisoner of the Mountains*: *Non-Professionals* (1986), *Freedom Is Paradise* (1990), and *I Wanted to See*

Angels (1992). But the difference in Bodrov's use of amateurs here is signal, for their roughhewn, red-cheeked faces make up a kind of human scenery that underscores this picture with history—with the history of similar faces that populated the isolated, stubborn, struggling region of Chechnya before the czars as well as throughout their reign, and which subsequently survived the seventy-odd years of the so-called New Soviet Order.

The people remain, and their *aul* or village in *Prisoner of the Mountains* remains much as it was when Tolstoy was a soldier there: a place of flinty, unpaved roads and clay huts with earthen floors, where wheat is still threshed by mules, men still travel on horseback, and dress codes, gender roles, the veneration of ancestors, and the rule of elders have persevered, unchanged, for many generations. These Chechnyans may not be prisoner to the Caucasus mountains, like their Russian captives, but they are in awe of the cruelly beautiful, grandly gaunt peaks that look down at them in stunning images (photographed by Pavel Lebeshev) with a chilling hint of blue-green. So much so that, in *Prisoner of the Mountains*, the Chechnyans step out onto their roofs in a paradoxical gesture of both deference and self-assertion toward the majestically uncompromising starkness that surrounds them. And so in awe are they that they have composed a plaintive yet celebratory ode to the Caucasus which forms half of the film's musical score: "We are the children of the mountains," the villagers sing, "The mountains will protect us."

The other half of the film's score counterpoints the first: beloved songs from past Russian military campaigns, such as the pre-Revolutionary "On the Hills of Manchuria" and World War II's "The Blue Kerchief," both of which are here ironically deployed. There is no such irony in the story "Prisoner of the Caucasus," which the elderly Tolstoy oddly thought was one of his two best pieces of fiction (together with "God Sees the Truth, But Waits," which was written at about the same time but is quite different in subject, if similar in intended theme: enlightenment through imprisonment); nor is the short story's portrayal of Russians and Caucasians as balanced as the motion picture's. Tolstoy's central concern was almost exclusively with the experience of one of his two Russian soldiers, the dashing, courageous officer Vania Zhílin, captured along with another officer, the stout and dullish Sasha Kostílin, in an ambush by raiding "Tartar" mountaineers.

"A Prisoner of the Caucasus" is related in the third person, from Vania's point of view. This means, of course, that we get his interpretation of people and events with virtually no narrative intervention from the inveterately economical Tolstoy, as in the following:

> Zhílin was very thirsty . . ., and he thought: "If only they would come and so much as look at me!" Then . . . [t]he red-bearded Tartar entered, and with him was . . . a smaller man, dark, with bright black eyes . . . and a short beard. He had a merry face and was always laughing. . . . The red-bearded Tartar . . . stood . . . playing with his dagger and glaring askance at Zhílin, like a wolf. The dark one . . . came straight up to Zhílin, squatted down in front of him, . . . and began to talk very fast in his own language. His teeth showed, and he kept winking, clicking his tongue, and repeating, "Good Russ, good Russ." Zhílin could not understand a word, but said, "Drink! Give me water to drink!" The dark man only laughed. (16-17)

Bodrov's cinematic adaptation does not employ such third-person narration—few fiction films do, of course, for the more we hear such a non-participating narrator on the soundtrack, the more we feel that we might as well be reading the story or novel itself. (Third-person narration is most often found in documentaries.) *Prisoner of the Mountains* slips naturally into the omniscient form endemic to the camera-eye, and it is this omniscience—the power to regard character and action from multiple points of view, or an all-encompassing perspective—that enables Bodrov fully to articulate elements of the drama which Tolstoy only touches upon, sometimes with a touch of heaviness. The relationship between Vania and Sasha is a case in point.

The screenplay demotes Vania from a bold, debonair officer to a newly conscripted private, naïve and reticent, while it changes his fellow captive from a plodding, overweight officer to a veteran, non-commissioned one, a sergeant who is at once clever, cynical, garrulous, and reckless as well as ruthless. Several objectives are thereby achieved: (1) greater contrast between two already different prisoners; (2) more balance in their relationship, since the film, unlike the story, depicts an enterprising Sasha as the initiator of escape, not a resourceful Vania, whereas the latter remains the one, on film as in fiction, who develops an affection for Dína, the girl who brings the Russians their daily rations; (3) greater dramatic tension in the scenario as a whole—a tension that itself stands in contrast to the film's almost leisurely observation of archaic Muslim customs and age-old Caucasian vistas—since the boyish Vania's affection for his "enemy," the thirteen-year-old Dína, dangerously if plausibly verges on love-cum-marriage in Bodrov's adaptation (and in the Caucasus, where girls still routinely marry in their early teens); and (4) less contrast or difference between the Russian prisoners and their Chechnyan captors, because the former are no longer members of an elite, not to say aristocratic, class of commissioned officers (who, in these days of high technology and helicopter evacuation, the Russian brass might have been more eager to rescue), even if they are citizens of a great military power, while their chief jailer—the fiftyish Abdul-Murat, Dína's father—is unquestionably a village patriarch.

The similarities between these rivals extend to parallelism in the plot and beyond, for, in *Prisoner of the Mountains*, the stern and proud Abdul-Murat does not kill his two Russian prisoners (only one of whom he wanted) after the guerrilla ambush because he hopes to exchange them for his schoolteacher-son, Dzaramat, a prisoner of the *Russians* whom he has not been able to ransom with money. In Tolstoy's story, Abdul-Murat is less sympathetic, for he has no son and is interested only in ransoming Vania and Sasha for monetary gain. Furthermore, in "A Prisoner of the Caucasus" there is no character called Hasan, a dumb eunuch whom Bodrov and his collaborators write into the script. Hasan guards the already shackled Russians, more or less around the clock, for Abdul-Murat, to whom he appears almost to be in indentured servitude. This added figure's real significance, however, lies in the genesis of his condition, which says as much about his Chechnyan master as it does about the Russian imperialists. For Hasan lost the power of speech as a prison inmate in Siberia, where he was sent for the murder of his adulterous wife, who was also Abdul-Murat's daughter and Dína's older sister—and where his Russian captors cut out his tongue, in addition to castrating him, because they felt he talked and sang too much.

The Chechnyan captors of Vania and Sasha do not castrate them, and they do not cut out their tongues—indeed, they could be said to give the Russians a voice in their own fates. After a failed attempt to exchange the two soldiers for Dzaramat—failed because Russian forces tried to trick Abdul-Murat, whom they consider to be just another scheming Chechnyan—the patriarch ignores pressure from his fellow villagers to butcher the Russians and instead makes his prisoners write letters to their mothers urging them to intercede on their sons' behalf. Vania does so, and his widowed schoolteacher-mother comes to his aid; Sasha writes home, too, but he knows his letter will never get a response, as he grew up in an orphanage where no one will remember him now, anyway. The letter-writing in the story, by contrast, is only an appeal for ransom money, and there the swaggering Vania deliberately misaddresses his letter so that it will not reach its destination, whereas the pathetic Sasha writes home a second time in Tolstoy's fiction in a desperate attempt to raise the rubles necessary for his release.

Maslov, commander of the Russian garrison in the nearby, occupied town where Dzaramat is being held, refuses to let Abdul-Murat see his son, and the military chief meets with Vania's mother only to advise her not to negotiate with the shifty locals. She does so anyway, yet to no avail: Abdul-Murat tells his fellow parent merely that he will try again to arrange a prisoner exchange. Then, immediately afterwards, Sasha and Vania escape—apparently inspired by a radio broadcast of "Go Down Moses" (ironically so, with its equation of the Chechnyan struggle with that of the ancient Israelites and Egyptians and, by implication, with the struggle of American blacks against their white racist oppressors) as performed by Louis Armstrong. In the process of fleeing, Sasha kills both Hasan and a shepherd whose rifle he steals; but the rifle turns out to be useless, as it contains only one bullet and the bumbling Vania fires it by accident, thus giving away his and his comrade's position to the pursuing Chechnyan rebels. Both Russians are recaptured, yet only Private Zhílin is returned to his Muslim master; Sergeant Kostílin gets his throat cut for the crime of murder.

Prisoner of the Mountains, 1996, dir. Sergei Bodrov

Nonetheless, Sasha does not disappear completely from the film. Through shared adversity, the bond of trust between him and Vania has grown so great (so great that, sensing his imminent execution after their botched escape, Sasha asks Vania to help support a son he had out of wedlock), despite the sergeant's at first utter contempt for his otherwise earnest subordinate, that Vania twice has visions in which a serene and solicitous Sasha appears. Are these visions attributable in part to the place where they occur, a Muslim place conceivably more mystical or spiritual than Russia proper, where religion was officially suppressed for decades under the rule of the Soviets? Bodrov wisely does not comment on this matter, but one can infer that Vania's visions are at least in some measure a result of the remote, mountainous location, his long, enforced isolation, and his gradual, sentient education not only into the ways of his superior officer but also into those of a non-materialistic culture very different from his own.

As for Abdul Murat's son, he too is killed shortly after Sasha in an escape attempt—this one prompted by the shooting of a Chechnyan collaborator, Mamed, by his own father, who especially buys a Russian pistol from a pawnshop in order to do the job. This old man, according to Abdul-Murat in Tolstoy's story,

> was the bravest of our fellows; he killed many Russians, and was at one time very rich. He had three wives and eight

sons, and they all lived in one village. Then the Russians came and killed seven of his sons. Only one son was left, and he gave himself up to the Russians. . . After [shooting and killing him, the old man] left off fighting and went to Mecca to pray to God; that is why he wears a turban [and] is called 'Hadji' . . . He does not like you fellows [Vania and Sasha]. He tells me to kill you. (26-27)

Indeed, this village elder called Hadji has taken at least one shot of his own at the two Russian prisoners, in the story as well as the film. That one missed, but the one aimed at Mamed struck not only him but, figuratively speaking, the loyal Dzaramat as well. For the latter—who, to repeat, does not appear in Tolstoy's "Prisoner of the Caucasus"—conceived the idea to escape only during the pandemonium surrounding the slaying of Hadji's traitorous son, and, in the act of fleeing, Abdul-Murat's own son gets hit by a bullet to the back as, tellingly, *Vania's* long-suffering mother looks on in horror.

Because of Dzaramat's death, Dína reports to Vania in the solitary confinement of a stinking pit, he will be executed the next day. She then betrays her father—or, depending on your point of view, honors her burgeoning affection for Vania—by giving the Russian the key to his shackles. In order to protect Dína, however, he refuses to run away in Bodrov's adaptation, and is subsequently taken into the mountains to be shot by Abdul-Murat. But this father cannot shoot a stricken mother's only son, or his beloved daughter's own love, so he fires into the air, then turns around and starts walking home. As a stunned Vania wanders away on the vast Caucasian slopes, four Russian helicopter gunships appear overhead, on their way to a retaliatory strike against Abdul-Murat's village—not to a merciful rescue of the lone Private Zhílin.

While martial music blares on the soundtrack, the repatriated and in some ways still innocent Vania fondly recollects, in voiceover, his experiences as a "guest" of the Chechnyan people. To some of them he became deeply and unforgettably attached, he says, while for many of their customs he developed an increasing respect, even as they did for his "alien" skills as a mender of watches and a crafter of bric-à-brac. One of those crafted items, all of them presented to Dína, is a beautiful wooden bird with movable wings, which the grateful girl hangs from the ceiling of her and her father's small home, and which plainly symbolizes not only Vania and Sasha's will to freedom but also the Chechnyan people's.

The Vania of Tolstoy's story carves gifts for Dína as well, but they are dolls without the symbolic import of the bird, which is to say without an import that attaches equally to Russians and Chechnyans alike. This is the problem with the short story in general: it displays something less than mutual compassion for the combatants in this longstanding regional conflict. Tolstoy called "A Prisoner of the Caucasus," together with "God Sees the Truth, But Waits," a "Tale for Children." And in its uncomplicated view of the world, along with its emphasis on Dína's material accumulation as opposed to her spiritual bonding, "A Prisoner of the Caucasus" certainly seems designed to appeal to the child in all of us, particularly as its ending differs from the resoundingly poignant one of the film version.

In the story, Sasha is not slain after he and Vania are recaptured, because the former did not kill either an innocent shepherd or Hasan. Afraid that her father will give in to his compatriots' demands that he cut Vania's throat, Dína frees him from his outdoor dungeon after fattening her favorite with cakes and cherries and cheese, while Sasha remains shackled in the pit on account of illness and fatigue. Then Vania successfully escapes, arriving back at his Russian fort after an all-night journey and an averted skirmish with at least three enemy horsemen. "He went on serving in the Caucasus," Tolstoy flatly concludes, and "a month later Kostílin was released after paying five thousand rubles ransom" (43). As for Vania's last-minute promise to Dína that he would never forget her, no further mention of it is made in the story—unlike the film—nor of the girl herself or, most importantly, of her father's reaction to her perfidious act.

Since the Dína-Vania relationship provides the gist of Bodrov's narrative, if not Tolstoy's, it was imperative that both roles be well cast. Bodrov found Susanna Mekhralieva in a school in Dagestan, not far from Chechnya, and her performance as Dína is exemplary in its ease, simplicity, and understatement. The director naturally found Sergei Bodrov, Jr., in his own family, and, as Vania, he gives an equally unsentimentalized but tremendously affecting performance of great faith—youthful faith in a caring universe—reminiscent of the World War II-draftee from Grigori Chukhrai's *Ballad of a Soldier* (1959), another young Russian (played by Vladimir Ivashev) thrown into the maelstrom before he has had time to live. This was Bodrov, Jr.'s, screen début (he was killed in 2002 in a rock-and-ice slide while shooting a film in the mountains of North Ossetia), which was followed by his role as the combat veteran-become-civilian-murderer in both parts of Balabanov's *Brother* (1997, 2000)—a chilling gloss on the possible fate of his character in *Prisoner of the Mountains*.

Oleg Menshikov, for his part, went on to become one of the biggest stars in Russian cinema. Prior to *Prisoner of the Mountains*, this actor was familiar to American audiences through his sterling work as the Stalinist policeman in Nikita Mikhalkov's otherwise languid *Burnt by the Sun*, which won the Academy Award for Best Foreign-Language Film in 1994 (part II was released in 2010). Here, playing the quite different character of Sasha, Menshikov brings to the role the doomed raillery and easeful cocksureness of a man convinced at once of his own superiority and his common mortality: a combination Errol Flynn and Martin Sheen, as it were.

Oleg Menshikov and Sergei Bodrov, Jr., deservedly shared the prize for Best Actor at the Sochi Kinotavr, today the leading Russian film festival, where *Prisoner of the Mountains* won the Grand Prix for best picture, which it also garnered, along with four other awards, at the 1997 Nikas (the Russian Oscars). This powerfully affecting film received, in addition, the Crystal Globe at the Karlovy Vary International Festival, as well as the International Critics' Prize and the Public Prize at Cannes, but it was subsequently beaten out for the 1997 Academy Award for Best Foreign-Language Film by the Czech director Jan Sverák's insipid *Kolya* (another tale about the encounter between two initially incompatible people, in this instance a middle-aged Czech man and a little Russian boy).

The choice of *Kolya* over *Prisoner of the Mountains* should not surprise anyone, though, given the Academy's predilection for the maudlin and mannered over the measured yet moving, whatever a motion picture's national origin may be. In fact, had Sergei Bodrov made a *faithful* adaptation of Tolstoy's tendentious, sometimes puerile "Prisoner of the Caucasus," his *Prisoner of the Mountains* might well have won the Oscar—an irony perhaps grimmer, in the end, than the film itself.

WORK CITED

Tolstoy, Leo. *Twenty-Three Tales*. Trans. Aylmer Maude. London: Oxford University Press, 1928.

BIBLIOGRAPHY

Allen, W.E.D., and Paul Muratoff. *Caucasian Battlefields: A History of the Wars on the Turko-Caucasian Frontier (1828-1921)*. New York: Cambridge University Press, 1953.

Allworth, Edward, ed. *Central Asia, 130 Years of Russian Dominance: A Historical Overview*. Durham, N.C.: Duke University Press, 1994.

Beumers, Birgit. *The Cinema of Russia and the Former Soviet Union*. London: Wallflower, 2007.

Birnie, Ian. "End Game." *Filmmaker: The Magazine of Independent Film*, 5.2 (1997): 54-55.

Brower, Daniel, and Edward Lazzerini, ed. *Russia's Orient: Imperial Borderlands and Peoples, 1700-1917*. Bloomington: Indiana University Press, 1997.

Broxup, Marie Benningsen, ed. *The North Caucasus Barrier: The Russian Advance Towards the Muslim World*. New York: St. Martin's Press, 1992.

Brunette, Peter. "War Is (Still) Hell." *The Village Voice*, 42 (Feb. 4, 1997): 69.

Dawisha, Karen, and Bruce Parrott, eds. *Conflict, Cleavage, and Change in Central Asia and the Caucasus*. New York: Cambridge University Press, 1997.

Denby, David. "Blue Route." *New York Magazine*, 30 (March 3, 1997): 53-54.

Deweese, D. A. *History of Islam in Central Asia*. Leiden, Neth.: Brill, 2000.

Dunlop, John B. *Russia Confronts Chechnya: Roots of a Separatist Conflict*. New York: Cambridge University Press, 1998.

Farber, Stephen. "Foreign Serviceable." *Movieline* (8 March 1997): 46+.

Ferraro, Michael X. "*Prisoner of the Mountains*." *American Cinematographer*, 78 (April 1997): 79-82.

Frye, Richard N., and Bernard Lewis, eds. *The Heritage of Central Asia:*

From Antiquity to the Turkish Expansion. Princeton, N.J.: Markus Wiener, 1996.

Gall, Carlotta, and Thomas de Waal. *Chechnya: Calamity in the Caucasus.* New York: New York University Press, 1998.

Goldenberg, Suzanne. *Pride of Small Nations: The Caucasus and Post-Soviet Disorder.* London: Zed Books, 1994.

Graffy, Julian. "Soldier, Soldier." *Sight and Sound* (8 March 1998): 34-35+.

Grant, Bruce. "The Good Russian Prisoner: Naturalizing Violence in the Caucasus Mountains." *Cultural Anthropology*, 20.1 (Feb. 2005): 39-67.

Henze, Paul B., et al. *The North Caucasus Barrier: The Russian Advance towards the Muslim World.* New York: St. Martin's Press, 1992.

Hoberman, J. "Russians Are Coming." *The Village Voice*, 42 (Feb. 4, 1997): 69.

Hunter, Shireen T. *The Transcaucasus in Transition: Nation-Building and Conflict.* Washington, D.C.: Center for Strategic and International Studies, 1994.

Klady, Leonard. "*Prisoner of the Caucasus.*" *Variety*, 363 (May 20/26, 1996): 38-39.

Klawans, Stuart. "Border Crossings." *The Nation*, 264 (Feb. 17 1997): 35-36.

Layton, Susan. *Russian Literature and Empire: Conquest of the Caucasus from Pushkin to Tolstoy.* 1994. New York: Cambridge University Press, 2005.

Menashe, Louis. "*Prisoner of the Mountains.*" *Cineaste*, 23.1 (1997): 47-49.

Matsumoto, Jon. "*Prisoner of the Mountains.*" *Boxoffice*, 133 (Feb. 1997): 59.

Neff, Renfreu. "*Prisoner of the Mountains.*" *The Film Journal*, 100 (Jan./Feb. 1997): 85-86.

Plakhov, Andrei. "*Kavkazski plennik (Prisoner of the Mountains).*" *Cinemaya: The Asian Film Quarterly*, no. 33 (Summer 1996): 37-39.

Simon, John. "Wars Near and Far." *National Review*, 49 (June 2, 1997): 56-58.

Stackpole, John. "*Prisoner of the Mountains.*" *Audience*, no. 194 (April/May 1997): 32.

Stojanova, Christina. "Russian Cinema in the Free-Market Realm: Strategies for Survival." *Kinema: A Journal for Film and Audiovisual Media*, no. 11 (Spring 1999): 25-42.

6

Literature Become Cinema:
Notes on Three Emblematic Adaptations

As many commentators have noted, film is closer in form to fiction than to theater. Like fiction, film can move easily through time and space, and, like fiction, film employs narration—sometimes in the first person, through subjective camera and voiceover; rarely in the third person, through the anonymous commentaries that accompany certain documentaries; and most often and most naturally in the omniscient mode, which enables a filmmaker to cut from a subjective point-of-view shot to a variety of objective shots, from a single reaction in close-up to the simultaneous reactions of several characters in medium or full shot. (Every picture may tell a story, but every moving picture is "told"—by a narrator called the camera.)

Unlike fiction, or I should say in a more powerful way than fiction, film can go inside human beings to explore interiority. It does this through the voice and the voiceover, through the close-up, and through the ability to present multiple states of consciousness, as Federico Fellini does in *8½* (1963): present awareness, memory, dream, and daydream. A novel could do all this, of course, but its words wouldn't have the immediacy and effect of film, the power of the image and its accompanying sound. To be fair to the novel, the Russian filmmaker and theorist Sergei Eisenstein has shown how such cinematic innovations as fades, dissolves, and parallel editing were in fact taken directly from the pages of Charles Dickens. And to praise the novel, it has learned from film, as has poetry: a number of critics have remarked upon the cinematic qualities of much twentieth-century fiction and poetry, including Joyce's *Ulysses* (1922) and Eliot's "Love Song of J. Alfred Prufrock" (1915).

As for the adaptation of fiction into film, the chief problem for the adaptor is that of narration, and I'd like now to treat three forms of fictional adaptation: those of first-person narration and third-person narration, and that of epistolary (or multiple first-person) fiction to drama as well as to film. Let me begin by discussing the adaptation of novels written in the first person. As I suggested earlier, omniscient narration is almost inevitable in film: each time the director moves his camera—either within a shot or between shots—we are offered a new point of view from which to evaluate the action. Many films employ first-person narrative techniques, but only sporadically, because in order to produce continuous first-person narration on film, the camera would have to record all the action "subjectively," through the eyes of a narrator. The problem with such a subjective point of view is that it creates frustration in the viewer, who wants to *see* the hero. In fiction, we get to know the first-person narrator through his words, through the judgments and values he expresses through those words. But in movies, we get to know a character by seeing how he reacts to people and events, and unless the director breaks the first-person camera convention, we can never see the hero—we can only see what he sees. So the solution for the adaptor of a first-person novel is to include just enough first-person narration—usually in the form of voiceover—to remind us from whose point of view the story was originally told.

This is what James Ivory and Ruth Prawer Jhabvala attempt to do in their 1993 film of the novel *The Remains of the Day*, whose subject is the life of an emotionally and sexually repressed butler as it dovetails with that of his employer, a well-meaning but wrongheaded aristo-twit who, in the mid-1930s, secretly works to appease Hitler, avoid war, and preserve England's rigid social hierarchy. In other words, this is a work dealing chiefly with issues of politics, class, and sexuality. The novel (1989) was written by Kazuo Ishiguro, who was born Japanese but bred English; it was supposed to have been adapted to the screen by Harold Pinter, but Ivory discarded Pinter's script in favor of Jhabvala's.

Pinter has proved himself adept at adapting novels with first-person narrators (e.g., *The Go-Between* [1970], *The Proust Screenplay* [1977], and *The Heat of the Day* [1989]), something that is made difficult by the natural omniscience of the camera eye. The solution is obviously not to use a first-person camera throughout, to show only what the narrator can see and never the narrator himself, nor to employ large chunks of first-person voiceover narration; what the camera eye must do as much as possible is *see as the narrator in the book does*, see selectively that is, as if it were using the narrator's eyes. This is a neat trick, a kind of imaginative leap, and it can be made only by a screenwriter who is genuinely creative in her own right yet spiritually faithful to her source. Ruth Prawer Jhabvala, alas, is not such a scenarist, though she isn't without a certain skill.

The story of her screenplay begins in 1958, shortly after Lord Darlington's death and the sale of his palatial manor, Darlington Hall, to a solitary, rich American. Stevens, the butler, is staying on to work for the new owner, Mr. Lewis, but with a staff reduced from twenty-eight at the climax of the British empire to four during its present decline. Stevens is thinking of adding to that staff one Miss Kenton, the former (superbly efficient) housekeeper of Darlington Hall, who has recently sent him a letter (parts of which she reads in voiceover, and to which Stevens responds with his own letter read in voiceover) implying that she would like to return to her old position. So, having been given a week's vacation by his new employer, together with the use of the American's car (a Daimler, not the novel's Ford), he sets out from Oxfordshire on a journey to the West Country to meet Miss Kenton. She's been Mrs. Benn for the past twenty years, during which time Stevens has not seen her, and by now has a grown daughter, but her marriage is in trouble. Miss Kenton seems to be searching for something, then, to be reaching out, and so does Stevens. As he rides through the countryside to his appointment with her, he flashes back to their relationship—or non-relationship—in the past, as well as to his role as master servant in a house once brimful of statesmen and ambassadors.

It was Stevens' role as servant, as server of Lord Darlington rather than fulfiller of himself, that got in the way of any personal relationship he might have had with Miss Kenton. A love seemed to evolve between these two household workers who never so much as call each other by their first names, but it remained unacknowledged and unexpressed—at least on Stevens' part. There is no real acknowledgement of its existence by Miss Kenton either, but there is some expression of feeling, which unexpectedly

The Remains of the Day, dir. James Ivory, 1993

gets underscored in the film. Indeed, even Stevens' feeling gets expressed in the movie version, which recasts Ishiguro's exquisitely balanced tale more as doomed romance than as political allegory.

This is a direction Pinter, with his latter-day political engagement, may have reversed, and a direction the normally reticent Ivory has apparently chosen to take in the condescending belief that the lower orders of society are more given to venting their emotions. For example, during one of their nightly meetings to discuss the management of the house, Miss Kenton responds to Stevens' question "Are you with me?" with the excuse that she is very tired. She is tired, of course—tired of meeting with him under these circumstances, solely to discuss work—but this meaning of "tired" remains subtextual in the novel. In the film, Miss Kenton directly expresses the sentiment that she wants to *be* with Stevens, not merely to talk with him about the discharge of their servants' duties.

The next day, her day off, she has a date in a pub with Tom Benn, a former butler who wants to marry her and open his own boarding house in Clevedon-by-the-sea. There is no such scene in the book; it fractures the first-person perspective of Stevens; and it's almost immediately followed by another insertion, Miss Kenton's desperate revelation to Stevens of her impending engagement, to which he reacts by hastily leaving the room. Later, after she becomes formally engaged, he impatiently offers her his "warmest congratulations," for "there are matters of global significance taking place upstairs and [he] must return to [his] post." Then, in the process of fetching drinks for Lord Darlington's guests, Stevens drops a fine bottle of port—one more "emotional" event that does not occur in Ishiguro's novel—peremptorily replaces it with another, and proceeds to deliver it.

But he must pass Miss Kenton's room in order to do so, and here again the film tellingly diverges from its source. This is what the author understatedly writes, in the first-person voice of Stevens:

> As I approached Miss Kenton's door, I saw from the light seeping around its edges that she was still within. And . . . that moment as I paused in the dimness of the corridor, the tray in my hands, an ever-growing conviction [mounted] within me that just a few yards away, on the other side of that door, Miss Kenton was at that moment crying. As I recall, there was no real evidence to account for this conviction—I had certainly not heard any sounds of crying—and yet I remember being quite certain that were I to knock and enter, I would discover her in tears.

In Ivory's film, as you might guess, the door does get opened and Stevens discovers Miss Kenton in tears, only to advise her that some household article wants dusting! Further, after the butler departs, the camera remains on Miss Kenton, regarding her heartbroken face in a way that Stevens could never bring himself to do.

The camera does this once more near the end of *The Remains of the Day*. Stevens and Miss Kenton have had their meeting and character-history has proved to be human destiny: the aging butler will return to his butlering without ever having brought up the subject of their dormant love, and the now matronly housekeeper will go back to her marriage and the promise of a grandchild from her expectant daughter. As he puts Miss Kenton on a bus in the novel, Stevens notices that she is crying and comforts her with some pleasantries—nothing more. As he puts her on that same bus in the film, Miss Kenton is not yet in tears. For heightened effect, we see her crying through the window of the departing bus as Stevens does; then, after he leaves the frame, we get another shot of her face receding in tears. From whose point of view? The omniscient camera-as-narrator, or Ivory-cum-Jhabvala as italicizers of emotion.

This team even manages to inject heat into the novel's politics, or to put its heart where Ishiguro's head has prevailed. Before departing for the West Country, for example, Stevens is sent by Ivory and Jhabvala on business to the local general store, where he denies ever having known Lord Darlington, whom the clerk has decried as a Nazi sympathizer. No such scene occurs in the novel, and its effect is to change Stevens from an obtusely loyal, blindly trustful servant to a shifty timeserver masquerading as a man of conscience. En route to Clevedon, Stevens has a similar encounter—embellished by the filmmakers—with a doctor at an inn, where customers mistake the butler for a gentleman on account of his proper diction and dignified bearing. Dignity is the mark of a true gentleman, several villagers agree in the book, but one farmer argues that "Dignity's something every man and woman in this country can *strive for* and get. . . . Dignity's not just something for gentlemen" (emphasis mine). On screen, this gets reduced to "every Englishman has the *right* to be called a gentleman."

The high-born doctor arrives, senses Stevens' working-class origins beneath his superficial dignity and acquired speech, and gets him to admit, in the film, that he is "in service" at a great house in Oxfordshire. Inevitably, their cinematic conversation comes around to Lord Darlington of Oxfordshire, whom the doctor pillories for his virtual collaboration with the Nazis, and with whom Stevens once again disavows any acquaintance. Then he relents and tells the truth: he was proud to have served Lord Darlington but his job was just that, *to serve*, not to agree or disagree with his employer's political views. He goes on to say that, in attempting to accommodate Hitler, Darlington made a mistake for which he later sincerely repented; whereas he, Stevens, once made a mistake too—but one that he can correct rather than lament. The teasing implication, of course, is that his mistake was a matter of the heart rather than politics: to have repressed his love for Miss Kenton, which he will shortly express to her in Clevedon.

Stevens' words here are a complete reversal of what he says in the novel, *two days after* Miss Kenton's departure by bus, to a man sitting next to him on a pier in Weymouth:

> Lord Darlington wasn't a bad man. He wasn't a bad man at all. And at least he had the privilege of being able to say at the end of his life that he made his own mistakes. His lordship was a courageous man. He chose a certain path in life, it proved to be a misguided one, but there, he chose it, he can say that at least. As for myself, I cannot even claim that. You see, I *trusted*. I trusted in his lordship's wisdom. All those years I served him, I trusted I was doing something worthwhile. I can't even say I made my own mistakes. Really — one has to ask oneself — what dignity is there in that?

Stevens appears less politically correct in this speech, since he calls Darlington courageous if misguided; but he also appears more emotionally honest because he speaks of his own mistakes as irremediable in addition to undignifying, as inherent in his character as the narrative has established it. And they are *mistakes*, not one mistake, the use of the plural serving to conflate Stevens' relationship to Lord Darlington with his relationship to Miss Kenton. For the two relationships, and the butler's mistakes in them, are indeed related, as is Stevens' first-person perspective to the novel's thematic intent.

Ironically, Stevens gets to speak for himself in Ishiguro's tale, whereas in the past he had always allowed Lord Darlington to speak for him or at least to speak in his place. But in speaking for himself, he only reveals the tragicomic extent of his political capitulation and emotional barrenness, his substitution of a life of peripheral protocol for one of direct involvement. Being a butler, for Stevens, has been an act of selfless fealty toward a lord, not a mere profession or business — moreover, toward a lord engaged in great undertakings designed to secure England's future. He has allowed nothing to come between him and his duty to Darlington, not even the love of Miss Kenton (for which he unconsciously substitutes the reading of sentimental romances), so satisfactory has his relationship with his master been. And Lord Darlington, for his part, has allowed nothing to come between him and his duty to his country, not even the love of a wife, so satisfactory has his life of (behind-the-scenes) public service been. As a member of the household staff at Darlington Hall, Miss Kenton serves Stevens even as he serves his lord and his lord serves the state. The problem with this hierarchy of faithful service, however, is that it permits no room for second-guessing, and second-guessing is what the actions of both master and butler so desperately require. When Miss Kenton tries to question the actions of her "betters"—particularly in the dismissal of the two Jewish maids—she is rebuffed.

Ishiguro means, I think, to make Stevens' blindness—both to Darlington's political naïveté and Miss Kenton's emotional warmth—stand as a metaphor for England's blindness to its own national character and destiny. Just as Stevens trusted in Lord Darlington, Darlington trusted in his, and his country's, ability to broker a lasting peace with the Germans where no one else had been able to do so. That is, he and his associates—who recall the members of the notorious if somewhat mythologized "Cliveden Set" (a 1930s aristocratic, Germanophile social network not only in favor of the appeasement of Adolf Hitler but also in favor of friendly relations with Nazi Germany)—placed their trust in the cachet of British empire and aristocracy, as did Prime Minister Neville Chamberlain after them. They were mistaken to do so because, as Hitler clearly saw, the empire and its royalty were headed for extinction. Stevens thought he was serving the empire by denying himself, but all that he really did was *deny himself*, deny the love that could have given his life some dimension. He unquestioningly accepted the class system and his insulated place in it, and his reward, like that of many of his countrymen high and low, was a life of lovelessness if not brutality, of coldness if not desolation, of constriction if not misery.

Stevens' singular detachment or self-enclosure is well conveyed by the novel's first-person perspective, which naturally permits no other points of view to interject themselves, least of all the omniscience of the author; and which furthermore allows Stevens to create his character, as well as its social significance, by indirection, without resort to psychologizing on the one hand or historicizing on the other. One of the problems with Ivory's film, as I've indicated, is that the omniscient camera *does* intervene and perhaps had no choice but to intervene. In doing so, however, it sacrifices Stevens' integral tunnel vision without providing any compensatory light.

If it is ironic that Stevens finally gets to speak for himself in the novel of *The Remains of the Day*, it is doubly ironic that a butler is made to serve as England's national symbol. Or perhaps it is appropriate in the postwar period, if only the butler were not so proudly subservient as this one. For the postwar period in Britain was a time, if not for the dismantling of the class system, then for a definite questioning of its premises—a questioning brought on by the very war the Tory Darlington had tried to avoid, which gave new experiences, freedoms, and responsibilities to proletarian soldiers that they weren't so willing to relinquish upon their return from the fighting abroad. Instead of serving in the war, Stevens served his lord at home, where, he tells Mr. Lewis, over the years the world—in the form of Darlington's political confreres and social peers—had always come to his door. Lewis responds that his butler should now get out and see the world for himself; and Stevens does so, even if that world is limited to the beautiful English countryside through which he drives on his way to the West Country.

The year of his trip to Clevedon-by-the-sea is 1956 in the book, July 1956 to be exact, which the filmmakers have changed to 1958 in keeping with their recasting of the narrative more as doomed romance than as political allegory. The "Suez Crisis" occurred in 1956 as a result of Egypt's nationalization of the Canal in July and expulsion of British oil executives together with embassy officials from the country in August. Great Britain sent an invasion force to retake the Suez Canal in October, but this final attempt to reassert its traditional imperial influence ended with a whimper when English troops were forced to leave Egypt under the threat of United Nations sanctions.

For Stevens the end of empire does not seem imminent, which is one reason he doesn't mention the unfolding crisis over the Canal in his story. But the title of Ishiguro's novel refers both to the remains of Stevens' own day—to the quiet evenings following his daily yeoman's service as well as to the lonely retirement that awaits him—and to the twilight of British imperialism. And the onset of that twilight is signaled by the year 1956. Why change it to 1958, especially when the filmmakers have gone out of their way in another instance—the changing of Stevens' West-Country destination from Compton to Clevedon in order to echo Cliveden—to literalize the book's political suggestiveness?

The twilight of British imperialism tends in general to get moved back to its heyday or sunshine in Ivory's film, partly because of Tony Pierce-Roberts' cinematography, which appears celebratory instead of elegiac, lush rather than weathered; partly because of the movie's ending, which instead of finding Stevens sitting alone on a seaside bench in the evening (as the novel does), shows him back at Darlington Hall the next morning going about his duties, which happen to include the cliché of releasing a trapped pigeon into the verdant beauty of the surrounding countryside; and partly because of the film's documentary-like sequences.

These sequences show, even glory in, how a great manor is run, from the butler's ironing of the morning paper page-by-page to the scullery maid's cleaning of the cutlery, from the elaborate preparation of meals to the equally elaborate accommodation of numerous important guests. The camera does remain somewhat removed through all of this, yet one can't help thinking that the preoccupied Stevens would never take the time to scan the place and process of his work in such loving detail. Nor, as I've already pointed out, would he regard Miss Kenton in the way the camera does: lingeringly and lovingly. In the novel, she's a figure of imagination, created by words, a player in Stevens' internal drama whose face we never see. In the film, Miss Kenton takes on a life of her own, and that life with *its* drama detracts a bit from Stevens' own.

Next I'd like to consider the adaptation of a short story written in the third person: John Huston's last film, *The Dead* (1987), based on the last short story in James Joyce's collection *Dubliners* (1914) and the last story Joyce ever wrote. Nearly all of Huston's films are based on novels, plays, or short stories, and James Agee was right to conjecture in 1950, when Huston was shooting *The Red Badge of Courage,* that the director "lacks that deepest kind of creative impulse and that intense self-critical skepticism without which the stature of a great artist is rarely achieved. A brilliant adaptor, he has yet to do a Huston 'original,' barring the war documentaries."

Agee added that the better the original material, the better Huston functioned as an artist. This is because Huston was a faithful adaptor, not a loose one. He didn't seek to put his own stamp on source material; he tried to be as faithful as possible to the original, to re-create the literature in filmic terms. The loose adaptor *does* seek to put his own stamp on original material, to interpret it independently, and consequently he often works with lesser literary sources—sources, that is, that leave room for improvement, for expansion or refocusing. Huston stayed away from these, as the following sampling of his films will attest: the aforementioned *Red Badge of Courage* (1951), *Moby Dick* (1956), *The Bible* (1966), *Wise Blood* (1979), *Under the Volcano* (1984), and finally *The Dead*.

The problem for the faithful adaptor, of course, is that sometimes filmic equivalents for the literary can't be found. If prose could easily be translated into film, then it would lose some of its distinctiveness as prose. The following example from Joyce's story makes my point:

> A light fringe of snow lay like a cape on the shoulders of his overcoat and like toecaps on the toes of his galoshes; and, as the buttons of his overcoat slipped with a squeaking noise through the snow-stiffened frieze, a cold fragrant air from out-of-doors escaped from crevices and folds.

Gabriel Conroy and his wife, Gretta, have just entered the Dublin home of Gabriel's two aunts, Kate and Julia Morkan, for their annual dinner party-dance on the Feast of the Epiphany. We get none of Joyce's effect here in the film in part because *we see Gabriel himself*, all of him, and he is what captures our attention; in the story the words quoted above create a picture, and Gabriel's physical distinctiveness is missing from that picture. Joyce's emphasis is on the snow, which plays an important role in the story and is introduced at this moment.

Aside from the fact that cold, fragrant air escaping from crevices and folds can't be filmed, to have cut to the fringe of snow on the shoulders of Gabriel's overcoat and on the toes of his galoshes would have been to italicize that snow in a way that the prose does not do. Joyce's prose is a *description* that, in the course of the story, gains symbolic importance. Huston's cutting to the snow, had he done so, would have been to give it symbolic portent immediately, to direct us forcibly to its significance, and this would have been too much. With a choice between too much and too little, Huston wisely chooses too little: we see *Gabriel*, the shoulders of whose overcoat and the toes of whose galoshes are in fact covered, in turn, with a fringe of snow. But too little is not enough, and "enough" could only be contained in prose.

Huston faced another problem in filming Joyce's "The Dead" that was solvable but that he nonetheless did not solve. Joyce wrote in the third person—a non-participating narrator tells the story from the point of view of Gabriel's consciousness, as in the following:

> Gabriel felt humiliated . . . by the evocation of this figure from the dead, a boy in the gasworks. While he had been full of memories of their secret life together, full of tenderness and joy and desire, she had been comparing him in her mind with another. A shameful consciousness of his own person assailed him. He saw himself as a ludicrous figure, acting as a pennyboy for his aunts, a nervous well-meaning sentimentalist, orating to vulgarians and idealising his own clownish lusts, the pitiable fatuous fellow he had caught a glimpse of in the mirror.

Few fiction films employ a third-person narrator, and those that do don't employ much of one, because the more we hear him, the more we feel we might as well be reading the story or novel itself (third-person narration is most often found in documentaries). Third-person narration is usually translated into the more immediate interior monologue and we hear it in voiceover as we see the character; again, though, we can't hear too much of it or else our visual experience will be thwarted.

Now Joyce wrote "The Dead" in the third person for a reason, best described by Allen Tate:

> The author suppresses himself but does not allow the hero to tell his own story, for the reason that "psychic distance" is necessary to the end in view. This end is the *sudden* revelation to Gabriel of his egoistic relation to his wife and, through that revelation, of his inadequate response to his entire experience. Thus Joyce must establish his central intelligence through Gabriel's eyes, but a little above and outside him at the same time . . .

Perhaps Huston thought that Joyce's "psychic distance" would be destroyed by translating third-person narration into the interior monologue of Gabriel Conroy, for we hear Gabriel speak in voiceover only toward the end of the film, after Gretta has fallen asleep in their hotel room. Huston was wrong, however, if he did think this, because film, through the very device of framing the action, is ideally suited to maintaining the "psychic distance" of third-person narration at the same time that it periodically translates the third-person narration of fiction into interior monologue on a soundtrack.

Huston keeps his camera back for the most part in *The Dead*, using it to objectively frame the action rather than to subjectively enter it, but he fatally damages his film by not allowing us, through voiceover, to enter Gabriel's consciousness at significant moments. We cannot know, from Huston's film and from the performance of Donal McCann—and we should *not* be presumed to know the story—that Gabriel regards his aunts as only two ignorant old women, that he considers his fellow party guests vulgarians, that he pities his wife the loss of her youthful beauty when she feels no such pity for herself. The *narrator* tells us these things in the story because we must know them if we are to appreciate both the size of Gabriel's ego and the extent of his "recognition" at the end, his movement outside himself into an expansiveness that includes "all the living and the dead," that includes the room in which he's staying as well as all of Ireland and even the universe, throughout which he imagines snow softly falling.

These criticisms made, I must say that *The Dead* is a delight to look at and to hear, in music and in the music of Irish accents. Alex North, who did the score for Huston's *Under the Volcano* and is best known for the scores of *A Streetcar Named Desire* (on screen) and *Death of a Salesman* (on stage and on screen), has composed delicately and evocatively. North has captured in his music the double nature of Joyce's story as a lament for Gabriel and a hymn to him, to the gentle, moving epiphany he achieves at the end. Fred Murphy's cinematographic world, for its part, is filled not so much with color as with light—lamplight or night light. Murphy's palette consists largely of browns, grays, and blacks, and it is his intimate lighting during the party scenes that makes these colors mingle and dance,

The Dead, dir John Huston, 1987

while it is his cold lighting during Gabriel and Gretta's coach ride back to the hotel and in the hotel room itself that makes these colors congeal and recede, to be surrounded by the whiteness of snow's blanket.

I cannot be as positive about the performances of Donal McCann as Gabriel and Anjelica Huston as Gretta, but, as is often the case in film, this has less to do with the performances themselves than with the film of which they are a part. Gretta is too prominent at the dinner party and dance, as she is not in the story—Huston cuts back and forth a number of times between her and her husband when she is dancing and he is not, and when she, unlike him, is unsettled by the recitation of a poem called "Broken Vows" (not part of Joyce's story). Huston does this to try to convey possessiveness and insecurity on Gabriel's part, but in the process he diminishes the effect of Gabriel's reversal at the end. Joyce's point is that, up to the moments of reversal and recognition, Gabriel is completely wrapped up in himself and in his role as his aunts' favored guest. The result of Huston's distortion of the story is that his daughter injects into Gretta a preciosity or self-consciousness that isn't part of her character and a remoteness that shouldn't be part of her character until much later, when she hears the tenor Bartell D'Arcy (a guest at the party) sing "The Lass of Aughrim" and is reminded thereby of Michael Furey, a boy who had once been in love with her in Galway and who used to sing the same song. Michael died at seventeen and, Gretta later says to Gabriel, " I think he died for me."

Donal McCann is hindered, as I have pointed out, by the absence of his interior monologue on the soundtrack until the end of the film, and he simply doesn't have it in himself to tell us physically—facially and gesturally—what Joyce does in words. Add to this the fact that McCann's eyes aren't expressive, whereas Gabriel's are "delicate and restless," and that he's not helped by the omission of the character's "glimmering gilt-rimmed eyeglasses," and you have an actor hamstrung less by his own shortcomings than by his director's shortsightedness. Before his death, John Huston did his part in the unsuccessful campaign against the "colorizing" of black-and-white movies. I wish that he had been as faithful to Joyce's "The Dead" as he wanted Ted Turner to be to his *Maltese Falcon*.

Lastly, I'd like to treat what I call an omnibus adaptation—of fiction to drama to film—and the case in point is *Dangerous Liaisons*: a novel by Choderlos de Laclos (1782), from which Christopher Hampton took his play of the same title (1985), and from which Hampton then derived his screenplay for Stephen Frears's motion picture called, appropriately enough, *Dangerous Liaisons* (1988). Laclos's novel *Les Liaisons dangereuses*, for its part, is a product of its age in two senses: it is in epistolary form, a dominant narrative mode of the eighteenth century, and it embodies the conflicting philosophical and political impulses of this, the so-called age of reason.

On the one hand, the French *comédie larmoyante* and *drama bourgeois*, as well as the English sentimental comedy, sentimental tragedy, and sentimental novel, were arguing along with Rousseau that man was by nature good and could remain so by following his instincts—that is, the promptings of his heart; evil persons, on their side, might be reclaimed (at the same time they might be punished) if their hearts could be touched, if the callus of their vice could be penetrated to reveal the soft skin of their virtue. On the other hand, the Marquis de Sade was arguing that the "promptings of the heart" were in fact the product of reason, of teaching and socialization, not of instinct, which modeled itself after the chaos of the world and obeyed the laws of desire.

Sentimental literature was designed, of course, to appeal to the growing middle-class audience, to assist that audience in developing its own, self-congratulatory moral code and social ethic. Anti-sentimental literature—in the form of the libertine novel of eighteenth-century France and the British Restoration comedy of manners before it—was designed, by contrast, to confirm the shrinking upper classes in their unsentimental self-knowledge as well as in their ability to use their superior intelligence to outwit others and *liberate* themselves: from repressive moral codes, from political domination, from social subservience of any kind. Sexual intrigue and indulgence play such a great role in this literature partly because, for the idle and wealthy, gaming is the natural pastime, and sexual gaming is the most natural pastime of all.

Christopher Hampton's screenplay for *Dangerous Liaisons* happens, happily, to be faithful to the time period as well as the setting of the original. There are seven major correspondents in Laclos's *Les Liaisons dangereuses*, moreover, and all of them appear as characters in Frears's *Dangerous Liaisons* as well—characters who remind us of their origins in epistolary, or multiple first-person, fiction by periodically exchanging letters with one another during the film. (The very first shot is of someone's hands holding a letter, which itself bears the title of the film.) The chief characters are the Marquise de Merteuil, a young widow and arch manipulator of men; the Vicomte de Valmont, her former lover and an inveterate womanizer; and the Présidente de Tourvel, the young and pious wife of a magistrate (a Présidente, or presiding judge) away on business in Burgundy, and the closest we shall come to a bourgeoise.

Then come Cécile de Volanges, the young and innocent daughter of Madame de Volanges, who has recently arranged the girl's marriage to the Comte de Gercourt, a former lover of Merteuil's; Madame de Volanges, confidante to Merteuil (her cousin), the Présidente de Tourvel, and Rosemonde, and one of Valmont's many previous sexual conquests; the Chevalier Danceny, a young music tutor and suitor for Cécile's hand as well as the eventual lover of Merteuil; and Madame de Rosemonde, Valmont's eighty-year-old aunt, who is the Présidente de Tourvel's close friend and the owner of a country estate between which location and Paris the action alternates.

The plot—and what a plot, given its seven "narrators"—hinges on Merteuil's desire for revenge against Gercourt for his engagement to Cécile, and on Valmont's desire for yet another night in bed with Merteuil. As part of her plan, Valmont agrees to seduce the fifteen-year-old, convent-brad Cécile, but regards this as such an easy task that he won't accept Merteuil's renewed favors unless he is also able to bed Tourvel, whose religion and virtue present him with a real challenge. Valmont succeeds easily with the young virgin, as he predicted, but must work so assiduously at seducing Tourvel that after he finally does, he realizes that he is as passionately in love with her as she is with him. Merteuil realizes this, too, and refuses Valmont his night in bed on the ground that he has breached the rules of their game: to achieve purely sexual consummations that are then rapidly and dispassionately severed.

Valmont severs his relationship with Tourvel but Merteuil still refuses him his prize, so jealous is she of his love; Valmont counters by arranging the first sexual liaison between Cécile and Danceny, Merteuil's own most recent conquest; and Merteuil retaliates by telling Danceny of Valmont's affair with Cécile. Danceny kills Valmont in a duel, but before dying the vicomte hands over his letters from Merteuil and Tourvel to the young man, thereby exposing the marquise's machinations and causing her public humiliation. Tourvel has retired to a convent, where she lapses into madness and dies; Cécile, who miscarried Valmont's child, will eventually enter a nunnery as a postulant; and the remorseful Danceny will opt for a life of celibacy as well, by joining the Knights of Malta.

In Laclos's novel, Merteuil soon contracts smallpox, becomes so disfigured that she loses an eye, then loses a lawsuit and with it her fortune, whereupon she flees Paris for Holland. In Hampton's dramatic adaptation as in the film version, we see none of this. We last view Merteuil on stage playing a game of cards (just as we saw her at the start of the drama) as the shadow of a guillotine falls on the rear wall of the theater—a somewhat heavy premonition of the French Revolution and the beginning of the end of the aristocratic class. Hampton's film ending is lighter in touch than both his stage ending and the ending of the novel, and it fills in the "sentiments" that Laclos had only outlined.

The last shot of *Dangerous Liaisons* is a close-up of Merteuil in front of her dressing-table mirror, removing her make-up after her humiliation at the opera, where her former friends booed her as she stood alone in her box; the film had begun with a shot of her face in that same mirror as she was preparing to make herself up. The implication is that there are two Merteuils: the heartless, egotistical one "made up" in the mirror, and the real woman beneath with a heart and with love to give rather than desire to slake. After Merteuil removes the last of the make-up from her pale face, she stares blankly—at herself—and tears begin to fall as the screen slowly fades to black. She cries at her own ruin, her own folly, but also at the death of Valmont, for whom she had begun to have genuine feelings.

Valmont, for his part, tearfully declares before his death both his love for Tourvel and his sorrow for the licentious life he has led: "Her love is the only real happiness I have ever known"; "[Danceny] had good cause [to slay me]; I don't think that is anything anyone has ever been able to say about me." Ironically, it is Valmont's love for Tourvel that gets him killed in Hampton and Frears's interpretation. As he duels with Danceny, Valmont flashes back to his lovemaking with Tourvel even as the film cross-cuts to the scene of her

Dangerous Liaisons, dir. Stephen Frears, 1988

being bled with leeches in the convent; their deaths thus become visually intertwined with their love, or their love becomes a kind of death. Tourvel dies of her love, and Valmont dies of his: clearly the superior swordsman, he lets his guard down at one point as his memories of Tourvel overtake him, and Danceny takes the opportunity to run him through. Our final look at Valmont is from on high, along with, by implication, a judgmental God: in a stunning high-angle shot, we see him lying on his back in pure white snow, his servant and Danceny hanging over him and a long, thick trail of blood leading randomly away from his body.

Like sexual gangsters, Merteuil and Valmont have had their way, up to a point, and like dutiful spectators, we have thrilled to their exploits, up to a point—the one where moral duty intervenes and we assent, with God, to their penitence and punishment. Religion triumphs at the end of the filmic *Dangerous Liaisons* more than revolution, sentiment more than slaughter, conversion more than conquest. The greater truth of Hampton's movie ending, as opposed to his stage ending, is that the bourgeoisie assimilated, rather than assassinated, the aristocracy (even as the twentieth-century cinema did to the nineteenth-century theater, and that theater itself did to the eighteenth-century novel); that the sentimental view of life outflanked, rather than outmatched, the anti-sentimental one.

Sentimentalism acknowledged that good souls like Tourvel could be tempted to commit evil precisely because they were so good and trusting; and that even souls as evil as Merteuil could be made to see the error of their ways, precisely because their evil had finally consumed them together with their victims. If Sade's "instinct" obeyed the dictates of universal chaos, then sentimentalism's "heart" obeyed the dictates of providential design, and that design is adumbrated more by the omniscience of film form than by the discontinuous first-person narration of the epistolary novel, let alone the absence of narration in the drama.

In *Dangerous Liaisons*, we see events as they happen from the point of view of an omniscient camera/narrator not bound by time, space, or self-interest; we get Laclos's fragmented and disordered fiction, told by several people who don't know the whole story, converted into a complete and ordered film, told by someone who knows all. At the same time, Stephen Frears does his best to preserve the immediacy, intimacy, and secrecy, even solipsism, of the letter-form by shooting much of *Dangerous Liaisons* in close-up, going so far as to rack focus—to alter the plane within a shot—in order to isolate a character in medium close-up in the foreground of the image while turning the background (of which Frears has given us a compensatory glimpse) into a blur.

The "epistolary" close-up alternates with Frears's omniscient, and highly skillful, cutting among scenes to give us what Laclos's novel really cannot—as no other novel could, either—and what Hampton's stage adaptation could only awkwardly attempt to convey (especially without resort to simultaneous staging): the paradoxical sense that we share in the immediacy of the confidences exchanged at the same time as we are in the hands of a silent divinity who overhears, and oversees, everything. *We* put together the pieces Laclos gives us when we read the 175 letters of the novel, or as we watch the eighteen scenes of Hampton's theatrical version; as we see the film, someone else is putting the pieces together, for us as well as for the characters.

I'd like to close not by arguing for the overall superiority of film as an art form—it is superior in some ways, inferior in others, which I have been careful to leave out of this discussion. What I would like to say, however, is that film was certainly *the* art form of the twentieth century and promises to dominate the twenty-first as well, and that's because it's the one technology that is—or at least can be—absolutely humanistic in its outcome. It can put many of the technological impulses, cravings, and interests of our age at the service, not merely of the machinery of sensation, diversion, and profit, but of the mystery of the human spirit as well. I'm speaking about film at its best, of course. Why it often isn't at its best is a subject complicated by the commerce of the world, and one better left for another day.

WORKS CITED

Agee, James. "Undirectable Director [John Huston]." 1950. In *Agee on Film: Reviews and Comments*. New York: McDowell Obolensky, 1958. 320-331.

Hampton, Christopher. *Dangerous Liaisons*. London: Faber & Faber, 1985.

Ishiguro, Kazuo. *The Remains of the Day*. New York: Viking, 1989.

Joyce, James. "The Dead." In Joyce's *Dubliners*. London: Grant Richards, 1914. 151-194.

Laclos, Pierre Choderlos de. *Les Liaisons dangereuses*. 4 vols. Paris: Durand Neveu, 1782.

_____. *Dangerous Liaisons*. Trans. P.W.K. Stone. Harmondsworth, U.K.: Penguin, 1961.

Tate, Allen. "Three Commentaries: Poe, James, and Joyce." *The Sewanee Review*, 58 (Winter 1950): 1-15.

7

The Theater-of-Film of Hans-Jürgen Syberberg

The films of Hans-Jürgen Syberberg (born 1935) are at times annoying, confusing, and overlong, but they are also ambitious and compelling. In no way is he ever conventional or commercial: critics and audiences have alternately labeled his work brilliant and boring, absorbing and pretentious, and his films today are still rarely screened. Stylistically, it is difficult to link Syberberg with any other filmmaker or cinematic tradition. In this regard he is an original, the most controversial of all the New German directors, and a figure who has long been at the vanguard of the resurgence of experimental filmmaking in his homeland.

Not unlike his (late) contemporary Rainer Werner Fassbinder, Syberberg's most characteristic films examine recent German history: a documentary, for example, about Richard Wagner's daughter-in-law, who was a close friend of Hitler (*The Confessions of Winifred Wagner* [1975]). But especially "historical" is his trilogy covering one hundred years of Germany's past, including *Ludwig II: Requiem for a Virgin King* (1972), which portrays the mad king of Bavaria who was the patron of Wagner and a builder of fairy-tale castles; *Karl May* (1974), which deals with the life of the famous author of Westerns who himself had never seen the American West; and, most famously, *Hitler, A Film from Germany*, also known as *Our Hitler* (1977). Seven hours and nine minutes long, in four parts and twenty-two chapters, *Our Hitler* effects a synthesis of Brecht and Wagner, of epic defamiliarization and operatic pathos. (Brecht's influence began relatively early in Syberberg's artistic life: the latter's 8mm sound film of the Berliner Ensemble at work in the 1950s—a film blown up to 35mm and released in 1970 as *My Last Move*—is the only record of that group during the Brecht period.) Syberberg's Hitler is painted as both a fascist dictator who could have risen to power at any point in time in any number of political climates, and a monstrous movie mogul (called "the greatest filmmaker in the world") whose version of Griffith's *Intolerance* (1916) would be *The Holocaust*, with himself in the leading role.

Syberberg unites fictional narrative and documentary footage in a style that is at once cinematic and theatrical, mystical and magical. His films might easily be performed live (*Our Hitler* is set on a stage, and *The Night* [1985] was in fact performed live—more on this later), but the material is so varied that the presence of the camera is necessary to translate the action thoroughly. Additionally, this director is perceptibly aware of how the events that make up history are ultimately comprehended by the public via the manner in which they are presented in the media. History is thus understood more by catchwords and generalities than by facts; as a result, in this age of mass media real events can easily become distorted and trivialized. Syberberg demonstrates this in *Our Hitler* by presenting the Führer in so many (dis)guises that the viewer is often desensitized to the reality that was this mass murderer.

Our Hitler, a.k.a. *Hitler, A Film from Germany*,
dir. Hans-Jürgen Syberberg, 1977

None of Syberberg's later work has earned him the visibility, let alone the acclaim, of his earlier films. Since *Parsifal* (1983), his version of the Wagnerian opera that was his most widely seen work, he has collaborated with one of that film's stars, Edith Clever. Their artistic ventures have included a number of theatrical monologues, a few of which have been videotaped or filmed. The series commenced with *The Night*, a six-hour long examination of how an individual may act or what an individual may ponder deep into the night—the literal night as well as the figurative one that resulted from (among other events in the history of the West) the holocaust of the Second World War. This examination continued into the nineties with *The Bad and Happy Lot of Art after World War II* (1991).

Syberberg's latest work of which I am aware, a video installation titled *Plato Cave Memory* (1997), itself continues to pursue his major filmic theme—Germany's collective remembrance of things past—in addition to exploring the following important subjects: the relations between theater and film, and by extension among film, video, and computer-enabled digital technology; the relationship of the *Gesamtkunstwerk*, or "total work of art," to the particular arts of closet drama, literary fiction, and lyric poetry; and the juxtaposition of artistic "shadow worlds," in Plato's cave as in Syberberg's own films, to the material world of transitory reality, on the one hand, and the ideal realm of immutable eternity, on the other.

In this essay, I would like to examine the two works by Syberberg that best exemplify what I describe in my title as the "theater of film": *Parsifal* and *The Night*. Let's begin with the earlier picture, whose subject shouldn't surprise if you know Wagner's *Parsifal* (1882) and if you have seen Syberberg's *Our Hitler*. (The connection between Wagner and Hitler is the fact that the Führer venerated Wagner's works and saw them as embodying true German ideals.) No, you should not be surprised by Syberberg's choice to make a film of Wagner's work; nor should you be surprised by this director's general approach to his subject. But this *Parsifal*, among its fascinations, does have a surprising new aspect—to which I shall return.

Syberberg's obsession with Wagner has long been familiar. The first film of his to be shown in the United States, *The Confessions of Winifred Wagner*, was a 104-minute condensation of the five-hour interview, made for German television, that he conducted with the composer's daughter-in-law. Wagner, musically and otherwise, is present in several other Syberberg films. And one of the most vivid images in postwar German cinema occurs in *Our Hitler*: the toga-clad Hitler rising from a grave that has a stone marked "RW." In Syberberg's view, then, *Parsifal* must be the most representative of Wagner's works, the most beautiful but silly, exalted yet pretentious, noble at the same time it is vicious—all the contradictions that Syberberg patently finds in German character and behavior.

Wagner himself, of course, is prototypical of a great deal that both repulses and fascinates about Germany. On the one hand there is Wagner, the maniacal, blood-and-iron, anti-Semitic Teuton. On the other hand, there is Wagner, the titanic genius whom the young Nietzsche saw as the new Prometheus restoring Dionysian flame to a pallid civilization. (And the older Nietzsche never really recanted. As Thomas Mann remarked, "Nietzsche's [later] polemic against Wagner pricks on enthusiasm for the composer rather than lames it.") Eric Bentley, in that masterwork *The Playwright as Thinker*, goes as far as to pair Wagner with Ibsen as one of the two great modern exponents of tragedy. Yet this is, inseparably, the same Richard Wagner who inspired Adolf Hitler, and whose anti-Semitism is sometimes seen as Syberberg's own.

Wagner's score for *Parsifal*, which (I think) Syberberg uses uncut, is a succession of marvels that coalesce into a gigantic marvel; yet the libretto, or poem as Wagner called it, is itself less than completely cogent. The atmosphere may be as spiritual as anything in Wagner, but he explicitly intended the work as an Aryan, anti-Semitic allegory. (Further contradiction on that point: the first conductor was a Jew.) Moreover, it is an allegory that idealizes (again) Wagner's view of male innocence beset by the temptations of woman: as in Tannhäuser's enslavement within the Venusberg in *Tannhäuser*; or in Siegfried's cutting open the armor of the sleeping Brünnhilde, in the third part of the *Ring of the Nibelung*, and exclaiming naïvely, "*Das ist kein Mann!*" Be that as it may, the Parsifal-Kundry encounter in Act II is still one of the most perceptive rites-of-sexual-passage in drama. (Kundry entices Parsifal by speaking of his mother—more than a decade before Freud.) Writing from Bayreuth in 1889, Bernard Shaw had this to say on the subject: "And that long kiss of Kundry's from which [Parsifal] learns so much is one of those pregnant simplicities which stare the world in the face for centuries and yet are never pointed out except by great men."

No wonder, then, that Syberberg, only one of a number of German artists who have simultaneously loved and loathed their country, should respond to *Parsifal*. Nonetheless, a question persists. No, not the question of Syberberg's purported anti-Semitism or ultra-nationalism, the political nature of which does not interest me. The question that persists is an *aesthetic* one, and one that leads to the surprise mentioned earlier. Why did he film a work that was already famous in another medium? His previous films had been entirely his own creations. Here, Syberberg did begin with a new recording of *Parsifal*, but, except for bits of music rehearsals under the credits and a few snatches of random voices after the finish, he simply supplied visuals to accompany that recording. Why?

The answer begins to be suggested by the following statement of his, from the original press kit for *Parsifal*:

> Just as the composer [Wagner] was inspired by a legendary evocation of the Middle Ages in his desire to express ideas which were of his own time, I am basing my approach on the fact that the work is one hundred years old and that I can therefore describe its significance through time.

Ascribe the hubris of that last phrase to the energy which an artist needs in order to do anything serious at all—no one knowingly creates just for next week—and Syberberg's approach becomes clearer while we watch the film. This view of *Parsifal*, as a classic text chosen by a later artist for contemporary definition, puts his film in a *theater* tradition, not a cinematic one. That is the surprise. And his film derives, fundamentally, from Adolphe Appia.

Appia (1862-1928), the Swiss theatrical designer and visionary, had revolutionary views of production that have hugely influenced Western theater in the twentieth and twenty-first centuries— particularly non-illusionistic dramatic practice. Not only did he emphasize the role of light—to Appia, the visual counterpart of music—in fusing all of the stage's visual elements into a unified theatrical whole, but he also argued that artistic unity requires that one person control all the elements of production, and thus he helped to strengthen the role of the director (especially what has come to be known as the "concept" director) in the theater. Appia's strongest love was for Wagner; all his life, in fact, he worked on designs for Wagnerian productions. Few of them were ever realized—he participated in only six actual productions of any kind during his entire career—but they changed the theater's way of seeing.

Appia was shocked by the old-fashioned staging and design at Bayreuth, which had been prescribed by the composer. He wrote in *Music and the Art of the Theatre* (1899) that

> Wagner made but one essential reform. Through the medium of music he conceived of a dramatic action whose center of gravity lay inside the characters and which at the same time could be completely *expressed* for the hearer.... But he did not know how to make his production form—his *mise en scène*—agree with his adopted dramatic form.

Though Appia never stopped dream-designing for a theatrical revolution of Wagner that would fit the revolution in the music, he did get three Wagnerian production chances, half of his whole practical career. One of them was *Tristan and Isolde* for Toscanini at La Scala in 1923, and neither of the others was *Parsifal*. But his unrealized designs for *Parsifal* figure prominently in the treasury of his work.

Syberberg's film of *Parsifal* does not in any detail come from Appia, but ideationally it is the result of an intent that began with Appia and has since flourished. To wit: Appia was the first conceiver of productions who re-created the inside of his head on stage, rather than reproduce the world outside realistically, classically, or even romantically. What he wanted to reify on the stage was his imaginative response to a work of art. And that, exactly, is Syberberg's basic intent in *Parsifal*, though of course his response is his own—nothing like Appia's.

Syberberg puts before us, then, not just a film of the opera, however symbolic or impressionistic, but absolutely everything that *Parsifal* evokes in him, about art and politics and history, about theater and cinema, about the possible exorcism of the demon Wagner himself. While Wagner's rich, almost extravagant music floods our hearing, Syberberg feeds our eyes with as much as he can crystallize of what that music—that music's very existence—has done to him. To be sure, the *Parsifal* story gets told well enough, but this is not a consistent "eccentric version," as a modern-dress or science-fiction adaptation, for example, might be. What we are really watching, in addition to the *Parsifal* narrative, is a cascade of connections, the play of associations hauled out by other associations in Syberberg's mind.

Some of the elements in his film are easily understood, perhaps too easily. When Gurnemanz leads Parsifal to the castle in Act I, for instance, they go backward through German history as represented by an alley of flags, beginning with the swastika. Behind Klingsor in Act II, the watchtower of a concentration camp can be seen. The waxworks-museum heads of Marx, Nietzsche, and Wagner himself are sometimes part of the décor; so is a three-dimensional facsimile of André Gill's famous caricature of Wagner—inside a human ear, hammering away. At one point Parsifal is even seen against a ridge that turns out to be Wagner's face in horizontal profile. Amfortas's wound, moreover, is an entity quite separate from his body, so that it seems to be a possession more than an affliction. Syberberg represents it by a thick, folded napkin on a pedestal next to the ailing king's couch: the bleeding gash is in the napkin. (It suggests a vulva, and thus the wound, which he got from Kundry, may be a figure for carnal seduction.)

Most of the film's actions and details, however, must be taken only as phenomena that affect us or don't—not as elements to be explicated. For one thing, most of the roles are mimed with lip-synch. (Two of the performers we see happen also to be singers on the soundtrack; the text is naturally sung in German, with subtitles.) That in itself is neither novel nor troublesome. But Syberberg goes further: he chooses to have Parsifal mimed first by a stripling, adolescent boy and, then, after Kundry's kiss, the role is mimed by an even younger girl, with Reiner Goldberg's strong *Heldentenor* coming out of the mouth of each Parsifal in turn. At the end, the boy and girl embrace chastely.

I don't believe that this device "means" anything; it's intended to jar preconceptions and provoke new response, not to fill out any pattern, Freudian or otherwise. As is the device of dolls that are suddenly used as characters and then discarded. Or the one of the Flower Maidens posed immobile, against rocks, while they sing of caressing Parsifal. The penultimate image itself is of a skull, crowned with a bishop's miter, lying on the ground. The last image is of Kundry, her arms and long hair embracing or entwining a small wooden model of what I take to be the Bayreuth Festspielhaus. And much more, all of it intended only to represent Syberberg's visions, or visionary response to *Parsifal*—for us to absorb, to use, if we can and will.

Contrapuntally, as in *Our Hitler*, Syberberg insists on a kind of Brechtian candor throughout, to keep us aware that fabrication is part of his process. Everything is played against a black cyclorama, on which slides are often projected. (Compare this device, used here on a sound stage as it was in *Our Hitler*, with the use of theatrical backdrops in Syberberg's *Ludwig II*, where such scenery crystallizes the theatricality of Ludwig's life and the "performance" of that life, his passion for the theater as well as his devotion to Wagner.) The lighting of a scene often changes while we watch. And almost all the scenery is meant to look like scenery. Sometimes, for example, we see the floorboards of the film studio. Near the end, projected on the cyclorama behind one scene, there is even some film footage of the conductor, Armin Jordan, shot during the recording session. (Jordan, who has conducted in many European opera houses, here leads the Monte Carlo Philharmonic Orchestra and the Prague Philharmonic Choir.)

Yet, in the midst of this torrent of images combined with Syberberg's "exposé" of image-making, most of the performances are quite traditional. The Gurnemanz here is much younger than usual, but he is nonetheless the poem's Gurnemanz, beautifully played by Robert Lloyd. (Lloyd also sings the role beautifully; the other singer who appears on screen is Aage Haugland, the Klingsor.) Amfortas is feeling, mimed—by the conductor himself, to the accompaniment of the good baritone of Wolfgang Schöne. And Yvonne Minton sings Kundry powerfully, while that miraculous actress Edith Clever mimes this problematic role with an intensity that holds its tensions in fiery focus. (The recording, by the way, is fortunately in Dolby stereo, but, spatially speaking, Syberberg elects to use the "old" screen size, which is one-third wider than it is high.)

The most significant previous film of an opera was made only eight years before *Parsifal*—Bergman's *Magic Flute* in 1975—and a comparison of this work with Syberberg's own reveals a paradox. To Bergman, Mozart's opera was a *cinematic* challenge: by means of the camera, he therefore combined a conventional stage performance both with the presence of an audience and with backstage data to create a purely filmic locus for the work. By contrast, Syberberg, who had never worked in the theater until *The Night*, strives in *Parsifal* to make film into theater.

Distant from Appia yet evolved from him, Syberberg puts his "definitive" theatrical production on film because, in several senses, it would not be possible in an actual theater. Aided by designers of exceptional talent, he has created a sweepingly personal, expansively idiosyncratic vision of *Parsifal* that nonetheless places his film in a venerable theatrical line: a director's "statement" of a classic. In spite of a camera that is almost always slowly moving in or away, panning or traveling, this work, then, is much less like pure cinema than a superb (television) film of a production in a hypothetical (but oversized) theater.

Syberberg's final—or perhaps first and foremost—comment on *Parsifal* is that he filmed it at all. For *Parsifal* has a unique history: beginning with its première at Bayreuth in 1882, it was zealously guarded as a sacred work, to be performed only in the hallowed atmosphere of Bayreuth, not on profane stages elsewhere. And except for some concert versions, this "edict" was carried out for twenty-one years. Then the Metropolitan Opera in New York took advantage of inexact international copyright law to produce *Parsifal*, despite German cries of profanation, on Christmas Eve, 1903. (A chartered Parsifal Limited train came from Chicago, while the *New York Evening Telegram* produced a *Parsifal* extra.) Other "profanations" followed in other cities, in the United States as well as abroad, until 1914 when the Bayreuth copyright expired and *Parsifal* became unrestrictedly available to every opera house throughout the world.

And then, one hundred years after *Parsifal*'s original production, Syberberg makes a "mere" film of it—something that can be shown anywhere, at any time. But this fact, too, holds a contradiction. By making his film, and making it in his particular way, Syberberg has utterly destroyed any remaining fake pieties about *Parsifal*. At the same time he has tried, through belief in the pertinence of his vision/version of the work, to consecrate it anew for the present-and-future, protean theater of film.

A true adventurer in film, Syberberg pressed on after *Our Hitler* and *Parsifal*—which teemed with images and characters and devices and fantasies—with *The Night*, which is mostly set in one place and, through all of its six hours, has only one performer. Yet—another contradiction—this film is not a whit less adventurous than the earlier two and, through different modes and stimuli, teems just as plentifully. However, unlike *Our Hitler* and *Parsifal*, *The Night* had fewer theater showings in North America: several in Chicago, some in Montreal, and then four in New York (where I saw it). No regular theater showings followed, then or now, which is a sadness I'd rather not dwell on here.

The Night consists of a prologue and two sections, with an intermission after Part I. Following the prologue, of a half hour or so, the credits appear, a number of authors are listed, some album pages turn, and then we move to Part I and the only setting used thereafter. Part II begins with a similar listing of authors, some album pages, and a return to that same setting. (The prologue is in pale colors, as shot by Xaver Schwarzenberger; the rest is in black and white.) From the authors whom he names, Syberberg has culled, touched up, and interwoven—with some autobiographical material—a skein of language intended to circumscribe the night of his title: the long night of Western culture.

That he includes more than Europe in this night is patent from the start. The prologue, spoken in a large, rubble-strewn room in a battered Berlin building, is the speech of the American Indian chief Seattle when he signed a peace treaty with Washington, D.C., in 1855. His words envision the end of his people and their ways, but Seattle warns the white man that, though the Indians may disappear from view, their spirits will continue to inhabit the land. Syberberg dabs this speech with present-day (mid-1980s) references that ensure topicality and ensure also that the words apply to Europe as well as the United States. The speaker is the great German actress Edith Clever, clad in a simple dress and holding a dark, rough cloth about herself. Only then come the credits—after Clever finishes speaking.

We now move to a placeless place: a floor of gleaming black gravel, a white circle of light at its center and a small white cloth in the light, with a cloak of darkness surrounding everything. In the light, acutely varied by the cinematographer Schwarzenberger, Clever spends the next five-and-a-half hours—close to us or with the camera at differing distances and angles, her body statuesque or sinuous depending on the angle and the light, her torso curved away from the camera-eye into architectural form, her body self-caressed in recollections of Eros, her presence immediate, her presence godlike, as she speaks, intones, sings, mourns, and eulogizes through the medium of the text that Syberberg has prepared. As far as the film reveals, Clever, or Clever's character, is the sole survivor of a long, glorious, *and* atrocious history, and before she too disappears into the black all around her, she offers a threnody.

The text, often accompanied by sections of Bach's *Well-Tempered Clavier* in Sviatoslav Richter's hands, moves through literature that is mostly German—Hölderlin, Goethe, Heine, and Nietzsche, as well as Schiller, Kleist, Novalis, and Heidegger—but with minglings of other cultures translated into German. (Prospero's farewell to his art, from *The Tempest* but in German, is transfixing.) The tone ranges from Wagner's crawling pleas for help from his patron Giacomo Meyerbeer, to his slimy spewings to King Ludwig about "Jewry in Music"; from the sight of a child's toy in Clever's hand to her sublime reciting of a poem in which humankind asks Jesus if his father is still alive, to which the son of God, his eyes streaming with tears, replies that we are all orphans now.

Courage is one hallmark of Syberberg's film work, and that hallmark is visible in *The Night*. He wants to burst through order and plunge into the unknown, the possibly chaotic, there to forge a new aesthetic order. Since he did this differently in his previous two films—*Our Hitler* and *Parsifal*—no fixed criteria will help the spectator to navigate Syberberg's artistic ventures. Sometimes, I must admit, *The Night* escaped my powers of attention during my sole viewing of it. For the film doesn't aim at a relentless, concentrated march toward spiritual nakedness and existential nullity like

Acropolis, the titanic theater production by Jerzy Grotowski from the mid-1960s, which conducted its own requiem. (*Acropolis* took the concentration camp at Auschwitz for its setting, and, for its "plot," the building by the prisoners there of the gas chamber in which they will be consumed.) *The Night*, six times as long, does not march and only fitfully exalts.

Principally, the film *remembers*, but its memories wander in addition to both fondling the past and grieving over it. Certainly it has passages that repeat notes already heard. Certainly, too, it vibrates more fully for someone (like me) familiar with German literature in German. But even such a person would not find every moment in *The Night* tense and fraught with meaning: I, for one, did not. Yet it is a facet of Syberberg's experimental daring—not an excuse for avant-garde idling—that, instead of shaping a drama, he has in effect enclosed a preserve or park, of time, in which to linger and remember and even nod in the last remaining light. One factor in this film, however, did sustain me through its length, and it was surely a part of Syberberg's design from the beginning. *The Night* must have been conceived, that is, with the prospective collaboration of Edith Clever in the principal—and, it's worth repeating, the lone—role.

Clever is known in the United States chiefly through the films *The Left-Handed Woman* (by Peter Handke) and *The Marquise of O.* (Éric Rohmer's version), and, as previously mentioned, through Syberberg's *Parsifal*, where she mimed Kundry so intensely that, although it was not her singing voice we heard, it seemed to be. What is not known in North America is her theater career, mostly with the Schaubühne in the former West Berlin. I have never seen Clever on stage, but I know that she has played leading roles in Schiller (*Kabale und Liebe*), Goethe (*Torquato Tasso*), Middleton and Rowley (*The Changeling*), Ibsen (*Peer Gynt*), and Aeschylus (*The Oresteia*), as well as in Gorky, Brecht, and Botho Strauss. In 1983 she played Gertrude in *Hamlet*.

I cite all of these instances prior to Clever's work in *The Night* because they are quite clearly the sources of her spiritual or imaginative endowment (not to speak of her physical resources), the simple majesty with which she makes her very first movement, utters her very first word in this, Syberberg's eighth film. I know of no better actress or actor in the world than Edith Clever, and few are her peers; but *The Night* is not a display vehicle, a "one-woman show" where the woman herself, or generic "woman," is the focus. Clever is completely and wondrously in union with what is happening in the film. So much so that her art *in itself* is as much a manifestation of the culture that *The Night* embraces and indicts, as much both an exhilarating triumph and a profound grief, as any of the words in the text.

Clever performed *The Night* a few times in a small Paris theater in 1984, and in a conversation I once had with Syberberg, I asked if it had been planned as a theater piece, then filmed. No, he responded, *The Night* had been planned as a film, but when this Paris theater offered to produce it, he accepted. The stage setting was much like that of the film, and French subtitles were projected high above, on the dark wall behind Clever. The production was done in two evenings—three-and-a-half hours, then two-and-a-half hours—each evening without intermission. "And," said Syberberg proudly, "although there was a prompter there, Edith never needed him, she never faltered." I replied that I supposed the stage darkened from time to time—if only to give Clever a momentary breather—in the way that the film goes to black and then resumes at a different angle or distance. "No," said Syberberg, "the pauses in the film of *The Night* are there only because the film runs out in the camera-magazine."

That Paris engagement was Syberberg's first theater work, and for me it underscored that, volitionally or not, he was further exploring—on screen as on stage—what I earlier called, in reference to *Parsifal*, the "theater of film." Two passages in the film of *The Night* especially mark this exploration: two Wagnerian excerpts, one from Isolde's *Liebestod*, the other from Brünnhilde's "Immolation Scene" in the *Twilight of the Gods*. In both instances, we hear a full orchestra playing as Clever sings. She has nothing like an operatic voice; she merely sings pleasantly. (Syberberg did tell me, however, that a Wagnerian conductor he knew was struck by the accuracy of her entrances and tempi and phrasing.) The point is that, with her modest singing voice, Clever acts those excerpts in a manner that illuminates them as never before.

Wagner himself asked the impossible: wonderful singing *and* wonderful acting. A major Wagnerian production gives you the first, plus passable acting. Clever, who could not possibly do the first, supplies what is always missing from the second. As I watched her perform in *The Night*, I suddenly wanted to see a Wagnerian "theater of film" in which Clever would give us, in this manner, the missing dramatic element to add to our memory of musically great Isoldes, to name just one heroine—which is not the same (if you think about it) as her miming a character, however convincingly in the case of *Parsifal*'s Kundry, to the accompaniment of another woman's operatic voice.

All of the above is to emphasize that, for me, Syberberg is seeking new empowerment for the arts he inherited in the arts he practices: theater and film, or film and theater. What persists after the long filmic threnody of *The Night*, as after the enduring theatrical conceptualization of *Parsifal*, is that Syberberg's search, in tandem with Clever, is the expression of an austere hope (but nonetheless a valid one) not only for the rebirth of the culture he is mourning, but also for the consecration of a theater of film. Why a *theater* of film? Because the filmmaker Syberberg paradoxically believes, as he said to me in our conversation, that film represents "the birth of *dead* light and *dead* images, of a plastic art that split the nucleus of the world into a series of views and angles, much as scientists split the atom, and thus disturbed the world in ways we all know." Only the human spirit can cohere in the face of such a disturbed world, ever veering toward environmental destruction and nuclear holocaust. And that spirit, that "grace of pure life," as Syberberg put it, can still be found—whole, shining, and undisturbed—in the living theater.

WORKS CITED and BIBLIOGRAPHY

Appia, Adolphe. *Music and the Art of the Theatre*. 1899. Trans. Robert W. Corrigan and Mary Douglas Dirks. Coral Gables: University of Miami Press, 1962.

Atkinson, Michael. "Syberberg's Unique Takes on German History." *Sight and Sound* (Dec. 2009): 87.

Berman, Russell A. "Hans-Jürgen Syberberg: Of Fantastic and Magical Worlds." In *New German Filmmakers: From Oberhausen through the 1970s*. Ed. Klaus Phillips. New York: Ungar, 1984. 359-378.

Brockmann, Stephen. "Syberberg's Germany." *German Quarterly*, 69.1 (Winter 1996): 48-62.

Brunette, Peter. "*Ludwig: Requiem for a Virgin King.*" *Film Quarterly*, 34.3 (Spring 1981): 58-61.

Buruma, Ian. "There's No Place Like Heimat (Nazism and the Work of Film Director Hans-Jürgen Syberberg). *New York Review of Books*, 37.20 (Dec. 20, 1990): 34+.

Cardullo, Bert. "Theater and Film, or 'Adolphe Appia and Me': A Discussion with Hans-Jürgen Syberberg." *Literature/Film Quarterly*, 38.1 (2010): 5-15.

Corrigan, Timothy. *New German Film: The Displaced Image*. Rev. ed. Bloomington: Indiana University Press, 1994.

Del Caro, Adrian, and Janet Ward, ed. *German Studies in the Post-Holocaust Age: The Politics of Memory, Identity, and Ethnicity*. Boulder: University Press of Colorado, 2000.

Diederichsen, D. "Spiritual Reactionaries after German Reunification: Syberberg, Foucault, and Others." *October*, 62 (Fall 1992): 65-83.

Elsaesser, Thomas. "*Hitler, Ein Film aus Deutschland* (*Hitler, A Film from Germany*): Film Review." *Sight and Sound*, 2.5 (Sept. 1992): 49-50.

_____. "Myth as the Phantasmagoria of History: H.-J. Syberberg, Cinema, and Representation." *New German Critique*, 24-25 (Fall-Winter 1981-1982): 108-154.

Erkkila, Betsy. "Hans-Jürgen Syberberg: An Interview." *Literature/Film Quarterly*, 10.4 (1982): 206-218.

Farmer, James Clark. *Opera and the New German Cinema: Between Distance and Fascination*. Ann Arbor, Mich.: UMI, 2003.

Green, Peter. *The Films of Hans-Jürgen Syberberg*. London: Goethe Institute, 1978.

Jameson, Frederic. "'In the Destructive Element Immerse': Hans-Jürgen Syberberg and Cultural Revolution." *October*, 17 (Summer 1981): 99-118. Reprinted in *Perspectives on German Cinema*. Ed. Terri Ginsberg and Kirsten Moana Thompson. New York: G. K. Hall, 1996. 508-525.

Joe, Jeongwon. "Hans-Jürgen Syberberg and His Film of Wagner's *Parsifal*." *The Opera Quarterly*, 22.2 (2007): 369-375.

Koshar, Rudy. "*Hitler: A Film from Germany.*" *The American Historical Review*, 96.4 (Oct. 1991): 1122-1124.

Miller, David. "Lost Life: Syberberg's *Hitler, A Film from Germany*." *Origin: Fifth Series*, 2 (Winter 1983): 55-61.

Monaco, Paul. "Across the Great Divide: Young German Cinema in the 1970s." *Mundus Artium: A Journal of International Literature & the Arts*, 11.2 (1979): 42-51.

Mueller, Roswitha. "Hans-Jürgen Syberberg's *Hitler*: An Interview-Montage." *Discourse*, 2 (Summer 1980): 60-82.

Olsen, Solveig. *Hans-Jürgen Syberberg and His Film of Wagner's "Parsifal"*. Lanham, Md.: University Press of America, 2006.

Phillips, Klaus. *New German Filmmakers: From Oberhausen through the 1970s*. New York: Ungar, 1984.

Santner, Eric L. "The Trouble with Hitler: Postwar German Aesthetics and the Legacy of Fascism." *New German Critique*, 57 (Fall 1992): 5-24.

_____. *Stranded Objects: Mourning, Memory, and Film in Postwar Germany*. Ithaca, N.Y.: Cornell University Press, 1990.

Schiller, Beatriz, and Rod Ott. "Interview with Hans-Jürgen Syberberg: *Our Hitler* as Visual Politics." *Performing Arts Journal*, 4.3 (1980): 50-58.

Sharrett, Christopher. "Sustaining Romanticism in a Postmodernist Cinema: An Interview with Hans-Jurgen Syberberg." *Cineaste*, 15.3 (1987): 18-20.

Snell, Marilyn Berlin. "Germany's Heart: The Modern Taboo; Interview with German Filmmaker Hans-Jürgen Syberberg." *New Perspectives Quarterly*, 10.1 (Winter 1993): 20-25.

Stewart, Heather. *Syberberg, A Filmmaker from Germany*. London: British Film Institute, 1992.

Wasserman, Steve. "Interview with Hans-Jürgen Syberberg." *The Threepenny Review*, 2 (Summer 1980): 4-6.

Part II

CONTEMPORARY CINEMA IN (RE)VIEW

8

Suffer the Children

Most of the best films about children are about boys: *Shoeshine* (1946), *Germany, Year Zero* (1947), and *Bicycle Thieves* (1948), for instance. Moreover, most of the best films about children were made by Italian neorealists, as well as by directors following their socially as well as politically realistic example, from Luis Buñuel with *Los Olvidados* (1951) and René Clément with *Forbidden Games* (1952), to Hector Babenco's *Pixote* (1981), Mira Nair's *Salaam Bombay!* (1988), Gianni Amelio's *Stolen Children* (1992), Samira Makhmalbaf's *The Apple* (1998), and Bertrand Tavernier's *It All Started Here* (1999). Now we can add a Russian to this list of Latin Americans, Frenchmen, Italians, Indians, and Iranians, makers all of "children's films." His name is Andrei Kravchuk, and his film is called *The Italian* (2005), in seeming homage to neorealism's country of origin. (Kravchuk was preceded in this style and genre by at least one fellow Russian, Vitali Kanevsky, with his 1989 film *Freeze. Die. Come to Life.*)

One of the questions that attends *The Italian* and the rest of the above-named films is less *why* they are about children (that's easy: often one can see a war-torn, religiously-divided, or economically-distressed society more clearly, more freshly, through the eyes of its youngest members) than *how* those children gave the performances they did. For, however lovely among film's powers its relationship to children may be (not children in the audience but those on screen), that relationship is also quizzical. Certainly something about performing before a camera stimulates a child's natural instinct to pretend. But all children play and pretend in one way or another; the real wonder is how, without knowledge and often without ambition, a child will behave on a movie set like a pro, in every sense of that word. I'm not necessarily talking here about

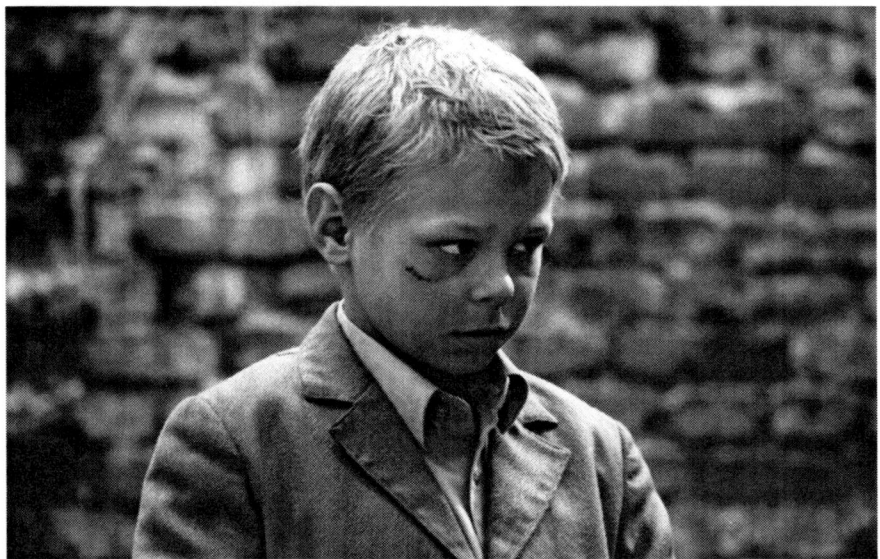

The Italian, dir. Andrei Kravchuk, 2005

those children whose parents want them to become film stars, because an extraordinary performance can come from a child without any subsequent career, such as the little girl in Jean Benoît-Lévy's *La Maternelle* (1932). The viewer is left wondering whether such a child remembers, later in life, that she had once moved thousands — in fact, still moves them.

And what about Kolya Spiridonov? This boy, who was nine or ten at the time *The Italian* was made, plays a six-year-old (named Vanya Solntsev) in the film's leading role, its mainstay part. Spiridonov had already been acting for two years prior to this movie, in several pictures that never made it to the United States. Still, with his pale blond hair, scrawny frame, and wide but tired, cautious eyes, there is no child-star quality about him. How did he create the thoughtful, oddly private performance that he gives in *The Italian*? As his director, Kravchuk probably wooed Spiridonov and won his confidence, but can that really account for the relative depth of this child's acting? Why did he *want* to do it well? Pleasing his director and his parents, being praised and having his ego massaged, yes, but where did he find the sheer understanding to play the part, and did he even realize that he had found it? It seems fitting to fantasize that the camera speaks a secret, attractive language to certain children who comprehend it and respond. If so, this is a conversation that the camera and the child can, and will, forever keep secret from all the grownups around.

Let's start with grownup number one in this case, Andrei Kravchuk. *The Italian* is his first solo feature: in 2000, he co-directed *A Christmas Mystery* (unseen by me), and he has also directed a few documentaries, made several short films, and done some work for television. One of Kravchuk's documentaries was about his teacher at the St. Petersburg Institute of Film and Television, Semen Aranovich (1934-1996), himself a documentary filmmaker who infused his feature films with authentic, documentary-like detail. (As we can see from *Summer Trip to the Seaside* [1978], where he recruited actors from juvenile correctional institutions or foster-care facilities in order to render more accurately his characters' harsh childhood experiences during the early years of World War II.)

What marks Kravchuk as a latter-day neorealist (also as a documentarian-become-fiction filmmaker) is that (1) he and his scenarist, Andrei Romanov, got the idea for *The Italian* from a newspaper article (the origin, as well, of a number of scripts by the best known of Italian neorealist screenwriters, Cesare Zavattini) about an orphan who learned to read and write so that he could find his biological mother; (2) Kravchuk observed children at real orphanages, and then, after deciding to shoot his film on location at the state-run Lesogorsky Children's Home near St. Petersburg (the director's own home town), he cast several of this institution's children in featured roles; and (3) despite shooting in color, Kravchuk and his cinematographer, Alexander Burov (who has also done exceptional work for the director Alexander Sokurov), use grainy or gritty, black-and-gray-dominated visuals to keep *The Italian* well this side of arrant tear-jerking.

The Italian begins with a striking image: a group of young children emerge like phantoms from the mist hovering over a bleak Russian bog, then proceed to push an SUV run short of gas to its destination—the crumbling orphanage where much of the film takes place, a children's home that is a lingering relic of the Soviet past, now lost amid the snow-covered expanses of Russia's vast northwest. A nearby highway bustles with commercial vehicles from an entirely different, profit-driven era of free-market enterprise as well as social mobility; and in this particular backwater, the truck drivers slow down only to satisfy their carnal appetites. Excluded from the "brave new world" epitomized by this well-maintained, cost-effective road, the orphanage's neglected and poorly educated charges survive in the only way they know how: by servicing the privileged highway population as prostitutes and car-washers. In other words, these children are wards of the state in name only.

The orphanage is run by the Headmaster (played by Yuri Itskov), a broken-down man who, in spite of being occasionally drunk, periodically unkempt, and frequently flustered, does the best he can, with limited resources, for the many youngsters abandoned by their parents to his care. The Headmaster notwithstanding, however, the real rulers of the orphanage are found in a group of older orphaned boys whose own leader is Kolyan (Denis Moiseenko). He and his gang operate out of a basement boiler room, where they run a variety of schemes from theft to pimping in order to get by.

Though we sometimes see younger kids punched and intimidated by these older boys, it's quite clear that none of this is done arbitrarily or out of cruelty. Instead, the boys are enforcing a code of conduct that demands honesty and the sharing of assets, all for the good of the group; treated as an equal despite his age, six-year-old Vanya himself contributes money to the group out of the tips he earns washing cars at a local gas station. Ironically, then, socialism is still alive and well in Russia—at least among children at the very bottom of the socioeconomic ladder, who have neither mothers nor fathers to look out for them but who have something comparable in their "brotherhood" of orphans. (It must be said, however, that there is always corruption at the top, and in this socialistic "state," it resides in Kolyan, who keeps a stash of money for himself and eventually uses it to purchase a motorcycle—an important asset giving him access to the superhighway of capitalism.)

The brightest moments in the lives of these bedraggled and lonely youngsters come when "Madam" shows up with well-heeled foreign couples who want to adopt a child. A wily and formidable woman with a portly and controlling presence (as played by Maria Kuznetsova, who acted the roles of Catherine the Great in Sukurov's *Russian Ark* [2002] and Lenin's wife in the same director's *Taurus* [2001]), she is the only frequent visitor from outside the confined space of the orphanage. Madam is also a ruthless capitalist entrepreneur, an illegal baby-broker who makes a comfortable living by selling orphaned children for adoption abroad. She thus regards every such international adoption as a financial transaction to be carried out exclusively for profit. In this business she not only has the pliable Headmaster firmly under her thumb, Madam is closely connected to the local authorities as well, who are more than happy (for a price) to help her satisfy the needs of—and navigate the Byzantine Russian courts for—wealthy Westerners in search of a child.

Two of those Westerners are Claudia and Roberto, an amiable Italian couple (the inhabitants of the stalled vehicle from the film's opening) who have come to Russia to look for a child to adopt, and whom Madam duly escorts to the provincial orphanage. Out of all the youngsters offered, they choose Vanya, and we feel we would do the same: tough-skinned but vulnerable, full of spunk yet deeply sensitive, matter-of-factly confident and self-aware at the same time as he is charmingly naïve (with his best friend, Anton [Dima Zemlyanko], he seriously discusses foreigners' buying up of Russian children for "spare parts"), Vanya is irresistible as, dressed in his best clothes and with both fear and anticipation on his face, he introduces himself to the Italians. They quickly settle the issue of money with Madam, but because of legal procedures and bureaucratic paperwork, it will be two months before the couple can take the boy home. The film takes place in those two months, during which all the other waifs in the asylum call Vanya "the Italian." These other orphans, jealous but resigned, consider him lucky to have been chosen for adoption, and so does Vanya—at first.

A few days later, though, a distraught woman (Darya Lesnikova) comes to the orphanage looking for her son, whom she had abandoned at birth and whom she is now desperate to reclaim. But she is told that the boy she looking for, who was Vanya's friend Mukhin, has recently been adopted by a European couple. Mukhin's biological mother then leaves in despair despite Vanya's attempts to comfort her; the next day, word reaches the orphanage that this guilt-ridden woman committed suicide by throwing herself under a train.

Now Vanya is not so sure about beginning a new life in another country with the Italian couple. Suddenly he has questions about who he is, who his mother is, and he knows he will never be able to find out after he leaves the orphan asylum. What if his own mother should happen to come looking for him, he asks himself? How would she ever find him if he has moved away to Italy? What then? In a second, Vanya has seen answered, with a dash of hope, the question that underpins any orphan's existence: "Why was I rejected?" (We are never told why Vanya's own mother gave him up, because her "psychology" or morality is not the issue here.) Sometimes the answer is that it was all just a mistake, and real parents do return.

Or they are found. And, despite the heartfelt, searingly honest attempts on the part of the other kids to convince the boy that birth mothers don't usually try to find the children they've abandoned (and even if they did, the kids, say, who would want to be with someone who had already deserted him once?), Vanya decides that he has to find his mother even if it means losing the Italian family. In order to find out where she is, however, he needs access to confidential records stored in the Headmaster's office; but he can't read, and the older kids won't help him until he can read his file for himself. Vanya therefore convinces Irka (Olga Shuvalova), a feisty teenaged orphan who earns money as a prostitute, to teach him. Then, with the help of some of the boys, he retrieves his personal file one night after the Headmaster has passed out from drunkenness.

From it he learns the name of the foster home for newborns, in a far-off city, where he spent his first few months. But that's all Vanya learns, and to discover more he will have to embark on a journey to that foster home. Again with the aid of Irka, he is enabled to do so: she buys him a train ticket (taking the money from Kolyan's stash) and he flees the orphanage just days before the Italian couple is to get custody of him—to become a Dickensian waif, out on the road in the strange, novel world of the twenty-first century. (Speaking of Dickensian waifs, *Oliver Twist* was filmed yet again—this time by Roman Polanski, of all people—in the same year *The Italian* was made: 2005.)

The remainder of this ninety-nine-minute film documents Vanya's search for his origins and ultimately his, and in a sense his country's, identity, as he traverses the hostile Russian terrain (with its perpetual wintry gloom of snow and ice and rain) and navigates through the various generational and social layers of what has become a deeply split society. During his trip by train, by bus, and then on foot, Vanya encounters kindness and sympathy, treachery and duplicity (being beaten and robbed at one point), but he remains unwaveringly focused on the goal of meeting his mother. He's not desperate or over-emotional in his quest, just determined and smart, persistent and resourceful—making full use of the wiles he has learned in six years of state confinement. Vanya especially needs those wiles (blending into crowds, hiding out, and even outrunning his pursuers) because, together with her mercenary driver-cum-bodyguard, Grigori (Nikolai Reutov), the fuming-mad Madam is in hot pursuit of him and the (potentially lost) income he represents. Not only do these two travel by automobile, but the automobile is an expensive Range Rover, bought from Madam's illicit child-adoption fees to replace her otherwise top-of-the-line, but Soviet-made, Volga.

Finally, Vanya reaches the foster home of his infancy, where he learns the address of his mother from the welcoming night-time supervisor (Rudolf Kuld), a World War II veteran of simple dignity and uncommon selflessness. She lives at apartment 3, 25 October Street (ironically, October 25th was the starting date of the 1917 Russian Revolution according to the Julian Calendar in use in Russia at the time [for the rest of the world, the date was November 7th]), the night supervisor reveals, and he further promises to adopt Vanya himself if the boy does not find or reunite with his mother in the end. He *does* locate her domicile, though not before a run-in on the street, in the rain, with Grigori, who, in a dramatic conversion worthy of Dickens (like much of this tale itself), turns from a pitiless bounty hunter into Vanya's compassionate ally—simply by letting the young fugitive go.

And go he does: right to the apartment where his mother lives. Before ringing the bell, he carefully smooths down his hair and straightens his clothes, in a moment of calm self-possession that recalls the rich inner lives of working-class people living out their existences under the watchful eye of the Dardenne brothers (in such films as *L'Enfant* [2005] and *The Son* [2002]). Previously unsmiling, Vanya now smiles, in close-up, and the up-to-now spare, even timid, notes of Alexander Kneiffel's ethereal score (which has relied mainly on the plink of piano keys, as if a child were trying to pick out a lullaby) swell to flood the soundtrack. But Kravchuk and Romanov abruptly end *The Italian* here, with a fade-out to a blank white screen, as Vanya narrates in voice-over a letter to his friend Anton, who was adopted by the Italian couple in his place.

To wit: we never see the boy's mother, let alone any reunion of this woman with her son. So we get no answers to the questions, "Has Vanya found his birth mother? If so, does she welcome her son with open arms or turn her back on him once again, turning him out into the street and sending him away?" The real question then becomes, of course, why does the film end in this way, denying us the emotional fulfillment of its own concluding, sentimental, even pathetic terms (unlike Valery Akhadov's *The Greenhouse* [2005], with its similar theme)? Is this ending a cheap trick, or is it part and parcel of *The Italian*'s overall artistic design—the design, that is, less of a heart-warming family movie (you can find that in the similarly-themed Brazilian movie *Central Station* [1998] and the Czech *Kolya* [1996]) or a Russian after-school special, than of a probing social-realist film that raises more issues than it resolves? Its numerous prizes—the "Cinekid Award," top honors at the "International Young Audience Film Festival," the "Deutsches Kinderhilfswerk Grand Prix" at the Berlin Festival—not to speak of its being nominated for Best Foreign-Language Film at the 78th Academy Awards, suggest the former genre. I think *The Italian* is the latter: a work that has popular ingredients, to be sure, but one that uses them, when all is said and done, to serious artistic ends.

Those ends naturally include the whole issue, or business, of the adoption of Russian orphans by foreigners. But Kravchuk and Romanov are not so interested in indicting the parents who abandon these children, the state that warehouses them, or even the ultra-nationalists who would rather see such youngsters spend their first eighteen years in a Russian asylum rather than be brought up, as part of a family, in a foreign country. For a social exposé of the melodramatic kind *The Italian* is not. It is, however, a political allegory at the same time as, on the surface, it is a kind of domestic drama that finally takes the form of a road film.

The first clue to the film's "deep structure" is its titular character's last name, Solntsev (close to the Russian word for "sun," *solntse*), which Vanya shares with the eponymous child protagonist of Valentin Kataev's 1944 socialist-realist novella *The Son of the Regiment*—this son being a wartime orphan adopted by the army and raised in an elite military school. Vanya's last name is thus doubly symbolic: not only of the ultimately failed Soviet social experiment, but also of the "sunny" future that might have awaited him, away from the frigid climes and dim prospects of his motherland, in Italy. The second clue to *The Italian*'s subtext is the name of the gang leader at the orphanage, Kolyan, which phonetically resembles the name of the character Tolyan from Pavel Chukhrai's film *The Thief* (1997), even as the authoritarian behaviors of these two figures mirror each other.

What these clues suggest is that *The Italian* is scrutinizing and consequently rejecting several successive models of social organization, as its naïve child protagonist bypasses the mistakes and inadequacies of the past to arrive at his own, post-*glasnost* ideal of human commonality. Those models include both the "new capitalism" of the economically exploitative Kolyan and the "utopian socialism" of the classless, motherless, and fatherless (if not stateless) brotherhood of orphans, as well as the "old totalitarianism" of the mercilessly domineering Madam. Madam's previous ownership of a Volga, for example—the Soviet car once accessible almost exclusively to Brezhnev-era political and cultural elites—traces her lineage back to the Communist *nomenklatura*. So do her methods of achieving her goals: her threats not only to lock up the willful, noncompliant Vanya in isolation, but also to send him to a home for the mentally retarded, followed by assignment to a labor camp, recall Soviet-era psychiatric abuses against political and intellectual dissidents. Madam is thus little more than the cynical, selfish functionary of a corrupt former regime—yet one clever enough to continue exploiting her country and her people up to the present in the guise of a free-market entrepreneur.

In this scheme, where does Grigori, Madam's chauffeur and bodyguard, fit? In a sense, with Kolyan and Madam herself, he completes *The Italian*'s new-capitalist triad. In the age bracket between his boss and the orphanage gang-leader, Grigori represents the *glasnost*-era generation that succumbed, under pressure from its "superiors," to the former Soviet elites' immoral re-appropriation of power and wealth. An obedient executor of Madam's orders throughout the movie, Grigori suddenly, and seemingly implausibly, changes his ways when he disobeys Madam by not returning Vanya to her custody. But Grigori's change of heart is not so implausible from the perspective of the film's political allegory. For that change, or conversion, appears to imply that his generation's squandered aspirations toward political morality, social justice, and—perhaps above all—personal responsibility are ultimately recoverable, and may even constitute the foundation of the ideal living arrangement sought by the child protagonist of *The Italian*.

That ideal living arrangement is not to be found in a children's home, and, apart from the obvious reasons for this, the patriarchal heads of both the Petersburg orphanage and Vanya's original foster home reveal why. Certainly neither is a bad man, as I've already made clear, but each is identified with his particular generation in such a way that he becomes part of the film's problem, as opposed to its solution. The Headmaster, for example—a disillusioned 1960s dreamer who ascribes his failure to become an elite fighter pilot, *à la* Yuri Gagarin, to the absence of a benevolent mentor by his side—may be uncomfortable with Madam's strong-armed tactics, but he himself delivers such an abusive tirade against the dejected young woman who comes to recover her child that he inadvertently causes her suicide.

The nighttime supervisor, for his part, also indiscriminately condemns mothers who choose to abandon their children at birth, for in his authoritarian model of self-sacrifice and civic duty—doubtless derived from his wartime service—there is no place for individual fulfillment, personal motivation, or self-justification. The supervisor's "collectivist" point of view is subtly suggested not only by the street on which his foster home is located ("Frunze," from the name of Mikhail Vasilevich Frunze [1885-1925], the "father" and ideologue of the Red Army) and his brand of cigarettes ("Belomorkanal," introduced in 1932 to commemorate the construction of the White Sea-Baltic Canal [abbreviated as *Belomorkanal*], which was the site of one of Stalin's first "re-education through labor" projects). It is also suggested by his surprise at learning that "Solntsev" is, in fact, Vanya's actual last name, the one he inherited from his biological mother—and not, like many a parentless newborn named by a doctor or a nurse, from a real or fictional Soviet war hero. (We, or literary types in general, may know that "Solntsev" derives from the last name of the protagonist of Kataev's novel, but Vanya's mother would not know and therefore obviously did not take her and her son's surname from this character.)

Vanya, of course, is not surprised at the origin of his last name. For he is a naïf in the best sense: a person with an inherent faith not only in the concept of family, but also in people generally; with a genuine capacity for love, compassion, and forgiveness; and, most importantly, with a sense of personal responsibility both for his own life and that of the human being (genetically) closest to him: his mother. Refusing to play into the latter-day nostalgia for Soviet state-ism or the contemporary Russian infatuation with unrestricted market capitalism, Kravchuk and Romanov hold up Vanya's instinctive belief system as the ideal model of social action. Vanya *takes charge* of his and his mother's lives, that is to say, thereby challenging the commonly held conviction about the ineffectualness of individual action in Russia, eloquently if fatalistically summed up in the phrase "*ot nas nichego ne zavisit*" ("nothing depends on us"). And, through the courageous example of Vanya Solntsev, *The Italian* admonishes its predominantly adult audiences in its native Russia to start taking responsibility for their own future—one that is clearly inseparable from the welfare of Russia's children.

The film locates the model community, then, in the nuclear family, representing it as the basic cell, or logical framework, from which to build a civil society in a truly democratic Russia. Will Vanya and his birth mother reunite and achieve that community at the end of *The Italian*? The "warmth" of their surname implies that they are destined to come together, whereas the "coldness" of the film's final image—a blank white screen—suggests the very opposite. (Similarly, the narrative point of view the filmmakers adopt—that of the six-year-old protagonist—conflicts with their almost always photographing him from above [instead of from a ground- or eye-level perspective], in high-angle shots that make this little boy seem even littler and less able than he is.)

In other words, Vanya's dreams of a sunny Motherland clash with the reality of the wintry Madam-culture he continues to inhabit. That is *the truth* of *The Italian*'s otherwise abrupt conclusion, an allegorical truth that extends to all of Russia's orphans. If you want emotional or cathartic closure, you'll have to find it somewhere else. And if you want to know what happened in the end to the real-life orphan whose story inspired Vanya's, read the Russian newspapers.

Along with the name Andrei Kravchuk, remember the name Bahman Ghobadi, the director of the "children's film" *Turtles Can Fly* (2004). As I watched this picture, I thought of two of its cinematic relatives, each of which shall frame my discussion of *Turtles Can Fly*. The first, as in the case of *The Italian*, is neorealism, and in particular Roberto Rossellini's neorealist film *Germany, Year Zero*, in which a twelve-year-old boy, trying to feed his family amidst the destitution of occupied Berlin, poisons his sickly father (played by the only professional in the cast, Franz Kruger) to lessen the burden. Unable to live with the deed, however, he throws himself from the ruins of a tall building—but not before poignantly finding a moment to play (yes, play, not pray) before killing himself.

The second work I recalled, as I screened *Turtles Can Fly*, is the "new" neorealist *West Beirut* (1998), a film by Ziad Doueiri about two Muslim boys and a Christian girl (all played by young people who had never before acted) growing up in the war-torn Lebanon of 1975. Here they manage to tease, quarrel, idle, snack, and bicycle like their youthful counterparts everywhere, at the same time as they take risks—amidst bombed-out buildings, rubble-strewn streets, military checkpoints, and frequent sniper fire—that even the most intrepid of schoolchildren would have trouble imagining.

In connection with Ghobadi's movie, I also thought of the contemporary Iranian cinema, what could be called the larger "picture" of which *Turtles Can Fly* is a part—a larger picture itself framed by such films around, or outside, it as the classic *Germany, Year Zero* and the contemporaneous *West Beirut*. For Ghobadi was born in Iranian Kurdistan and received his film education in Tehran, where, along with other experience, he was an assistant director for Abbas Kiarostami on *The Wind Will Carry Us* (1999) and acted in Samira Makhmalbaf's *Blackboards* (2000). Indeed, the threads that link many Iranian films may be found in Ghobadi's cinema as well. These pictures often focus, for example, on ordinary people caught in harsh circumstances brought about by sociopolitical, cultural, or natural forces. The devastation created by an earthquake, the wounds and traumas caused by war, the hardships heaped on the poor—these are powerful subjects. And such films manage to address them not with easy sloganeering or smooth sentimentality, but with both penetrating insight and a strong feeling of compassion for those who suffer.

Formally as well as narratively, moreover, Iranian moviemakers, like the Kurdish Ghobadi, have shown a genius for making virtues out of constraints. Since their films are cheaply made, they often have a surface simplicity that belies their subtle realism. And the fact that Western-style obscenity and sex are prohibited has meant not only that directors practice skillfully indirect, sometimes allegorical storytelling, but also that they search for subjects which go beyond the formulaic or the genre-specific. The Iranian specialty of films about children, for instance, is also a specialty of films not necessarily made *for* children, and this type of picture allows both for a form of oblique social commentary and for the depiction of intimacy—each of which would be difficult, if not impossible, to achieve with adult characters in censorship-burdened Iran. (Here is just a sampling of such Iranian "children's films": *The Runner* [1984], *Where Is the Friend's House?* [1987], *Children of Divorce* [1990], *The Jar* [1992], *The White Balloon* [1995], *The Mirror* [1997], *The Children of Heaven* [1997], *The Apple* [1998], and *The Color of Paradise* [1999].)

Bahman Ghobadi well knows about the relationship of children to film censorship in his part of the world, given the fact that he has taken up this Iranian—now Kurdish—specialty in at least two of his features to date. Since Ghobadi is a Kurd, he is one of a people who are, in a sense, stateless, because they live in a number of Middle Eastern states. Their nation of Kurdistan is apparently an entity to Kurds, however—if not always to the several countries across which it stretches (among them Turkey, Iraq, and Iran). And Ghobadi's *Turtles Can Fly* is his fourth film about Kurds that I know, as well as his third of five full-length films (on all of which he has served as both director and screenwriter). The other pictures of his about Kurds are *A Time for Drunken Horses* (2000), *Marooned in Iraq* (2002), and *Half Moon* (2006), the middle one of which, like *Turtles Can Fly*, also deals with a group of orphaned children trying to survive in extreme circumstances.

A Time for Drunken Horses deals a bit more heavily, though, with its family of young people trying to eke out an existence at the same time that they try to raise money for an operation to save their dying brother. There's no such heaviness or italicized sentiment in *Turtles Can Fly*, which is masterly as it courses before us with grace, control, love—and anger. The terrain is the barren, rocky hill country of northern Iraq near the Turkish border (which is fenced with barbed wire and guarded by machine guns). The time is a few weeks before the American invasion of 2003. The specific place is a refugee village of tents, in the midst of a brown landscape topped by an ice-blue sky and littered with the ruins of houses. (The ruins are not identified, but they may be leftovers from the Iran-Iraq war, which ended in 1988.)

The three leading characters of *Turtles Can Fly* are in their early teens: a smart operator nicknamed Satellite; a youth called Henkov, who lost both his arms in a mine explosion; and Henkov's sister, Agrin, gentle but desperately resigned to the grayness of her existence. They are joined by Pasheo, Satellite's nimble lieutenant, who, even though he has a crippled foot, runs around on crutches like an antelope; and by Rega, Agrin's three-year-old son (whom the armless Henkov sometimes carries—with the little boy's arms around his neck) and the product of her gang rape by soldiers of Saddam Hussein. The narrative has two main elements: Satellite's romantic interest in Agrin; and his efforts, along with the ragtag army of children (orphaned by the ethnic genocide or "cleansing" Saddam Hussein perpetrated against the Iraqi Kurds) this natural leader commandeers, to earn income in *dinars* or dollars from the excavation of unexploded "anti-personnel" mines, planted like seeds in the fields all around them—which he then sells to Kurdish middlemen, who, in turn, sell them for profit to the United Nations.

Accidents inevitably occur, as the legions of the scarred and disfigured in this film attest (even the resourceful Satellite is not immune). Throughout, the land mines are ironically called "American," because Americans sold many of them to Saddam

Hussein, who swamped northeastern (Kurdish) Iraq with the mines rather than use them against Iran, as intended. Yet the Kurdish adults we see—pompously ineffective or hopelessly lost—are awaiting the American invasion eagerly, as a possible correction to or improvement of a condition that includes no electricity, no running water, and no schools. Hence the reason why the elders engage Satellite: they need a satellite dish for their village's community television if they are to keep up with news of the impending war, and Satellite got his nickname for his expertise in procuring dishes from the black market. (He installs them as well, for a price.) Indeed, one of the few humorous moments in *Turtles Can Fly* derives from Satellite's handiwork: a village elder turns his head away when the young entrepreneur puts on a "prohibited channel" that shows a long-haired rock musician in concert.

Mostly the film's texture (and loosely textured it is more than tightly plotted) is composed of grim details, but Ghobadi embraces a range of feelings—proud, amorous, and terrible in addition to humorous—that swirl through these youngsters' lives. Moreover, he has an eye both for intimacy—the affection, the eating, the quarreling—and for vista. An example of the latter: at times, huge swarms of villagers, at times only children, flow over the hills in panoramic breadth, so as to suggest that these two groups live in vastly different figurative worlds despite the fact that they both literally occupy the same vast, harsh, and forbidding place. Ghobadi is helped here by Shahriar Assadi's cinematography, which is acutely placed in the chromatic spectrum. For its effect is of black and white, with only occasional hints of color—for instance, dim red stripes on Satellite's T-shirt. The overall visual impression of such imagery is that these characters, these people, live in the grainy, pallid, continuous present, occasionally touched by a variegated glimpse of an even worse past (the lurid sexual assault of Agrin, in a quick flashback) or a potentially better future (the arrival of the American colors at the end).

Satellite, for his part, is irresistibly optimistic about that future, as his appearance reveals: showing fuzz on his upper lip, wearing a pair of large-framed glasses, and sporting jeans, floppy sweat shirt, and a reversed (fatigue-issue) baseball cap, he rides a souped-up, colorfully adorned bicycle down muddy roads as he tends to

154   Formal Matters

Turtles Can Fly, dir. Bahman Ghobadi, 2004

his assorted money-making schemes. Henkov himself claims the power to see into the future in intermittent visions that are reliable compared to the inanities uttered by CNN's disembodied but endlessly talking heads. The very title of this film is a reference to one of the visions he shares with Satellite: that some day these Kurdish villagers will live in normal housing, free from tyranny of all kinds in their own private utopia, where even turtles can fly. If such a prophecy seems anachronistic, contrived, or fanciful to you as you read this, remember that the reality Ghobadi is depicting is so bizarre that, in its midst, a mystical oracle like Henkov turns out to be not so unlikely a thing. Is it, or he, any more implausible, after all, than a world where infants can toddle through minefields and red-colored fish swim at the bottom of sinkholes; where children treat their toothaches with kerosene, use gas masks as toys, and live in abandoned tanks near borders dotted with guard towers?

Whatever her brother Henkov's clairvoyance about the future, Agrin will have none of it: her world is unrelievedly bleak and her otherwise beautiful face meets it only with a vacant stare. From the opening shots of *Turtles Can Fly*, in one of which she leaps precariously from a rock, Ghobadi makes no secret of Agrin's ultimate fate. Understandably fearful of men in general, she has repeatedly discouraged the friendly advances of Satellite at the same time as she has wanted to abandon or destroy Rega, the man-child she love-hates so intensely. And, in the end, this ineffably sad young woman sadly capitulates to her *dual* fate: after killing her son by tying him to a rock and dropping him into a pond, she commits suicide by jumping off a cliff. Henkov finds her shoes on the cliff's edge, picks them up with his mouth, and simply walks off. Later a little kid presents Satellite with an arm from a Saddam statue (for which these street urchins paid a pretty price), as clean-uniformed, well-equipped, and well-fed American troops march into the area. But now Satellite is no longer sure of his optimism, let alone the American kind, with its promise of liberation, independence, and material welfare. So, as *Turtles Can Fly* concludes, its central character turns his back on the United States Army and, moving screen-left, quietly exits the frame.

Even as a film released in the same year, the Japanese *Nobody Knows* (2004), presented child abandonment from the point of view of the children abandoned, *Turtles Can Fly* presents war from the point of view, not of its perpetrators, but of its most vulnerable victims: children. They may appear to have the least power over their destinies, but here the poignancy is in the human control that characters like Satellite, Henkov, and Pasheo *do* exercise, as well as in the deadly decisiveness displayed by someone such as Agrin. Humanity survives in the surviving children at the end—or let us say that the *courage* to survive lives on—but at what price? This is the question we are left asking, such that *Turtles Can Fly* becomes a highly political film without turning into a politicized one that takes sides for or against any nation-state, even an aspiring one like Kurdistan. "Support our troops" might be the dictate of the conservative American patriot, then, but "suffer the children" is the mantra of this grittily primitive yet highly sophisticated Kurdish work of art.

Save for Ghobadi's films, however, there isn't much of a Kurdish cinema (only the additional names of the directors Hiner Saleem and Jano Rosebiani come to mind)—certainly not in the organized sense of an "industry," perish the word. Hence low budgets

(Ghobadi himself has produced or co-produced all of his pictures) and non-professional actors are the order of the day. But what wonders this director, like others before him and concurrent with him, works with his novices!—all of them non- or first-time actors, not merely non-professionals (which implies previous acting work as an amateur), and all the main ones children. The most disturbing yet admirable instance is the armless boy Henkov, who is played by Hiresh Feysal Rahman with flawless intensity, and about whose armlessness there can be no fakery (in a movie, happily, that cannot afford digital effects): we see the stumps. Avaz Latif is irretrievably distraught as Agrin, Henkov's sister, whom Latif makes compelling despite the more or less monochromatic nature of her character. And Soran Ebrahim has all the flash, wit, and energy, together with tacit depth, that Satellite requires. The dialogue these characters speak is mostly in Kurdish, with touches of Arabic and occasional dabs of English picked up from television—especially by Satellite, who, not without some justice, nonsensically translates any and all news as "It will rain tomorrow: this is a code."

In any case, "Kurd" or "Kurdistan" is no longer merely a code word for me that conjures up the much-betrayed political entity of Kurdistan—betrayed by Saddam Hussein, who poison-gassed its people (*his* people) in addition to mining their land in a megalomaniacal effort to "purify" Iraq and dominate the region's oil fields; and deserted, to its infinite discredit, by the United States, which broke promises of support for the Kurds when they needed it most: against the forces of American "ally" Saddam Hussein. (I do not have the space here to speak of the Kurds' vexed relationship with the Iranians or, for that matter, of their long and troubled history with the Turks.) Now, when I think of Kurdistan—a name you can't even find on many maps—I will think of its people, its customs, its geography, its children. And I will try to envision the day when Satellite's Kurdistan-of-the-imagination becomes a reality, where Kurds can thrive and even turtles can fly.

9

Engendering Genre

What creates a new genre, particularly in so relatively young an artistic form as film? The same thing that creates a new genre in other art forms—a combination of social perception and aesthetic revision, or social change and aesthetic impulse—with the exception that film, in Robert Warshow's words, is a more "immediate experience" than the other art forms. This means that it reacts to and reflects social currents faster than, say, the novel (whose rise in the eighteenth century is attributable to the rise of the middle class and with it a larger reading public). The drama can be just as fast in this sense as the cinema, both being "group" art forms that depend on the physical co-mingling, or communion, of spectators, but it cannot command the huge audience, worldwide, which is drawn to film and feeds off it in a mutually dependent or sustaining relationship.

When you combine film's speedy reaction-time (let us call it) with the continuing evolution of its form and technique (given its comparatively recent birth date of 1895), and then add the growing number of young artists who are drawn to filmmaking because of the relative ease, these days, of entering the field (again, partly the result of technical developments that, outside places like Hollywood, make moviemaking cheaper and easier)—well, you have a potent mixture that at any time can combust into a new genre or subgenre. To go back to the 1930s, when of course Hollywood or the American film "industry" was still king, think only of what the invention of sound and the rise of organized crime gave to us: the gangster film. Further, consider what the invention of sound, the concomitant need to engage Broadway dramatists to write sparkling dialogue, and the increasing independence of women produced: the screwball comedy.

This leads me to a consideration of the first of four film genres-in-the-making: the Holocaust film, which by now may already be "made." But its making raises a by-now familiar question: should there be a continual flow of movies on this subject? Do we need continual reminders of what happened at the death camps, or have images of Nazi atrocities been sufficiently burned into our collective memory? In short, is a Holocaust genre necessary? I hasten to add here that I am not one of those who believe that the enormity of the Holocaust is above and beyond presentation in artistic form, except in the most indirect or metaphorical way. I have never believed this, and maintain that those who do wish simultaneously to apotheosize the victimhood of the Jews and to deny the transformative powers of art. After all, if Christ's crucifixion can be depicted on film (in a veritable genre unto itself, as, relatively recently, *The Passion of the Christ* [2004] and *The Gospel of John* [2003] have shown us), so too can that of twentieth- and twenty-first-century Jews. The ultimate question in art, of course, is not *what* you present but *how* you present it, not so much the message as the medium.

Some have chosen to treat the Holocaust in documentary-film form, such as Alain Resnais in *Night and Fog* (1955), out of the apparent belief that no one could quarrel with the unvarnished truth, however horrible it might be. But Claude Lanzmann implicitly quarrels with Resnais in *Shoah* (1985), his nine-and-one-half-hour documentary on the Nazi extermination of European Jewry, by not including any imagery of his picture's central subject. We see interviews with survivors, with "former" Nazis, with Holocaust historians; we see the sites of the concentration camps. We do not, however, watch footage of the Jewish ghettoes, of the emaciated camp survivors, or of the piles of corpses, as we do in *Night and Fog* and numerous other films about the German atrocities. This is one way of saying that these atrocities are beyond representation, even in documentary form, and that to represent them is somehow to endorse them; that, before as well as after the Third Reich, such brutality on such a scale was and remains unimaginable, or, conversely, is conceivable only in the moral imagination. (Indeed, Lanzmann himself has said that "fiction about the Holocaust is a transgression; I deeply believe that there are some things that cannot and should not be represented.")

Other directors have elected to treat the Holocaust in fictional form (if that is the appropriate term), going as far back as Wanda Jakubowska's *The Last Stage* (1948) and Aleksander Ford's *Border Street* (1949), continuing with Andrzej Munk's *The Passenger* (1963), and stretching into the near-present with Andrzej Wajda's *Korczak* (1990), Agnieszka Holland's *Europa, Europa* (1991), Steven Spielberg's *Schindler's List* (1993), Roberto Benigni's *Life Is Beautiful* (1998), and Roman Polanski's *The Pianist* (2002). Each of these films, with the possible exception of the documentary-like *Last Stage*, is marred by broad or monochromatic characterizations and rhetorical gestures. All but one was shot in Poland, where today only a few thousand Jews are left out of the more than three million who lived there before Hitler's arrival in 1939. At least three make the fatal error of turning the Holocaust into a morality play that diminishes the humanity of Holocaust victims either by depicting the genocide of the Jews solely from the point of view of the German perpetrators (*Schindler's List*); by sugarcoating the camps themselves in the process of reaffirming the humanity of concentration-camp victims, and thus diminishing the guilt of the war criminals (*Life Is Beautiful*); or by managing to commit both these sins with its portrait of a man whose Judaism is largely an accident of birth, whose Christian girlfriend is anything but a Polish anti-Semite or Nazi collaborator, and whose life is saved by a kindly German officer with a saving love for classical music (*The Pianist*).

Yet another Holocaust film came along five years into the twenty-first century—one that I hesitated to see—but, among its other virtues, *Fateless* (2005) is an assurance to those of us who fear that the Holocaust is congealing into just another movie genre. There are several reasons why. First, the screenplay is by Imre Kertész, not some film-world hand (as in the cases of the three Holocaust pictures prior to this one)—adapted by this Hungarian Nobel laureate from his novel of the same name. Furthermore, the book is based on his own experiences beginning in German-occupied Budapest. In 1944, when he was fourteen, Kertész, who is Jewish, was deported to Auschwitz and was subsequently moved from this death camp to various labor camps. He was liberated by the Americans in 1945 and insisted on returning to Budapest rather than be resettled in the United States. The outline of Kertész's own story is also an outline of the film; and, though *Fateless* contains little that will be new to any informed viewer, it fascinates for all of its 140 minutes, never lapsing into the pitfalls of this particular "genre": exploitation, facileness, sentimentality.

The second reason for the truthfulness (in every sense) of *Fateless*, related to the first, is that it depicts the genocide of the Jews from the point of view not of the perpetrators, but of the victims themselves. And the director, Lajos Koltai (here making his directing début, but better known as a cinematographer on such pictures as *Mephisto* [1981] and *Colonel Redl* [1985]), is careful to remind us of his film's perspective aurally as well as visually. The boy who plays the fourteen-year-old character of György, for example, is given a good deal of voice-over narration as connective tissue. Perhaps more important, *Fateless* is marvelously concerned with faces—Jewish faces. Throughout the film, to be sure, long shots and panoramas, particularly of the prisoners *en masse*, recur as reminders of historical context; but principally Koltai wants his picture to have its being in the faces of the boy and all those he encounters, whom he *sees*. Every face thus becomes at least a minute—and in some ways imperishable—biography. Moreover, Koltai gives *Fate-*

Fateless, dir. Lajos Koltai, 2005

less an overall lingering or album effect by closing nearly every scene with a quick fade instead of a sharp and relentless cut.

Inevitably enough, Koltai chose an excellent cinematographer, Gyula Pados, and together they have provided *Fateless* with a visual texture that is (appositely) in limbo. The palette is muted, so that the film seems, most of the time, to hover between color and black-and-white. Color in the concentration camp scenes would have been upsetting; colors in the beginning or end would have made *Fateless* a "movie," like *Schindler's List*. Throughout, the very palette of this picture—black-and-white, in color—thus conveys an aura of captivity, of a world imprisoned between the two worlds of past and future. (The acting of Marcell Nagy as György does something similar: he doesn't act for the camera so much as he moves through an enclosing reality as if the camera weren't there, creating from within yet fixing himself without in a being, a total presence, that will last as long as film itself.) But captive to the budding Holocaust genre *Fateless* is not. Indeed, this film bursts through the bounds of genre to become itself, and itself alone. It does so not merely because of the talent of those (including the extensive, and flawless, cast) who are exploring this grave—one can almost say consecrated—subject, but because every moment in *Fateless* is treated as a unit of trust and even faith, in both senses of the word. Every moment, in other words, is a captive one.

The second of my four film genres-in-the-making is not so much the anti-narrative film as the feature film that bridges the gap between the non-narrative and the storied, the avant and the garde, the abstract or abstracted and the representational. There have been a number such of such films over the last five years or so, from the United States as well as abroad: Gus Van Sant's *Last Days* (2005), Jun Ichikawa's *Tony Takitani* (2004), Kim Ki-duk's *3-Iron* (2004), Michel Gondry's *Eternal Sunshine of the Spotless Mind* (2004), and Miranda July's *Me and You and Everyone We Know* (2005). We can add another one to this list: *Woman Is the Future of Man* (2005). Like *3-Iron*, Hong Sang-soo's film is from South Korea, and I propose now to treat it at length, as well as the new genre to which it is contributing.

In their own highly individual ways, each of the filmmakers cited above turns his or her attention away from plots, reducing their importance if not eliminating them altogether, and rediscovers the essential elements of cinematic form: the painterly image, the musical gesture, the poetic presence. A recurrent motif in the history of purely avant-garde film itself is the very idea that the medium need not have become a narrative, representational one at all, but could instead have modeled itself on other art forms, especially painting and music. A history of avant-garde cinema could be constructed in just such terms, counterposing the origins of orthodox or mainstream narrative cinema in literature and theater with the painterly, poetic, and musical origins of the first avant-garde experiments in film. So what Van Sant, Ichikawa, Kim, Gondry, July, and Hong are doing today amounts to a kind of aesthetic revisionism toward the displacement and deformation of linear narrative in favor of such techniques as visual collage, musical counterpoint, circus-like simultaneity, and poetic compression or distillation.

I would also venture, however, that this narrative reduction by contemporary filmmakers has as much to do with social perception as aesthetic revisionism. That is, these writer-directors are less interested in what their characters do next, and more concerned with the fact that, in any deeply committed sense, their characters don't really know what to do next. And it is in an attempt to depict this widespread, contemporary malaise (related to the general decline of religious belief and the ongoing crisis of geopolitics) that an increasing number of film artists are contravening traditional cinematic structure, with its cause and effects, its clear linkages, its neat exposition and tidy closure. They certainly are not all good artists merely because of such contravention—but some of them are, and all of them are disquietingly significant in the face of what appears to be a nameless void. It used to be called the existential Absurd, but such a highfalutin term seems out of place in this era of diminished intellect. In the paradoxical age of global terrorism, the Pax Americana, nuclear proliferation, renewed religious enmity between extremists of every stripe, and Communist holdout (did I miss anything?), let us simply call this current condition material oblivion or its equivalent, spiritual deprivation.

South Korea, of course, is south of one of the world's last, and most troublesome, Communist strongholds. And this is where Hong Sang-soo has been making films since 1996, after taking his undergraduate as well as graduate education in the United States.

He has made eleven pictures to date, the fifth of which is *Woman Is the Future of Man* (whose purposefully misleading title, incidentally, is lifted from a poem by the Communist-Surrealist French poet Louis Aragon). All of Hong's films overtly or indirectly subvert narrative expectations, in the first place through the elliptical editing of dual narratives by placing them, or parts of them, one after the other, such that story A and story B play off each other enigmatically and even abstractly rather than in clearly defined contrasts or carefully arranged juxtapositions. Furthermore, in Hong's *The Day a Pig Fell into the Well* (1996) and *The Power of Kangwon Province* (1998), characters only mentioned in the first story emerge in the second, thereby evoking eerie connections between friends and strangers that culminate in both pictures in mysterious as well as cruel deaths.

All of Hong's movies additionally feature filmmakers or film actors among their characters, and there may be a connection between this and the fact that Hong is a financially unsuccessful art-house director in a country addicted to blockbusters (one form of material oblivion) of the American as well as the Korean kind, and therefore predisposed to "obsess" not only over his own fate but also over the relationship between film and reality. The issue of art-house versus commercial cinema even gets raised in Hong's *Rashomon*-like *Virgin Stripped Bare by Her Bachelors* (2000), during an argument between filmmakers over a stolen camera. The tragedy in *On the Occasion of Remembering the Turning Gate* (2002) itself is set in motion when a movie actor begins to pursue a beautiful female fan. Similarly, in *A Tale of Cinema* (2006), which also includes a darkly funny film-within-a film, a failed director becomes dangerously obsessed with a rising star. And one of the main characters in *Woman Is the Future of Man* happens to be a man who went to America to study filmmaking (like Hong himself?)—in the process spurning the woman who loved him.

The two main characters in *Woman Is the Future of Man*, set in and around Seoul today, behave as if their lives have something other than material direction. Hunjoon, single, is the aspiring filmmaker who has just returned from the United States; Munho, married, is a university lecturer whose specialty is the history of Western art. Each young man, then, in his way, has career projects in mind that are designed to do more than merely make money, but

Woman Is the Future of Man, dir. Hong Sang-soo, 2005

Hong knows more about them than they know about themselves. These men's lives are actually emptier than they are willing to acknowledge—morally and spiritually as well as emotionally vacuous—and the shape and pace of Hong's film show it.

Consider, for example, the opening sequence of *Woman Is the Future of Man*. Hunjoon meets his old friend Munjo outside the latter's heavily mortgaged, gated, luxurious suburban home. Curiously, Munho never invites Hunjoon inside to meet the lady of the house; instead, he gives him a cursory tour of the grounds. And it is during this awkward moment of forced domestic exile, as it were, that Munho offers his recently repatriated college buddy a peculiar gift: an invitation to track through the season's first snowfall, which has accumulated on the front lawn. Accepting the offer, Hunjoon begins to walk exclusively in one direction before doubling back on his steps in order to leave only a single set of footprints in the snow. This seemingly incidental episode provides us with an introductory metaphor not only for the film's subject—the attempt to retrace or relive the past—but also for one of its themes, which is that we cannot recover or re-create the past, we can only repeat it (and its mistakes) in the present.

The very next scene then underlines and augments this theme. Munho and Hunjoon go to a restaurant where they sit at a table, east raw squid, drink rice wine, and talk for five or six minutes—in one wide shot, unedited and unvaried. What the two men reveal about their pasts, especially in regard to the same young woman, connects with their (sometimes strained) relationship and plans in the present; but it is the very persistence of the shot itself, the long take, that is Hong's overriding comment. For he is telling us, visually, that the two friends are static—not necessarily in their visible careers (though academic tenure, a kind of stasis, is Munho's only goal, and Hunjoon himself is ready to teach to pay his bills, since his film career is going nowhere—he hasn't even written his first screenplay yet) but in their most private beings.

Hong uses this device of the held shot, filmed at an equivocal distance, again—with these two and with other characters—for it is his means of depicting personal stagnation. Indeed, everything personal that occurs in *Woman Is the Future of Man*, in talk as well as external action, seems haphazard or desultory and therefore directionless, a mimesis of inner beings, of inner *voids*, that are covered over with a patina of purpose. This is true in the film even of sex, that most personal of acts, which happens here several times in several ways with the woman mentioned in the previous paragraph, but which seems only the fulfillment of social routine by the participants rather than the expression of lustful heat, let alone romantic desire. Over the restaurant table, in fact, Munho reinforces this idea by declaring, "Koreans are too fond of sex. They have nothing better to do. There's no real culture." (And one of the saddest indictments of another culture you will ever hear is this query by the woman—I have deliberately neglected to give her name, Sunhwa, because names connote identities, and, even more so than her two former boyfriends, she doesn't have one—in mid-intercourse to Munho: "Can I moan?")

Let me continue by detailing what else of a personal nature is revealed in the restaurant conversation, as well as in what passes for a plot in so meandering (though, at eighty-eight minutes, relatively short) a film as *Woman Is the Future of Man*. Like overgrown college boys, both Munho and Hunjoon each attempt, separately, to seduce an attractive young waitress at the restaurant under the pretense of being inspired to capture her beauty through their respective arts. Rebuffed, the two men quietly feign indifference by awkwardly looking off into the street and abstractedly focusing their attention on another woman, who is wearing a purple scarf. Bearing a passing resemblance to Sunhwa, the female figure from Munho and Hunjoon's past, the scarved young lady briefly makes eye contact with each man before turning away. This repeated incident of rejection involving an anonymous woman then gets the male friends to talking about their mutual conquest of Sunhwa, in an attempt to assuage their bruised egos.

Neither man has seen Sunhwa for years, but Munho knows that she settled down in a nearby town and works in the local hotel's bar as a cocktail waitress. We soon learn, in the film's first flashback, that Hunjoon dated her first; that, while dating Hunjoon, Sunhwa was kidnapped and raped by a boy she knew from high school who had just been discharged from the military; and that Hunjoon's self-gratifying idea of "cleansing" Sunhwa of this violation was to have sex with her himself after duly washing her nether regions. Still in flashback, he promises to keep in touch once he goes to study in the States, but Hunjoon does nothing of the kind, and the heartbroken, abandoned Sunhwa falls for Munho (in a second flashback) at a time when she is feeling most vulnerable.

Hong shuffles his time scheme when he starts using these flashbacks, leaping backward, then forward, and then back again—sometimes making us, and perhaps the characters too, wonder where we are. As when the film cuts from one moment in the past during which Munho and Sunhwa have a happy, flirty encounter, to a follow-up sex scene (after a few weeks or a few months? after several years?) in which, sex or no sex, they can barely tolerate each other's presence. Some scenes even appear to run, not in sequence like these two, but in parallel as it were. We observe Munho alone, for example, seated at the side of an outdoor sports arena, wrapped in a scarf; then we see him, bare-necked, approach a group of his students—at the same time, in the same place, with the same dazzling sun and glistening snow—and accept a scarf from *them*. How can both scenes be true or possible, except in reverse or in reverie—or in a movie like *Woman Is the Future of Man*, where what happens next matters less than what is transpiring in a kind of static, eternal, multidimensional present, or where what happens next is less important than what doesn't?

Back in the present, feeling his rice wine, Munho can't resist joining Hunjoon in the latter's quest to see Sunhwa. All three meet after she finishes her night shift at the hotel bar, as the men wait in a nearby restaurant, where they continue to drink—this time beer. The tensions between Munho and Hunjoon have increased, moreover, not only because of increased alcohol-intake, but also because of their divergent (yet equally erroneous or extreme), rivalrous views of Sunhwa: Hunjoon the errant romantic puts her on a pedestal, whereas Munho the serial adulterer sees her as an easy lay (like some of the female students of his whom he has seduced). Sunhwa nonetheless takes her pair of former lovers back to her apartment, where the love triangle repeats itself in a drunken ritual of stumbling dance, stale sex, primal betrayal, and painful humiliation.

If excessive drinking is the catalyst for deadlock and degradation in *Woman Is the Future of Man* (as in Hong's other films), however, it's in the lingering hangover that follows where the characters dwell—especially the two men. After Munho and Hunjoon both sleep at Sunhwa's apartment, they awake purporting to remember very little and then disperse to wander the city of Seoul: literally to wander, not to "find themselves" or get their bearings, as they try to "walk off" the blistering headaches that otherwise paralyze them. It is Munho in particular, looking for love in all the wrong places, whom we follow deeper and deeper into a perpetual night of soulless discontent, and whom we leave as, at one point, he simply stands there in the snow, idling.

As one can deduce from my description of this film, there is great danger in Hong's procedure. Dramatists learned long ago that it is risky to include just *one* static character in a play, because he or she may so easily bore the audience. In the cinema, Antonioni took such a risk, but to see how he used a static character dramatically, have a look at Giulia in the 1960 film *L'avventura* (to take just one example from his *oeuvre*). Hong may not use his static characters dramatically, but he does vary his picture's emotional tone if not its visual style to keep us guessing—and interested—for all of eighty-eight minutes. Even within one scene, the tone of *Woman Is the Future of Man* can shift from light satirical comedy (hinted at by Yong-jin Jeong's jaunty, light-hearted musical score) to grim realistic drama (expressed not only by the cinematographer

Hyeon-gu Kim's clinical, blue-dominated palette, but also by an icily observational camera-mode that does not allow for a single close-up, even—or especially—during sex scenes). This strategy works because, though from time to time we wait a bit impatiently for the next cigarette or the next disconnected chat with a woman, most of the time we are held by a conviction that Hong not only knows what he is risking, he is doing it for a grave, contemporary purpose.

That said, Hong insists on a frustratingly amoral stance in the face of his characters' actions and motivations, pitching them into one gray area after another (and some not-so-gray areas as well) yet abjuring every opportunity to comment on their response, or lack of response, to the tawdry situations in which they find themselves. This makes *Woman Is the Future of Man* a provocative and even disturbing experience, which nevertheless demands from its viewers a response—without the reassurance of much guidance on Hong's part. Moreover, the flat placidity of the performances (Yoo Jitae as Munho, Kim Toewoo as Hunjoon, and former Miss Korea Sung Hyunan as Sunhwa)—particularly of Sunhwa, who is a disconcerting blend of the pliable and the numb—doesn't give much away.

Nor does Hong's own "static" analysis of his film's title: "As the future is yet to come, it means nothing, and if the future is multiplied by man, the result is still zero." (Aragon's own title and poem, by contrast, were designed to express his passion for women and his vision for a society that would permit women to be more in charge of their own destiny.) So we are left with a negative and maybe nihilistic film that risks aesthetic tedium in the process of analyzing socio-cultural tedium. For me *Woman Is the Future of Man* succeeds as a poetic evocation not just of Korea's fractured soul, but of present-day anomie in general. Still, I can understand the argument that if Hong's cinema is the future of man, or the harbinger of film art, we should all drink to diminished expectations—women included.

The third of my four genres-in the-making is the film with unsimulated sex acts (as opposed to the simulated kind to be found in *Woman Is the Future of Man*)—not pornography, of course, which consists of explicit sexual acts that are gratuitous, or designed merely for viewer-titillation. The unsimulated sexual activity I'm

Engendering Genre   169

talking about is part of, or related to, a picture's (serious) theme, which may or may not be concerned with sexuality itself. So perhaps it's better to call the "film with unsimulated sexual activity" a subgenre, since sex itself—the sheer physical act of sex—need not be its focus. Sometimes it *is* the focus, as in the cases of Nagisa Oshima's *In the Realm of the Senses* (1976), Catherine Breillat's *Romance* (1999), and Michael Winterbottom's *9 Songs* (2004). But sometimes the sex is graphic at the same time that it's not the focus, or the sole one, as in Marco Bellocchio's *Devil in the Flesh* (1986), Vincent Gallo's *The Brown Bunny* (2003), and Carlos Reygadas's *Battle in Heaven* (2005).

Now sex is hardly novel in films these days, and it hasn't been since the 1960s, when mainstream cinema began pushing the boundaries as to what would be permitted on screen. (The depiction of sexuality in mainstream cinema was at one time restricted by federal law in the United States, as well as by self-imposed industry standards in Hollywood.) But most of the time, in the past as in the present, the on-screen sex is simulated. Increasingly, however, sex in otherwise non-pornographic movies is becoming explicit, as shown by this supplementary list of fiction features from the late 1990s and early twenty-first century, all of them featuring either fellatio, intercourse, or both: *The Idiots* (1998), *I Stand Alone* (1998), *La donna lupo* (1999), *Guardami* (1999), *Polax* (1999), *Giulia* (1999), *Baise-moi* (2000), *Intimacy* (2001), *Dog Days* (2001), *In the Cut* (2003), *Anatomy of Hell* (2004), *Antares* (2004), and *All About Anna* (2005).

We shouldn't be surprised by this development, since sex, even in seriously intended films (which still have to make money), sells, and since the cinema, like any other art form but especially a popular one, abhors a vacuum: what hasn't been done, will be done. Moreover, the cinema is the most "immediate" of aesthetic experiences in that, to a greater degree than the other arts (including theater), it reflects contemporary currents—social, political, psychological, sexual—the fastest. And what could be more contemporary than the amoral or non-judgmental stance of many Westerners (and, increasingly, of people from other parts of the world) toward fornication, promiscuity, and adultery—in some cases even sadomasochism and pedophilia? So if anything goes off-screen, why shouldn't anything go on-screen? (Do I need to add here that the overwhelming majority of cinematic sex scenes, unsimulated or not, take place between unmarried couples?) Indeed, why shouldn't it be the cinema's duty, as the most graphically representational of art forms, to reflect the new permissiveness and to reflect it as realistically as possible? Art may not be life, but when it's as lifelike as film, the temptation is to stop imitating reality and to start creating it.

The latest example of a film that creates its own sexual reality is *Battle in Heaven*, and I'd like to treat it here not only for its sexual candor but also for its narrative discursiveness. In a sense, this Mexican film combines both the second and the third of my genres-in-the-making. Indeed, Reygadas, whose second picture this is after *Japón* (2002), is said to have remarked that narrative is merely a marketing necessity for a movie and not integral to its making. This view, curiously like that of some nineteenth-century opera composers who merely wanted plot armatures on which to hang their arias, could not be more clearly expressed than in *Battle in Heaven*. Many of the things we see are more affecting—or disaffecting—than the almost haphazard story that connects them. Events here are simply chronicled, slowly, and often with atmospheric excursions.

For instance, during one scene of intercourse, the camera goes out the window and pans around 360 degrees to take in the whole of the empty courtyard of the apartment house in which the sex is happening, and only then returns to the couple, lying side by side yet silently objectified and removed from each other. This movement itself is an echo of the camera circling around the same couple, as she performs fellatio on him, from the start of *Battle in Heaven*—*before* the start, during the pre-credit sequence. The fact that an explicit act of fellatio begins this picture tells us, in fact, that the picture most likely will *not* be pornography. A porn director would tease a while and not put the act right at the beginning. If actual sex occurs at the start, the film is probably a serious work—promptly signaling to us that it will scorn convention. And a serious (if sometimes heavy-handed) work *Battle in Heaven* is, on the subjects of social class, religion, nationhood, and sexuality as they intersect with the kind of moral inertia familiar to us from Hong Sang-soo's film: a moral inertia that, in this instance, is symbolized by the encircling, entrapping movement of the camera.

A straightforward description of the plot of *Battle in Heaven* would make it sound like a *noir* crime thriller or even a tempestuous *verismo* opera, but here goes. Marcos, married, middle-aged, blank-faced, and potbellied, has been engaged as a chauffeur for the past fifteen years for an important Mexican general, work that includes driving his daughter, Ana, around Mexico City (and has done since she was a child). Now nineteen, lovely, sylphlike, Ana works part-time in a seedy bordello—not for the money, clearly, but as an act of rebellion, debasement, and masochism. (This last touch may suggest *Belle de Jour* [1967] to some viewers, but *Battle in Heaven* has none of the progressive, role-playing tension of Buñuel's film.) Marcos is the only member of Ana's household or her immediate circle who knows that she is leading a double life; and, because he knows her secret, he gets a little action of his own on the side, unbeknownst either to Marcos's wife or Ana's boyfriend. (Marcos and Ana are the couple in the sex acts described in the previous paragraph; their opening scene of fellatio, moreover, is reprised at the very end of *Battle in Heaven*.)

Marcos has sex with his wife as well in this film, but it's not pretty, even if Jesus himself watches from a painting on the wall: she weighs about 300 pounds, and, as he takes her from behind, we see their rolls of fat jiggling up and down. Reygadas is interested, however, more in what happens on the inside during sex than in what happens on the outside. Movies that concentrate on the outside in order to arouse us are pornographic, of course, and *Battle in Heaven* is not pornography. If Marcos and his wife are making love, the point is not to establish the fact that they are making love. What matters is what you can learn about their relationship from the *way* they make love. And, to that end, it's no accident that Marcos and his wife's scene ends with a loving hug, whereas Marcos and Ana's mechanical copulation ends with an extreme close-up of his uncircumcised penis losing its erection.

Such explicitness is part of *Battle in Heaven*'s meaning, for Reygadas is less concerned with bodies in the erotic sense than in the way that they, and their positioning, can be indicators of class. To wit: body shapes are influenced by economics, such that the folks without the money to dine well end up feasting on junk food instead, which sticks to their figures. Furthermore, Marcos lies passive be-

Battle in Heaven, dir. Carlos Reygadas, 2005

neath the controlling Ana during his sex with her, or the princess is on top and the peasant is on the bottom; whereas Marcos takes the dominant position during intercourse with his woman, or the chauffeur drives it home.

Chauffeur for a general or not, Marcos and his wife—who sells clocks and cakes from a blanket spread on the floor of a subway station—are desperate for money. And to get some, they have kidnapped a baby for ransom; but the infant has been accidentally killed in their custody, before its mother (an acquaintance no less) was able to raise the cash. The megapolis of Mexico City, a polluted and corrupt city with a population of over twenty million, suffers thousands of such kidnappings-for-profit each year, and these abductions are committed against the poor—as in this case—as well as the rich, with ransom demands as low as $1500. The couple regards the kidnapped baby's death as regrettable—not least because of the lost ransom money—but not catastrophic, one more grim fact in a life of grim facticity. In other words, they feel no pressing guilt despite the fact that they are members of the most guilt-laden religion in the world, Catholicism—*that's* the level to which moral standards have sunk in Mexico City. (The title, by the way, is an ironic allusion to the epochal battle between the rebel archangel Lucifer and God for control of heaven, in which Lucifer was banished for eternity to the flaming bowels of hell.)

But something begins to happen to Marcos after he confesses his crime to Ana, in the comfort of whose body he has tried to hide. That is, he starts suffering, not from Catholic guilt, but from a natural revolt once his new physical or "natural" partner learns *his* secret; and his inner, secret being revolts against his outer, openly material one. Ana urges Marcos to turn himself in to the police, but he puts off doing so until he explodes—and stabs her to death. He is not pleased, you see, with what she has been doing with her life, sinning against herself as much as the Church through her acts of prostitution. Marcos's wife is not pleased that—as her husband reveals to her—he admitted their crime to Ana. And Marcos himself is not pleased with his own doings as a kidnapper who is also guilty of involuntary infanticide. He's not happy, either, with the hard fact that, sex though they may have, he and Ana are from completely different worlds and can never be together on an internal, intimate level—except in another dimension, which can only be achieved through death.

The latter portion of *Battle in Heaven* deals with Marcos's deteriorating mental state combined with his wish to die, the way in which he looks for death, and the manner in which he's granted his wish. (A death-wish links *Battle in Heaven* with Reygadas's *Japón*, except that in the earlier film, which shows the influence of Abbas Kiarostami and Theo Angelopoulos, it is thwarted. In this work, a middle-aged painter from Mexico City who travels to a remote mountain village to commit suicide is mysteriously re-invigorated by the forces of the natural world that surrounds him.) The climactic set piece is shot amid an annual, and actual, pilgrimage of thousands to the shrine of the Virgin of Guadalupe (a dark-skinned incarnation of the Virgin Mary, and the patron saint of Mexico), where chanting priests lead a hooded Marcos, moving along on bloodied knees and in urine-soaked pants, on a *via crucis* to beg forgiveness—and to engender his brutal self-punishment.

For the Virgin's forgiveness is not enough for Marcos, as it is for his wife. He cannot absolve his crimes by turning himself in to the authorities or by going on a religious pilgrimage—alternatives that at first seem separate but cannot be separated in a country like Mexico, where the Church is sponsored by the state. A mysteriously willed death—not one at the hands of the police—is Marcos's only solution, where he can be reunited with Ana in heaven (or is it hell?) as she goes down on him in the reprised fellatio scene, with the difference that now no tears fall from Ana's eyes, Marcos is not wearing a condom, and he and Ana both declare their love for one another. (At the start as well as the finish, this scene is dissimilar in tone and visual design from the rest of the picture, being almost abstract in conception—with no set dressing and a blank, vaguely luminous background.)

Battle in Heaven is book-ended, moreover, not only by this ritualistic spectacle of oral sex, but also by images of the raising and lowering, the unfurling and collapse, of a gigantic Mexican flag. (It is Ana's father, the general, who supervises the daily flag ceremonies; and it is Marcos who ambles along after a parade of snappy Mexican soldiers at the morning ceremony, and who in his ambling makes his own kind of comment on the soldiers', and the general's, snappiness.) In between, we get an equally startling juxtaposition of the sexual and the political as a dramatic soccer match, charged with nationalist hyperbole, is revealed not only to be televised, but also to be the object of Marcos's viewing pleasure as he masturbates. The very last shot, of church bells—whose piercing ringing itself has been juxtaposed against, or drowned out by, the sound of a raging waterfall during *Battle in Heaven*—adds the final ingredient to the film's potent thematic mix.

If the above summary of *Battle in Heaven*'s action sounds plot-driven—contrary to what I've said—it isn't so much as it is mood-driven. And the mood is Marcos's. What is special about Reygadas's film is the way in which it articulates the rupture in reality that Marcos has experienced as a result of his crimes, with the plot details serving as coordinates in the mapping of a very particular existential terrain (an inner being in revolt, as I described earlier). It is in giving the audience direct perceptual access to Marcos's confused and vulnerable sense of the world, through subjective shots but also through objective ones that nonetheless convey his state of mind (such as a preternaturally silent shot in the mountains during which, surrounded by mist, Marcos appears—depending on the viewer's perspective—either to ascend into heaven or to be swallowed up by the clouds), that *Battle in Heaven* excels. The drama of the picture is not, at least up until the closing scenes, what the world will do to Marcos so much as how he will perceive that world through his ruptured consciousness.

It is significant, for example, that the audience sees nothing of the infant's kidnapping and subsequent death; instead, from the outset we are plunged into the world as Marcos experiences it in the aftermath of these two eruptions. The shambling, fattish, unprepossessing, relatively inarticulate yet strangely moving protagonist is thus put in the position of having to renegotiate his relationship to the world, of having to process feelings that refuse to clarify themselves and which he proves himself ill-equipped to handle. Rather than giving us a Hitchcockian configuration of paranoid reciprocation between the main character and his environment, however, Reygadas presents us with a space that appears relentlessly objective and detached even when it is imbued with the protagonist's subjectivity. And it is Marcos's inability to reconcile the tumultuousness of his inner conflict with the indifference of reality that *Battle in Heaven*'s cinematic style is meant to reflect.

This dislocation or disconnection is graphed through a series of impeccably conceived and sometimes extreme behaviors or gestures rather than through dialogue. As when, after his wife informs him by cell phone of the baby's death, Marcos goes to meet her in the subway, where the surrounding noises gradually turn into a blur and the frame tightens on him to convey both his distress and his powerlessness. (These feelings will continue to be conveyed during the film by John Tavener's cosmically aching score—a kind of low-level, horror-movie thrum.) Similarly, during a scene when Marcos is driving Ana home from the airport, all the sound is muted save for her gravelly alto, which serves to express both his obsession with her and his profound alienation not only from the world, from *her* world, but also from himself. And when we get a shot of the schleppy Marcos sitting alone, totally alien, in Ana's tastefully appointed apartment, what's suggested is the chasm that gapes between them and that is about to be bridged through violence. This shot itself can be imagistically related to another one in which a nude Marcos is framed against a white wall, standing still and facing forward, looking for all the world like a distended Francis Bacon model.

As one can deduce from the above shot descriptions, the actors in *Battle in Heaven* don't so much give performances as they are used by Reygadas as units in a sort of visually stirring (im)morality play. In fact, they are all non-professionals, as were the performers in *Japón*. Marcos, we're told, is an actual chauffeur; and Ana is played, under an assumed name, by the daughter of a well-known Mexican family. Such non-professionalism has led to comparisons with Bresson that seem to me strained. For in his films Bresson wanted to supersede acting, which he loathed; Reygadas is more like the Italian neorealists, who wanted acting but from non-actors. Bresson's actors were models for his ideas, that is, whereas Reygadas's performers are individuals who are permitted to bring their own distinctive personalities to the screen—with the result that our perception of them is based not so much on any authorially predetermined, closed-off description of character as on our subjective response to their very presence or being, as it relates to the cinematic world that surrounds them. In effect, then, Reygadas puts us, as spectators, in Marcos's position, or the aesthetic equivalent of his position as he attempts to navigate his way through his changed, and changing, world.

In its treatment of the bizarre as commonplace, its blend of the ordinary and extraordinary into undiscriminating existence, *Battle in Heaven* eventually even spins a mild hypnosis on us. The very grotesquerie of this combination has an effect because, for all its marriage of the sententious to the ludicrous, it tells us that we are in the presence of a director of quite perceptible talent, who is intelligently disturbed by the state of his nation. After a while, we accept as well the very *longueurs* in this otherwise unlengthy film (at ninety-eight minutes): the lengthy contemplation of the characters' faces or bodies, for example, which the cinematographer Diego Martínez Vignatti uses almost like rests in music. Contrast these shots, a number of them in extreme close-up, with Martínez Vignatti's beautiful yet paradoxically frightening long shots of Mexico City—grand or expansive images that themselves seem like achingly recited monologues, but which are nonetheless shot entirely in available light—and you'll get a good idea of the baroque tensions, the earthly-cum-epic oppositions, at work in *Battle in Heaven*. (In one of these wide, continuous shots with the city as a backdrop, we pass in Marcos's car from a run-down metropolitan area where people push carts alongside the road, to its polar opposite: another economic universe entirely, with lush green lawns, suburban stillness, and armed security guards who guide their employers from the comfort of their homes to the safety of their limousines.)

One of those tensions is extra-cinematic: I mean, how does a director engage individuals for roles like Marcos and Ana, since these people are not porn professionals? He must tell candidates, presumably unacquainted with each other, that they are to have various kinds of sex on camera, and I have to wonder what the conversations must have been like in which Reygadas convinced the real-life Marcos and Ana—Marcos Hernández and Anapola Mushkadiz—both to participate. Not to speak of the obese Mexican woman (Bertha Ruiz) with varicose veins, in addition to layer upon layer of flab, who plays Marcos's wife. Well, at least *Battle in Heaven* shows its sex in an unadorned, unromanticized manner, between the kinds of characters who would never engage in such activity in a Hollywood movie (Ana, yes, but not with Marcos). In addition, the film disregards the double standard regarding male and female nudity, for here we get to see the genitalia of both genders, but particularly the male's, before as well as after sexual intercourse.

The final genre of my four genres-in-the-making is the terrorist film. Indeed, the terms "terrorism" and "terrorist" seem to be two of the most frequently used words in the English language. Every day we encounter them in the media as they are related to some disaster, recent or new. It would be spurious to sigh for a past that was always tranquil; nonetheless, we cannot help feeling that the world has become much more continually ravaged with violence than it ever has been before. And almost always it is principled violence, at least in the minds of the assailants. Nowhere are those principles more galvanic than in the work of the suicide bomber.

I want to concentrate here on this sub-genre of the terrorist film, rather than, say, terror-by-hostage-taking as treated not so long ago in Marco Bellocchio's *Good Morning, Night* (2003, about the kidnapping and murder of Aldo Moro, former Italian prime minister and head of the Christian Democratic Party). And I will also leave aside such relatively recent big-budget terrorist films as Oliver Stone's *World Trade Center* (2006) and Steven Spielberg's *Munich* (2005), because their real subject is not the terrorist killers themselves but rather the havoc they wreak—and the vengeful, murderous, often melodramatic retribution they inspire.

No, my subject is a new one in the world of art: the suicide bomber himself—or herself. In film several years ago there were three such pictures released within months of each other: *Paradise Now* (2005), *The War Within* (2005), and *Day Night Day Night* (2006). The first two films wanted to transform the anonymous suicide bombers—in the first instance, two Palestinians, in the second, a Pakistani—that we read and hear about in news reports into fleshed-out individuals, tremulous yet consecrated. The directors of *Paradise Now* and *The War Within*—Hany Abu-Assad and Joseph Castelo, respectively—seem almost to have had in mind the following words of Ralph Waldo Emerson as they made their movies: "Great men, great nations, have . . . been perceivers of the terror of life, and have manned themselves to face it. Without an understanding informed by empathy, we are not manned to face the new world in which we find ourselves." Though both Abu-Assad and Castelo know that not many viewers will sympathize with their protagonists, they also know that it is possible to see such young men, despite the murders they commit, as still more members of the human race enmeshed in the coils of history.

Day Night Day Night, however, is in a way more daring than *Paradise Now* and *The War Within*, than the earlier Indian film *The Terrorist* (1999, dir. Santosh Sivan), or even John Updike's contemporaneous novel *The Terrorist* (2006), for that matter. For this picture does not explore political and social motives or spiritual consecration; indeed, it is almost completely uninterested in the reasons for its protagonist's behavior. *Day Night Day Night* merely and sheerly enters her state of mind as if it were entering a chamber, a ritual, a locus of possibility. Hence there can't really be any question of identifying, or not identifying, with this young woman. She *is*, we are, she *does*, and we watch her do it.

Day Night Day Night is the first fiction feature written and directed by Julia Loktev (who has also made a feature-length documentary, *Moment of Impact* [1998]). The movie is divided into two parts: preparation and action. The first part, or half, has a visual and nearly silent quality that suggests an "interior" documentary about a person—in this case, a nineteen-year-old woman who is going to carry a bomb on her body. She is never given a name during the ninety-four minutes of this picture; and her intense, dark-eyed face (or that of the actress Luisa Williams, in her screen début) itself contributes to her anonymity in its ethnic indistinctness, for she could be Middle Eastern, Russian, Mediterranean, or Latin American. Whatever her ancestry, she and most of the people with whom she is allied speak uninflected Northeastern American English.

We first see her carrying a bag and a tennis racquet. (Soon we understand that the racquet was intended to mislead anyone who might be watching.) She gets into a car and is driven by a tacit chauffeur to a motel in New Jersey; once in her shabby room, the chauffeur draws the curtain and leaves. The young woman says nothing when she is alone. She sleeps, then scrubs herself thoroughly. The next day, three hooded and masked men arrive, and, treating her most courteously, they prepare her for her job. We don't know yet definitely what it is, but we begin to suspect when the three men pray (a prayer in which their female accomplice does not join). She is carefully instructed in a false identity—name, address, family background, and so on; outfits are tried on and discarded until one is chosen. The woman then surrenders her cell phone. She is eventually led blindfolded from the motel to a secret location, where a yellow backpack containing explosives is strapped on her shoulders and she is shown how to detonate it.

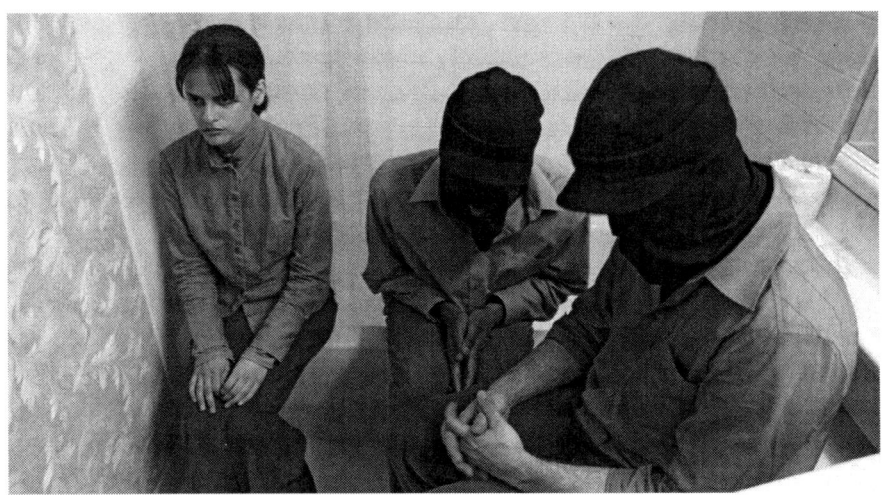

Day Night Day Night, dir. Julia Loktev, 2006

Through all these proceedings the young woman is obedient and unquestioning. Then part two of *Day Night Day Night* begins, as she leaves her collaborators and enters Manhattan via the Port Authority Bus Terminal, where sound effectively enters the picture. The chaos as well as the claustrophobia of the city now intrudes, and she is jostled like the handheld camera that follows her along 42nd Street to Seventh Avenue. Colors intensify, while the soundtrack is abrasively jangling. Eventually, the woman makes her way by train to Times Square, where she intends to activate her bomb. On her way, in and out of the subway, commonplace things occur. She buys some pretzels, then a candied apple. She is neither blithe nor tense, showing no sense of approaching finality. She simply has stepped into this role of suicide bomber as she might have stepped into her clothes.

What is particularly chilling is that the woman seems to have accepted this task as a reasonable way to deal with problems of her own—problems only intimated by the unsettled emotional weather on her face, where determination, rage, uncertainty, bravado, modesty, and panic are among the feelings that flicker over her slightly feral features. (Once she murmurs something about "meeting him," but whether "him" is a man or a deity is not clear.) Toward the end, after a minor mishap with a young man who tries to pick her up,

Engendering Genre 181

she tries to talk, via pay phone, with several people. They cannot be reached, but she *is* able to make a collect long-distance phone call to her parents, who sound like a typical, concerned middle-class mom and dad. Afterwards we see the lights of Manhattan against electrically starred skies. And then the picture abruptly ends—in Times Square.

Thus have Julia Loktev and Luisa Williams taken *Day Night Day Night* out of the realm of physical terror into conceptual abstraction. Their daring is that they do not explain: they show. Their picture is a minimalistic distillation of a state, a condition, which could, if needed, be attached to one set or another of suicide-bomber motivations. Here, then, uncannily, is *das Ding an sich*—and all the more terrifying for it. Like their female bomber's victims, we are left not knowing precisely when a bomb, *this* bomb, will explode, or exactly why this woman has chosen to kill herself and others in such a way. This obviously is not traditional, character-driven empathy, but it is identification of a strangely perverse kind. For the film places us in the role of victim at the same time as it makes us witness to our victimizer. Now that's entertainment.

That brings an end to this particular genre-watch. As I conclude, I am reminded of the term "genre painting," which refers to a work that realistically depicts scenes or events from everyday life. It got that name, of course, because painting hadn't always so depicted human life. A Vermeer genre painting from the second half of the seventeenth century, for example, portrayed human figures of the lower orders, albeit anonymously; it treated them as types rather than unique personalities. Furthermore, the genre painter made no judgments: he was interested, above all, in the objective contemplation of everyday life. (That a seamstress, water girl, or lacemaker could become the subject of a genre painting is certainly not an indication of any improvement in the lot of the worker or peasant at the time; rather, such depiction was a signal of a curiosity on the part of the middle-to-upper classes about the daily lives of those beneath them, and—more important—a sign of the beginning of a desire on the part of early modern artists to embrace everyone and everything as their subject matter.)

Oddly enough, each of the four otherwise "extreme" pictures under consideration here could be said to contemplate everyday life as well, though each (with the notable exception of *Woman Is the Future of Man*) of course implies some judgments. But they all have more or less ordinary people at their centers; all these figures are meant to be emblematic in addition to being "unique" or "individualized"; and the dailiness of everyday life in these movies remains "daily" even when it occurs in a death camp or a brothel instead of a restaurant, a bar, or a living room—sometimes remaining so to the point of dramatic (or should I say pictorial?) stasis. In other words, *Fateless*, *Woman Is the Future of Man*, *Battle in Heaven*, and *Day Night Day Night* are all essentially realistic or naturalistic films, whatever new genre each may be helping to forge and despite any temporal experimentation it may conduct. And I like the fact that, at least in painting—motion pictures, after all, are serial "paintings," or a succession of still images in motion, as their name indicates—the term genre is connected with such realistic or naturalistic representation.

It's as if, two centuries before the invention of cinema, and with it the ultimate incarnation of realism and naturalism as artistic styles, European genre painters, well, had envisioned the creation of the genre of genres: film, the democratic art as it were, which gives equal importance to every face, speaks the universal language of visual images, and puts all the world at every human being's disposal. In a world without technology, these painters naturally were not yet able to respond to the question, "In a world without film, what would you create?" as Michelangelo Antonioni did, with a single word: "Film." Seventeenth-century artists knew this word, too, but for them, paradoxically enough, it was only a layer of paint designed to cover up, cloud, or even obscure, unlike the pellucid film on which the genre art of today is printed—or, better, brought to light.

10

Westward Faux

Once the richest and most enduring genre of Hollywood's repertoire, the Western is now beyond revisionism and mere decline: it seems to me to be dead. Nearly sixty years ago, Robert Warshow could write that the Western "presents an image of personal nobility that is still real for us." But this claim could hardly be made today; our tolerance for the Western's rigid formulas and limited characterizations has all but disappeared. When the classic chase and showdown sequences could generate no further variations, the vitality of the form was sapped. This generic self-exhaustion was abetted, as well, by the rise of what became known as the revisionist Western—the "shoot-'em-up" that undermines its own conventions.

To some extent, revisionist or self-conscious Westerns have been around since the turn of the twentieth century. The Edison Company's 1905 film *The Little Train Robbery*, for example, was a parody of its own success just two years earlier with *The Great Train Robbery* (which itself grew out of a nineteenth-century American theater that was rife with Western dramas). And the "adult" Westerns of the late 1940s and early 1950s, like *The Gunfighter* (1950) and *High Noon* (1952), showed their own form of self-consciousness by concentrating on the psychological or moral conflicts of the individual protagonist in relation to his society, in an effort to make cowboys more "realistic" in contrast to the heroic, idealized figures of such epic Westerns as *The Covered Wagon* (1925) and *Stagecoach* (1939). To be sure, the latter-day revisionists also aimed at realism— by showing the hypocrisy, violence, and meanness presumably missing from previous Western movies. Yet this alleged recovery of the "real" Old West actually amounted to little more than a revision of cinematic history, for filmmakers merely substituted new myths for the old ones.

Sam Peckinpah was the leading mythmaker of the revisionist movement, beginning with such early films of his as *The Deadly Companions* (1961) and *Ride the High Country* (1962). He shattered the image of personal nobility by having over-the-hill stars—William Holden, Ernest Borgnine, Randolph Scott, Joel McCrea—play distinctly ignoble, over-the-hill cowboys. Their weary, cynical, even mercenary screen *personae* thus cast as much doubt on the actors' own careers as on frontier history. Peckinpah's masterwork *The Wild Bunch* (1969), for instance, used *armed robbers* at its center, or Westerners who, having outlived their role and milieu subsequent to the closing of the American frontier, became outlaws rather than the victims of industrio-technological progress. His intent in featuring such thieving gunmen was not to glorify criminality but to enhance his own mythmaking. The first of these new myths was that the West gave the romance of the robber—the mounted robber—a panoply of glamour; the second was that the illegal behavior of such a criminal could be likened to the legal behavior of rapacious civilians (especially entrepreneurs) and marauding soldiers.

The invidious historicism of this kind of film was most apparent in *Little Big Man* and *Soldier Blue*, both released in 1970. Each of these pictures purported to offer enlightened commentary on racism and (by implication) the Vietnam War (even on sexual liberation)—all in the context of a cowboy movie in which the hostile Indian savages of the cinema of the 1930s, the 1940s, and most of the 1950s were suddenly presented as a race of gentle, intelligent, defenseless people upon whom the United States military establishment, through the agency of its cavalry troops or "horse soldiers," had committed genocide. (The analogy with the 1968 My Lai massacre, in which hundreds of unarmed Vietnamese civilians were murdered by American soldiers, was inescapable and deliberate in *Little Big Man* as well as *Soldier Blue*.)

Of course, the genocide against the American Indians was depicted as graphically as possible in these films, as was carnage in other revisionist Westerns like *Will Penny* (1967) and *Monte Walsh* (1970). For the intent of these pictures was not only to rewrite history, but also to revise (with the help of new technology) the conventions for the depiction of violence: to insist, for the first time in the history of American cinema, that the human body is made of real flesh and blood and does not have the resilience of rubber; that arterial blood spurts rather than drips demurely; that bullet wounds leave not trim little pinpricks but big, gaping holes; and, in general, that violence has painful, unpretty, humanly destructive consequences, rather than leading to a "polite" death that is simply a state of terminal sleep.

But, as we all know, the explicit violence that was such a large part of the revisionists' vision—particularly Peckinpah's—quickly passed from revolutionary innovation to accepted convention to exploitative cliché, becoming in the process as formulaic as the less graphic action it was intended to supplant. So much so that it, and the Western, became ripe for the very kind of revisionism found long ago in *The Little Train Robbery*: parody, as evidenced in such films as *Cat Ballou* (1965), *Waterhole No. 3* (1967), *Butch Cassidy and the Sundance Kid* (1969), and *McCabe and Mrs. Miller* (1971). This parody was intentional, but there was also the unintentional kind to be found in movies like *The Missouri Breaks* (1976) and *Goin' South* (1978), whose revisionist thrust gets lost in the mugging, clowning, and sheer self-indulgence of its star performers, Marlon Brando and Jack Nicholson respectively. (Nicholson appears in *The Missouri Breaks* as well, but there he looks restrained opposite the absurdly bizarre, foolishly flamboyant, bloatedly overweight Brando; in *Goin' South*, Nicholson's own tomfoolery is complemented—if that is the word—by John Belushi's buffoonish and ultimately patronizing performance as a Mexican deputy.)

These two pictures were eventually followed by a corrective of a kind, Clint Eastwood's *Unforgiven* (1992), which has been described as "the last great Western." Well, it's probably the last try to create a real Western, I'll say that. But *Unforgiven* is spoiled by its own form of self-consciousness: its self-advertisement as a moral reconsideration of the role of violence in previous Eastwood films, hence its forced attempt to de-romanticize Western gunfighting. This movie is also spoiled by its treatment of the oppressed lot of women, the loneliness of un(in)tended children, and adult illiteracy in a desperate bid to inject some social significance, or thematic heft (which includes a down-on-his-luck black cowboy, Morgan Freeman, in a co-starring role opposite Eastwood), into a tired genre.

Was there ever any hope for the future of the Western, once it had begun to parody itself? Yes, some hope could once be found in a phenomenon that paralleled revisionism and which might be termed the cross-fertilization of genres. This cross-fertilizing was first demonstrated in John Sturges's *The Magnificent Seven* (1960), a version of Akira Kurosawa's *The Seven Samurai* (1954) set in the American West. (Kurosawa himself had been inspired by John Ford's Westerns.) In both films, seven hardened warriors (gunmen in Sturges's adaptation) fallen on hard times are driven to risk their lives, at first for a price and then increasingly out of a sense of honor, to defend the inhabitants of a small rural village from plundering by bandits. But *The Magnificent Seven*, unlike its superior artistic source, was a huge popular success and sparked an international trend toward *samurai* imitations that ultimately produced the "spaghetti Western"—violent, fateful films of the American West starring American actors which were shot in Italy or Yugoslavia by Italian moviemakers.

The master craftsman of the spaghetti Western was Sergio Leone, whose *Fistful of Dollars* (starring Clint Eastwood)—a direct, almost scene-by-scene and sometimes even shot-by-shot copy of Kurosawa's *Yojimbo* (1961), itself reputedly a version of Budd Boetticher's *Buchanan Rides Alone* (1958)—started the cycle in 1964. The films of Leone (who followed up his first hit with *For a Few Dollars More* [1965] and *The Good, the Bad, and the Ugly* [1966]) and his many Italian imitators tended to be stylish (featuring dynamic montage), musically innovative (with scores by Ennio Morricone), and excessively bloody, graphically depicting for the first time on screen the impact *and* exit wounds produced by bullets. Perhaps chiefly for their extreme violence, the spaghetti Westerns were enormously successful in the United States and produced a number of American-made imitations (for instance, Ted Post's gratuitously brutal *Hang 'Em High* [1968], also starring Clint Eastwood).

Spaghetti westerns also played a major role in conditioning American audiences to accept the new levels of violence that were to emerge toward the end of the sixties not only in Peckinpah's apocalyptic *Wild Bunch*, but also in the 1967 gangster film *Bonnie and Clyde*. (*Bonnie and Clyde* was directed by Arthur Penn, who also made *Little Big Man* as well as the earlier, "adult" Western *The Left-Handed Gun* [1958], a re-telling of the Billy-the-Kid legend notable for its portrayal of the outlaw as a psychologically troubled, misunderstood youth.) But Leone himself finally resorted to parody, rather than revitalization, of all the mythic-cum-romantic themes of the traditional American Western in *Once Upon a Time in the West* (1968), even if his cross-fertilizing tendency continued into the 1970s with *Red Sun* (1971), which co-starred Charles Bronson (once voted the world's most popular star) and Toshiro Mifune, Japan's leading male actor at the time and himself the star of several *samurai* movies (including *The Seven Samurai*).

During this decade, such international exchange continued apace with films like *The Stranger and the Gunfighter* (1974)—a joint Italian-Spanish production made in Hong Kong and starring Lee Van Cleef, veteran of countless cowboy movies, as well as Lo Lieh, a king of the Kung-fu spectacular—and *Breakheart Pass* (1975), another Charles Bronson movie that itself is an instance of generic swapping: this time through a reworking of Agatha Christie's detective fiction *Murder on the Orient Express* (1934) in the form of a Western. The swapping, or the exchange, even continued into the 1980s when the Australian Bruce Beresford (more on Australia shortly) went to southwest Texas to shoot *Tender Mercies* (1983), which was about a down-on-his-heels country-and-western singer named Mac Sledge, or a Westerner with a guitar instead of a gun.

Alas, the hope that once spurred the cross-fertilization of the Western is itself by now long since dead. But the spirit that informs the genre, along with its legendary characters, its myths, its values, and its historical associations, is far from dead, though that spirit often turns up in unexpected forms and in previously unvisited places. (This was true, as well, of the Western's stage equivalent a hundred years ago or so, when Puccini converted a corny American melodrama into the opera *La Fanciulla del West* [*The Girl of the Golden West*, 1910]). It reappeared not so long ago in three films, two in unexpected forms and one in a place that has not quite been unvisited but is hardly worn.

The first is *Down in the Valley* (2005), which uses its unexpected form to sobering intent. It depicts the effect that a film genre can have on a person's mind, and thus also reveals the mental hunger that had been nourished by this movie model. A previous instance in another genre is Travis Bickle in *Taxi Driver* (1976): a forlorn man who needs to behave like a movie tough guy, a kind of urban vigilante, in order to flesh out his puny life. In *Down in the Valley*, as its geographically accurate yet mythically resonant title suggests, the self-dramatization is Western.

A young man named Harlan Carruthers arrives in Los Angeles from South Dakota in full cowboy persona, with Gary Cooper courtesy and chivalry, a lasso, and two Colt revolvers. He has no ambition to work in films (any more than Travis had, even though some of Harlan's soliloquies—performed solo in his room, like Travis's in *Taxi Driver*—suggest that he is rehearsing a part). Apparently, Harlan just wants to play his movie role in real life, in the area that spawned so many Westerns. Later he accidentally encounters the filming of a Western, but even though he is in Hollywood, he never wants to fulfill his fantasy on screen—he just wants to live it.

Eventually, Harlan gallantly throws over his bread-and-butter job at a filling station to go to the beach with a pretty adolescent girl

Down in the Valley, dir. David Jacobson, 2005

named Tobe, and he wears his Stetson hat the whole time. His gentle, strong-man behavior attracts the girl, and a torrid affair ensues. Her father—a policeman—is displeased, though Harlan fascinates Tobe's kid brother. The ins and outs of the plot turns that follow, accordingly, are not hard to follow. They abut on two matters: on the one hand, there is Harlan's imitation Westernizing, including some horseback sequences, all of which entrances Tobe (and her brother); on the other hand, there are the father's objections, increasingly futile. Tobe's attraction to the fantasist is a mirror image of Harlan's own need for fantasy, and is a testament as well to the power of the Western in the cultural history of the United States.

The story of *Down in the Valley* winds along until, inevitably, shootouts arrive: fantasy, in this case (again, as in the case of *Taxi Driver*), leads to fatalities. Yet, looked at with a smidgen of rationality, this film doesn't make any sense. (And there are unexplained details, such as where Harlan's expensive saddle came from.) But since it's about a young man whose life doesn't make any sense, rationality is probably not the right criterion in this instance. Mythology *is*, and Harlan Carruthers is a dream-intoxicated being (brought to life here by the redoubtable Edward Norton) who believes in everything he says, no matter how silly or dangerous it sounds, and despite the fact that at the finish he is only a case who has met a case's end.

What he suggests, en route, or what his author-director David Jacobson meant him to suggest, is that the absence of genuine Westerns on screen has not wiped them out. They survive in the world's mind. They persist because we still have a craving for them—for the spectacle of their action, the romance of their quest, and the nobility of the Westerner himself.

Australia is not a place previously unvisited by such nobility, quest, or spectacle, yet it is still so novel a locale that an Australian Western has an odd effect. It reminds us of what should be obvious similarities between that country and the United States: huge space in the west, for example; an indigenous population that was treated roughly by invading whites; and invading whites who themselves were fleeing rough treatment of a kind in their own native land. The Australian film I'd like to consider, *The Proposition* (2005), is set in the late nineteenth century, so a "captain of lawmen" can still have an ambition we have often heard voiced by Western lawmen in American movies: to civilize the wilderness, along with its savages. Moreover, even though much of this captain's action is conducted against natives, he has an Aborigine scout at his beck, just as U.S. regiments in the Old West had Indian scouts.

The screenwriter of *The Proposition* was Nick Cave, who here remembers some of his country's history and at the same time lets it remind him of Sam Peckinpah, whose unique—or uniquely violent—contribution to the Western is adopted by Cave with only limited success. The reason is that, a good deal of the time, he simply wallows in the fact that a Western movie licenses violence, whereas Peckinpah, no matter how violent his films became, always kept in mind the rationale behind it. The very first scene, for instance, plunges us into a whirlpool of killing led by the captain and his men against outlaws, and it is exploited from every angle, for every possible ferocity, by the director, John Hillcoat, and his cinematographer, Benoît Delhomme.

When the fight is finished, with the outlaws defeated, the captain offers the captive outlaw Charlie Burns a proposition. Charlie's brother Arthur has escaped; but if Charlie will kill Arthur by Christmas, the captain will spare their other brother, Mikey, who is a prisoner and will otherwise be hanged. Hence the proposition of the film's title and the presupposition for the action, violent or otherwise, that will follow. As story ideas go, it's not entirely original—you can find a variation on it in Westerns where a former outlaw, now a sheriff, must kill a brother, or a friend, who is still an outlaw. But that's not the problem so much as the fact that the film never comes to any point or purpose. It's hollow, finally, and this despite the firm performances by Ray Winstone as the captain and Guy Pearce as Charlie Burns, despite the miraculous John Hurt in an eccentric role that was put in just for spice (though such an addition should have immediately signaled the aesthetic dubiousness of the whole enterprise).

Some might argue that *The Proposition*'s aim was to show the civilizing of the outback, or to depict the cruel treatment of the Aborigines (and, apart from the Burns-brothers plot, there is plenty of that). But these are not the film's motives, just the excuses for its existence, for its wallowing in violence and for its exploitation of

The Proposition, dir. John Hillcoat, 2005

the visual paradox that Westerns allow. To wit: almost all the riding and fighting and rumination take place against settings of extraordinary beauty, the setting sun being one of Hillcoat and Delhomme's chief assets. A scene near the end and the final scene consist of two of the Burns brothers seated outdoors, their backs toward us, contemplating action as they watch the sun set. The problem with such scenes, of course—especially when the filmmakers over-rely on them—is that, unlike the characters, we start to "goggle" more than "contemplate"; and that the setting thereby becomes less of a character or force in the narrative than just another pretty picture gratuitously juxtaposed against the ugly or thrilling or suspenseful one that is the film's action.

The visual paradox that Westerns allow is again on display in *Brokeback Mountain* (2005), where it works a little better than it did in *The Proposition*. The landscape in which most of the film takes place is majestic, thrilling (ostensibly Wyoming, but actually the Canadian Rockies), and the cinematographer (Rodrigo Prieto) presents the scenic marvels of this place to us as if they were resplendent gifts. But not gratuitous ones, for here the interweaving of the grand landscape with the narrative has a peculiarly synesthetic effect, absent from *The Proposition*. This is because *Brokeback Mountain*'s story is intimate—indeed, it's a Western romance—and the poignant lyricism of the movie's romantic theme winds almost musically through a cosmos otherwise shaped by only grand chords.

Oddly enough, *Brokeback Mountain* was directed by a Chinese, Ang Lee, a filmmaker nevertheless at home in the West as well as the East (born in Taiwan, he received both his undergraduate and his graduate education in the United States), as his major credits before this picture make clear: *The Wedding Banquet* (1993), *Eat Drink Man Woman* (1994), *Sense and Sensibility* (1995), *The Ice Storm* (1997), *Ride with the Devil* (1999), and *Crouching Tiger, Hidden Dragon* (2000). *The Ice Storm* and *Ride with the Devil* were each ultra-American pictures, the one about Connecticut suburbanites, the other about the Civil War. Despite their American ease, their societal comprehension, if you will, I didn't care for either film; and I took away the feeling, especially after seeing the martial-arts extravaganza *Crouching Tiger, Hidden Dragon* (not to speak of his comic-book adaptation of *Hulk* [2003]), that Lee was an industry gun-for-hire as opposed to an independent *auteur* with a vision. I still feel this way, but that won't keep me from saying that, precisely because of his remove from the subject at hand, as an artist, a Taiwanese, and a man, Ang Lee was the right choice to direct *Brokeback Mountain*.

The screenplay by Larry McMurtry and Diana Ossana, based on (and faithful to) a 1997 short story by Annie Proulx, is about two cowboys who become lovers. In 1963 in Wyoming, two young ranch hands named Ennis Del Mar and Jack Twist are hired to spend the summer tending a thousand sheep up on Brokeback Mountain. (Shepherds though the men are, through much of the film they call each other "cowboy," and we do see them later with cattle.) Ennis and Jack had not known each other previously, and they don't spend a lot of time together now. Ennis sleeps somewhere off near the sheep, and Jack bunks away from them in a pup tent. One inclement night, however, they share the tent after sharing a bottle of whiskey. There has not been the slightest hint of physical attraction between the two men up to this point, nor is there now as they bed down together. Nonetheless, during the night, they find themselves—the phrase is apt—having sex.

Brokeback Mountain, dir. Ang Lee, 2005

In the morning Jack and Ennis are their customary laconic selves as they go about their jobs, but they are both marked for life—by love. That is, on this morning after their first sexual experience, they virtually decide they *must* be in love. They specify to each other that they are not "queer," so the condition that allows them to be themselves without shame is to believe that they are in love. And they are, as truly as two people can be, yet they are grateful for it because this spiritual union licenses them to continue their beddings, and helps to justify each man to himself. Over the remainder of the summer, Jack and Ennis's sexual and emotional relationship deepens, although they part ways at the end of their job. Later on, through the years—up to 1983—they continue to meet as often as they can, despite the fact that in time both men marry and father children.

The film traces the men's torment when separated, their happiness at reunions, and their near-pride in their private selves: in short, the delicacy and pain and almost unbearable joy experienced by the two. Their marriages themselves are not so totally blissful—

Ennis's wife, for example, has seen the two men kissing—but they seem to accept marital trouble as part of the price they have to pay for their secret truth. Jack does broach the subject of creating a life together on a small farm, especially after Ennis's wife divorces him, but Ennis refuses to move away from his two daughters and fears that such an arrangement can only end in tragedy (as it did for a gay couple who were tortured and murdered in the town where he grew up). So, unable to be open about their relationship, Jack and Ennis settle, after a bitter quarrel-become-desperate embrace, for their infrequent meetings (separated not just by months but sometimes by several years) on camping trips in the mountains.

Alas, their story does not finish as they might have wished: it couldn't, given the world in which they live. But their relationship from beginning to end has a texture so finespun that it seems, more than the story itself, the purpose for which the film was made. *Brokeback Mountain* does not contain the slightest suggestion, by contrast, that its purpose is to chronicle a psychological case or a social problem. And that, as an aspiring work of art, is *its* problem, for, on the evidence of both Proulx's story and Lee's film, Jack and Ennis, in addition to being adulterers, are *bisexuals*—not homosexuals. (Just one of the pieces of bisexual evidence: after his divorce, instead of declaring his total "availability" to Jack, Ennis begins dating an attractive waitress he has met at a diner he frequents, though Ennis continues to see Jack as well.)

The film, like the short story, completely avoids this issue—that monogamous marriage, be it of the heterosexual or homosexual kind, presumes faithfulness or at least openness (not cheating as we see Ennis and Jack engage in it), and it cannot tolerate bisexuality (for a bisexual marriage would necessarily involve at least three partners!). The movie chooses instead coyly to treasure two human beings who, as it sees them, and as unlikely as we may have thought it for these two men, find themselves fixed in a discomfiting yet thorough passion that the filmmakers (and Annie Proulx) thoroughly affirm. Jack and Ennis may inhabit a world—the world of the Western—which vaunts macho masculinity and even loneness or isolation (not to mention the Westerner's personal integrity as expressed in his code of honor); nonetheless, they seem secretly fortified by their mutual fate instead of self-sacrificially rejecting it or openly questioning it.

Brokeback Mountain's coyness in this matter seems designed to pander to the gay community, to which (among other "communities") its producers successfully marketed the film as a tragic, albeit same-sex, love story, as opposed to a social-problem picture about the difficulty of living an openly bisexual life in a society that venerates the institution of marriage as well as the pureness or absoluteness of sexual categories—not to speak of the difficulty of surviving in a West-world that prides itself on the bashing of anyone who even appears to be gay. (The poster for *Brokeback Mountain*, incidentally, was inspired by that of James Cameron's *Titanic* [1997], which the producers chose as a model after looking at the posters of what they considered to be the fifty most romantic movies ever made.) And a neat trick this was on the part of the film's marketing team, for neither *Brokeback Mountain*'s two leading actors, nor its director, nor the author of the story on which it is based, nor its screenwriters are gay. Those actors are the late Heath Ledger, an Australian who for this picture mastered a Western accent and bearing, and who gave Ennis a solidity through which his new experience shivers like a crack through a rock; and Jake Gyllenhaal, who creates in Jack a man of dogged sensitivity, one who has not previously lived by emotional finesse but now finds himself capable of it and will not relinquish it.

Ang Lee was the right choice to direct Ledger and Gyllenhaal, and to film the screenplay as written (not as I wish it had been written, by an *auteur* or writer-director), not only because he's neither from the Western hemisphere nor a Western American and hence has no "investment" either in traditional or non-traditional Western conceptions of masculinity. Lee was also the right choice because he has shown himself in the past to be a consummately tasteful, acutely sensitive director of actors: witness, for one, Emma Thompson's performance as Elinor Dashwood in *Sense and Sensibility*, which is buttressed by her comments about Lee's directing in the diary she kept during filming (published by Newmarket in 2002).

Moreover, given that the film of *Brokeback Mountain* had to have handsome young heterosexual stars to insure its commercial success outside the gay market, it also had to have someone directing them who was sensitive to their needs as actors; to the general current of emotional need that floods around all men and women (but especially two men as isolated as these shepherds are for an entire season on Brokeback Mountain), and which looks for reification, for person and place, in one or another sort of gender relationship that may or may not include sex; and the film needed someone sensitive to the needs of the overarching narrative itself. This movie adaptation further required someone who knows, as the characters of Ennis and Jack do and as does any real-life bisexual, that the line between acting "straight" and playing "gay"—especially for a cowboy-type who happens to fall in love with another man—is very thin indeed. That someone, again, was Ang Lee. (See *The Wedding Banquet* for additional evidence.)

Well, so now we have a gay or—my preferred term in this instance—a bisexual Western (Western in spirit, anyway) on our hands, trying in the twenty-first century to deal with some of the themes of the traditional American Western: rugged individualism, individual freedom, and self-reliance versus family values, individual restriction or constraint, and family-dependence; physical allegiance to nature, wilderness, and the environment versus moral commitment to the community, society, and civilization. But even a "domestic" Western like *Brokeback Mountain* is not as new as it seems, save for its homoerotic wrinkle. In 1971, for example, Peter Fonda made (and starred in) *The Hired Hand*, in which a drifter, who had been roaming from town to town with his close friend and fellow wanderer, decides to make amends to the wife and daughter he abandoned seven years before by returning to them—offering to do penance by working on the family farmstead as a hired hand. (Fonda's sister, Jane, went so far as to call *The Hired Hand* "the first feminist Western.")

But *The Hired Hand* was still a real Western, replete with Western violence when the Fonda character ultimately has to choose between responsibility to his blood relatives and the obligation to aid his friend-in-need. *Brokeback Mountain* is an imitation of the genre, *Down in the Valley* an imitation-of-an-imitation, and *The Proposition* a bloody anachronism. The Western is dead. Its ghost still haunts us. Long live the West of our imaginations.

11

Odd Couples, or Unelected Affinities

What a relief: a niche of film reticence amid filmic uproar. All around us swirls a steady stream of gargantuan movies, Styrofoam epics with megatons of special effects, gleefully inane adolescent pictures, horror films that are really horrible, children's films that are more childish than childlike. We do not actually have to see these movies (I see as few as possible) in order to feel pounded by them. But every once in a while a few cinematic refuges come along, and those discussed here are uniquely related and unique—even the British one (*Enduring Love*) that, on its surface, depends on the conventions of the stalker-thriller genre.

Kitchen Stories **(2003).** The first of these films, *Kitchen Stories* from Scandinavia, has more than two characters, but in effect it is a two-man story. Written (with Jörgen Bergmark) and directed by Bent Hamer—a Norwegian who received his film education in Stockholm and, as of 2010, had made six features (*Kitchen Stories* is his third) in addition to a number of shorts and documentaries—this movie takes place for the most part in an isolated farmhouse in Norway in the dead of winter. That sounds grim, and in a visual way it certainly is grim, as Philip Øgaard's cinematography takes full advantage of the snowy landscapes and uncongenial interiors with their reduced palette of color. But the base of *Kitchen Stories* is comedy, for it is in some measure a wryly humorous satire on scientism. (And the film's comedy is aptly introduced by color: the look of the picture is so pallid at the start that we could think we were in a world of black and white, until there suddenly appears a tractor painted fire-engine red. This jolt itself is funny.)

In Sweden in the 1950s, a group of sociologists is studying traffic patterns in kitchens. Their latest study, which took some years, discovered that in a single year the average Swedish housewife, in her own kitchen, walks enough to take her all the way to the Congo. The sociologists' trade joke is that they hope to reduce her trek so that it will take her only to northern Italy. Now they are about to observe the traffic patterns of single males in the kitchens of Norway. Clearly the arbitrary sacredness of social studies, which are sometimes more heavy than helpful, is being gently kidded here. But this is merely where *Kitchen Stories* begins.

One of the observers, a middle-aged man named Folke Nilsson, is sent to Landstad in Norway to study a bachelor farmer named Isak Bjørvik. This farmer, about Folke's age but perhaps older, had previously agreed to the study because he was promised a horse as advanced payment—an animal that turned out to be a painted, arts-and-crafts item, not the real horse Isak needs to replace his sick (and ultimately euthanized) one. So it takes some days before the disappointed bachelor responds to the knocking on his door. (Folke lives outside the house in a trailer he had brought.) At last the taciturn Isak admits the persistent scientist. Neither of these two is colorful—that's something we have already deduced. What will hold us, as day after day of the study slowly goes by, is the resident— and irreducible—humanity in each man.

Conversation here between subject and observer is understandably meant to be sparse, even as their space is constricted (a constriction emphasized by the editing); but in this instance the conversation is ultra-sparse: Folke is quiet by professional discipline, Isak through idiosyncratic temperament. Essentially, all that Folke does is sit on a high chair in a corner of the farmhouse kitchen— something like a tennis referee's perch—and make notes on, as well as diagrams of, Isak's movements around the room. (These movements themselves are not particularly busy, since Isak's meals are meager—by choice, one feels—and therefore do not require much preparation. Folke, in his trailer, eats better, especially since an old aunt sends him packets of food—and drink—by mail.) Little by little, however, the "scientific" distance between the two men narrows, much to the dismay of Folke's supervisor Mr. Malmberg, who calls occasionally and must then report back to *his* supervisor, Mr. Ljungberg.

Kitchen Stories, dir. Bent Hamer, 2003

In sum, Folke and Isak become friendlier—but without any of the syrup (musical or otherwise) that usually accompanies such transitions. It is human curiosity, not welling affection, which brings the two men so close that, for instance, Isak can admit that he drilled a hole in the floor of his bedroom above so that he could observe the observer in the kitchen. Then, when Folke gets sick and must retire to his trailer, Isak does him the courtesy of tracing his own kitchen movements in Folke's notebook. In time, Mr. Malmberg becomes so dissatisfied with his employee's conduct that he fires him. This leads to an unexpected result, yet one that grows logically out of everything we have seen: Isak dies suddenly (several times he has said, almost as if he were grateful for it, that he believes the date of one's death is always predetermined) and, as spring returns, Folke takes his place not only at the farm but also in the sole human relationship Isak seems to have had prior to Folke's arrival: with a friend named Grant, who himself owns a farm nearby and who earlier had been jealous of Isak's relationship with Folke.

Hamer may begin *Kitchen Studies*, then, by lightly mocking the seriousness with which the field of social studies takes itself. But he is obviously also interested in the nature of his locale: there is plenty of nationalistic teasing between Swedes and Norwegians, for example (each of whom seems to speak or at least understand the other's cognate language, by the way), and some of it goes beyond teasing. At one point, Isak soberly notes that, not unlike social scientists, the Swedes were neutral observers during World War II, whereas a Norwegian like Grant was placed in a concentration camp for his resistance to the Nazi occupation of his homeland (an occupation indirectly abetted by the collaborationist Finns, about whom neither the Norwegians nor the Swedes in this film have anything good to say). In that camp, Grant learned to repair—of all things—dolls, and the fact that during the film he uses his own hair for one such repair gruesomely suggests that during the war he may have "borrowed" hair, clothing, and the like from his fellow prisoners (dead or alive) for similar patching.

The subject of incarceration or isolation itself is not unrelated to one of Hamer's concerns in *Kitchen Stories*, which is with what happens to two human beings in the pseudo-laboratory situation that the film proposes (a situation that is bizarre, to be sure, but apparently not so far from the realm of possibility). Part of the theme is our growing awareness of what it has been like for these two men to be alone, to have spent their adult lives, up to this point, more or less exclusively in the prison-houses of their own minds. We *see* that Isak is solo, of course, but only when conversation between the two finally comes does Folke reveal that, except for his food-supplying aunt, he too is all by himself.

Thus, beneath the laconic relationship between these men, even after it becomes a bit more talkative, is the tenet that, especially in an odd situation like this one, two can make a multitude. And one man, limited though he may be to a single place and sporadic human contact, can trace the arc of human existence. (This aspect of *Kitchen Stories* made me think of Samuel Beckett, another author whose grimness is texturally comic, even though Folke and Isak have little of the philosophical or metaphysical dimension to be found in the pair in *Waiting for Godot* and *Endgame*, or in the lone protagonist of *Krapp's Last Tape*.)

Following from all of the above, I wondered about the impulse behind the making of *Kitchen Stories*. Hundreds of films are made around the world every year that cannot hope for mass response, that exist chiefly because their creators willed them into being. *Kitchen Stories* is one of them. It attempts no broad appeal; it has wit, but that wit is dry; it has depth, but such depth relies on the viewer's desire to plumb it. The juxtaposition of the two males may—probably will—serve to suggest the awakening of latent homosexuality in two lonely men, but so far as we can see, Folke and Isak are never aware of this incursion. (The two central actors, Joachim Calmeyer as Isak and Tomas Norström as Folke, are prime instances of how to resist such a psychosexual temptation without sacrificing interest—for interesting they both are without being in the least charismatic.) Bent Hamer, who (in his mid-forties when he made *Kitchen Stories*) presumably knows as much about such matters as we do, apparently wanted to make his movie without reference to or motivation in sex—possibly because he knew that, if he did so, for some viewers this would become its only subject.

Son Frère (2003). The Frenchman Patrice Chéreau (born 1944) directs plays (since 1964) as well as films (since 1974) in a double career that, at least in shape and intent, is comparable to the late Ingmar Bergman's. (Indeed, Chéreau also directs for opera and television—even having produced the operas *Wozzeck* and *Lulu* for TV—and he also acts from time to time.) It seems fair to conclude that, because his theater dossier includes so many classics—*Phaedra*, *Peer Gynt*, and *Hamlet* among them—the dramatic and cinematic arts function symbiotically for him, as they did for Bergman: in a kind of mutually enriching balance. Like Bergman, Chéreau appears to use film to do what he cannot do in the theater—work in close, with a physical intimacy that the stage doesn't comparably permit. In fact, his previous film was called *Intimacy* (2001), during which the camera was virtually in bed with a man and a woman so as to capture the heat of sex, in the act.

But, as of 2003, the three films of Chéreau's ten features that had come to the United States—among them the fairly widely distributed *Queen Margot* (1994)—were a long way from Bergmanesque quality. For this reason it is pleasant to report that *Son Frère* (*His*

Son Frère, dir. Patrice Chéreau, 2003

Brother) is a real achievement: delicate, perceptive, somewhat muted or low-key but nonetheless strong. (So much so that I eagerly look forward to his next picture, *Trois Soirées*.) The screenplay, adapted by Chéreau and Anne-Louise Trividic from a 2001 novel of the same title by Philippe Besson, deals with two brothers, both around thirty, whose lives have diverged, especially because the slightly younger one, Luc, is gay. Events push them together when Thomas, the elder, contracts a rare and incurable blood disorder — indeed, one from which he can die at any time, as the result of a hemorrhage.

Although Thomas has a devoted girlfriend, the intensity of his trouble, and of his fright, makes him seek his brother's help, as caregiver — with Luc's very estrangement as well as his concern to keep him company. (Thomas may foresee that his girl's devotion will wane and they will split, just as do Luc and his boyfriend.) The film proceeds to move in and out of a Paris hospital (where Thomas's doctor is reminiscent of the psychiatrist in Bergman's *Persona* [1966]), the brothers' apartments, and the coast of Brittany near the family home, where the landscape and ocean view prompt memories of boyhood fun together with friction. But the real setting of *Son Frère* is Thomas's illness as it runs its fatal course from winter to summer.

Thomas's blood disease thus becomes the ambience in which the two men find out more about each other and, of course, about themselves. Glimmering outside this dark ambience is a suggestion that the illness is a clarifier. It is not a blessing in disguise, not a metaphor for something else, but part of the traversal of life that affects the ill person and those who care. Particularly in this case, where the illness is terminal and where roles are reversed, as it were. I mean that given the fact of Luc's homosexuality, you would expect him to be fatally afflicted with AIDS (like many other gay men his age)—not his straight brother to be struck down by a blood disorder that seems to come out of nowhere. (Surely Philippe Besson and his adaptors are playing on this conventional expectation.) Indeed, Thomas and Luc's father remarks on this very subject during a visit to the hospital, when he says that Luc is the one who should have become so sick because he would find it easier to cope—or does he mean easier to explain, given his younger son's sexual preference and the chief way in which AIDS has been spread?

Whatever the father means, dialogue is less a part of *Son Frère* than silence, gesture, and sound (crashing waves, clanking siderails on the hospital bed). And does Chéreau ever take his time during this picture's ninety-five minutes! Within the expected temporal frame of a film (and an hour-and-a-half is about right), the flow of minutes to which we are accustomed, he lingers, he observes, he absorbs, he rests for the duration of a mood. The most obvious instance of this—all of this—occurs in the hospital scene where Thomas is being prepared for surgery by two nurses. He lies naked on his bed, and gently, amiably, they shave his armpits, his chest, his pubic area. Chéreau's purpose is not terror or indignity here (or in the scenes that show blotches, blood, sweat, scars, stained sheets, decaying flesh, and protruding bones). Rather, he wants to dramatize the idea that, inside this shaveable torso, this mere thing, is the nexus of sensibilities, radiated and received, that transforms an objectified person into a complex human being. Chéreau's patience during what otherwise would be a perfunctory scene (easily and smoothly reduced in length through editing) thus transforms its commonplace action into a small but moving epiphany.

As the brothers, Bruno Todeschini (who reportedly lost twenty-six pounds to play the part of Thomas) and Eric Caravaca (Luc) evoke perfectly the sense not that they have begun and are fulfilling a film, as two separate characters, but that they have joined these two men at this particular stage in their long relationship—the kind of relationship that is crucial to, but all too often missing from, a work with so late a point of attack. Their deepening knowledge of their disparate but connected (and connected now even more in the sense that Luc has given up his job to be with his brother) private lives is the quintessence of *Son Frère*, and it itself is only deepened by the editor François Gédigier's relentless use of close-ups.

The cinematographer Eric Gautier gives an all too apposite pale, sepia-toned quality to those and other shots, even as Marianne Faithful occasionally sings snatches of a soulful song called "Sleep" on the soundtrack—the only music used in a film whose delicate, unsentimental, almost uninflected portrait of human compassion, mortal agony, and restored brotherhood *je n'oublierai jamais. Son Frère*, indeed. *Lequel des deux est-ce?* That is, which, or whose, brother?

Gabrielle (2005). Patrice Chéreau's *Trois Soirées* finally arrived in the United States, re-titled *Gabrielle* and made with the same team that created *Son Frère*. *Gabrielle* was adapted for the screen by Chéreau and Anne-Louise Trividic from a story by Joseph Conrad titled "The Return." First, some background on that story.

In 1897, Conrad, who had written three novels that dealt with Asia and the sea, decided to write a story quite different in setting and tone—"a London story," he called it. "The Return" was indeed drastically different from Conrad's previous work: it concerned a wealthy London couple and their marital crisis. The material had some relation to what English dramatists—Arthur Pinero and Henry Arthur Jones, for instance—were trying to do at the time, possibly influenced by Ibsen: they were looking at marriage with new candor and understanding, rather than with the conventional, formal criteria of the past.

Conrad's adaptors have changed the scene to Paris but have remained in the late Victorian era, and though they have added material, they have concentrated on the quintessence of the couple's lives that Conrad captures so keenly:

They skimmed over the surface of life hand in hand, in a pure and frosty atmosphere—like two skillful skaters cutting figures on thick ice for the admiration of the beholders, and disdainfully ignoring the hidden stream, the stream restless and dark; the stream of life, profound and unfrozen.

Conrad's story and this film deal with a moment when that stream is no longer hidden.

The husband, Jean Hervey, rich and generally content with his judgment and aplomb, not especially interested in emotions, has been married for ten years. (Conrad says five years: perhaps the film doubles the span to fit the two leading actors.) One late afternoon he returns from work to the mansion, prodigally staffed with servants, where he lives with his wife, Gabrielle. The screenplay here adds a sequence about the previous Thursday evening, one of the Thursdays when the Herveys entertain with large formal dinners. This flashback is like a large helping of the formalities—the ice skating—that constitute their lives.

When Jean gets home this afternoon, Gabrielle is not there. Upstairs he discovers a letter that she has left for him; he reads it and learns that Gabrielle has left him for another man. Then comes the Conrad touch: after Jean has gone through some spasms of shock, Gabrielle returns. As the title has foretold, this is the crux of the story. She admits an affair with the other man. She had left today to live with him, but she cannot go through with it; she calls the letter a mistake. The long scene that follows between Gabrielle and Jean is the heart of Conrad's story and this film.

Love, what that word can mean, in all its iridescent gleamings; self, in all its proud and petty aspects; marriage and the various ways in which one can comprehend it—all are elements in this fascinating, painful scene. It can best be summarized by saying that these two people move here through a drama that is larger than they would have expected themselves to be capable of, a drama that shakes their very beings. We can infer that Gabrielle was the first to explore the stream beneath the ice and that her action has now compelled Jean, too, to take the plunge. Late in the film (and story) comes a line that discloses much of their relationship before the plunge: of how they have been living and why she attempted to change. Gabrielle had wanted, she thought, a more fully charged life, but on her way to the other man, she had realized that such a life would be too demanding. When Jean at last declares his love, Gabrielle says, "If I had believed you loved me . . . I would never have come back."

So much of this adaptation is engrossing that the script's additions are jarring—Jean's near rape of Gabrielle on a stairway, her disrobing in their bedroom so that sex may reunite them. (The sex doesn't happen.) Moreover, after their intent at the start to keep their troubles from the servants and others, they quarrel publicly the next evening—one of their Thursdays (and the third "evening" in the film's original title, *Three Evenings*). These scripted interpolations, though they can just possibly be mined out of Conrad, still smack of moviemaking. Cinematically, too, there is a puzzle. Chéreau moves recurrently through three visual modes: black and white, color, and a sort of blue overlay. (All are superbly handled by Eric Gautier's camera.) The blue shading first occurs just after Jean reads the letter. We think that Chéreau is tinting the shot to fit the mood, but this pattern is quickly disturbed. And the result is that we never quite understand why he is using any one of the three modes at any particular moment.

But, aside from these inexplicable color variations, Chéreau's directing is fine, as it was in *Son Frère*. He is a master of two kinds of movement: he moves his camera with an assurance and relevance that are in themselves exciting; and, uncommonly for a film director (but not for a man of the theater), he moves his actors within any shot like a discerning choreographer. Crowning all this, he has drawn exceptional performances from his two principals, Isabelle Huppert and Pascal Greggory.

Huppert is not by usual disposition an emotional actress. Much of her best work has seemed to rely on the camera to find and convey what is deep within her (as in *The Judge and the Assassin* [1976]), and when this doesn't succeed (in *Madame Bovary* [1991], for example), the effect verges on stolidity that is out of place. She is sexy, of course, but aloof, and only occasionally does she cut loose (see *The Piano Teacher* [2001]). In this latest picture, Huppert gives Gabrielle an extremity of emotion that is so extreme, she has to find her feelings as she goes—which makes them all the more affecting.

Gabrielle, dir. Patrice Chéreau, 2005

Greggory, by contrast, creates a Jean who metamorphoses. At the start he is somewhat smug, yet insidiously enviable, and as the film progresses he works changes on this initial persona which amount in the end to a sensual pilgrim's progress. Accompanying Huppert and Greggory throughout is Fabio Vacchi's score: all of it chamber music that, appositely, lurks tactfully beneath the chamber drama.

Enduring Love **(2004).** Quietly, almost politely, English filmmakers over the past twenty to thirty years have been developing a sub-genre in social heterodoxy. These films do not violate convention; they completely ignore it. Two instances: Stephen Poliakoff's *Close My Eyes* (1991), about a man who accepts his wife's incestuous affair with her brother; and Anthony Harvey's *Richard's Things* (1980), about a widow who discovers that her lately deceased husband had a mistress, seeks out the mistress in curiosity, then eventually is seduced by her. Common characteristics of this sub-genre are acting that is spotless and directing that itself has a neatness about it, as if the filmmaker wanted to emphasize the bizarreness of his story by presenting it in an especially acceptable format or context.

Roger Michell's *The Mother* (2003, with a script by Hanif Kureishi) certainly fit into this sub-genre, since it concentrated on the affair between a recently widowed grandmother, in her late sixties, and a man half her age—who also happens to be the boyfriend of her daughter. So, too, to some extent does Michell's latest picture, *Enduring Love*, fit the sub-genre beneath its stalker-cum-thriller trappings and horror-film score (by Jeremy Sams, in homage to Bernard Herrmann). This is because it shows—not only like *The Mother* and other British films of social heterodoxy, but also like the 1997 Ian McEwan novel of the same name from which *Enduring Love* is adapted (and like the rest of the Englishman McEwan's fiction)—how easily the shells that encase us all in normality can be cracked, and how the stripped or uncovered person turns out to be someone whom he or she would not have expected to discover inside.

In a previous screen adaptation of a McEwan novel, *The Comfort of Strangers* (1991), a seemingly blithe English couple visiting Venice meet a suave Venetian, and in the course of time the young, not-yet-married pair find themselves shorn of their shells and considerably—nay, traumatically—transformed. Now, in *Enduring Love* (whose screenplay was written by the playwright Joe Penhall, even as the script for *The Comfort of Strangers* was done by Harold Pinter), the psychosexual process of the earlier McEwan novel-become-film, broadly speaking, is frighteningly repeated. The surprise here is not the quality of the scenario but the continued growth of Roger Michell as a director after a promising start with an adaptation of Jane Austen's *Persuasion* (1995), only to be followed by the froth of *Notting Hill* (1999) and the foolery of *Changing Lanes* (2002). Yes, now he's working from good material again; still, Michell directs with understanding, restraint, and just the right amount of punctuation to create a kind of analogue for McEwan's swift, spare, cool prose (as in his use of overhead shots to suggest vulnerability, fatalism, and remove).

Enduring Love begins with a pair of lovers, Joe Rose and Claire, a university lecturer and a sculptress, picnicking in the exquisite English countryside of Oxfordshire, just about to pop the cork of a champagne bottle—even as Joe may be about to pop the question of marriage. Then, as in much of McEwan's fiction, a most unlikely

Enduring Love, dir. Roger Michell, 2004

thing happens that is nonetheless possible, as this elegantly pastoral scene is interrupted by a dizzyingly kinetic event. A huge red, hot-air balloon plunges from the sky, throwing out the pilot as it bumps onto the ground yet leaving a boy in the basket as a gigantic gust of wind sends the balloon airborne again.

Joe had rushed to grab a rope to hold the balloon down and was joined by several male passersby. He and most of the men manage to let go of the wind-blown balloon while it's still low, but one of the men hangs on too long and is killed by his fall to earth. (Later we learn from this man's widow, in keeping with the general tone of the sub-genre of heterodoxy, not that she mourns him but that she suspects her late husband of having been involved in an affair at the time of his death.) Another of the rescuers then implores Joe to join him in a prayer for the dead (including the boy who dies, unseen, minutes later when the balloon crashes). A man of reason, a scientist and a secularist, Joe is not the prayerful type; still, he lets himself consent. Thus does this other man enter Joe's life, through a bizarre, random accident and the first of several instances of persuasion in the film.

The other man is Jed Parry, a Welshman who is lanky and long-haired and insidiously cajoling. We never learn what Jed actually does or how he supports his rather mangy existence, which is probably part of the point: *Joe* quickly becomes what he "does" and the spiritual or emotional support for Jed's being. Joe isn't much interested in the disheveled Jed at first, but the latter pursues him obsessively. A few days after the balloon incident, Jed phones Joe in his London flat, saying that he is just across the street in a park, and pleads to see his new acquaintance again. Out of some sort of compassion combined with curiosity, Joe goes down to meet him and, as in their subsequent meetings, Joe does nothing to encourage Jed, yet the Welshman keeps turning up, to the point of stalking him—in restaurants, bars, and bookstores, one day even appearing at a desk in the back of Joe's college classroom. In a slippery, reptilian way, he has begun to wind himself around Joe's life in the belief that God, through the "sign" of the balloon, meant him to do so.

Jed's persistence has an effect on Joe's relationship with Claire and, tangentially, on other friendships (including one with a happily married couple, invented for the film as foil figures, who have three grandchildren). At first, and at second and third, we wonder why Joe doesn't report the stalker to the police. But after a while we sense that though Joe never speaks a word of interest in the man, something about the almost rhapsodic Jed is engaging him—if only Jed's connection to the fatal balloon accident, over which Joe is racked with guilt, obsessively trying to analyze his role in or responsibility for it. So otherwise engaged is Joe that he withdraws into an alternative world, becoming increasingly hostile, temperamental, even paranoid.

Moreover, if the genially creepy, deeply entreating Jed simultaneously attracts and repels him, Joe starts having a similar effect on his colleagues, students, and loved ones. Claire, in particular, sees something in the man she loves and considered marrying that she realizes was merely latent before the hot-air balloon's (and Jed's) appearance: someone in fact terrified of love and smugly disengaged from emotion, an intellectual control-freak whose fundamental fear of real intimacy has been yanked into daylight, as it were, by the ropes of that same balloon. (Tellingly, Claire sculpts Joe's bust only when she has become as detached from—and aesthetically objective toward—him as he is from her.)

There's another latency as well, unsuspected by Claire. Early on *we* suspect that under Jed's verbiage and sinuosity there is a strain of the homoerotic, one matched by Joe, and that this is a part of the latter's attraction-repulsion relationship with the Welshman. In a sense, Joe realizes that he's being stalked by a detached, self-loving version of himself, and this realization both infatuates and infuriates him. Matters come to a head, at last, in a climactic scene that confirms our suspicion of the rage as well as the rapture. Jed stabs Claire so as to have Joe all to himself; Joe lets Jed lock lips with him and then stabs his *doppelgänger*; Jed survives the stabbing (as he must, one could say, if Joe himself is to persist in his present state), only to be committed to a psychiatric hospital; and Joe and Claire finish their picnic, complete with champagne and ring (but he doesn't propose this time, either).

This climax may stretch credibility for some, but hardly in comparison with so much other film violence—particularly of the kind found in the finale of *Fatal Attraction* (1987), itself based on a short story called "Diversion" (1979) by the British writer James Dearden. (McEwan's own ending—including a "happy" appendix in which, after splitting up, Joe and Claire get back together and adopt a child—was both quieter and more heterosexually conventional, in that Joe shoots Jed in the arm so as to keep him from knifing Claire.) After all, the whole point of Roger Michell's picture (which had McEwan's blessing, since he was its associate producer) is that the Joe of the opening has become someone else, or has become who he really is; and in so visual a form as film, we must *see* this—with all the phallic implications of the knifing of Jed—which we do. The college instructor, with a sympathetic lover and that clutch of wine-bibbing, intellectual friends who are the stock company of any English movie about academia, is visibly changed under the pressure applied by Jed—this catalytic stranger who keeps telling Joe how much he cares for him. (Hence the double meaning of the title: how love endures, as well as how one must sometimes endure love.)

Daniel Craig, who was the carpenter-lover of the sexagenarian woman in *The Mother*, plays Joe with a wired exasperation which convinces us that his repeated encounters with Jed are gradually cracking him open. (And Craig does this without the benefit of his first-person narration in the novel, without the benefit even of some of it translated into voice-over commentary, though Roger Michell does sometimes employ a Steadicam strapped to Joe's shoulder, different aperture speeds, and fish-eye lenses to give us this protagonist's subjective, increasingly harried view of the world.) Rhys Ifans comes naturally by his Welsh accent, which is used immediately in *Enduring Love* to place him apart; but he starts out with an even larger advantage, which understandably was less obvious in his role as Hugh Grant's roommate in *Notting Hill*, a romantic comedy. Namely, Ifans has a faintly repellent yet eerily intrusive quality about him—let's call it an intrinsic combination of the pathetic and the psychopathic—so that his performance of Jed begins with the effortless authenticity or believability that it requires.

Ifans and Craig are both helped by Harris Zambarloukos's cinematography, which captures an uncharacteristically sunny England (with coolly bright colors that favor the look of an upscale furniture showroom) as a counterpoint to the dark drama playing out between Jed and Joe. Neither actor is helped much, unfortunately, by Samantha Morton, who has a good deal to do as Claire—for all this character's quiet or reserve—but does none of it interestingly. Morton is merely an obedient actress: she does what the script and the director ask her to do without bringing something more—a color, a wrinkle, a perception—to the table. And, since she is the odd-woman out in *Enduring Love*—there wasn't really such an on-screen presence in either *Gabrielle*, *Son Frère*, or *Kitchen Stories*—"something more" was asked of her, if only to act as a counterpoise in the love triangle. Odd *couples*, indeed.

12

Serious Sex

The treatment of sex in most contemporary films is exploitative and unnecessary—isn't this true? Of course, you can't really even think about such a subject without remembering Hollywood's earlier handling of sex. For many years there was no sex on screen. You had to supply for the filmmakers what they were unable to put in their films. In the James Jones novel *From Here to Eternity*, for example, the hero goes to a brothel near Pearl Harbor and meets a young tart whom he likes. In the *film* (1953) made from the novel the young man goes to what looks like a sorority house, and the girl, played by the wholesome Donna Reed, at the end of their conversation, to indicate that intimacy is in the offing, takes off one earring. The viewer is supposed to fill in the rest.

But not today: you see it. Yet I'd go so far as to say that I can think of only a few steamy bedroom scenes that seem to me essential to the films they're in, where if they weren't present, you'd feel that something important was missing. Among that small number of films, I think of *Enemies* (1989), made from the Isaac Bashevis Singer novel. In that picture it's vital that we *see* the violent sex, because the participants are both concentration-camp survivors, and you have to see them relishing and affirming, and in effect reclaiming, what had been taken away from them, in order to understand what has actually become a part of their characters. Of how many other films, recent or not-so-recent, can you say that?

Nonetheless, even when it appears gratuitous in a movie, sex can be very helpful. For a filmmaker who wants to treat a subject that might seem insufficiently interesting to some viewers, a strong sexual element can serve as hook and medium. As multiple instances have shown, the sexual element can bring along with it the background material that may have been the first reason for making the picture. The reasons why sex can be used in this way are not difficult to fathom, for the average moviegoer, watching the nude body of an actor going through the motions of sex, feels privy to the private experience of the actor, and he therefore identifies with one or another participant in the lovemaking. By contrast, the average filmgoer watching a violent episode isn't identifying with the participant on screen, imagining what it would be like to kill all those people (or be killed by them). Indeed, it's impossible to take very seriously the unbelievable, almost comic-book violence in most films, whereas audiences take very seriously the sex scenes.

This is why otherwise serious directors include them, sometimes only the hint (later unfulfilled) that they will occur, in order to arouse interest in a subject that has little or nothing to do with sex. The Lebanese director Ziad Doueiri is one recent example of such a director, in his second feature, *Lila Says* (2004), as well as his first, *West Beirut* (1998). *Lila Says* was co-adapted by Doueiri from the highly controversial, bestselling French novel of the same name published in 1996 but of uncertain authorship. (Purportedly, it was written by its nineteen-year-old, first-person narrator, whose name—in the fiction itself as well as in the byline on the book's cover—is given only as "Chimo.") The story of *Lila Says* provided Doueiri with the chance to make a film about the problems of Muslim young people, in particular North African Arabs, in France today. This is the background, in any event, though it was probably the first point of the enterprise; the foreground, this picture's sexual element, provided a means to make the sociological subject (with its issues of racism, assimilation, religion, and poverty) viable in filmic terms. (By contrast, the sociology of Arab underclass frustration is moved to the foreground in Matthieu Kassovitz's *La Haine*, or *Hatred* [1995].) Nonetheless, the sexual element in *Lila Says* is not gratuitous, it's trenchant; while the narrative concerning the status of Franco-Arab youth manages for its part to register strongly.

The novel of *Lila Says* was set in Paris in 1996, and at least half of it dealt exclusively with the problems of Muslim immigrants in this urban, Western setting. Doueiri moved the film to Marseilles in the southern portion of France, which is more Mediterranean; he gave some structure to the chaos of Chimo's first-person narration by organizing the movie's plot, not around the problems of Muslim immigrants *per se*, but around the problems of an interracial or cross-religious romance; and Doueiri set his film in the present, that is, in a post-9/11 world, where a Muslim's eyeing of a Christian woman has taken on new meaning. At the start of the picture, Chimo is trying to record in notebooks the experiences that, in extensive flashback accompanied by considerable voice-over narration, form the substance of *Lila Says*. He is, you see, a budding writer, and *Lila Says* becomes the visual presentation of his writing.

Chimo lives with his mother in the "Panier" neighborhood of Marseilles, an Arab ghetto whose narrow, gloomy streets are made to look distorted and menacing by the (12mm) wide-angle lens through which the cinematographer John Daly shot them. Like his three best friends—also Muslims, of course—Chimo is jobless if not completely aimless; his father has run off with a French woman, so it is his mother (with whom he is close) who supports the teenager. Though he and his crew have pious friends, none of these boys seems serious-minded enough either to engage with Islam or to reject it. Like the legions of idle, unemployed, immigrant and second-generation youths who populate the poorer quarters of French cities, Chimo spends much of his time, not praying in the local mosque, but hanging out on the street with his buddies and occasionally getting into trouble.

But Chimo the would-be artist has a sensitivity and an intelligence, a reflectiveness and an awareness, for all his inner anger about his marginalized social status, that set him apart from his aggressively boorish friends. He is also handsome, so it comes as no surprise that a beautiful sixteen-year-old non-Arab girl named Lila, blonde and proud of her blondness, sets her sights on him. She has just moved into Chimo's run-down neighborhood, where she lives with her aunt. And Lila turns that neighborhood upside-down with her unbridled expression of her (newly discovered) sexuality, including a penchant for riding her moped around in dresses well above the knee—occasionally without underwear—and a gift for sexually frank gab. Recklessly indifferent to her effect on Chimo's pals, especially his hot-headed best friend, Mouloud (not to speak of the effect Lila's sensuality has on her eccentrically religious lesbian

Lila Says, dir. Ziad Doueiri, 2004

aunt), Lila wants to spend time only with the otherwise diffident, even emotionally wary, Chimo.

Their relationship begins in tight, soft close-up one day in a park as she asks this dark-haired, olive-skinned young man to admire her blue eyes and flaxen tresses. Then Lila quickly proceeds from chat to provocation as she boasts of her body and asks Chimo if he wants to see her pubis (my word, not Lila's). Paralyzed by her candor—and sensitive enough to be unsure whether this girl's talk is an invitation to action or a substitute for it—Chimo doesn't immediately respond, which is apparently what Lila counted on and what, in some sort of presentiment, attracted her to him. When he finally says "yes," she teases him with the option of a "long look" or a "short look." The scene ends with Lila on a swing in the park, riding up high; she is not wearing panties, so Chimo can glimpse at length what she promised.

They often meet again, sometimes through her arrangement, sometimes through his, and each of their meetings is filled with torrid accounts of her wild sexual past, which she says embraces group sex as well as amateur pornography. These hot tales are clearly meant to arouse Chimo, though Lila is almost relying on his innate delicacy to keep him from making moves. Still, in their peculiar, oblique way, this racially diverse pair grows steadily closer, until the film's most effective scene: an erotically charged moped ride, with Chimo driving and Lila sitting more or less in his lap, through Marseilles' port area. Set to the music of Air's "Run" and edited (by Tina Baz) into a fantastically fluid series of shots, this extended sequence becomes an ethereal vision of sexual awakening and initiation, as Lila masturbates Chimo at the same time as a voyeuristic Steadicam follows the couple in a cinematic equivalent of the extreme rush he gets from her.

Chimo's friends, in particular Mouloud—the leader of this feral pack—get something of a rush from Lila, too. They have frequently seen her on the mean streets of Marseilles, have taunted and badgered her, and seem particularly ardent because she is blonde and non-Muslim—therefore a special conquest. Indeed, these young men interpret Lila's every gesture, including giving them the cold shoulder, as a teasing come-on. They also know little of Chimo's closeness to her, and, as Muslim males who place the bonds of friendship above romance, they are disgusted when they learn of it. So disgusted that rather than let a woman come between Chimo and him, Mouloud—joined by two other mates of his—decides to place himself between Chimo and Lila. Spurred on by the rumor of Lila's nymphomania, this trio accomplishes its aim in the most literal or physical way possible: by gang-raping her.

What we learn from this heinous act is what we suspected all along about young Lila's "past": that her "sexploits" were nothing but girlish fantasies, that her come-on is a put-on, that her virginity is—or was—intact. Far from being just a predictable or melodramatic climax to this tale, then, the gang rape is a kind of tragic meeting of minds, or bodies: of Lila's sexual fantasies and male rape-fantasy; of female sexual equality, identity, and self-ownership and the masculine subversion or negation of it; of the soft-core subjectivization of lust and the violent objectification of it. Chimo is left only with the roiling emotional legacy of his romance with Lila, which prompts the scribbling in his notebooks that we see him do in the present.

As at the end of *West Beirut*—with which *Lila Says* shares not only its coming-of-age or rite-of-passage narrative, but also its friendship between two males that is tried by the arrival of a young woman—we are left asking, where will Chimo and his mother go? What will they do? Prompted by Chimo's teacher, his mother (acted by the same lovely and elegant woman who played the protagonist's mother in *West Beirut*) had encouraged him to submit some written work to an arts school in Paris (where the novel of *Lila Says* eventually saw its first publication) so that he might win an all-expenses-paid scholarship to go there and hone his craft. And Chimo's initial contact with Lila had inspired him to do just that—write and submit—even as her rape provided him with the impetus to complete his novel.

But was the Chimo of the film really able to do so on his own in ghetto-ridden Marseilles, where, he had said, he'd look less like a loser if he remained among other losers? (And what of his mother, who, despite her attractiveness, is driven to experiment with her hair in an attempt to get some male attention and end her mourning for her dastardly departed husband?) Or did Chimo in fact move to more cosmopolitan Paris, where, depending on your point of view, he learned either how to objectify, or capitalize on, Lila in a kinder, gentler way—through the pages of a book—or how to memorialize-cum-mourn her through the cathartic act of putting her life into words? The novel, after all, is named after her, not him. And the French title, *Lila dit ça*, makes Lila's own "ownership" of her story clearer: not "Lila says," which in English satirically implies both whimsicality and imperiousness; but, literally, "Lila says that," which warmly suggests the fondness of recollection.

Whatever Lila says, certainly it is the ambiguity of her character, up to a point, which has fueled the drama of Doueiri's film. And understandably that drama, or dramatic interest, is helped by the central conceit of *Lila Says*: a *female* teenager who spouts off about sex, how she likes it, when she wants it, where she does it. Doueiri himself has said that though an image may be worth a thousand words, in this film "a word is worth a thousand images—it's all in the language." And all the more so, one might add, because there is no nudity in *Lila Says*, which rediscovers fully clothed sexual tension as it was first exploited, thanks to Kathleen Turner's contours, in *Body Heat* (1981). But there *is* Lila's face, which is made to look even more sumptuous and more mysterious—indeed, nearly interactive—by often being photographed in close-up through the same wide-angle lens that John Daly trains on Chimo's and her environment. (The peculiar advantage of such a lens is that at the same time it enables you to see the character up close, it also allows you to take in the background out of which this character has emerged.)

Lila's lips, moreover, are not always spouting lascivious words: during an almost abstractly choreographed scene in a cemetery, for example, Doueiri charts the impulses behind Lila's ever-evolving relationship to Chimo, as well as the reasoning behind her aggressively sexual stance, not with dirty words but with stolen glances. Such an elliptical exchange of idea and emotion extends not only to this film's *tour-de-force*, Lila and Chimo's love scene on the moped, but also to a scene at the local market, when Chimo's mother comes to her senses about Lila's youthful character—about the plain truth behind the startling façade—as she watches the girl try to buy some fruit. In fact, it could be said that Doueiri relies too much, not on Lila's prurient talk, but on the musical soundtrack that accompanies the "silent" sequences: in addition to Air's "Run," three songs from Vanessa Daou's "Zipless" CD together with a richly wrought original score by Nitin Sawhney.

Still, Doueiri has cast his film acutely, so there's no question here, as in so many teen flicks, of his relying on music to substitute for, or cover up, poor acting. Chimo is played by Mohammed Khouas, who, for all his character's seeming passivity (or narrator's stance), manages to blend social truculence with a poetic sensitivity that verifies the end of the affair—and the story. Vahina Giocante, for her part, is perfect as Lila. She's no conventional sexpot, so all the comparisons of her to Brigitte Bardot in *And God Created Woman* (1956)—like the descriptions of *Lila Says* as a multicultural, teenaged *Betty Blue* (1986)—seem to me to be off the mark. In the role of Lila, Giocante simply appears to be an appealing, if odd, adolescent—a kind of sexed-up Emma Thompson with blond hair but without the intelligence that Thompson herself (like Katharine Hepburn before her) has made sexy. Chimo has that intelligence in this picture, but, even so, Lila's intoxicating (if concocted) mixture of gamine innocence and womanly worldliness proves too much for him.

Doueiri handles the encounters of this pair with sufficient empathy to make the explicit sexual parley seem only the way in which they get to know each other. So much does he succeed that when Lila asks Chimo, "Would you like to see my pussy?" she might as well have been saying, "Would you like to have a cup of coffee?" And Doueiri avoids the contrived cinematic nature of most paradoxical love—as when the couple are an Israeli and a Palestinian, a white person and a black—by making this encounter seem inevitable given the dysfunctionality of Lila's parentless family life as well as Chimo's fatherless one (and given the fact that his father ran off with a non-Arabic French woman), the constricted environment in which they both live, and the ability of the wide-angle lens to keep that environment lingering always in the background even as the love story plays itself out in the foreground. What Doueiri never does, however, is hawk a naïve liberal's vision of social integration and cultural immersion—he leaves that to Hollywood, which has been selling this particular perniciously sentimental bill of goods at least as far back as *Guess Who's Coming to Dinner* (1967) and, in the same year as *Lila Says*, in *Spanglish* (2004).

But it is to England, not Hollywood, that we now venture, for there we find another film which (1) doesn't hawk a naïve liberal's vision of social integration and cultural immersion, in this instance with reference to class, breeding, and education; (2) uses adolescent sex, not gratuitously, crassly, or salaciously, but as a means to investigate a subject that transcends the carnal; and (3) deploys a kind of love triangle, not only to set its thematic perceptions in worldly order, like *Lila Says* and *West Beirut* before it, but also to set them in quasi-religious relief. This new British film is unpromisingly titled *My Summer of Love* (2004), but the lack of promise in the title, we soon discover, may be intentional and is certainly ironic, since this is no average teenaged vacation romance or coming-of-age story. Its director is Pawel Pawlikowski, who adapted his screenplay (with the assistance of Michael Wynne) from a first novel by Helen Cross (2001).

Pawlikowski is Polish-born but has been living in England for a number of years and has had his directing career there. After some BBC documentaries, he made his first feature, *Last Resort* (2000), a Kafkaesque tale about a Russian mother and son seeking asylum in Britain yet trapped, in a holding camp, in immigration limbo. I do not use the adjective "Kafkaesque" lightly, since Pawlikowski's sensibility owes little to the sober social realism of Ken Loach or Mike Leigh; despite its gritty naturalistic texture (surely the product of its director's documentary past), *Last Resort* reminds one more, in its world view, of the black absurdism of Central European satire. The texture of Pawlikowski's second feature, *My Summer of Love*, is quite different—dreamy and shimmering—but its world view, if not darkly comic, is darker than this picture's pervasive sunlight (turned into an active, nearly physical presence by the cinematographer Ryszard Lenczewski) would give anyone reason to believe. Thus, like any good director (including Ziad Doueiri), does Pawlikowski not so much change his cinematic style as suit that style to his present subject.

That subject is triggered by what one might call the destabilizing power of adolescent sexuality—a power you can also find at work in Peter Jackson's prototypical *Heavenly Creatures* (1994) and in Bernardo Bertolucci's *The Dreamers* (2003), as well as in several films made shortly after *My Summer of Love*, from the American Miranda July's *Me and You and Everyone We Know* (2005) and the Argentinean Lucretia Martel's *The Holy Girl* (2005) to the Sundance pictures *Pretty Persuasion* (2005) and *The Chumscrubber* (2005). The adolescents in the case of *My Summer of Love* are two sixteen-year-olds, Mona and Tamsin, from West Yorkshire, in the north of England. Mona is a working-class girl who lives above a former pub that her evangelical older brother, Phil (an ex-con), has turned into a religious meeting house; she never knew her father and her mother is dead of cancer. The upper-class Tamsin (home from boarding school for the summer) lives with her well-to-do family in a manor house across town, though that family itself suffers an often absent mother as well as a philandering father and an older sister who has died, it seems, of anorexia. As in the case of *Lila Says*, the meeting of these two is almost inevitable in a place so small, or constricted, and in this instance so otherwise devoid of teenagers.

Also as in *Lila Says*, this meeting across class lines is inevitable because of each girl's dysfunctional or incomplete family situation. Tamsin, for example, might as well be living alone for all that she sees of her mother and father—at home or at school. Mona, for her part, may have a brother if no surviving parent, but she wonders where the old Phil has gone now that he has given over his (once

My Summer of Love, dir. Pawel Pawlikowski, 2004

violent) life to Jesus. With little to do but ride her motorless moped across the moors now that her married lover, Ricky, has dumped her, Mona encounters Tamsin one day as both are out riding, except that the latter is atop a beautiful white horse. And out of a mixture of boredom, curiosity, and intuitive sympathy, the two opposites do what they are proverbially supposed to do: they attract, start spending time together (including excursions on Mona's moped, newly motorized courtesy of Tamsin), and soon become intimate.

Mona and Tamsin's relationship moves not only from the sisterly to the sexual, but beyond: into a kind of mystical love, the kind of feverish, all-consuming, naked intimacy that makes everything else seem insubstantial. With the aid of his cinematographer, Pawlikowski visually renders both this worldly insubstantiality and the otherworldly intensity of the girls' relationship in one scene shot in almost complete darkness, as each of two silhouetted figures vows to kill the other (and then herself) should she stray. Otherwise, the dreaminess or unnaturalness (depending on your perspective) of Mona and Tamsin's connection is impressionistically rendered through long tracking shots, tight close-ups, and abrupt shifts in perspective that pull the viewer into a private world which is simultaneously erotic and eerie—even as the Yorkshire countryside, the scene of many of this couple's revels (which include drinking, smooching, and skinny-dipping), is made by Lenczewski's lens to seem at once brilliant gorgeous and hazily oppressive, euphorically exhilarating and unnervingly entrapping.

The scariness, oppressiveness, or confinement of this world comes partly from the outside, in particular from Phil's desire to save Mona's soul as well as her body from Tamsin's devilish temptations. (Phil's fervor, which in one aspect leads him to build a gigantic cross and carry it up a hillside along with his down-at-the-heel disciples, in another aspect makes him vulnerable to both the sophisticated beauty and the sophistic spirit of Tamsin, who is thus able to blunt his threat to her link with Mona.) But the real challenge to this lesbian *eros* comes from inside, from the volatility of Mona's and Tamsin's contrasting temperaments. Mona the realist confronts her unhappy prospects—a future, as she puts it, of working in a slaughterhouse, winding up with a boyfriend who is a real bastard, getting fat as she churns out a slew of mentally defective kids, and waiting for menopause or cancer to make things even worse—with grim, truculent wit. Tamsin the fantasist is more operatic, weeping over her sister's death and her father's adultery yet self-indulgently looking forward to a grand career as a lawyer.

Nonetheless, while it lasts, the girls' relationship is cemented not only by sexual exploration but also by Mona's desire to learn from the more widely knowledgeable Tamsin, for all the gaping social divide between them. "Have you read Nietzsche?" she asks Mona (who later goes home to tell Phil and his Bible-study group that God is dead). "You'd like him. Also Freud." Tamsin tells her, as well, about Edith Piaf (whose weepy if haunting lyricism is heard over the closing credits), and, after inviting Mona into her opulent home, she plays the cello for her entranced friend, identifying the music as Saint-Saëns's "The Swan"—to which Mona straightforwardly responds that she lives above The Swan, the name of the pub her parents once ran. There is comic pathos in Mona's ignorance, to be sure, but there are also tender pride and stubborn persistence in her efforts to educate herself, and these are the qualities of hers that appeal to Tamsin.

At least for a time, in any event. For both girls, it seems, realize that life has already assigned them roles they don't much care for (hence one reason for their small acts of vengeance against those whom they see as having locked them into these roles: men, in the persons of Ricky and of Tamsin's father), and their summer romance thus becomes for both—though for Tamsin much more than Mona—not so much a way of escaping as a way of imagining escape. Though of course they don't see it this way, their mystical kind of love is for them what his passion for Jesus is to Phil, namely a role he has been playing as a way of not playing another one—the "old Phil" he is desperate to elude. *My Summer of Love*, you see, is also the story of Phil's love affair with Jesus, and it is the counterpoint between his story and the two girls' that lifts this film above so many other pictures that depict the wonder of adolescent emotional discovery.

This counterpoint also lifts Pawlikowski's film above Cross's novel, into an arena where the collision of sex and religion, the differences of social class, and the potency of the northern English landscape immediately bring to mind the fiction of D. H. Lawrence. For the character of Phil is the director and Michael Wynne's invention, even as the movie's plot is a slimmed-down version of the book's (which—set as it is in the summer of 1984 as opposed to the 2003 of the screen version—is burdened by references to the nationwide miners' strike of that year and the ever-present threat of nuclear war, as well as by a serial-killer subplot). In Phil's case, as opposed to that of Mona and Tamsin, something like tragedy breaks through to upset his (let us call it) comic-romantic balance, as he gradually if reluctantly comes to acquiesce in his sister's view that the old Phil is finally inescapable.

Indeed, it is a prank of hers, in which Mona claims, "I am the Antichrist!" that precipitates Phil's return to violence and ultimately ends his flirtation with Jesus, which now seems as doomed as Mona's with Tamsin. "Get out!" he says to his fellow worshippers in the ex-pub. "You're all fakers!"—which is just the word that Mona had earlier applied to her brother in his pretense to piety, and which is an echo of what Tamsin called Phil after playing the role of his temptress just to see if she could do it: a "fucking fraud." And for this fraud or faker, at his age and with his background, the loss of his hopeful alternative self is bound to be devastating—far more so than the girls' loss of their alternate selves as they return to their old lives and recover from the end of the affair.

A first affair, or *premières amours*, in the case of Mona and Tamsin, which makes their final scene or sequence together especially poignant. As summer comes to a close, Mona is dead set on leaving home with Tamsin, running away, and honoring her end of their mutual avowal of a lifetime of love for each other. With this plan in mind she goes to her friend's place, only to find Tamsin's mother packing up her daughter's stuff in preparation for her return to boarding school; upset, Mona is ready to flee but Sadie—the older sister who, in Tamsin's perfervid imagination, had died of anorexia—adds insult to injury by asking for her shirt back (clothing that Tamsin had given to Mona). Finally escaping from the manor house, Mona goes to a creek where the couple used to swim, Tamsin follows, and, after she admits that "killing" Sadie was an exercise in poetic license, the two girls slide into the water.

Yes, they soon kiss, but it's not the picture that then fades to black: Tamsin herself almost does so as Mona attempts to drown her friend before desisting, getting out of the water, and walking alone down a long dirt road. Thus does the summer end as it had to end, as both girls knew it had to end—and not just because of class distinctions, though certainly they play a large part in splitting Mona and Tamsin up. We are left with a concluded lyric whose lyricism depended, in a way, on its conclusion as well as its counterpoint: on the brisk scent of Yorkshire air with which we're left, on the soft fragrance of inevitable parting that we are left to savor, on the cold reality we know is the legacy of a life lived without make-believe.

Aptly, *My Summer of Love* won the Michael Powell Award for Best New British Feature at the 2004 Edinburgh Film Festival, for, like Powell's work, Pawlikowski's film marries romance to realism, creepiness to funniness, and the earthly visual realm to the realm of the fantastic or even the supernatural. That marriage is aided not only by the serenely shimmering musical score provided by the electropop group known as Goldfrapp, but also by the performances of two actresses who are talented beyond their earthly years. Tamsin is played by the young but somewhat experienced

Emily Blunt, a coolly enigmatic, dark-haired beauty who has a precocious, imperial quality imparted by the slight sneer that hovers above her full lips. The lighter-haired Mona is Natalie Press (in her film début), who is more homespun or coarse-grained in appearance but whose sullen vitality is evidence of an individual searching for herself—not a type taken from the shelf for routine display.

Blunt and Press are both complemented by Paddy Considine in the tricky role of Phil, who is both a catalyst of, and participant in, this film's drama; whose inner torment must barely be contained by his newfound spiritual discipline, which itself suppresses any capacity on his part for genuine human connection; and whose character carries the terrific weight of incarnating this picture's equation between avid religiosity and adolescent fantasy, naïveté, or reverie. Anyone who thinks this is just retread work by Considine need only see his lesser performances in *In America* (2002) and *Cinderella Man* (2005), as well as his quite different effort in Pawlikowski's *Last Resort*, where he embodies English decency as an arcade manager who befriends the Russian émigrée and her child.

My Summer of Love, by the way, was shot on a budget of only about three million dollars; I'm guessing that, more or less, the same is true of *Lila Says*. And has anyone noticed that the "French" picture was made by a Lebanese working in France, whereas the "English" one was directed by a native Pole; that, additionally, each man, at this point in his career, had made two feature-length films of some artistic ambition, yet of relatively modest cost? I bring these matters up for the usual reasons: they remind me of the overall immodesty of the commercial American cinema (though, elsewhere in the West, the French, especially, make their share of movie trash) and all the money it spends each year on duds (*artistic* duds, that is, which, more often than Hollywood would have you know, turn out to be box-office failures as well). The American cinema has always functioned in this way; that is why it properly calls itself "the industry"; and that is why most of its products are quickly disposable.

I know that this situation isn't going to change as long as rampant capitalism is the order of the day and a boom-or-bust mentality rules the film business. But it's nice to dream, and occasionally to have that dream turned into reality by small gems like *Lila Says* and *My Summer of Love*—made, again, by transplanted directors from countries whose own national cinemas are either small or virtually non-existent. They remind us, these men and their movies, of the possibilities (some would say responsibilities) inherent in film art—particularly an art shorn of the gratuitousness of violent sex, or one, let us say, that knows how to use sex to achieve what it wants.

Postscript

I'd like to add a brief comment here on two films from France, relatively big-budget ones compared to *Lila Says* and *My Summer of Love*, both of which also attempt to use sex to a higher thematic end. *Heading South* (2005) and *The Bridesmaid* (2004) may be relatively big-budget pictures, with at least one certifiable international star on display in the former, but each was made by a serious director and therefore deserves some consideration.

It was with his second major film, *Time Out* (2001), that Laurent Cantet established himself as a serious artist. With his third, *Heading South*, Cantet paradoxically both buttressed his reputation and

Heading South, dir. Laurent Cantet, 2005

undermined it a bit. The setting is Haiti—Port-au-Prince—in the 1970s, the time of Baby Doc Duvalier. Most of the film takes place at a resort hotel on the beach, and most of it concerns two well-to-do white women from America, who speak French and spend summers there. They partake in what is apparently a recognized summer sport: liaisons with young Haitian men who furnish attention and sex in return for generous gifts.

The more experienced of these women is Ellen, played by Charlotte Rampling (for whom, by now, unconventional morality seems a habitat), who is back for her sixth summer. Her black companion is young Legba, who had previously attended a woman named Brenda. After an absence of three years, Brenda returns and seeks him out again. No serious rivalry erupts between Ellen and Brenda for Legba, but there are irritations and discontents. This portion of the film proceeds as a case study in exploitation, with wealthy women utilizing native poverty for their satisfaction when and as long as it suits them—a glandular instance of global capitalism.

But the very first sequence suggests another theme. The majordomo of the hotel, Albert, is waiting at the airport for Brenda when a native woman approaches him and asks him to take her fifteen-year-old daughter—just to take her, to protect her from people who will probably soon kidnap the daughter after they murder the mother. Albert politely declines; and we move with Brenda to the beach for the sex story. For a time—too long a time, in fact—that grave opening seems simply an odd way to approach the sexual exploits of the white women.

Then the sociopolitical theme that was predicted in the opening finally begins to seep into the story. But it is murkily handled, and what Cantet obviously intended is never quite realized. He clearly wanted to juxtapose the hedonism of the visiting women and the wretched state of native life, including that of the pampered Legba. But the social irony is never justly realized; the effect is almost of a jigsaw puzzle that we are left to assemble. If only Cantet and Robin Campillo (who based their screenplay on stories by Dany Laferrière) had balanced the sexual and political elements in *Heading South* more acutely, the result could have been searing.

The Bridesmaid similarly has two strands, the sexual and the everyday or the pedestrian, but here they are neatly balanced. This film was made by Claude Chabrol, who by the time he died in 2010, had nearly sixty features to his credit (he made three more full-length pictures after *The Bridesmaid*). Though there are variations in quality among his films, Chabrol reached such heights as *This Man Must Die* (1969, about a man who hunts down a hit-and-run driver who killed his small son) and *Landru* (1963, based on the same character as Chaplin's Monsieur Verdoux).

The Bridesmaid, which continues this *auteur*'s thematic interest in crime and guilt and shadowed lives, itself ranks high on the Chabrol roster. The first two minutes affirm his mastery. The film opens with a ride down a seaside street in an uninteresting neighborhood that ends at a house in front of which stand some people and a television reporter. She tells us of a crime that has been committed there. As she talks, the image converts into the screen of a television set, and the camera pulls back into the living room of some people who are watching. Thus, gently, we are reminded that crime is ready to appear anywhere, at any time, and that this imminence is nowadays a subliminal part of ordinary lives. In our minds, that opening becomes increasingly freighted as the film unfolds.

We are in the home of Christine, a widowed hairdresser in her fifties, and her three children. Philippe, in his late twenties, is an executive in a construction firm; Sophie, twenty-three, is soon to be married; Patricia is a typically "difficult" adolescent. All of them are going to dinner that evening with Christine's boyfriend, Gerard, a man in his fifties, and Christine asks if she may give Gerard the life-size sculptured head of a woman in their garden that her male friend has admired. All agree, so they take it along, and we can be sure that this head will figure in what is to come. (The closing credits roll over that head.)

At Sophie's wedding Philippe meets Senta, the bridegroom's cousin, who is a bridesmaid. She is quiet but not reticent. This is quickly demonstrated when she follows Philippe home—he had to leave the wedding early—and very soon maneuvers him into bed. Their affair continues at Senta's house, which she owns. Though it is large, she lives in the crummy basement. On the floor above, her stepmother, a dance teacher, practices the tango with her partner; above that are large rooms filled with white-sheeted furniture. Senta's cool-hot intensity, the force with which she tells Philippe that

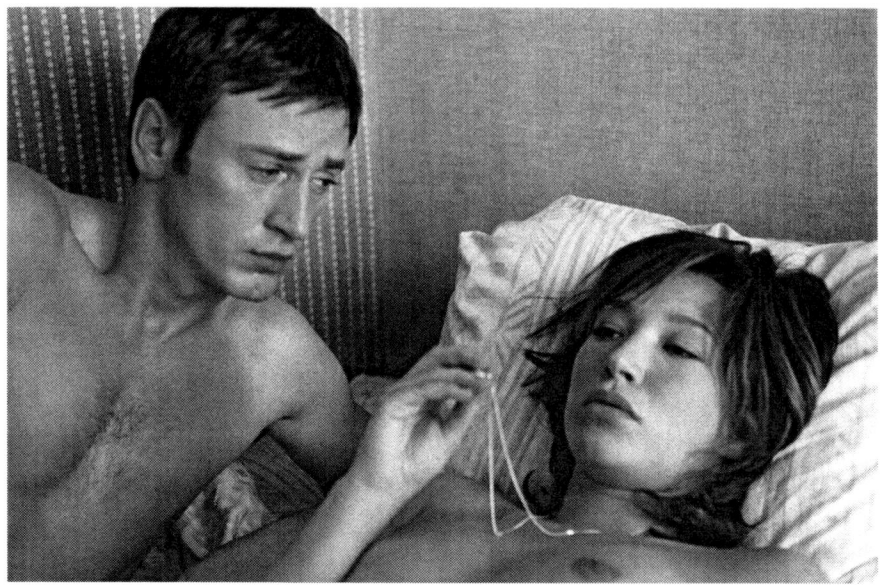

The Bridesmaid, dir. Claude Chabrol, 2004

she has been waiting for him all her life, that she loved him at first sight, is intoxicating to Philippe and lifts him to her state of passion.

In the course of time she recounts, truthfully or not, her lurid past in other countries. She says that she is now a would-be actress in (nearby) Paris and that, when she can't get acting work, she poses for porn photos. He accepts all these matters as part of her unique being. After they are deeply involved with each other, however, Senta tells Philippe that they have reached the plane where each of them must kill someone to prove the sublimity of their love. This pseudo-Nietzschean formula, elevating them beyond good and evil, at first amuses him. But she is serious, and he is so fevered to please her that he pretends compliance. Next day a murder is committed down on the docks, and, using it as a convenience, he boasts to her that he did it. She believes him. She then feels that she must fulfill her obligation.

The screenplay, adapted by Pierre Leccia and Chabrol from a novel by Ruth Rendell, dramatizes intoxication by passion—how it can take lovers, particularly when one of them is already quite strange, into places that had been unimaginable. Chabrol surrounds this affair with the quite mundane troubles of Philippe's family, and these troubles have a double effect. They seem small compared with his consuming affair with Senta, and they also seem precious as fingerholds on normalcy. Chabrol also makes a character out of Senta's weird house itself, where the tango sometimes goes on above the darkening lovers.

The two lovers are so well acted that their story, and its finish, are incredibly convincing. Benoît Magimel, who was Isabelle Huppert's young lover in *The Piano Teacher* (2001), gives heat to all the shades of feeling that come Philippe's way. Laura Smet, unbeautiful but sexy, creates a Senta who is driven by forces that she can't control and is glad of it. Thus did Chabrol insure the power of this dangerously difficult film with perfect casting.

13

Windows on the World

Film is the only narrative art form using words that is almost instantly available, through the subtitling of dialogue, to virtually every person in the world. This truth has been highlighted all the more by the rapid and steady replacement of film reels by videotape cartridges and DVD disks, as the media through which most people now view most of the movies they see—formats that have brought about a major increase in the accessibility of a wide range (temporal as well as geographic) of cinematic art. (This system itself is slowly giving way to one in which all films will be immediately accessible to our home video monitors over computer lines activated by a centralized digital database.)

I'm not going to wax too philosophical here on the crucial differences among these substances of transmission, but I will say this: that the images on celluloid film are *there*, visible to the naked eye, empirically and verifiably present, while the images on videotape, say, exist only as magnetic signals to be electronically decoded; and that video and DVD images are smaller, squarer, and less finegrained, their light not projected from behind the viewer and reflected on the screen, but self-contained and self-generated (which in a curious way makes us less "present" to the image, since we ourselves are not within or before the apparatus that produces it). Something has undeniably been lost in this process, for if film, as a mechanical reproduction or copy, constitutes in Walter Benjamin's analysis the final stage in the disappearance of the aura that clings to the singular, hieratic work of art, what stage do videotape and DVD represent? Still, it's hard to feel *too* bad about these developments. Though something essential to the pleasure of movies may now be irretrievably gone, something has also been gained.

Certainly the analysis and teaching of film have been vastly aided by video technology. But video technology, as well as the television that preceded it, has led to another sanguine development: a decline in the number of feature-length Hollywood films released (for theatrical exhibition) each year, as the cinema becomes more globalized than it has ever been before. As evidence of this, I present two pictures released in the United States around the same time: a movie by an African, from Chad, who received his film education in France (of which Chad was a colony until 1959), and a movie by a Turk who received his film education in Italy (where he now lives).

Abouna (*Our Father*, 2002) was made by Mahamat-Saleh Haroun, one of only two Chadian filmmakers at the time. *Abouna* is Haroun's second picture (he has since made three fiction films and one documentary); his first feature as a writer-director, *Bye-Bye Africa* (1999), was an agonized, quasi-fictional exploration of the difficulty of making movies in this central African country. Reversing the perspective of *Bye-Bye Africa*, in which the director himself took the leading role of an expatriate filmmaker returning from Paris to his native country, *Abouna* is an authentic mixture of who Haroun is, where he has been, and where he may be going.

In N'Djamena, the dry, dusty, tropical capital of Chad, an errant father, after going to a non-existent job for two years, abandons his family—an event that is apparently quite common in this poor country. *Abouna* begins with a shot of this man, walking into the desert landscape, turning to look (ambiguously) into the camera, then vanishing off over the dunes into neighboring Cameroon: possibly to seek work, perhaps to escape humiliation, though we never find out the precise reason for his disappearance. For, despite the film's title, Haroun's interest is primarily in the relationship between the man's two *sons*, the lighthearted and optimistic Tahir, who is fifteen years old, and dreamy, sad-eyed, asthmatic Amine, who is eight; and in the older boy's coming of age under less-than-opportune circumstances.

While their mother seems stoically resigned to her new situation, the boys resolve to find their missing parent. Their enthusiasm is kindled when, skipping school one day to go watch a movie (the film theater is the best building in town), they see an actor, his face turned away from the camera, who Amine is certain is their

Abouna, dir. Mahamat-Saleh Haroun, 2002

vanished father. The boy calls out, "Papa, look at me," and miraculously the man turns around to greet his children—not Tahir and Amine, but two other boys who, a few seconds later, bob into the frame. (This is not the first, nor will it be the last, of *Abouna*'s grimly comic moments.) Later the brothers sneak back into the theater (whose posters for Chaplin's *The Kid* [1921], Idrissa Ouédraogo's *Yaaba* [1987], and Jim Jarmusch's *Stranger than Paradise* [1984] quietly advertise the range of Haroun's cinematic influences) and make off with an enormous reel of 35-millimeter film, which they take home and unspool in search of their father's image. This otherwise innocent, absurd transgression proves too much for their proud yet harassed mother, who proceeds to send her sons off to an Islamic boarding school in the distant countryside—a place of utter tedium and harsh discipline (including severe beatings).

Tahir and Amine promise each other that they will look for their father as soon as they can escape the Koranic-Muslim school, but their initial escape attempt fails, and the brothers' thoughts soon turn to making their way eventually to the coast at Tangier, Morocco. (Chad is Africa's largest land-locked country, a fact emphasized by the poster of the sea the boys' father sends them, which they pin on the wall and raptly contemplate only after they have ushered their schoolmates out of the room.) That is, until Tahir falls in love with a radiant, deaf-mute girl who lives near the school. He alone finally succeeds, like his father, in running away—accompanied by his girlfriend. Amine's asthma has proved fatal, while, back in N'Djamena, the boys' once implacable and stately mother—an imposing, capable figure on her scooter in flowing, peach-colored robes—is descending into catatonic madness. *Abouna* finishes with the runaway young couple in search anew of Tahir's father, as well as in quest of a larger life. (In Chadian Arabic, by the way, "Abouna" means "our father" not only in the familial sense, but also in the spiritual or religious one.)

Tahir may, like his father, escape the chaos and hardship of life in Chad, but there's no suggestion that he's being as irresponsible as his elder. Indeed, in taking on responsibility for the deaf-mute girl (whose name we never learn) there is an indication that he just may grow from a generous, bravely determined boy into a decent and dependable man. Certainly one sign of his awakening maturity was his decision to remain playful and buoyant (yet ever solicitous) around Amine, despite his younger brother's rapidly declining health—itself tied to Amine's broken-heartedness not only at the loss of their father, but also at their failed attempt to escape the isolated Koranic school.

In its juxtaposition of country against city, of the village school with urban life in N'Djamena, *Abouna* thus invokes one of the commonest tropes of sub-Saharan cinema, only to avoid the schematic dichotomy to be found in Ouédraogo's *Samba Traoré* (1992) and his fellow Burkinian Drissa Touré's *Laada* (1991). In those films, there is a culture clash between the big city and little hamlets, whose wholesome, traditional values become tarnished and then forgotten amid any metropolis's mean, noisy, crowded streets. In *Abouna*, by contrast, Tahir and Amine seem at ease in N'Djamena, which, for all its temptations, seems to lend them the support of an extended family, while the brothers appear lost and disaffected in the countryside—not because it is lesser or less sophisticated, but, paradoxically, because they are out of their "natural" element in such a place.

Beyond *Abouna*'s tweaking of the urban-rural trope, there's an allegorical level to this local tale, the first evidence for which was the magical Pirandellian moment when "Dad" seemed to greet his startled boys from the movie screen with a cheery "Hi, kids, how are you?" War-torn, perpetually unstable, and seemingly ever affected by one humanitarian crisis or another, the nation of Chad may itself be a young "son" (independent only since 1960) in search of a paternalistic father or controlling authority figure other than the autocratic Chadian rulers it has had up to now: perhaps an omnipotent, all-beneficent God, perhaps the stabilizing if stifling hand of former colonial power France (nearly palpable during *Abouna* in the French into which the characters fall easily and frequently), maybe even (especially in Haroun's own case) the tender mercies of a sanctified national cinema. Haroun doesn't italicize this allegory, but the parallels between Chad's hardship and the hardships of Tahir and Amine—all of them co-authored, if you will, by state, mosque, and family—are clear enough.

The charm of *Abouna*—and that is the word, despite its almost melancholic quality in this instance—is that it unfolds at its own deliberate pace, in time with the unpredictable rhythms of childhood. One minute we get frenzied activity, the next torpid passivity, or a kind of combination of the two—as when a simple walk across an open field is abruptly punctuated by the two youngsters' jumping on their hands and continuing their stroll with their feet in the air. The result is an elliptical narrative of contemporary African childhood in which the emphasis is much less on key events in the story (some of which occur off-screen) than on offhand moments of understated poetry, like the little scene where Tahir and Amine journey down-river (the very river across which lies yet another path to neighboring Cameroon, the brothers' cherished "somewhere else") with their uncle in a canoe as birds swoop down from trees as if to join them.

Some of that poetry can be found in shots that exclude the two boys and their mother altogether: empathic close-ups of the faces of townspeople, open and appealing, appear throughout; lingering long shots of green-and-ocher landscapes dot the film; and simple shots of windows and doorways recur often enough to become a visual leitmotif for the brothers' wistfulness, their longing for everything, or anything, that is beyond this place. One of the most moving moments in *Abouna*, for example, occurs during the scene of Amine's death. Rather than dwell on the dying boy or the grief of his brother, Haroun cuts away to a window in the wall of their darkened hut, through which we glimpse a patch of light shining down on the bare earth outside. Contemplating this almost abstract composition in total silence, the camera slowly pulls back as though it itself were gradually letting go of life—an image and a movement at once poignant and redemptive.

As one might have guessed, there is a level of stillness to *Abouna*'s images that may be typical of African films, of the tempo of African life, but which is complemented here by a quietness, or relative absence of dialogue, that is as refreshing as it is apt. For there can be no ratiocinative, logocentric explanation for a father's abandonment of his family—especially for his young children. And nowhere is this truth clearer, nowhere is the hegemony of language or linguistic discourse more undercut, than when the boys' mother complains that their father is irresponsible, mixing in one French word—for "irresponsible"—with her Arabic. Amine wonders what this foreign term means, and, after a frustrating consultation with the dictionary, Tahir explains, "It means just that: someone who is not responsible." "So," Amine surmises with some relief, "our father was not responsible for leaving."

More than in most sound pictures, then, *Abouna*'s pictures alone tell its story, and that means its cinematography must be much more than serviceable. Abraham Haile Biru's is exquisite as it uses a palette of saturated primary colors, as well as earth tones, to create a series of careful compositions that capture the dark underside of this filmic rite of passage. This Biru manages to do—creating a strange sense of unease in the process—by training his camera on the sharply defined shadows of his sun-drenched locations at the same time as he makes his images give off a warm orange glow. Biru's stark yet sumptuous visual style is aided by the Malian musician Ali Farka Touré's haunting, meditative score, which the solo acoustic guitarist Diego Mustapha N'Garade injects with a lilt that makes it (like the movie itself) the opposite of depressing. And, of course, *Abouna* would be nothing without its actors—particularly

Ahidjo Mahamat Moussa as Tahir and Hamza Moctar Aguid as Amine—all of them non-professionals.

The obvious advantage of Haroun's using locals in his film (though, happily, he may not have had any other choice) is that they don't have to learn how to be at home in a new environment: N'Djamena *is* their home and they are therefore completely at home in it. Another, not so obvious advantage is that, in a movie which is less wrenching, spoken drama than visual rite of initiation, the performers must give themselves over to the rite more than they must create character and emotion, must be subsumed by the tale more than they must dominate it, must behave naturally more than they must super-naturally act. And this the untrained Chadians are supremely qualified to do.

Especially qualified is Moussa in the role of Tahir, where, with equal parts bravado, vulnerability, and credulousness, he shows the brats in Hollywood how children really behave. (As a host of other youngsters have done before Moussa, from Robert Lynen in *Poil de Carotte* [1932] and Enzo Staiola in *Bicycle Thieves* [1948] to Aida Mohammed-Khani in *The White Balloon* [1995] and Mohammed Chamas in *West Beirut* [1998].) Naturally, Moussa and the other cast members—notably Mounira Khalil as the deaf-mute girl (whose first present from Tahir, a pair of earrings improvised from peanut shells, makes her beam with speechless joy)—are assisted in their work by the movie camera, which, almost through the simple act of framing, has a way of conferring dignity and even grandeur on the simplest, most unassuming of human lives.

Frames, or windows, of a similar kind play a part in an Italian film called *Facing Windows* (*La finestra di fronte*, 2003). It was written by Gianni Romoli and Ferzan Özpetek, who directed. Özpetek has made three previous features, and has had theater experience. It shows in the empathy and skill with which he handles his actors, who warmly enhance a not-so-startlingly-original idea for a motion picture.

In contemporary Rome a young woman, Giovanna, is walking home one afternoon with her husband, Filippo, when they meet a man in his eighties, well-dressed and dignified, who holds out money to them. He is lost, he says, and will pay them to help him figure out where he is. They decline the money, and then Filippo

Facing Windows, dir. Ferzan Özpetek, 2003

drives the man to the nearest police station. The place is so crowded, however, that Filippo has to bring him home for the night. Giovanna is nervous about having this odd stranger in their apartment with their two children, but he is so quiet, often so abstracted, and always very well-mannered, that she becomes reconciled.

Giovanna, we soon see, is the center of the story: the old man is one of the forces that eventually affect *her*. Another is a young man who lives in an apartment across the way, whom she often watches from her kitchen window. The following evening after work, she is to drive the old man back to the police station, but she stops first to deliver some cakes that she has made for a neighboring café. (She has a job as an accountant, but baking is her avocation.) There she meets the young man who lives across the way—Lorenzo, as she learns—who tells her that the old man has just left her car. Lorenzo helps her to look for him; and they find him sitting quietly, thoughtfully, beside one of those ubiquitous Roman fountains.

Lorenzo and the old man aside for the moment, Giovanna is solidly married to a basically gentle man who is a good father, though she and her husband have a continual litany of bickering (in part because Filippo is only sporadically employed) under their affection. She is discontent, however, not because of the bickering but simply from having lived for nine years in the same set of circumstances and feelings. Now two catalysts have arrived to affect her.

First, the old man, whose thoughtful comments about Giovanna's avocation linger in her. When at last he finds his way back to his home and she traces him, she finds out that he is a master in his profession—a famous pastry chef named Davide who treats his work as a high *vocation*. Urged by him, Giovanna follows her own gifts in this calling, which is treated, however peripheral it may seem to the world's gravity, as a locus for high standards. The second catalyst is Lorenzo, who, she learns, has been spying on her, too. He is in love with her, and she responds—almost. But his adoration of her apparently reminds Giovanna finally of the value of her workaday marriage. The real windows in the picture's title, then, are the openings on herself, on life, that these two men have offered her—one of which she takes.

Özpetek himself warmly enriches this modest work through his direction. First, every scene in *Facing Windows* seems to be a distillation of all the matters that led to it, rather than a mere presentation of the scene's content, which spells the difference between a pedestrian or superficial director and one who comprehends the breadth as well as depth of his material. Second, Özpetek is able to give life to somewhat worn cinematic devices, like coyly moving the camera around his characters as they talk. His circling of the dinner table when the elderly Davide has his first meal in Giovanna's apartment thus becomes a moment of communion instead of directorial display.

Davide is played by the only actor in the cast possibly familiar to cinephiles: Massimo Girotti, who worked with most of the great Italian directors (Rossellini, Visconti, Antonioni, Germi, Pasolini, Bertolucci) through a great era of Italian film (circa 1942-1972). Girotti died on January 5, 2003, at the age of eighty-four, and *Facing Windows* was his last movie. It is dedicated to him, a handsome, magnetic, genuine actor whose performance here makes the past (a haunted, even shadowy one in the case of Davide, who is revealed to be a homosexual survivor of the Nazi death camps) part of the present and thus lends the picture a quasi-mythical, dreamily evocative atmosphere. So much so that Giovanna's window on the world becomes, through Girotti's eyes—which begin and end the film—a window to the soul: of man, of Italy, of the cinema. So much so, moreover, that Özpetek's *Facing Windows* could be called *Our Father*, in Girotti's honor—and Haroun's *Our Father* could itself be called *Facing Windows*, in homage to a world alive with imaginative possibility.

14

A World on Film

So many American movies came his way each week that James Agee, writing for *The Nation* in the 1940s, sometimes published "round-ups," or omnibus reviews in capsule form, in which he would humorously demolish dozens of these latest offerings from Hollywood. Here are three of my favorite (and representative) such capsules, from a column published on April 24, 1948:

> *All My Sons*. The Arthur Miller prize-winner. A feast for the self-righteous; Ibsen for beginners; for the morally curious a sad bore. . . . Entirely well-intended and sincerely acted; but not an interesting play, and certainly not a movie.
> *The Miracle of the Bells*. As pernicious a gobbet of pseudo-religious asafetida as I have been forced to sniff at, man and Sunday-school boy. I hereby declare myself the founding father of a Society for the Prevention of Cruelty to God.
> *The Search*. A displaced mother and child seek and find each other in American Germany. . . . Sometimes sweet or touching, but pathetically mild and unimaginative. . . . At one point, while starving children grab for bread, a lady commentator informs one that they are hungry, and that the bread is bread.

But Agee also wrote omnibus reviews of the best movies released in the United States during the previous year, such as his column of January 10, 1948, in which he singles out no fewer than thirteen films for judicious praise. They are Jean Vigo's *Zero for Conduct* (1933), Chaplin's *Monsieur Verdoux* (1947), De Sica's *Shoeshine* (1946),

Luigi Zampa's *To Live in Peace* (1946), André Malraux's *Man's Hope* (1945), John Ford's *The Fugitive* (1947), Elia Kazan's *Boomerang!* (1947), David Lean's *Great Expectations* (1946), Carol Reed's *Odd Man Out* (1947), Eisenstein's *Ivan the Terrible* (1944), René Clair's *Man About Town* (1947), Cocteau's *Beauty and the Beast* (1946), and Edward Dmytryk's *Crossfire* (1947). Is it possible that so many films of quality were released in New York in the space of a year (some of those releases understandably having been delayed until 1947 on account of their country of origin)? Agee does not remark on this phenomenon, as he would not in the pre-television age (which was ending even as Agee was writing).

I propose to imitate the laudatory Agee in this chronicle (though I shall do so in an extended form rather than an encapsulated one), but you, dear reader, should not be surprised by the absence of American pictures from my own list of relatively recent films worth seeing. For most of these Hollywood products, most of the time—even (especially?) when they are sincere and high-minded—are perfectly lousy "art." Their target, particularly when they are reverently changing the very salt (or, alternately, the dregs) of the earth into so much stale saccharine, is the big, soggy heart of the middle class, which doesn't know anything about art—that is, about mind, clarity, and imagination—but which certainly likes what it knows.

What follows, then, is a round-up of international films, arranged under two thematic categories, which have been released in the United States over a five-year period. Enjoy the movie.

Emigrés.

***Djomeh* (2000).** This Iranian film was written and directed by Hassan Yektapanah, who has been an assistant to Abbas Kiarostami. It's a simple picture that achieves its largeness by concentration rather than by size, by a belief that every human face is important (not just a movie star's) and that atmosphere is rooted in culture (not spectacle). Djomeh is a twenty-year-old Afghani émigré in Iran who works on a small dairy farm owned by a man named Mahmoud, works hard, and lives simply. He has seen—but, in our sense of the word, has not met—an Iranian girl named Setareh, the daughter

Djomeh, dir. Hassan Yektapanah, 2000

of a shopkeeper in a nearby village, and he is smitten. Most of the story is concerned with Djomeh's efforts to propose to this young woman, efforts that must proceed through a fixed protocol.

Plenty of pictures have treated the subject of star-crossed love, between persons of different races or religions or politics. But *Djomeh* is much less a love story than an account of the self, Djomeh's self (as the film's title indicates): who he is, how he hopes and cares, his persistence in a quest that would be difficult in any case but is aggravated by his foreignness to this country. Ironically, and artfully, the concentration on self in this film augurs a fate, a future, for Djomeh in which loneliness or loneness will have some part; thus the conclusion of the narrative is, in a way, embodied in the isolation of the protagonist throughout.

That isolation is itself augmented by the vast brown landscape, which the cinematographer Ali Loghmani manages to enlist in the drama, as well as by the frequent use of an automobile interior (a device borrowed from Kiarostami) as a kind of particularized space, or pressure chamber, for intensified dialogue between the driver of a car and the person sitting opposite him. The core of

Djomeh, then, is not in camera cleverness or performative display, but in its humility in the face of an equally humble subject and in the dignity that its restraint, or patience, can inspire.

Let us not leave out the humanity to be found in the film's characters, who are acted by persons—Jalil Nazari as Djomeh and Mahmoud Behraznia as his boss—committed to empathic revelation rather than pyrotechnic exhibition, to spiritual distillation instead of superficial diversion. These two may be non-professionals, as are many of the actors in the Iranian cinema, but they quietly profess far more than do their noisy, noisome counterparts in the juvenile Hollywood cinema.

Otomo (1999). Here is another film about an émigré, similar to *Djomeh* in that there's built-in drama between the lone outsider and the insiders, in that fatefulness plays a role in the action; but this is also a different work—quite different. For Otomo is a victim, the victim-as-hero (not to be confused with the twentieth century's anti-hero, who has the capacity to make choices but may choose *not* to choose), the man who didn't have a chance or a choice.

Otomo is a German film about a black man. Frieder Schlaich, the director, wrote the scenario with Klaus Pohl (the playwright-screenwriter who later wrote *The Farewell* [2000], about the last days of Bertolt Brecht's life); they based it on actual events that occurred in Stuttgart in August 1989. A West African immigrant (one among many thousands of "guest workers" in Germany), jobless, broke, nearly hopeless, makes his way through what turns out to be the last day of his life. The man is known by his German name of Albert Ament, but—as we learn near the end—his original African name is Frederic Otomo. Hence the film's telling title.

At the start Otomo checks out of a sort of shelter, whose clerk treats him as a friend. Then, on a streetcar en route to look for a job, he gets into a dispute with the conductor because he feels that he is being unfairly treated. Otomo spends the rest of the day evading the police while he looks first for work, then for transport to Holland. This day—capped by the desperation of a final scene between Otomo and five policemen—is seen as inevitable, the climax of a long struggle, the end of an *agon* that would be Attic were it not for the fact that the protagonist, unlike a tragic hero, does not have the

Otomo, dir. Friedrich Schlaich, 1999

freedom to choose his fate. Still, Otomo's last day sums up his life, or at least that life's potential (as briefly seen when he opens up a bit during an encounter in a park with a young girl and her youngish grandmother).

Much of the sense of size, or potential, in this account of an immigrant worker comes from the performance by Isaach de Bankolé. He was first prominently seen in Claire Denis's *Chocolat* (1988), where he displayed a reticent power that visibly pervaded his character, particularly through his sculptural face. (In the 1990s, Bankolé appeared in two Jim Jarmusch films: *Night on Earth* and *Ghost Dog*.) In *Otomo*, that power, that authenticity of feeling, is again on display, where it is poignantly contrasted with the implication of powers that dog him—as in the long shots of Otomo seated alone on one end of a bench or of him moving down a cheerless, empty street. Bankolé has a performative appeal and Schlaich a directorial gift (like his German predecessors Werner Herzog and Wim Wenders) that make us want to share Otomo's experience, because we know we cannot reverse it.

Films-within-Films.

Goodbye Dragon Inn **(2003).** Apropos the disappearance over time of the traditional movie theater, the Taiwanese movie director Tsai Ming-liang gives us *Goodbye Dragon Inn*, a sort of farewell to the kind of film that once played in such places (or in some cases, "palaces"). It is set in a Taipei movie house that is showing a costume drama full of swordplay, a 1966 opus called *Dragon Inn*. The theater is large, and only a handful of people are in the audience: one is a Japanese man apparently cruising for a pickup, and another is an old man who, we can infer, was an actor in the picture that is up on the screen. The only other person of note is the ticket-taker, a young woman who limps: her steps, as she moves around the concrete-floored theater, are part of Tsai's aural structure. (She is played by Shiang-chyi Chen, who was the protagonist of Tsai's *What Time Is It There?* [2001].)

Throughout *Goodbye Dragon Inn* we get glimpses of the gorgeously arrayed actors on the theater's screen, and most of the dialogue that we hear is from that film, echoing through the huge auditorium and along the concrete corridors around it. The first line of present-time dialogue—*Goodbye* dialogue itself—doesn't come until about halfway through Tsai's film, when one man says

Goodbye Dragon Inn, dir. Tsai Ming-liang, 2003

to another, "Do you know this theater is haunted?" After *Dragon Inn* finishes, *Goodbye Dragon Inn* concludes. One person leaving the theater says, "Nobody goes to the movies anymore." The ticket-seller puts up a sign reading "Temporarily Closed." Then she walks home in the rain.

Most of what Tsai shows us are shots of the theater's concrete corridors and the projection room and various nooks, all cold, bare, and usually empty. He thus emphasizes, sometimes rather strongly, the difference between the ornate film that the theater is showing and the bleak theater itself, which is nothing like the great luxury theaters of the past with their pipe organs and painted clouds, earth-toned frescoes and velvet curtains, opulently upholstered seats and richly appointed snack bars. The inner film's swashbuckling is further contrasted with the almost tangible stasis of the shots of the theater auditorium, which are so devoid of camera movement that they come close to being still photography, visited occasionally by a few people.

Clearly Tsai is bidding farewell to escapist cinema, in this case to its action genre, and is asking his audience to join him—if only because such "epics" belong on the big screen (one, again, that is gradually disappearing) and not at the end of a picture tube. He means to replace such films with reality or realism, on screen as in life: the concrete floors, the dank corridors, the rhythm of the ticket-taker's limp, the falling rain outside. This is precisely why the film theater in *Goodbye Dragon Inn* is so stripped-down and jury-rigged: pretending to be nothing more than an empty room in which to sit and watch a movie, it makes us aware of how place persists when all the trappings of setting, or of art, recede. Indeed, this bare house with its few spectators reminds us, subliminally at least, of what it means to *be* in a place, as opposed to use it, embellish it, pass through it, or go past it. Such a place thus becomes a call for a type of art that not only places its maker squarely in the world to which he belongs, in all its dailiness and corporeality, but also, through its recording of the surface of the everyday, evokes for its viewers the wonder and mystery of that world's presence, its invisible yet persistent pointing to something besides, or beyond, its palpable self.

This "call" on the part of *Goodbye Dragon Inn* is hardly new in the world of art or the art film. Of course, Tsai is too intelligent, and too honest, to believe that he is replacing fiction with reality. He knows that the sequence of images he has presented of this Taipei theater, where the old-fashioned *Dragon Inn* is being shown, is only one set of realistic selections and arrangements—necessarily limited, however artful. But Tsai *is* proposing that his art should concentrate on more apposite fictions, on concentrated or distilled inquiry rather than diverting escape and compensatory fantasy. To be sure, *Goodbye Dragon Inn* is not free of *longueurs*, but, as in much modernist work in almost every field, these stretches are deliberate assaults on conventional expectation. And, for this viewer at least, they are refreshingly, replenishingly, welcome—especially after a film like Pedro Almodóvar's *Bad Education*.

Bad Education (2004). This film, like much of Almodóvar's recent work, leaves the spectator with the sense of a writer-director concocting complexities for the sake of—well, concocting complexities. I have never been a big fan of this Spanish director's movies, but at least some of the early ones—like *Dark Habits* (1984) and *Matador* (1986)—tried through ruthless ridicule and scornful comedy to slash open the hypocritical guises of Spanish conventions (including some in religion). Soon, however, Almodóvar began to invent intricate plots instead of creating thoughtful narratives, plots sometimes so bizarre that, in the hands of someone more discerning, they could become sarcasm about plotting. As a matter of fact, a summary of even one of these stories would sound like a satire of the story.

Bad Education suffers in this way, just as Almodóvar's *All about My Mother* (1999) did before it: the more recent work "reads" like too many pieces of a puzzle put together in something other than lucid design. Basically, *Bad Education* is about two young men, one a film director (possibly modeled after Almodóvar himself) and the other an actor, who were once classmates in a parochial school and who meet again professionally. In flashback we see their homoerotic attachment at school and their molestation by a priest. Yet to attack the censors of homoeroticism and the sexual abuse of boys by Catholic priests is no longer enough material for Pedro Almodóvar, as it once might have been. Now not only must he adorn his picture with homosexual activities (as unwelcome, and unnecessary, as the

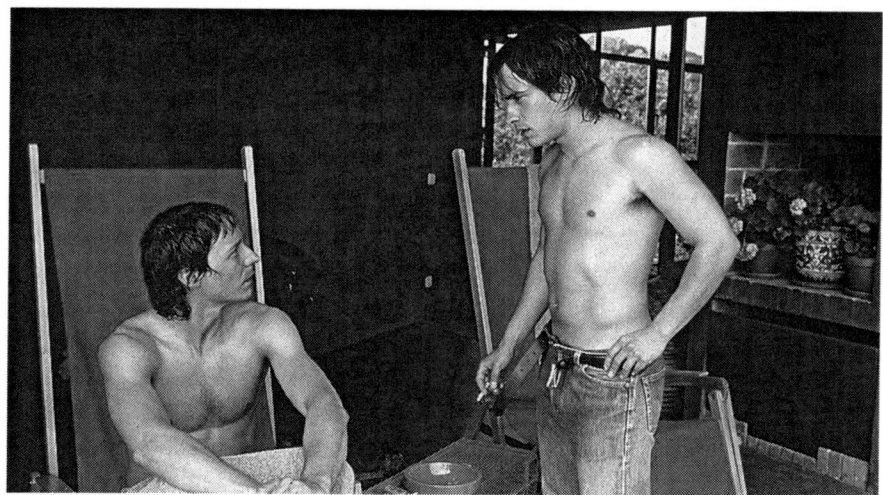

Bad Education, dir. Pedro Almodóvar, 2004

heterosexual activities in other, comparably worthless contemporary films), he has to set this account, told in the two time-planes of past and present, in a Pirandellian conundrum about reality versus illusion.

The actor, you see, has written a story about the pair's boyhood love, and the director films it; and matters become so convoluted (including the convolution of cross-dressing) that we have questions about which is the director's film and which is the actuality underneath it. But these questions lead not to revelation or epiphany, as in the best work of this kind (most of which has occurred onstage, in the play-within-a-play), but only to pretentiousness and preening. For all its adroitly composed scenes and more than competent acting, then, *Bad Education* is yet another movie from Almodóvar that only a postmodern narcissist could love: a work whose cinematic self-reference or –reflexivity never gets beyond the confines of its *auteur's* own hyper-inflated self. Once considered the *enfant terrible* of European, if not world, cinema, Pedro Almodóvar (born 1951) will now have to settle for one or the other: depending on your perspective, he's either acting like a child or he's a terrible director.

Sex Is Comedy **(2002).** This is a film about the making of a film. It was written and directed by Catherine Breillat, a Frenchwoman born in 1948, who is also a novelist; she has been making movies since 1975, but this is the first of her pictures to come my way. (The second one I have seen, *Anatomy of Hell* [2004], strains much too heavily to maintain Breillat's reputation as a sexually frank *auteur*.)

Films about filmmaking—its joy and heartbreaks but mostly its glamour—began almost with Edison. In the 1970s, however, the self-loving film took on a new aspect: it concentrated on the director, the very director of the framing film, let us call it. So, egocentrically, Fellini put himself in *The Clowns* and his *Roma*; Lindsay Anderson appeared in *O Lucky Man!*; and, in *Day for Night*, Truffaut played the director of a movie called *Meet Pamela*.

But as early as 1963, with Fellini's *8½*, another kind of film-about-filmmaking made its entrance: the meditation on the work (and sometimes the life) of a movie director and on the faculties of film. In 1983, Bergman gave this kind of picture a new twist in *After the Rehearsal*: made by a theater director of world renown who was also a film director of global stature, it took place on a stage and explored relationships between a theater director and two of his actresses—yet it was done on film. Now comes *Sex Is Comedy*, which does not approach Bergman's film (let alone Fellini's) in depth or scope—it's more in a league with Tom DiCillo's clever, amusing look at a low-budget movie-in-progress, *Living in Oblivion* (1995)—but which itself explores relationships between a film director and two of her actors.

We never, and never need to, learn much about the film that is being made within Breillat's framing picture. *Sex Is Comedy* concentrates on only two of the inner movie's scenes. In the first one, a couple (played by Grégoire Colin and Roxane Mesquida) do some kissing on a beach; in the second, they make love on a bed. The beach scene happens to be shot on a cold day, so, although the director and crew are bundled up, the lovebirds, lying on the sand in bathing suits, have to generate their own heat. The second scene, in which the young man deflowers the girl, is rife with subtler difficulties connected less with the embarrassment of total nudity than with the actors' dealings with the director, as well as with their own lives outside these roles. (For more on the latter subject, see another French film: Yvan Attal's *My Wife Is an Actress* [2001].)

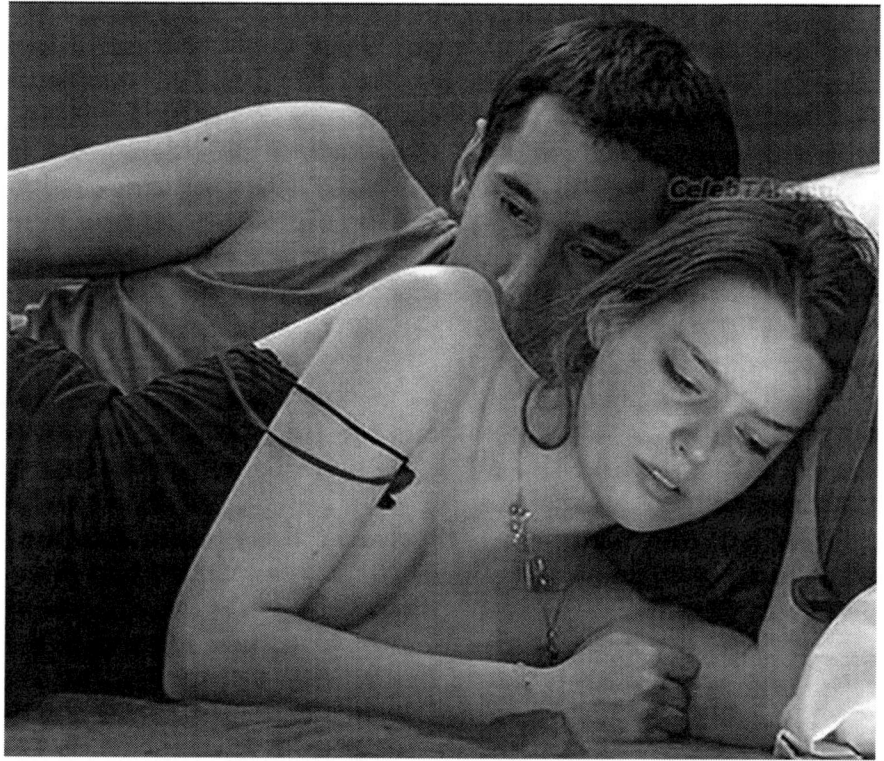

Sex Is Comedy, dir. Catherine Breillat, 2002

The action of *Sex Is Comedy* being relatively slight, then, the substance of Breillat's film is in the director's perceptions about her job—not merely the directing itself, but the personal valences (actor-to-actor, actors-to-director, director-to-crew) that shift and combine in the chemistry of creation. As for the perceptions about directing, I'll note two here. The first concerns a perception on the part of the director about *acting*. At one point, the director (incisively played by Anne Parillaud, best known for her starring role in Luc Besson's *La Femme Nikita* [1990]) says, much to the consternation of every performer, that actors can pretend in most scenes of any script but that in sex scenes no fakery is possible. "Your ass is your ass," she comically declares in one explanation of why "unfaked" sex (for those who observe it in person, like everyone on a movie set) is incongruously funny.

Of course, in non-pornographic pictures like this one, the sex itself is *simulated*; the director's point is that the further two actors advance *toward* the sex act, the less individual and more objectified (and therefore funny) they become—hence the harder it is to sustain the illusion of character, which makes the actor naked in the figurative as well as the literal sense. This is no small point, and is the real reason why explicit, lengthy sex scenes in a non-pornographic film are, from an artistic point of view, pointless. But not in this film-within-a-film, because here the sex leads to a revelation about the art of acting and one condition under which that art cannot thrive.

The second, and larger, perception about directing is implicit in the very method by which *Sex Is Comedy* proceeds. The director is present throughout the making of the film-within-the-film, just as Catherine Breillat was there during the making of the film-outside-the-film, as it were. Thus, unlike the theater director who is finished when the curtain goes up and then can only watch, the film director is present while we watch her film almost to the same degree as an orchestral conductor is present as he leads his orchestra in the performance of a piece of music. Breillat may be invisible, but she was there during every moment of the making of what we see; and, if the sound was re-recorded, she could even have spoken to the actors while they acted (which in fact was standard practice during the silent-film era).

Therefore, even though nothing in *Sex Is Comedy* is greatly moving, nor is intended to be (with the exception of the moment when, after the sex scene, the actress—who, like the actor, is otherwise an experienced professional—sobs uncontrollably and the director embraces her), it moves us to add one member to the cast of every film: the director. Or, at the very least, to think of this person as the leader of any motion picture's first, on-set, and engendering audience.

Part III

CLASSIC CINEMA (RE)CLASSIFIED

15

Without a Prayer:
Vengeance Is Mine and the Cinema of Shohei Imamura

I

Shohei Imamura was born in Tokyo on September 15, 1926, and died there on May 30, 2006. Too young to fight in World War II, he was nonetheless, like all Japanese, heavily affected by its aftermath. The son of a physician, Imamura was nearly nineteen when the global conflict ended, and that year—1945—marked his entry into Tokyo's reputable Waseda University to study Western history. During this period, the social upheaval of the American Occupation opened his eyes to a new world entirely different from the one in which he had been brought up. While at the university, he earned his living by buying black-market cigarettes and alcohol from American troops and selling them to his professors. Imamura recalled that "this was the only time in my life I was well off, although I spent all I made on drink. I was surrounded by prostitutes and other low-life types" (Quandt, 111). Accordingly, many of his early films focus on characters from the lower orders—prostitutes, pimps, pornographers, and black marketeers—who act out of what could be called financial impulse but is better known as basic survival instinct.

Imamura was one of a generation of young directors, including Nagisa Oshima, Yoshishige Yoshida, and Masahiro Shinoda, who in the early 1960s became known collectively as the New Wave (*nuberu bagu*) of Japanese cinema. The term, coined by critics to draw parallels with the French *nouvelle vague*, was somewhat artificially imposed, since none of the Japanese directors saw themselves as belonging to a broad, cohesive movement akin to the one associated with Jean-Luc Godard, François Truffaut, Jacques Rivette, and Eric

Rohmer. For their part, Imamura, Oshima, Yoshida, and Shinoda made films as individuals, with different filmmaking philosophies and under different production conditions.

Yet similarities do exist among the individual practitioners of the Japanese New Wave, and these similarities go beyond their shared status as young directors practicing a new, very different style of filmmaking from that of the previous generation. For one thing, Imamura received his training at a major studio, as did Yoshida, Shinoda, and Oshima. The latter three apprenticed at Shochiku, whereas Imamura quickly jumped from Shochiku to the newly re-established Nikkatsu studio when it started production again in 1953. During their early years at the studios, all four men served as assistant directors, as part of the *sempai-kohai*, or senior-junior, mentoring system that was the norm in the Japanese film industry until the late 1970s.

During his brief spell at Shochiku, Imamura worked as one of five assistants for the now internationally renowned master of Japanese cinema Yasujiro Ozu on the films *Early Summer* (1951), *The Flavor of Green Tea over Rice* (1952), and *Tokyo Story* (1953). However, the older director's well-ordered world and scrupulous portrayal of the Japanese middle class were the very antitheses of what Imamura sought in his cinema. As he himself put it, "I wouldn't just say I wasn't influenced by Ozu. I would say I didn't *want* to be influenced by him" (Bock, 289). Fortunately, after moving to Nikkatsu, Imamura found a more compatible mentor in the person of Yuzo Kawashima, a director little known outside Japan but highly regarded at home for films such as *The Sun Legend of the Tokugawa Era* (1957). Kawashima's fondness for low-life settings and ribald humor proved a far more decisive influence, and the two men soon became close friends and soul-mates. Imamura later even wrote a book about the older director, titled *Life Is But Farewell: The Life of Yuzo Kawashima* and published in 1969.

The younger directors of the Japanese New Wave were united in railing against the big studio productions of the 1950s: family-oriented dramas laden with sentimentality and nostalgia, as well as with a sense of what Oshima termed "postwar victimization" (Quandt, 111). Oshima, Shinoda, Yoshida, and Imamura viewed the maudlin and conservative films of the directors who embodied the Golden Age of the 1950s—Kenji Mizoguchi, Mikio Naruse, Keisuke Kinoshita, and Ozu—as refusing to address subject matter and political issues relevant to the *après guerre* generation of which they themselves were a part.

The New Wave directors' break with filmmaking traditions manifested itself both technically, through their use of real locations and experimentation with documentary-style shooting, and in their choice of subject matter, as they focused on the underprivileged masses and the social injustice to which such lowly people were subjected. It was natural enough—for these filmmakers as for many others—to hold such strong, left-wing political views in the early 1960s. The Communists had opposed the expansionist plans of the militarist government before and during World War II, and thereafter they were all for the discontinuation of the Japanese imperial system, since they saw Emperor Hirohito as someone who had been complicit with the wartime regime.

Like Nagisa Oshima, Imamura eventually left the studio where he had made his first seven films and formed his own production company, Imamura Productions. Whereas Oshima, however, had departed from Shochiku under something of a black cloud after the company pulled his *Night and Fog in Japan* from distribution in 1960, Imamura's final three films of the 1960s—*The Pornographers* (1966), *A Man Vanishes* (1967), and *The Profound Desire of the Gods* (1968)—were all distributed by his former employers, Nikkatsu. In an interview with Audie Bock, Imamura succinctly summed up the crucial difference between himself and Oshima: "I am a country farmer, Oshima is a samurai" (289). While the latter's work belongs to a more polemical, essayistic tradition, tackling issues with intellectual rigor and singular focus in such films as *A Town of Love and Hope* (1959), *Death by Hanging* (1968), and *Diary of a Shinjuku Thief* (1969), Imamura presents us with a wider, more emotionally encompassing picture.

That is to say, Imamura's narratives unfold on broad canvases, packed with detail and teeming with life. Like a cinematic equivalent to the medieval Flemish painter Pieter Brueghel, this Japanese *auteur* makes his characters vulgar and absurd, yet full of a boundless energy that the screen can barely contain within the confines of the frame. Capturing from a god-like perspective the particulars of the lower-class world in all their glorious disorder, Imamura draws our attention to aspects we might otherwise have missed, as if he were a scientist gazing at the organisms in a sample of pond water on a microscopic slide. In 1984 the French critic Max Tessier even went so far as to label him "Japan's Modern Entomologist" (Quandt, 45), and it's an analogy that fits his work well.

Imamura actually named his 1963 film—about an impoverished country girl lured to the big city to make her living as a prostitute—*Nippon konchuki*, or, literally, *Entomological Chronicles of Japan* (commonly known in the West as *Insect Woman*). Its script was motivated by the appearance of an insect circling his ashtray as he sat down to write, which he felt was a similar situation to the one in which his main character would find herself. Indeed, insect and animal metaphors feature heavily in much of Imamura's work. *Pigs and Battleships* (1961), for example, is set around an American naval base in the town of Yokosuka during the occupation years, when the impoverished masses must eke out their existence by ravaging through pig refuse-containers set outside the perimeter fence of the base. There also local girls turn tricks for the American interlopers and a massive black market converges around the sale of stolen slabs of pork meat. The movie culminates in scenes of rioting rabble and warring black-market gangsters, intercut with shots of pigs running wild through the neon-lit streets surrounding the U.S. base.

Unholy Desire (1964), for its part, makes heavy use of two visual metaphors—a caged mouse and a silkworm—to suggest both the wretched experience of a lower-class housewife stuck in a loveless, only semi-legitimate marriage and her newly awakening awareness of her ability to use this situation to her advantage. The writhing creature that lends its name to *The Eel* (1997)—similar in expressive function to the oversized carp that thrashes around in the cramped aquarium of *The Pornographers*—itself serves as a visualization of the primordial subconscious of the film's guilt-wracked protagonist, who has just been freed from prison after serving time for violently murdering his wife.

Imamura thus sees his characters as being deeply connected, like their fellow denizens of the natural world, to the immediate environment in which they find themselves. And he takes great pains to depict it faithfully, without making even the basic assumption that it is environment that forms and shapes man. Rather, Imamura's characters remain somewhat unformed or unshaped, almost anonymous beings who blend into the background—like animals that would camouflage themselves.

II

Although Shohei Imamura had made his film début some two decades earlier with *Stolen Desire* (1958), until *Vengeance Is Mine*—an unflinching portrait of a callous psychopath, released in 1979—the director remained virtually unknown outside Japan. Much of his anonymity can be attributed to the fact that Nikkatsu, the studio that financed his early work, showed little interest in distributing his films to overseas markets. Even though *Insect Woman* had been entered into competition at the 1964 Berlin Film Festival (winning a Best Actress Silver Bear for its lead, Sachiko Hidari), previous to this event only Imamura's 1961 picture *Pigs and Battleships* had seen distribution in the West—in France, as *Filles et Gangsters*.

Still, Imamura was hailed in Japan as one of the most visionary moviemakers of the 1960s, due to a series of works that explored the gray areas between the rational and the irrational, man and beast, personal experience and official history, and the illusionary objectivity of documentary versus the unconcealed subjectivity of fictional narrative. Though critically as well as publicly established at home, Imamura had nonetheless experienced difficulty in adapting to the changed filmmaking climate of the 1970s in Japan. Moreover, *Vengeance Is Mine* was his first fiction film since the costly failure of *The Profound Desire of the Gods* (a.k.a. *Tales from a Southern Isle*) for Nikkatsu in 1968.

The Profound Desire of the Gods was a 170-minute epic whose lengthy on-location shoot sent the production's budget spiraling out of control. The film depicted a primitive tribe living in near-Stone Age conditions on a remote island (one of the Ryukyu chain), far from the Japanese mainland at the southern extreme of the Okinawan Archipelago. The tribal community there, ruled by superstition, is forced to face the future when an engineer, sent as a delegate from his company in Tokyo, arrives on the island with the aim of constructing a water mill. With this community serving as a microcosm for Japan-the-nation, *The Profound Desire of the Gods* saw Imamura pursuing his interest in anthropological subject matter (an interest betokened by the very subtitle of *The Pornographers: Introduction to Anthropology*), analyzing society through the behavior and interactions of its members—and finally deploring the coming of Western industrial development and religious practice to the Ryukyu Islands. However, the emotionally taxing shoot and the disappointing performance of this film at the box office nudged Imamura away from large-screen cinema for a while, with *The Profound Desire of the Gods* effectively serving as an end-marker in general for the period known as the New Wave of Japanese film.

Imamura then spent much of the 1970s making documentary works, many of which developed the concerns of *The Profound Desire of the Gods* into studies of national identity, or the nature of "Japanese-ness." The three-part *In Search of Unreturned Soldiers* (1971, 1975) looked at the lives of those who had remained overseas in the areas of Southeast Asia to which they had been posted during the Pacific War, opting to stay behind rather than return to Japan. *Karayuki-san: The Making of a Prostitute* (1975) revealed the hidden history of girls from Japan's outcast *burakumin* (or *eta*) class who were forced to find work as prostitutes in the nation's overseas colonies during the early decades of the twentieth century—a subject to which Imamura would later return in the fiction film *Zegen* (1987).

By the end of the decade, however, the director felt that he had reached the limits of what he could express through documentary, and was eager to return to the world of dramatic fiction—albeit fiction firmly rooted in fact. His script for *Vengeance Is Mine* was based on Ryuzo Saki's biographical novel of the real-life sociopath Akira Nishiguchi (called Iwao Enokizu in the film), who for seventy-eight days roamed Japan committing a string of grisly murders until his arrest on January 3, 1964. But Imamura was aware that in order to realize his story on film, on a suitable budget, certain concessions would have to be made. This was because, while studios throughout the 1960s had appeared willing to grant an unprecedented amount of creative leeway in order to nurture their more talented filmmakers, the tastes of Japanese audiences in the 1970s had turned more conservative, and at the same time the rising yen was forcing the film industry into a crisis of confidence.

Produced by Imamura Productions (the company he founded in 1965), *Vengeance Is Mine* needed the large distribution network that only a major company could provide, so Imamura approached Shochiku for funding. At the time, it was seen as one of the more conservative studios—famed for its long-running and perennially popular *Tora-san* (or *Otoko wa Tsurai yo!*) series starring Kiyoshi Atsumi and directed by Yoji Yamada—but Shochiku was now eager to strike out into more adventurous territory. Imamura, along with the screenwriter Masuru Baba, honed the script for several years until it was at a level in which Shochiku was willing to invest. Moreover, in spending additional time researching the Nishiguchi criminal case, these *auteurs* turned up a few details that both the novelist Saki and the police had missed.

III

Before continuing, let me first synopsize the action of *Vengeance Is Mine* for those who may not remember it or may be unfamiliar with the film altogether. At the start of the movie, the brutally murdered bodies of Tanejiro Shibata and Daihachi Baba, who had been collecting money for the Government Tobacco Monopoly Corporation, are found near a railroad station, having been robbed of 410,000 yen. Among the suspects is one Iwao Enokizu, a driver who had once worked for the distribution end of the Tobacco Monopoly. In gathering evidence about the killings, the police discover additional information about the type of man Enokizu really is—one who, for example, had earlier raped a woman bar owner and then forced her to live in his apartment as a sex slave. In fact, everyone who knows him attests to the fact that he is a "sex maniac."

The police visit Enokizu's home in Beppu, where his family—his father, Shizuo; his mother, Kayo; and his wife, Kazuko—all promise to do their best to find him. According to Shizuo, he, his wife, and his daughter-in-law are all devout Catholics, but ever since the war when Enokizu saw his father beaten up by the military and their

Vengeance Is Mine, dir. Shohei Imamura, 1979

fishing boats seized by force, the son had lost his own faith in God. Since that time Enokizu has been shuttling back and forth between prison and home, where he seldom stays for long. His wife and two daughters rarely see him and Kazuko must sell eggs to support the family.

At this point in *Vengeance Is Mine*, Enokizu turns up in Hamamatsu and settles down at the Asano Inn, where he claims to be a professor at Kyoto University. Occasionally he visits nearby Shizuoka University in the company of a prostitute, acting all the while as if he enjoys mocking the police on his tail. Continuing his stay at the Asano Inn, he begins a relationship with the female owner of the place until she and her mother find out that he is an impostor wanted by the police for murder. To protect himself, Enokizu winds up killing both of the women and selling their possessions in order to get money to escape. He does so, to Chiba, where his sphere of activity widens as he pretends to be an attorney at District Court and swindles an old woman out of the bail money for her detained son. Later he robs and murders an actual lawyer—an elderly man he meets by chance in Tokyo.

Meanwhile, the police have set up a nation-wide dragnet and circulated Enokizu's picture throughout the country. Nonetheless, for several more weeks Enokizu continues to travel throughout

Japan, committing fraud and victimizing women, until he is finally arrested (after a tip-off) in Kyushu. Eventually convicted and sentenced to death, Enokizu is visited for the last time by his father. But all that the son can say to the man who gave him life is "Seduce my wife. Instead of murdering others, I should have killed you!" After Enokizu's execution, his wife and his father go to a cliff overlooking Beppu Bay and mercifully scatter his ashes to the wind. But the family still gets no final peace, for, after Enokizu's mother dies, his father finds himself attracted to the son's widow. Yet Shizuo's religion forbids him to do anything about it, even though Kazuko herself is attracted to her father-in-law . . .

With both a higher budget and a more conventional structure, not to mention a considerably more nihilistic subject than hitherto had been the norm for this director, *Vengeance Is Mine* seems at first glance a world away from the ironic social commentary of Imamura's early works, which celebrated the effusive, irrepressible energy of downtrodden, low-life characters and their communities. This film, by contrast, achieves a bleak but chilling efficiency, and it does so largely through the portrayal of its central character, Iwao Enokizu, a man without a visible shred of humanity who is not averse to brutally murdering those who have the misfortune of getting too close to him, or who otherwise happen to stray into his path. With his dominating central performance of this role, Ken Ogata would become Imamura's actor of choice during the 1980s in the films *Eijanaika* (1981), *The Ballad of Narayama* (1983), and *Zegen*.

Vengeance Is Mine may initially appear distant from the humanism, and humor, of Imamura's earlier as well as later works, yet the angle from which this *auteur* approaches the film's material—with its flat, documentary-like stylization, lack of moral judgmentalness, and rigorous attention to characterological as well as environmental detail—highlights a number of threads that run throughout Imamura's *oeuvre*, threads that developed from his own experiences growing up in the ruins of postwar Japan. *Vengeance Is Mine* itself depicts the changing face of postwar Japan in a manner that appears oblique but in fact is highly arresting. As Imamura himself declared in the original brochure accompanying the film's release by Shochiku, "By describing this man's crimes in every respect, I have attempted to grasp today's era and the root of mankind living in my country in the present. Inside this man, could there be nothing except hollowness? I think that in him I can see the forlorn soul of today's Japanese."

With the approach of 1964's Tokyo Olympics—an event that came to symbolize the arrival of total modernization in Japan— forming the backdrop of *Vengeance Is Mine*, we see a man of self-made rootlessness who has turned his back on the three mainstays of authority or order in Japanese society: the Emperor, the father, and religion. Iwao Enokizu's ready adoption of disguises, complete rejection of established society, and sneering contempt for the values of restraint exercised by his father, all reflect a new Japan whose fugitive identity is as unstable as it is difficult to redirect. As Enokizu criss-crosses the country in search of a freedom or transcendence he knows he will never attain, he is also mapping out the darker corners of a nation in social as well as political transition, unwilling to confront directly its jingoistic, empire-building past.

With *Vengeance Is Mine*, Imamura thus moved his magnifying lens away from the plight of the unrefined masses to the dilemma of the newly emerging *petite bourgeoisie*. His focus, Enokizu, is a soulless construct who denies his roots in the endless search for a new self. He spits in the face of his father, Shizuo, who, in an early flashback, elicits the anger of his young son when, under physical threat, he gives up his fishing boats to the imperial navy during World War II. The use of such flashbacks to tell the story over several distinct time periods, and from a number of different points of view, adds something of a psychological element to Enokizu's characterization—one willfully absent from Imamura's earlier films. And that element is plainly visible (or "invisible") when, during Enokizu's time spent evading the police through various masquerades as a lawyer and university professor, he not only severs contact with his family but also keeps his true identity secret from everyone he encounters—including Haru Asano, the woman with whom he otherwise shares a bed.

Appropriately, given the film's flashback structure, multiple sequences of *Vengeance Is Mine* are shot from a distance—and from slightly above eye-level—yet Imamura uses telephoto or long lenses to keep us physically close to the figures on screen. In such a way, the director displays an objectivity and moral ambivalence that are at odds with the actions of the protagonist he depicts; he refuses, in other words, to manipulate his audience into any moral interpretation of events. Indeed, in a rigorous effort to steer viewers away from just such a moral interpretation, he includes material that might fall outside the scope of any other filmmaker's treatment of this subject. Imamura revels, for example, in his characters' petty foibles and inconsequential words or acts—minor things that may reveal much about their personalities, but that say little about their deeper motivations or any thematic intentions on the part of this *auteur*.

Released in the United States only six months after its Japanese première, *Vengeance Is Mine* proved far more commercially oriented than Imamura's earlier artistic experiments, despite its lurid subject matter, and the film's success led to its director's international breakthrough. His name brought to prominence among cinephiles worldwide, Shohei Imamura was later to score further success when *The Ballad of Narayama*, a radical reworking of the folk legend (in which, in an isolated and impoverished village in northern Japan, an old woman who can no longer do a full day's work observes a long tradition by abandoning herself to a snow-covered mountaintop rather than strain the limited resources of her son's family) first filmed in Kabuki-style in 1958 by Keisuke Kinoshita, won the Palme d'Or at the Cannes Film Festival in 1983. Then, in 1989, Imamura's *Black Rain*—a Hiroshima film about how, in the aftermath of the atomic bombing, radiation sickness binds a family of sufferers together in mutual sacrifice and support—itself won the Ecumenical Jury Prize at Cannes. When *The Eel* won the Palme d'Or at the same festival eight years later, Imamura became one of (at the time) only three film directors to win this grand prize a second time.

Grueling yet compelling, naturalistically staged yet meticulously stylized, *Vengeance Is Mine* succinctly bridges the later phase of Imamura's filmmaking career and his earlier one. A painstakingly matter-of-fact depiction of a man whose actions place him outside the realm of human comprehension, it is a pivotal work from one of the most significant directors in the last half century of world cinema. And, unlike the merely grisly (and American) *Henry: Portrait of a Serial Killer* (dir. John McNaughton, 1986), *Vengeance Is Mine* is a film whose cold, clinical presence retains the power to chill, to haunt, and to evoke to this very day.

CHRONOLOGY of the Prolonged Crime Spree of Akira Nishiguchi (known in *Vengeance Is Mine* as Iwao Enokizu)

14 December 1925: Born on Nakadori Island in the Goto Islands.

18 October 1963: In Fukuoka Prefecture, killed two people (Tanejiro Shibata and Daihachi Baba) and stole approximately 410,000 yen.

19 October 1963: Watched a baseball game at Hewadai Stadium in Fukuoka.

22 October 1963: Went to confession at a church in Saga.

24 October 1963: Feigned suicide on the Utaka Ferry in Tamano, Takamatsu.

28 October-1 November 1963: Stayed at the Asano Inn in Hamamatsu posing as a professor from Kyoto University.

7 November 1963: TV scam at a nursing home in Hiroshima.

15-19 November 1963: Stayed at the Asano Inn in Hamamatsu. Killed Haru Asano and her mother, Hisano; on 18 November pawned their clothes and jewelry. Pawned their phone on 19 November and fled.

3 December 1963: Committed fraud in Chiba by stealing criminal proceeds and bail money at Chiba District Court and Chiba Prison. Also stole a Lawyers' Registry.

7 December 1963: Used a travel-expenses scam to swindle a haberdashery in Monbetsucho, Sarugun, out of 15,000 yen and some underwear as well as other clothing.

9 December 1963: Swindled a securities company in Tokyo out of 40,000 yen in bogus fees and fled.

19-23 December 1963: Stayed at the home of an elderly lawyer in Tokyo, pretending to be looking after the house in his absence. Killed this man, Kyohe Kagashima, upon his return.

3 January 1964: Stayed at a chaplain's house in Tamana posing as a lawyer. Arrested in Kyushu after a tip-off.

11 December 1969: Executed at 10:05 A.M. at Fukuoka Prison.

BIBLIOGRAPHY: Shohei Imamura and Japanese Cinema

Bock, Audie. *Japanese Film Directors*. Tokyo: Kodansha International, 1978.

Burch, Noël. *To the Distant Observer: Form and Meaning in the Japanese Cinema*. Rev. and ed. Annette Michelson. London: Scolar Press, 1979.

Desser, David. *Eros Plus Massacre: An Introduction to the Japanese New Wave Cinema*. Bloomington: Indiana University Press, 1988.

Hunter, Jack. *Eros in Hell: Sex, Blood, and Madness in Japanese Cinema*. London: Creation Books, 1998.

Iles, Timothy. *The Crisis of Identity in Contemporary Japanese Film: Personal, Cultural, National*. Boston: Brill, 2008.

Kawamoto, Saburo. *New Trends in Japanese Cinema*. Tokyo: Japan Foundation, 1986.

McDonald, Keiko. *Cinema East: A Critical Study of Major Japanese Films*. Rutherford, New Jersey: Fairleigh Dickinson University Press, 1983.

Nolletti, Arthur, Jr., and David Desser, ed. *Reframing Japanese Cinema: Authorship, Genre, History*. Bloomington: Indiana University Press, 1992.

Phillips, Alastair, and Julian Stringer, ed. *Japanese Cinema: Texts and Contexts*. New York: Routledge, 2007.

Quandt, James, ed. *Shohei Imamura*. Toronto: Toronto International Film Festival Group, 1997.

Sato, Tadao. *Currents in Japanese Cinema: Essays*. Trans. Gregory Barrett. Tokyo: Kodansha International, 1982.

Washburn, Dennis, and Carole Cavanaugh, ed. *Word and Image in Japanese Cinema*. New York: Cambridge University Press, 2001.

16

Modish Artifice versus Modern Art:
Alain Resnais's *Last Year at Marienbad* in Light of Michelangelo Antonioni's *L'eclisse*

As I left the movie theater years ago after seeing *Last Year at Marienbad* (1961), I heard a man saying grimly to his wife, "Boy, I sure pity the critics on this one." He had evidently seen none of the tens of thousands of words already published at the time (and many more since) in Europe about this French film, where critics enjoyed themselves at sorting out its meanings.

Last Year at Marienbad is a relatively short picture—ninety-three minutes—directed by Alain Resnais, who made *Hiroshima, mon amour* (1959) immediately before it. He commissioned the original script from Alain Robbe-Grillet and worked closely on it with him. Robbe-Grillet was one of the three or four leading figures among the so-called New Novelists of France, and those who knew his two chief works, *Le Voyeur* (1955) and *La Jalousie* (1957), had something more than a glimmer of what to expect in this film.

It takes place in a huge baroque palace—actually Nymphenburg in Bavaria—which has been converted into a deluxe hotel. A man (never named—no characters are named) meets a young woman. He tells her that they met last year at Marienbad, or perhaps some place else, and were lovers. She denies it. Through a complex series of flashbacks, we see various versions of this past encounter as it may or may not have happened. The young woman is accompanied by a man who may or may not be her husband. The putative husband plays an implicative match game with the other man all through the film, always beating him. The latter insists that the woman leave the "husband" and go away with him, as he says he asked her to do a year ago. At the end, the man and the woman leave together—or maybe they don't.

Last Year at Marienbad, dir. Alain Resnais, 1961

The indefiniteness of this story is part of the very fabric of *Last Year at Marienbad*. Resnais and Robbe-Grillet disagreed publicly at the time of the film's release about whether the pair actually did meet the year before, and far from being embarrassed by differing views about their collaboration—as, say, their American contemporaries Billy Wilder and I. A. L. Diamond might have been—this director and screenwriter apparently took their disagreement as a certificate of success. This film, they claim, is like a piece of sculpture that may be approached from many angles—and hence be all things to all men.

But the gauzy story is only one note in the work's tonality. Resnais said that, before shooting *Last Year at Marienbad*, he drew up a complete chronology of its events on graph paper; while he was shooting, he told actors that the scene at hand followed a certain other scene in time sequence yet would not appear there in the final editing. The plainest point of the film, in fact, is that it does not intend to tell a chronological story. It tries to isolate and reproduce the emotions of its situations, drawing (as all our minds do constantly) on the past and the possible future, as well as on a temporal zone where we put elements of past and present into combinations that may never have happened and may never happen but which influence us nonetheless. *Marienbad* is thus an attempt to make visible the intangible—the lightning play of mind and memory and impulse.

To describe Resnais's method in detail is as impossible as it would be unhelpful. Much more to the purpose is to observe that he uses a free range of cinematic devices: intercutting, sometimes so brief as to be subliminal; swift series of still shots; quickly successive scenes of a character in the same composition but in different clothes and different lighting; and repetitions of whole sequences from the same or different viewpoints. (He even repeats one zooming close-up of the young woman in more and more intense light to the point of almost white overexposure, presumably to simulate the increasing intensity of the image in the narrator's mind.) The other guests in the hotel sometimes freeze motionless as the protagonists move among them, sometimes behave normally, sometimes are seen to speak but cannot be heard. At one point, we watch a duo of string musicians sawing away while we hear an organ playing. Occasionally the hero—the first man—recalls on the soundtrack an episode that is not quite what is happening before our eyes; later, the episode is repeated more or less as he had previously described it.

As in Robbe-Grillet's novels, the film's planes of time dissolve, resolve, and re-dissolve continually, like prisms in a kaleidoscope. And the most realistic detail—a statue's face, a broken glass—by its juxtaposition with other shots, takes on an unreal, suggestive quality. Kafka once said that "the strings of the lyre of modern poets are endless strips of celluloid," and the film of *Last Year at Marienbad*, an imagist poem, is proof. It is neither a narrative nor a drama but an endeavor to render subjectivity corruscatingly whole on the screen.

Anyone familiar with fantastic, surrealist, or "experimental" movies will recognize all the cinematic effects described above. Technically, there is little new in the film, as Resnais himself was the first to declare. He and Robbe-Grillet have used their method, not as inventors, but as devotees. They felt, as others have felt before them, that the conventions of art lay a false logic on the mercurial inner life of man, that plot contrivances are the real obscurantism, that the only lucidity is to present inner life as it is. I assume that it is to emphasize this belief that the filmmakers have placed their unconventional work in a highly conventional setting: a place and gardens that are the result of imposing strict order on nature.

Resnais's film style is much like Robbe-Grillet's prose. The latter writes in orderly grammatical sentences, not in expressionistic fragments or rhapsodies; his fracture of tradition comes from the content and sequence of sentences. Just so, Resnais almost never uses distortion, or freak shots, or double exposures; virtually every frame in *Last Year at Marienbad* is a clear and lovely photograph. To use an analogy from painting, Resnais has combined the loneliness of a surrealist vista by de Chirico with the exploded time of Picasso's cubism, but with this simple yet important difference: he has not distorted any of his elements. It is as if he were willing to accept orderly surfaces because it is the disorder beneath those surfaces that interests him; he seeks the disorderly true reality under the orderly false reality of the surface.

That said, the continuing critical search for meaning in this film is, to me, meaningless. Let us define "meaning," for our purpose, as the belief about an aspect of life that strikes us as basic or residual in a work of art after the initial emotions and sensations it arouses have passed. In this sense, *Last Year at Marienbad* has no fundamental meaning. Archibald MacLeish's familiar line tells us that a poem should not mean but be; a film, Resnais obviously thinks, should not mean but *see*.

A somber search for meaning is always the curse of an unusual work like this one. The analysts and aesthetes approach it with pigeonholes and cross-references at the ready, seemingly more interested in explaining it than in experiencing it. But the authors in this case want us simply to let the film happen to us, not to ferret out symbolized theses, not to compare it with plotted movies as we watch, any more than in a love affair of our own we would constantly compare it with a movie love affair. In this ostensibly arty film, Resnais and Robbe-Grillet are trying to remove what they feel are the barriers that art erects between maker and viewer. This film, they imply, is what it *does* to you: a congress of sensations; no more, perhaps, but no less and no other. Nevertheless, one analytical question must be raised: does *Last Year at Marienbad*, in the process, open up artistic immediacies to truth or is it simply a case of art anarchy?

Let me qualify my answer at the start by saying that I'm glad the film exists and is still seen, but I believe that this kind of film is self-limiting and eventually futile. My belief does not derive from accepted definitions of art: the fallacy in Resnais and Robbe-Grillet's style is that if it is followed absolutely rigorously, it leads not to art but to madness. This is because no one moment of time *can* be completely stopped; no one encounter or thought *can* be traced in all its permutations and ramifications. James Joyce's novel about one ordinary day in the life of one ordinary man is a titan's masterpiece; still, any reader can find gaps in the inclusiveness of *Ulysses* (1922). Art that tries to set down everything, and to set it down as it occurs, must end like a man trying to pick up too much and dropping what he has. Every honest artist who ever lived has known that he told partial lies, that he had to settle for less than he could see or know in order to reveal *something*, and that he therefore ended up compromising reality with some kind of abstraction or arrangement.

The Resnais-and-Robbe-Grillet alternative is to reject the contrivances and selectivity of art; but, far from being a move of liberation, this is, in fact, the most slavish realism. It tries to reproduce actual inner life instead of distilling it, as even the most Zola-esque naturalism does. The logical end of this director-screenwriter's method, its ultimate purity, is to see that there is falsity in any attempt to reproduce the truth, no matter how faithful; that for full, uncontaminated emotional truth, each audience member must go himself to Nymphenburg and hover in time between present and past, among varying shades of reality. Pressed to perfection, such a quest for fidelity to life cannot be satisfied by anything but life itself, of which art must always be only a delegate. This true-map-of-the-mind style, arising from a hatred of tired formula and fakery, inevitably founders, then, on the faintly sophomoric failure to distinguish between life and art.

Further, the possibilities of extension of self or self-knowledge, provided by other artistic styles, are negligible here. A work like *Last Year at Marienbad* is, in its way, only a "recognition" film, like a television domestic comedy in which you watch kids who behave just like yours at home. When all is over, you are not deeply moved or mentally stimulated; you have spent most of your time checking whether or not Resnais and Robbe-Grillet's representation of the functions of the mind and imagination corresponds with your own experience.

About the acting itself in this film there can be small comment. The actors here are usually not asked to be much more than elements in pictorial compositions, required to stand thus and look thus, rarely with emotional development or transition in any one shot, scene, or sequence. Giorgio Abruzzi, who plays the man, has a genuinely romantic face; Sacha Pitoëff, the other man, has a mysterious death-head's face. There is really not much more to be said about them. Delphine Seyrig, the young woman (whom Resnais also featured in *Muriel* [1963]), is handsome, but we are sometimes distracted from the emotion her face is supposed to evoke because her attitudes keep reminding us of those displayed by fashion models. Thus do chic photographers pose their girls in rich settings, even to the averted head and the ineffable secret sorrow that seems inseparable from *haute couture*. (Indeed, Seyrig's gowns are by Chanel.)

For myself, there is infinitely more reward in films from the same period by (for a paramount example) Michelangelo Antonioni, who by the 1960s is equally disgusted with stale formulas but who replaces them with new and appropriate abstractions, with new art, rather than with figurative mental recorders. Because he is interested in character (as *Last Year in Marienbad* is not), he involves us to a degree that disembodied reproduction of inner processes can never reach. Strictly speaking, Antonioni rearranges and distorts certain realities as Resnais tries not to do; but Resnais's efforts lead only to duplication of experience, while Antonioni's freshly seen artistic order results in illumination of experience. After *Marienbad*, I knew more about Alain Resnais and *his* search for reality; but after *La notte* (*The Night,* 1961) and *L'avventura* (1960), I knew more about myself.

Let me explain by using Antonioni's *L'eclisse* (*Eclipse,* 1962) as an example, and by using Monica Vitti's character, and acting, in this film as a focal point. *L'eclisse* appeared the year after Jean Rouch's *Chronicle of a Summer, Last Year at Marienbad,* and Jacques Rivette's *Paris Belongs to Us;* it was released in the same year as Luis Buñuel's *The Exterminating Angel* and Jean-Luc Godard's *Vivre sa vie;* and *L'eclisse* premiered one year before *Muriel* and Godard's *Contempt*—a period, in short, when large thematic statements and major narrative innovations were often coming together in the cinema. *L'eclisse* also came as the climax of Antonioni's loose trilogy about Eros, art, business, and emotional alienation, preceded by *L'avventura* and *La notte*. And in some ways it upped the ante of his provocative modernism by being the most radical of the three films in both its defiance of narrative conventions and its chilling poetry of absence and desire.

L'avventura's central mystery—the disappearance of a major character, Anna (Lea Massari), on a volcanic island during a luxury cruise—is never solved, and its narrative focus shifts part of the way through the film to Anna's best friend, Claudia (Monica Vitti). (This device anticipates the shock tactics of Hitchcock's *Psycho* soon thereafter, whereby Vera Miles "replaces" Janet Leigh.) *La notte*, adhering to a time sequence of almost twenty-four hours, has a more conventional shape, though most of its middle consists of a seemingly directionless narrative shift. *L'eclisse*—beginning with the termination of one love affair and ending with the apparent scuttling of another—appears at times to consist of nothing but narrative drift, and the fact that none of the film's characters, including the two leads, Vittoria and Piero (Vitti and Alain Delon), appear during the final sequence only adds to the impertinence. (Some American exhibitors were in fact so troubled by this ending that they lopped off the entire seven minutes.)

This eerie yet stunning climax brings to a head Antonioni's preoccupation with objects and places as they overtake and supplant people—a preoccupation that already figures in such sequences as the visit to the volcanic island in *L'avventura* and the helicopter's buzzing outside the hospital window near the beginning of *La notte*, as well as in the scene at the start of *L'eclisse* after the couple's morning break-up, when various objects in the room, and a tower seen outside through the window, momentarily seem to displace them. In all three cases, the viewer is suspended in what initially feels like narrative digression but may in fact be a dispersal of the narrative in an unforeseen direction, away from the characters and into the setting. That is, into yet another perspective in a series of perspectives which suggests a narrative equivalent to cubism. Significantly, had Antonioni had his way with *L'eclisse*'s story and not been overruled by his producer, it would have yielded two features rather than one, exploring the same events from the separate viewpoints of Piero and Vittoria.

But it is Vittoria who is the film's focus. And all the more so because she is played by Monica Vitti. *L'avventura* was her first film

L'eclisse, dir. Michelangelo Antonioni, 1962

with Antonioni. She was a little-known actress; he had directed some remarkable films. But this was the one that made him famous, and it made her famous along with him. Their names became inseparable as their collaboration continued in *La notte*, *L'eclisse*, and *Red Desert* (1964). For, unlike other actresses who achieved notable collaborations with film directors (Lillian Gish with D. W. Griffith, Marlene Dietrich with Josef von Sternberg, Godard with Anna Karina), Vitti is identified with the director-as-beholder behind the camera, whose gaze she doubles. Not that Vitti isn't beautiful and worthy of being beheld for herself. But her presence is less commanding than that of Gish, Dietrich, or Karina, her beauty more tentative, which is in keeping with the unsettled, questioning beauty of Antonioni's visual style. And in Vitti's films with him, she is therefore as much beholding as beheld.

Other male directors have adopted the point of view of a female character, but none has made a woman his surrogate in the way that Antonioni made Monica Vitti his. "I especially love women," he once said in an interview,

> Perhaps because I understand them better? I was born among women, and raised in the midst of female cousins,

aunts, relatives. I know women very well. Through the psychology of women, everything becomes more poignant. They express themselves better and more precisely. They are a filter that allows us to see more clearly and to distinguish things.

Antonioni's tendency to filter our perceptions through the perspective of a woman was already manifest in such accomplished early works of his as *La signora senza camelie* (*The Lady without Camelias*, 1953) and *Le amiche* (*The Girlfriends*, 1955). But it reaches a culmination in his films with Monica Vitti, which display a peculiar intimacy between director and actress (similar in some ways to that between Godard and Karina and no doubt in both cases having something to do with the fact that director and actress were intimate in real life). Paradoxically, though Antonioni is rarely viewed as a director of actors, he should be (quite unlike the subject of the first part of this essay, Alain Resnais), and I would argue that *L'eclisse* features the most expressive, exuberant performance by Vitti in any movie she ever made. Indeed, the achievement of this subtly structured masterpiece would be unthinkable without her.

The distinctive interrogative gaze of Antonioni's camera, it follows, is paralleled by the gaze of Vitti's major characters in his films—Vittoria in *L'eclisse*, Claudia in *L'avventura*, Giuliana in *Red Desert*. Take the first stock-market sequence in *L'eclisse*. Vittoria, after having been up all night in a draining quarrel with the lover she has decided to leave, arrives at the stock exchange, the Borsa in the center of Rome, looking for her mother and wishing to talk to her about the love affair that has just ended. But her mother is too preoccupied with financial matters to talk about personal ones, and Vittoria instead observes the hectic activity of the exchange as an uncomprehending outsider, taken aback yet curious about its strange spectacle in which great energy is unleashed in the mad pursuit of money. Her position is exactly the observing position of Antonioni's camera. (In the second, longer visit to the stock market, the camera goes there with an insider, Piero, the stockbroker with whom Vittoria starts a new love affair, but all the same its point of view remains that of an outsider—especially after the heroine turns up, once the market crashes—immersed in the turbulent proceedings without knowing quite what to make of them.)

Monica Vitti may well be described as an actress of the gaze, both the gaze she turns on the world and the gaze the world turns on her. Every performer, of course, is there to be looked at, on display before an audience of *voyeurs*, if you will. But just as Antonioni's films enact a special way of looking, so too does Vitti's special quality as a performer arise from the way in which she looks at things, as well as the way she is looked at and aware of being looked at: in a word, from the interplay between her as the subject and the object of the gaze. In both positions, she is visibly a little self-conscious, as if she always felt on her the eye of the beholder and responded in kind with her own beholding. Just as Antonioni, then, is, more than a director of scenes, a director of *attention*, so Vitti is a performer of attention, which she pays to her surroundings and receives from Antonioni's camera—and from an attentive audience—with much the same inquiring, responsive intentness.

Watch her, for example, as she watches a Borsa trader who, after losing a lot of money, goes to a café, takes a tranquilizer, and draws flowers. Or as she pauses, while walking with Piero, to gaze at a good-looking young man passing by: like Antonioni's camera, Vitti is open to distraction here as a way of paying attention to the world around her. Or watch when she arrives early at the corner where she is to meet Piero and has time for a private preamble to the meeting, bringing the place, the passersby, the unfinished building mirroring her own sense of suspension, into commerce with her consciousness. Or when, in the most tranquil sequence in *L'eclisse*, Vittoria takes a plane ride to the Verona airport, another public place she invests with her subjectivity and somehow makes private. She feels at ease for no particular reason during her visit to this nondescript provincial airport, where a man drinking beer at the bar looks at her and she looks at the people and the place, the airplanes on the ground and in the sky, with a reflective contentment that just manages to hold off emotional anxiety. Nothing happens in such scenes except an experience of awareness, awareness of the world and of the self in transaction with the world (something quite different from what I earlier described as Resnais's disembodied reproduction of inner mental processes); and that is Monica Vitti's specialty as a performer.

Ingmar Bergman once told an interviewer that he considered

Antonioni—along with the Danish filmmaker Carl Theodor Dreyer—an amateur and Vitti a talented but technically insecure performer. The truth is that Bergman is a master of conventional technique, the way a good professional does it, by the rules; and that Antonioni—like Dreyer—is the kind of artist who goes his own way in disregard of the rules and achieves an unconventional mastery. The conventional camera is a storyteller that knows the story and picks out for us at each moment just what we need to see; this can even be said of Alain Resnais's cubist-like camera in *Last Year at Marienbad*. But Antonioni's lens continually explores the alternative, the stray aspect, the revising angle, the newly revealing moment. And its inquiry into appearances, its searching rather than knowing apprehension of things, finds its acting counterpart in the similarly searching Monica Vitti—even as, from a reverse angle, as it were, Resnais's lovely but empty photographs are matched by the superficial beauty of Delphine Seyrig. Vitti's engaging yet diffident verve consorts with the uncertain beauty, the arresting tentativeness, the detached intensity of Antonioni's images. And what Bergman calls her insecurity—a fair enough term for Vitti's characteristic tinge of self-consciousness—she makes into a style of performance, one that could not be better suited to her partnership with Antonioni.

As a director, Antonioni gained renown as the maker of films short on action and long on the spaces in between. But even if nothing much is happening, those empty spaces, those intervals of an uncertain modernity, are fraught with intimations of something that happened or is about to happen, narrative paths that have been taken or may be taken. And though Vitti inhabits those spaces provisionally, quizzically, in the way of someone who feels like a stranger in her own land, she nonetheless brings a lively presence to that landscape of absence and a sense of narrative expectancy (let us call it), a search for connection in the midst of alienation. Troubled inquiries into the shifting appearances of our shared reality, the films of Michelangelo Antonioni are modernist mystery stories, and Vitti's characters in them are something like detective figures.

Antonioni's camera itself is a kind of detective. His method of looking at things "consists in working backward," as he has explained, "from a series of images to a state of affairs," whereas most filmmakers start with a state of affairs—a story or the ingredients for one—that determines their choice of images. But Antonioni is a detective faced with a mystery too large and implicative to admit of a solution. Even at the end of *L'eclisse*, when the awaiting camera registers, around the suburban corner where the protagonist couple are supposed to meet, the uneventful daily passage from afternoon to evening, daylight to twilight, twilight to darkness, a clipped series of images (centered around both the absence of Vittoria and Piero and a recapitulation of motifs associated with them) holds any conclusion in unsettling abeyance.

It is almost as if Antonioni has extracted here the essence of everyday street life that serves as a background throughout the picture, and once we are presented with this essence in undiluted form, it suddenly threatens and even oppresses us. The implication is that behind every story there is a place and an absence, an unsolvable mystery and a profound uncertainty, waiting like a vampire at every moment to emerge and take over, sucking the very life out of the story. And if we combine this place and absence, this mystery and uncertainty, into a single, irreducible entity, what we have is the modern world itself, the place where all of us live and which most stories are designed to protect us from—including the kind, like Alain Resnais's *Last Year at Marienbad*, that pretend with their quasi-photographic realism to do the very opposite.

BIBLIOGRAPHY

Antonioni, Michelangelo. *Interviews*. Ed. Bert Cardullo. Jackson: University Press of Mississippi, 2008.

_____. *The Architecture of Vision: Writings and Interviews on Cinema*. Ed. Carlo di Carlo, Giorgio Tinazzi, and Marga Cottino-Jones. New York: Marsilio Publishers, 1996.

_____. *Michelangelo Antonioni: A Introduction*. Trans. Scott Sullivan. New York, Simon and Schuster, 1963.

Armes, Roy. *The Cinema of Alain Resnais*. London: Zwemmer, 1968.

Arrowsmith, William. *Antonioni: The Poet of Images*. New York: Oxford University Press, 1995.

Brunette, Peter. *The Films of Michelangelo Antonioni*. New York: Cambridge University Press, 1998.

Callev, Haim. *The Stream of Consciousness in the Films of Alain Resnais.* New York: McGruer Publishing, 1997.

Cameron, Ian Alexander, and Robin Wood. *Antonioni.* 1968. New York: Praeger, 1971.

Chatman, Seymour. *Antonioni, or, The Surface of the World.* Berkeley: University of California Press, 1985.

_____. *Michelangelo Antonioni: The Complete Films.* London: Taschen, 2004.

Cowie, Peter. *Antonioni, Bergman, Resnais.* London: Tantivy Press, 1963.

Kreidl, John Francis. *Alain* Resnais. Boston: Twayne, 1977.

Leutrat, Jean-Louis. "*L'Année dernière à Marienbad*". Trans. Paul Hammond. London: British Film Institute, 2000.

Lyons, Robert Joseph. *Michelangelo Antonioni's Neo-Realism: A World View.* New York: Arno Press, 1976.

Monaco, James. *Alain Resnais and the Role of Imagination.* London: Secker and Warburg, 1978.

Perry, Ted. *Michelangelo Antonioni, A Guide to Reference and Resources.* Boston: G.K. Hall, 1986.

Rohdie, Sam. *Antonioni.* London: British Film Institute, 1990.

Sweet, Freddy. *The Film Narratives of Alain Resnais.* Ann Arbor: UMI Research Press, 1981.

Ward, John. *Alain Resnais, or the Theme of Time.* London: Secker and Warburg, 1968.

Wilson, Emma. *Alain Resnais.* Manchester, U.K.: Manchester University Press, 2006.

17

Re-reading the Rules:
Renoir's *La Règle du jeu* Reconsidered

It may not be remembered that before World War II, and even for some time after it, Jean Renoir was by no means ranked as the supreme French film director. Marcel Carné, René Clair, Jacques Feyder, and Julien Duvivier were all considered at least his equals, or even his superiors. His work, by comparison with theirs, was felt to lack polish and dramatic shape; both technically and morally, Renoir's movies seemed rough, often tentative or self-questioning. It was only around the early 1950s, with the advent of the *Cahiers du cinéma* school of *auteurist* criticism, that Renoir's stock began to rise even as that of the other 1930s directors (with the sole exception of Jean Vigo) fell. Speaking for his fellow *Cahiers* critics and New Wave directors, François Truffaut hailed Renoir as "the father of us all" (cited in Wakeman, 944-945).

During the heyday of *Cahiers du cinéma* and the *politique d'auteurs*—the so-called *auteur* theory—the young French cinema was rejecting the established criteria of cinematic merit, which had much to do with literary orthodoxy and which celebrated such cinematically barren but financially successful films as Marcel Pagnol's popular pre-war trilogy *Marius, Fanny, César* (all three adapted from Pagnol's own plays). The *Cahiers* critics favored a cinema of authorial primacy for the writer-director that ignored the pedigree of literary antecedents preferred by their elders. And the critical impulse that brought *auteurism* into vogue prepared the way for the intensely personal cinema of the *nouvelle vague*, the New Wave of critics-turned-filmmakers who shocked the bourgeoisie at the same time as they energized French moviemaking.

That the *Cahierists*, who hoisted the "auteurial" flag and gave the world the New Wave, venerated Renoir above all other French filmmakers is not a surprise. Renoir took chances, made films on risk or instinct, insulted political sensibilities, challenged the Hollywood studio system during his self-imposed wartime exile, and actually managed to make some interesting movies in the United States despite the best efforts of American producers not to understand him. Certainly, few today would dispute Renoir's status as one of the greatest of all filmmakers, and most would accept that the films made between 1932 and 1939 (from *Boudu*, that is, to *La Règle du jeu*) consist of his best work and some of the best work ever committed to the screen.

Indeed, Renoir's pre-war films were received, upon re-release, with an enthusiasm they had rarely received the first time around. This was particularly true of what, along with *La Grande illusion* (1937), many today consider his very best work: *La Règle du jeu* (1939). It had initially been attacked by hostile Parisians as frivolous, clumsy, and downright incomprehensible, yet *La Règle du jeu* (*The Rule[s] of the Game*) is now generally regarded as a masterpiece.[9] There is a strange side to the film, however. What most critics and reference books say concerning it—and they tend to say much the same thing—does not, to put it bluntly, square with the facts.

Let me quote from the *New Oxford Companion to Literature in French* (1995): *La Règle du jeu* is "about an aristocratic house-party that is a microcosm of the corruptness and exhaustion of French society on the eve of World War II" (684). Here is Philip Kemp, in the liner notes to the 2003 BFI DVD of the film: "The seemingly elegant, old-world gathering is riven with rancour and hatreds, social, political, and racial. The rules of the game are designed to exclude those who fail to grasp the unspoken assumptions behind them." According to Celia Bertin, in her biography *Jean Renoir: A Life in Pictures* (1991), Renoir "wanted to tell the story of people dancing on a volcano. . . . He knew that the slaughter of rabbits and pheasants prefigures the death of men. War was inevitable, and he was thinking about it all the time now" (161; as Bertin also tells us on page 156, however, Renoir "felt the need to express his anxiety by imagining what he called 'a happy drama' [*un drame gai*].")

From *French Cinema from Its Beginnings to the Present* (2002), by Rémi Fournier Lanzoni, I shall give a longer extract, along much the same lines:

Re-reading the Rules 287

This fantasy is a mundane massacre, and a sharp vision of prewar social degeneration, with a hint of several theatrical traditions (Beaumarchais, Musset, Marivaux). . . . This comedy, which veered inescapably into a dramatic finale, illustrated a series of ruptures in the social order. For example, the scene showing the senseless carnage of rabbits in the forest became an omen for the disproportionate combats that occurred a few weeks later all over Europe, and it exemplified society's plunge into pointless violence. . . . Throughout the film, viewers can feel that the rise of the impending threat of a possible world conflict, coupled with a deep apprehension of hostile foreign neighbors, had generated a defeatist mind-set about the prospects for the future of France. (92, 94)

What on earth, one asks oneself, is one to make of this? It seems quite baseless. None of the characters in Renoir's film even mention war or the future of France; and it is not clear how a massacre of rabbits, or indeed of anything, can "become" an omen. Still, that did not deter Alexander Sesonke, writing for Criterion in 2003, from opining something similar to what Lanzoni says:

By February 1939 it no longer seemed evident that the surrender of Czechoslovakia to Adolf Hitler at Munich "saved the peace." Soon a sense of doom would hang over Europe. In this atmosphere Jean Renoir, anticipating war and deeply troubled by the mood he felt around him, thought he might best interpret that state of mind by creating a story in the spirit of French comic theater, from Marivaux to de Musset, a tradition in which the force that sets every character in motion is love and the characters have no other occupation but to interfere with this pursuit.

Here is Christopher Faulkner, echoing Sesonske two years later—and finding yet another omen for the world war to come, not in the rabbit hunt, but in the hunt (from Renoir's *La Vie est à nous* [1936]) that prefigures *it*:

288   Formal Matters

> *The Rules of the Game* is a report on the condition of French society on the eve of the Second World War. . . . The film exposes the hypocrisy, ignorance, cynicism, and moral turpitude of a society in the face of what it perceives to be imminent threats to its security. . . . The hunt sequence [itself] recalls a scene in Renoir's *Life Is Ours*, in which members of the upper class dressed for the hunt take target practice at cardboard cutouts of French workers. The war . . . can [thus] be understood as class war as well as international war. (302-303)[10]

Moreover, what is all this that Philip Kemp tells us about the "elegant, old-world gathering" at the Marquis de la Chesnaye's chateau being "riven with rancour and hatreds, social, political, and racial"? As to race, there is only a single brief reference to it in the film. One of the servants at the downstairs dining table says that it should be remembered that Chesnaye is a "Yid" (meaning that his mother was Jewish), but the Chef avers, firmly, that nevertheless the Marquis (played by the same actor who played the wealthy Jew Rosenthal in *La Grande illusion*: Marcel Dalio) has "quality." That he has "class" is also what the elderly General (who, if anyone, might have been expected to harbor social prejudices) is quick to affirm in Chesnaye's defense, when a guest hints that the Marquis has told a lie. Apart from this, one would seek in vain for signs of "rancour and hatreds," any more than of Celia Bertin's "volcano."

As for the *New Oxford Companion*'s "corruptness and exhaustion of French society on the eve of World War II," one is struck by the zest and energy, the noisy and joyous *brio*, of Chesnaye's guests on their arrival at La Colinière (the country estate where Renoir's story takes place). It sets the tone for the excited swiftness, the sense of ceaseless movement, running through the film and complemented by Renoir's ever mobile camera. Nor is any of the guests, so far as one can see, noticeably "corrupt." Yet the tendency to see them as such goes back a long way: Gerald Mast, for instance, writing in 1973, declared that "the tendency to see [*La Règle du jeu*] as a purely satirical indictment of a corrupt social system dominates the reviews written since the reconstructed print of the film appeared in 1959" (69-70). And Robin Wood, in 1984, argued that the film was detested when it first appeared precisely because it was "satirizing the corruption of the French ruling class on the brink of the Second World War" (390).

The structure of *La Règle du jeu* is a descendant of the comic French theater of the eighteenth century, and that should tell us something more about its subject matter than what the critics have deduced. An opening title quotes Beaumarchais, one of the comic dramatists of that century, and all during the film there are echoes of other dramatic works from centuries in addition to the eighteenth—works by Marivaux and de Musset, also Molière and Feydeau, even Shakespeare and Jonson, indeed many masters of classical comedy.[11] It is therefore no accident that the film's major-domo, one of the figures of competence and order, is named Corneille, the great French neoclassical *tragedian*, who placed duty before passion.

La Règle du jeu manipulates throughout the devices of classical comedy. There are parallel actions on the part of masters and servants, the activities of the lower classes being a "vulgar" and low-comic mirror of those in the upper ones. As in classical comedy, the subject matter is love—requited and unrequited; requited and then unrequited; unrequited and then requited—as well as the consequent errors of love—jealousy, misinterpretation, and misunderstanding. The narrative of the film plays several interlocking love triangles against the background of the two societies—that of the masters and the servants. And it does so with a fondness for the theatrical group shot in which several characters are linked and the continuous re-framings, along with the entrances and exits, ensure that the spectator's gaze is constantly transferring itself from character to character, action to action, as it would be in the theater—with few close-ups and point-of-view shots.[12] There are even such classical comic devices as the interwoven chase (various lovers weaving in and out of rooms searching for their own beloved), the mistaken identity arising from a piece of clothing (Lisette's cloak and Octave's raincoat), and the farcical slap in the face and kick up the backside (the fights between André and Saint-Aubin, André and the Marquis de la Chesnaye).

Most like the classical theater, and in fact like any traditional French play, *La Règle du jeu* is composed of five acts. The overall structure of the film, as in classical comedy, is to introduce the individual human pieces in the early acts, to bring them together shortly thereafter, to scramble them in the middle acts, and then to sort them out for the conclusion. The great difference, of course, between Renoir's film and classical comedy—a difference that he deliberately manipulates—is that his film contains a number of events, characters, and themes not usually found in traditional comedy. Whereas traditional comedy often ends with a party, a dance, and even a marriage, Renoir chooses not to end his film with a party but to add a serious, melancholy, and altogether catastrophic act after the party ends. This inspired juxtaposition of serious material and comic devices is ultimately what gives *La Règle du jeu* its dramatic power, its human complexity, and its intellectual richness.

The leading character in the film, the Marquis de la Chesnaye, himself is an impressive and most attractive figure. By a neat little directorial stroke we are made to see that he is the product of a strictly aristocratic upbringing. When his valet brings him his coat and scarf, he takes them without a glance, as if quite unaware of the valet's existence. But, on a personal level, he is not at all what this might lead one to expect. The Marquis is enlightened and egalitarian, a hater of all barriers—including social ones; and, being a man of feeling, he is also a masterly handler of human crises. He is evidently a magnificent host, having arranged for his guests, in addition to a hunt, several brilliant little fancy-dress entertainments on his private stage. The film is, among other things, a warm tribute to him and his values.

It is for Chesnaye a "rule of the game" that, if somebody falls in love with one's partner and the love is returned, it is contemptible to nurse vindictive feelings, and even more so to act on them. In this he contrasts with a friend of his, André Jurieu, a young aviator. André is in love with Chesnaye's wife, Christine, and is determined to make a tragic and public business of it. Chesnaye himself has for several years, unknown to Christine, had a mistress, Geneviève—a fact that Christine finds out by accident during the hunt. She is looking through binoculars and catches sight of them kissing. (It is actually a farewell kiss, for the relationship has cooled.) But Christine proves to adhere to her husband's "rule of the game" quite as firmly as he does; and, indeed, as the fruit of some frank conversation, she and his lover Geneviève are soon the best of friends. (They agree that he has only one grave fault: he smokes in bed.) Chesnaye's love for Christine has actually revived, but her own feelings are in a muddle. She does not know what she wants; or rather, what she really wants is to have a child.

Chesnaye's "rule" is an excellent one but more suited to a leisured aristocrat than to someone like the gamekeeper Schumacher, who has to work for his livelihood. It is one of Schumacher's grievances that he so rarely can see his wife, Lisette, who, as Christine's chambermaid, spends much of the time with her mistress in Paris. Another of his grievances is that Chesnaye has recently encountered a wily poacher named Marceau at La Colinière, and, being greatly taken with the man, has taken him into his household. Marceau is trying to seduce Lisette, and the jealous Schumacher, finding the two in each other's arms, chases Marceau through the house, threatening to kill him. Chesnaye comes to the poacher's aid this time, but soon Schumacher is again pursuing Marceau, revolver in hand (though some of the house guests, at first disconcerted by the spectacle, assume that it is all part of Chesnaye's program of entertainment).

Eventually it becomes plain to Chesnaye that André has won Christine's affections, and, forgetting his "rule" for a moment, the Marquis gets into a fistfight with him. Then, coming to his senses, he is full of abject apologies for his shameful behavior. With his handkerchief, Chesnaye solicitously helps brush the dust off André's jacket, which has suffered in the scuffle, and soon the two are as good friends as ever. We are approaching the climax of the film when Christine, beset by André, tells him that she will run away with him if it can be done this very instant, without further ado. But he, too, has a "rule": Chesnaye is a friend and his host, he says, and it would simply be impossible to take such a step without telling him first.

Christine is then seen strolling with Octave in the gardens, in the chilly night air, and she not only describes her situation with André but also says that it is really not André she loves but Octave himself. For a minute or two, the bumbling and self-doubting, yet warm-hearted Octave (played by Renoir himself) is convinced and

La Règle du jeu, dir. Jean Renoir, 1939

believes that she is ready to elope with him; but he is brought to his senses by Lisette, who joins them and tells him angrily that he is too old for an affair with her beloved mistress. Christine is anxious at this point not to have to return to the chateau, and Octave tells her to take refuge in the conservatory. They put Lisette's cloak round her for warmth, and Octave promises to fetch her own cloak for her from the chateau. André now appears, asking where Christine is, and Octave—silently renouncing all his own hopes—urges him to join her, putting his own coat round André's shoulders.

Meanwhile Schumacher, reconciled in his misery to Marceau (for Chesnaye has dismissed them both), has fetched his shotgun and is sitting with him, watching the scene from the shadows. He is misled by the cloak into thinking that the woman in the conservatory is his wife, Lisette; and when André—whom he mistakes for Octave—approaches, he shoots him. Summoning his guests to the steps of the chateau, Chesnaye tells them the news and, with his usual resourcefulness, explains that the killing was

Re-reading the Rules 293

an accident—as of course, in a sense, it was. Naturally, the group willingly and unemotionally agrees to accept what Chesnaye says as a gentlemanly display of good form.

Told like this, the plot of *La Règle du jeu* is surely not—not at all—what the critics' account of it would have led us to expect. I used to be puzzled by their interpretation, but I now think it derives from a misunderstanding. After the film, to Renoir's bewilderment and dismay, went down extremely badly on its first showing in 1939, being hissed and jeered at, he decided either to give up filmmaking or to leave France. The reason for the bad reception, it appears, is that—for a predominantly left-wing audience, rightly obsessed, as Renoir himself was, by the imminent threat of a world war—*La Règle du jeu* was far too sympathetic towards the French aristocracy, and in particular towards the Marquis de la Chesnaye.[13] Thus, the lacerating reflections about the "degeneracy" of French society that critics find in it represent what (in their view) Renoir *ought* to have expressed, though in fact he did not.

Renoir's own account in his autobiography, *My Life and My Films*, of how *La Règle du jeu* came to be conceived is that it was inspired by French eighteenth-century music—Couperin, Rameau, Mozart. Indeed, we are given a few bars of Mozart's "Three German Dances, K. 605" at the beginning and the end of the film. (It is complemented by what one could call the "visual" music in *La Règle du jeu*, which comes from Renoir's depth-of-field shooting, enabling the staging of simultaneous foreground and background actions that often operate like counterpoint in music.) He had developed a great liking for such music, and it made him wish to film the "sort of people who danced to it" (169). They would, in the nature of things, have been aristocrats, and their outlook would very likely have been a "libertine" one. It would, he felt, be interesting to see what such people would be like if transposed to modern times. Renoir was, as he himself said, meaning to create a *drame gai*, a light-hearted drama in the style of *The Marriage of Figaro* (1784).

Accordingly, after the film's credits, these are the lines we are shown, on a placard, from Act IV, scene 10 of Beaumarchais's play:

> Coeurs sensibles, coeurs fidèles,
> Qui blâmez l'amour lèger,

> Cessez vos plaintes cruelles:
> Est-ce un crime de changer?
> (Weak of heart, faithful hearts,
> Who condemn light-hearted love,
> Stop your cruel complaints:
> Is it a crime to change?; my translation)

Since we know from Renoir's own words that he was at this time, 1939, quite alarmed (as were many other intelligent people) by the terrifying prospect of a new world war, we can deduce that his film was clearly intended as an antidote to, or escape from, such alarm or anxiety. That in places it would, nevertheless, be extremely poignant, should not surprise anyone familiar with Beaumarchais's *Marriage of Figaro* (itself performed on the eve of the French Revolution but, like *La Règle du jeu* in relation to World War II, offsetting this cataclysm rather than foretelling it) or especially Mozart's 1786 operatic version of it.

After all, Renoir knew that the perfect grace and orderly, delicate perfection of the eighteenth century (the century that produced Mozart, Chesnaye's chateau, his aristocratic way of life, and his mechanical music boxes) could no longer exist in the twentieth century, with its airplanes, automobiles, radios, telephones, mass destruction, and empowered masses. To prefer the stability of the old order to the terrifying instability of the new disorder (as do the two aristocratic military officers, one French and one German, in Renoir's other masterpiece, *La Grande illusion*) is both human and understandable. It is also, unfortunately, an anachronism, and therefore a human impossibility. Still, even though the lower classes' dream of material ease and democratic freedom may point the way in which the world will go, the aristocratic ethos of *noblesse oblige*, of gentlemanly honor and chivalric spirit, embodies what the world will lose by going there.

In addition to knowing something about the onrush of modernity, Renoir knew that the order or rules of society and the chaos of passion are both necessary for human survival, that each threatens the existence of the other, and that neither of the two can be excluded from a meaningful life. The human condition for Renoir in *La Règle du jeu* is thus a delicate balance between the demands of order and spontaneity. But failure at this balancing act is as inevitable as the act itself. Man must juggle the two demands and he must also fail to juggle them perfectly, for they cannot ever be juggled perfectly. And the idea that human beings have been assigned an impossible task at which they are doomed to fail is one of the major components of the film's tone, contributing to the cold, acidic current, the black, grim, even tragic thread, which winds through this sometimes farcical comedy. *La Règle du jeu* may be light-hearted, then, but darkness nonetheless runs all through it.

In the face of the terrible reception given to the film, however, Renoir began to have misgivings about its nuanced lightness, as he tells us in *My Life and My Films*. All he had had in mind originally had been "nothing avant-garde but a good little orthodox film," and he had been utterly dumbfounded at finding that "the film, which I wanted to be a pleasant one, rubbed most people the wrong way" (172). This reception made him begin to ask himself, had he been right in making no allusion to the threat of war in his film? Did the film, perhaps, give a shameful picture of present-day France? He mentioned these wonderings of his to others, though he found no answer to them, and maybe they were the origin of later critical attitudes—including, rather startlingly, his own, for, in 1974 in *My Life and My Films*, he went so far as to call *La Règle du jeu* a "war film . . . that attacks the very structure of our society" (171).

In any event, Renoir did leave France (to the Nazis, as it were), which in the end may not have been very good for him as a filmmaker. As for the film itself, when it was shown again in the 1950s, the French—released from the pressures of the grave year 1939—fell in love with it (and not only they), and it quickly acquired its present very high reputation as one of the best movies ever made. Far from perceiving in *La Règle du jeu* evidence of the "corruption" and "exhaustion" in French society that led to the country's defeat and occupation by the Germans during World War II, audiences in France now blithely saw the film for what it was—not for what historicist critics, as well as the elderly, legacy-conscious Renoir, wanted it to be.

WORKS CITED

Bertin, Celia. *Jean Renoir: A Life in Pictures*. 1986. Trans. Mireille and Leonard Muellner. Baltimore: Johns Hopkins University Press, 1991.

Faulkner, Christopher. "*The Rules of the Game*: A Film Not Like the Others." In *Film Analysis: A Reader*. Ed. Jeffrey Geiger and R. L. Rutsky. New York: W. W. Norton, 2005. 300-317.

France, Peter, ed. *The New Oxford Companion to Literature in French*. New York: Oxford University Press, 1995.

Kemp, Philip. Liner Notes. DVD of *La Règle du jeu*. London: BFI Video, 2003.

Mast, Gerald. *"The Rules of the Game": Filmguide Series*. Bloomington: Indiana University Press, 1973.

Lanzoni, Rémi Fournier. *French Cinema from Its Beginnings to the Present*. New York: Continuum, 2002.

Renoir, Jean. *My Life and My Films*. Trans. Norman Denny. New York: Atheneum, 1974.

Sesonske, Alexander. Booklet Essay. DVD of *La Règle du jeu*. New York: The Criterion Collection, 2003.

Wakeman, John, ed. *World Film Directors: 1890-1945*. New York: H. W. Wilson, 1987.

Wood, Robin. "*La Règle du jeu*." In *The International Dictionary of Films and Filmmakers: Films*. Ed. Christopher Lyon. New York: Putnam, 1984.

BIBLIOGRAPHY

Bazin, André. *Jean Renoir*. Ed. François Truffaut. 1971. Trans. W. W. Halsey II and William H. Simon. New York: Simon and Schuster, 1973.

Bergstrom, Janet. "Jean Renoir's Return to France" (1996). In *Exile and Creativity: Signposts, Travelers, Outsiders, Backward Glances*. Ed. Susan Rubin Suleiman. Durham, N.C.: Duke University Press, 1998. 180-219.

Braudy, Leo. *Jean Renoir, The World of His Films*. 1972. New York: Columbia University Press, 1989.

Budgen, Suzanne. "Some Notes on the Sources of *La Règle du jeu*." *Take One* (Montreal), 1.12 (July-August 1968): 8-10.

Faulkner, Christopher. *Jean Renoir: A Guide to References and Resources*. Boston: G. K. Hall, 1979.

_____. *The Social Cinema of Jean Renoir*. Princeton, N.J.: Princeton University Press, 1986.

Gilliatt, Penelope. *Jean Renoir: Essays, Conversations, Reviews*. New York: McGraw-Hill, 1975.

Joly, Jacques. "Between Theater and Life: Jean Renoir and *The Rules of the Game.*" *Film Quarterly*, 21.2 (Winter 1967/1968): 2-9.

Lebovics, Herman. "Jean Renoir's Voyage of Discovery: From the Shores of the Mediterranean to the Banks of the Ganges." In Lebovics' *Imperialism and the Corruption of Democracies*. Durham, N.C.: Duke University Press, 2006. 34-59.

Leprohon, Pierre. *Jean Renoir*. Trans. Brigid Elsen. New York: Crown Publishers, 1971.

Lesage, Julia, "S/Z and *The Rules of the Game.*" *Jump Cut*, nos. 12-13 (Winter 1976-1977): 45-51.

Litle, Michael. "Sound Track: *The Rules of the Game.*" *Cinema Journal*, 13.1 (Fall 1973): 35-44.

Perebinossoff, Philippe R. "Theatricals in Jean Renoir's *The Rules of the Game* and *Grand Illusion.*" *Literature/Film Quarterly*, 5.1 (Winter 1977): 50-56.

Quarterly Review of Film Studies, 7.3 (1982): 199-280: Special issue on *La Règle du jeu*.

Rafferty, Terrence. "*The Rules of the Game.*" *New Yorker*, 66.19 (June 25, 1990): 80-92.

Reader, Keith. "Chaos, Contradiction, and Order in Jean Renoir's *La Règle du jeu.*" *Australian Journal of French Studies*, 36.11 (Jan.-Apr. 1999): 26-38.

Renoir, Jean. *Jean Renoir: Interviews*. Ed. Bert Cardullo. Jackson: University Press of Mississippi, 2005.

_____. *Jean Renoir: Letters*. Ed. David Thompson and Lorraine LoBianco. Trans. Craig Carlson, Natasha Arnoldi, Michael Wells, and Anneliese Varaldiev. London: Faber and Faber, 1994.

_____. *Renoir on Renoir: Interviews, Essays, and Remarks*. Trans. Carol Volk. New York: Cambridge University Press, 1989.

_____, Camille François, and Carl Koch. *The Rules of the Game*. Trans. John McGrath and Maureen Teitelbaum. New York: Simon and Schuster, 1969.

Snyder, John. "Film and Classical Genre: Rules for Interpreting *The Rules of the Game.*" *Literature/Film* Quarterly, 10.3 (1982): 162-179.

Tifft, Stephen. "Drôle de Guerre: Renoir, Farce, and the Fall of France." *Representations*, 38 (Spring 1992): 131-64.

Vincendeau, Ginette. "The Exception and the Rule." *Sight and Sound* 2.8 (Dec. 1992): 34-36.

Warehime, Marja. "Mixing Genres, May '68, and the Ghosts of History: Louis Malle Rewrites *The Rules of the Game.*" *Historical Reflections*, 24.2 (Summer 1998): 179-203.

Wood, George A., Jr. "Game Theory and *The Rules of the Game.*" *Cinema Journal*, 13.1 (Fall 1973): 25-34.

18

All That Glitters:
The Early Film Career of John Schlesinger

I'd like to argue in this essay that the progress of John Schlesinger (1926-2003) as a film artist, up to and including *The Day of the Locust* (1975), seemed dependent on whether he was willing to settle for surfaces (be they gleaming or glowering), or whether he would insist on an inner rationale and validity for his work: whether he would build upward from the most stringent perceptions toward a virtuoso display of them, or begin at the top with slickness and add just enough clever dialogue and facilely bitter comment to provide marketable *Weltschmerz* for all those in need of it. Alas, Schlesinger settled for surfaces—sometimes far less—in a career that, by the time of *Yanks* (1979) and *Honky Tonk Freeway* (1981) and continuing to *Eye for an Eye* (1996) and *The Next Best Thing* (2000), could only descend from so much slickness into lamentable sorriness. By considering this British director's first three, and best, films—*A Kind of Loving* (1962), *Billy Liar* (1963), and *Darling* (1965)—I propose to demonstrate how each of this trio of works holds both the promise of cinematic growth and the prospect of directorial delinquency into which Schlesinger would ultimately decline.

Let me start with *A Kind of Loving*, which stands as one salient piece of evidence for the growing belief in Britain in the early 1960s that a serious film was a film made in an industrial town. The British, let us remember, had taken a somewhat longer time than the rest of the Western world to admit the working man as a central character in art. (As evidence, compare the dates of novels by the Frenchman Zola and D. H. Lawrence, or of plays by the American Odets and John Osborne.) Having discovered the proletariat, however, British artists then placed themselves in danger of getting drunk on drabness, or of assuming that a work which contains sunlight and even a moderate amount of luxe is either frivolous or shallow. *A Kind of Loving* was one of the fruits of this then-flourishing gray tree of social realism. Like the films it followed—*Look Back in Anger* (1959), *Room at the Top* (1958), *Saturday Night and Sunday Morning* (1960), and *A Taste of Honey* (1961)—Schlesinger's picture was shot in the industrial north of England, once the center of the Industrial Revolution but, by this time, the center of what came to be known as the Angry Artistic Revolution, with all its "angry young men."

Based on a 1960 novel by Stan Barstow, himself a Yorkshire miner's son, and adapted for the screen by Keith Waterhouse and Willis Hall, *A Kind of Loving* is a cautionary tale of courtship and early marriage. The hero, Vic Brown, is a young draftsman struck by the blonde beauty of Ingrid Rothwell, a typist in the Lancashire engineering firm where he works. After a bus and movie-balcony courtship, they make love one day in her home when her mother is away. Instant pregnancy—that remote possibility so much more certain in fiction than in life—then occurs.

A few months later, the pair are married and are living in that home with the mother. Vic's feelings fluctuate between love sharpened by desire and revulsion sharpened by imprisonment. Ingrid, thriving as *mater* and warder, still worships him. The

A Kind of Loving, dir. John Schlesinger, 1962

mother-in-law hates him. An accident (Ingrid falls down the stairs) causes a miscarriage, and Vic feels trapped for nothing, as it were. Blow-up follows binge, and he goes to his adored, married sister for comfort—but she makes him face up to his responsibilities. At the end, Vic and Ingrid are settling into a small flat, free of the devouring mother, where they will make do with a "kind of loving." At least now their life together has a chance of its share of what the national weather service in England calls "sunny intervals."

The film of *A Kind of Loving* does have several virtues. The Hall-Waterhouse script refines and heightens Barstow's undistinguished novel, retaining the best of the book and extrapolating a few telling moments of its own. Here are some examples: the scene in which Vic's father, a railway worker, introduces him with taciturn pride to a fellow railway worker; and the scene where Vic goes into a druggist's to buy a condom, is unexpectedly waited on by a woman, then comes out sheepishly with a bottle of hair gel. Denys Coop's fine cinematography, moreover, makes the most of the black-and-white palette, devoid of sunlight, against which the action takes place. He transmutes grime and fog into a visual suggestion of the smell of tabloid newsprint.

Schlesinger, in this, his first full-length feature, shows quickly that he has compassion and perception as well as an eye for composition and for camera angles that underscore mood. If, at this point in his career, he lacks the sure subtlety and unfaltering pace of Karel Reisz (the director of *Saturday Night and Sunday Morning*), he is still much more secure than Tony Richardson (who made *The Entertainer* [1960] and *A Taste of Honey*), less dependent on the heavy-handed comment of background detail, less reliant on "shock" cuts—that is, a jump from one scene into the startling opening of the next, with the shock irrelevant to what follows. Because he was once an actor, Schlesinger understandably builds *A Kind of Loving* out of the interplay and rhythm of dialogue, rather than by means of intrusive editing or a hypodermic musical score. (The actual music, by Ron Grainer, is reticent and apt.)

As for the acting, Alan Bates plays Vic with such direct goodheartedness that even his recalcitrance affects us as the sulkiness of a child whom basically we like. His hushed infatuation and genuine puzzlement at its short life are equally touching. June Ritchie, who makes her début here as Ingrid, does not quite reach the depth of being helplessly but happily overwhelmed by her man that Shirley Anne Field conveyed in *Saturday Night and Sunday Morning*, but her performance is never false. As Ingrid's mother, Thora Hird acts with a bourgeois smugness that is perhaps this world's only justification for homicide. Mention must also be made of Bert Palmer, complete with National Health Service teeth, as Vic's affectionate father, and Pat Keen as the sympathetic but severe married sister.

It may come as a surprise, after such a list of virtues, that *A Kind of Loving* is a disappointment. For the first half an hour or so, it seems as if it is going to be a successful, honest picture on a subject that is almost always faked on film: courtship and marriage. The movie is honest enough but (1) the frankness of its dialogue and incidents is never really any more disturbing than the continual discovery that our own sons and daughters are highly sexual beings; and (2) the pregnancy, enforced wedding, and subsequent difficulties reduce the movie's impact—not because they kill romantic feeling but because they divert us from familiar universals to familiar plot. The line between truth and triteness is thin; *A Kind of Loving* crosses over it.

A more serious fault is the implication—in working-class locale and in naturalistic procedure—that the film is making a serious social comment. The secretary of the British Board of Film Censors at the time was pleased with *A Kind of Loving* because "it says that the anticipation of marital privilege is liable to produce great unhappiness not only for the boy and girl concerned but also for their families, and it also says that a sexual attraction, especially one that is variable, is not alone a basis for a successful marriage." Albeit clothed in itchy blue serge, this is a reasonable statement of the movie's implications from one point of view. But it is necessary to add that there is a little more to the matter than this. For *A Kind of Loving* quite clearly also states that, despite the universal dream of perfect freedom and ideal love, the forms of job and marriage provide an attainable life for many who might otherwise end in anarchic disaster. In short, the film proves that Thoreau's "quiet desperation" is often as much a haven as a prison.

But all this raises a further question as to the necessity of the picture's milieu to the proving of its point. To wit: Vic is out of

Billy Liar is that, unlike *A Kind of Loving*, it truly relies on its material, on the fundamental situation of its protagonist: there is minimal plotting, as such.

Let me hasten to add that several things *do* happen to Billy in the course of the story: the two girls to whom he is simultaneously engaged find out about it and throw him over; the girl he really likes leaves for London without him; his grandmother dies; and his pipe-dream of a big-city job explodes. But the emphasis of Schlesinger and his writers here is on organic development, not on contrivances of conflict and climax. The basic purpose of *Billy Liar* is to explore Billy's character, and the motions of the narrative are merely sufficient to put it on view. This, I must say, is intelligent risk-taking on the authors' part in a feature-length motion picture, and in this instance it is largely successful.

Billy is a clerk in a firm of undertakers, which profession we see from the inside. (In smarminess, at least, the British Way of Death on display in this film is not very different from the American one.) His problem is that he is normal, in his dreams and even his daydreams; but he is abnormal in the way that his daydreams influence his actions. That is, he cannot help lying even when there is no need for it, just to affect in some way the reality that he hates. When a neighbor, for example, asks about his father's health, Billy, for no reason, invents an illness and an operation. When complications follow, he lies more desperately. Similarly, he has pointlessly lied his way into his two betrothals to girls whom he in fact does not want to marry. Then, whenever matters become especially tight, he imagines himself in a trooper's uniform with a submachine gun, spattering his tormentors with bullets.

Schlesinger slips the film easily in and out of these fantasy sequences: the trooper flashes, or those of Billy's imaginary country, Ambrosia, whose dictator and defender he is. (Indeed, the chief bond between Billy and his beloved ones is their *mutual* imaginary country.) He also has a few visions about sex, about suffering in prison and writing it up, of the transformation of his middle-class parents into upper-class toffs. Additionally, we see Billy play-acting in real life, with his fellow clerks or alone in his boss's office, where he wallows in mimicries of various kinds. Moments like these—because they delve into byways of whimsy hard to define but universally true of every character—are the picture's best.

Billy Liar, dir. John Schlesinger, 1963

In terms of what he has to do during these moments, Tom Courtenay, who played the protagonist in Sillitoe and Richardson's *Loneliness of the Long Distance Runner* (1962), is versatile and funny. In terms of what he is, he lacks conviction. For one cannot believe that two girls would be fighting over this particular fellow and that the third, "liberated" girl would have chosen him above anyone else (before eventually choosing London over Billy, who elects to stay behind). Julie Christie (more on whom later), as this girl, is adequate but handicapped by the fact that she has been told—as a virtual unknown in 1963—that she is a striking new personality. Hence we get a great many fetching smiles from her throughout

Billy Liar. For their part, Mona Washbourne, Ethel Griffies, and Finlay Currie are excellent as various local types; and, as Billy's father, Wilfred Pickles has appropriate vinegar.

As one would have expected from a Hall-Waterhouse script, the dialogue is lean and swift, the characters generally well understood. The exception to this is Christie's role, which seems rootless and weakly motivated. There is also a weakness in the device of the funereal firm's Christmas calendars: 200 of them that Billy neglected to mail while pocketing the postage money, and has kept in his closet at home. Why are they so difficult to get rid of? And if it is difficult, why does he carry them back to the office itself, a few at a time, to flush them down the toilet? The sequence seems forced. Further, Schlesinger and his collaborators have a weakness for scenes in which a character sits down and thinks, on camera, until he reaches a decision. (Billy does it in his bedroom.)

In contrast, there are numerous subtle and felicitous touches in this film, like the dance band on the midnight train by which Billy and his girl plan to leave London. The musicians' sleaziness seems to predict what the future has in store for the potential runaways. Schlesinger knows how to get the most out of such a setting (there are also Billy's office, a cemetery, a hospital, and some sooty hillsides) and how to make scenes flow in and out of rooms, up and down stairs, through streets, like coursing water. In this increasing skill of his with film form, as with actors, there is the sense at this point in Schlesinger's *oeuvre* of a watchful, responsive talent.

That talent was also at work in the decision to remain faithful to the novel's treatment of social class. For, despite its North Country setting, *Billy Liar* is not just one more English social-realist film of the sixties, telling us of the plight—fixed or altering—of the working class. As is made clear with shots of council houses under the credits, the concern here is with the new middle class, enlarging in Britain as it had already enlarged in the United States, with the young included among this bourgeoisie deluded by the propaganda of possibilities into believing that all things were possible for them. (The facile comparison of *Billy Liar* with the American James Thurber's "Secret Life of Walter Mitty" [1939] does not hold: Mitty is a middle-aged, householding husband whose fate is molded and made, who knows it, and who dreams instead of drinking; Billy is still in the process of realizing his boundaries and has not yet quite reached them.) The mythology of advertising and the Benzedrine of mass communications implant and pump up this British variation on the American dream. Industrial democracy, in which all things are equally on sale to everyone, *has to* make Billy believe that all things are possible: so that he will buy the magazines, the television set, the latest record, the new ties, and keep on buying. After all, if these items make him look and act and talk like a star, maybe he can have a star's life.

But Billy will never leave his humdrum little street, despite his own modest idea of becoming a script writer for a comedian. First, there is no room at the top, or at least not that much. Second, only extraordinary luck or drive (more important than extraordinary ability) can blast him or anyone else upward. Some do it; many more do not and can, if they choose, console themselves with fantasies. What is needed, of course—then as now—is anger at the professional lies, the false promises of possibilities, which, even when realized, are not that much. After all, the few at the top who get their "pink Cadillacs" (a prized possession at the time) get them by pushing dope dreams of pink Cadillacs. Thus, although hampered (as noted) by major casting or character problems and minor plot deviations, *Billy Liar* is a good allegory of the striptease that the Bitch-Goddess Success performs, just out of reach, before she sends the wide-eyed watcher back to his solitary, less-than-solacing satisfactions. Whatever this picture's flaws, Schlesinger showed even more verity, humanity, and cinematic skill in it than he did in *A Kind of Loving*.

Subsequently, he made *Darling*, in which the skill is notably heightened—at some expense to the other qualities. *Darling*'s first effect is dazzling; its net effect is something less. Frederic Raphael wrote the screenplay from an idea by himself, John Schlesinger, and Joseph Janni, the producer. It concerns a modern English girl, a model with a model's vague ambition toward acting, who is intended as a contemporary symbol of moral undernourishment—something she is conscious of and regrets but is unable to do anything about. She is supposed to be telling her life story to a magazine (always a thin device, but all the more so in this case, since there is plenty in the movie that, at the time, could neither be told nor printed).

Married early, this young woman then falls in love with a writer and television interviewer, who leaves his wife and children for her even as she leaves her husband. After an abortion that affects her more than she expected, she begins an affair with a sleek public-relations man merely out of momentary boredom with the writer, who spends all his spare time working on a novel. When the writer finds out, he leaves her; she still loves him but is now cast adrift on an ocean of get-and-take. After various adventures, the young woman marries a rich Italian prince with seven children. Oppressed in her *palazzo* and still in love with the writer, she seizes a chance to fly back to London, where she sees him but is finally rebuffed.

As the heroine of *Darling*, Julie Christie (the "liberated" girl in *Billy Liar*) makes a strong impression. She has an expressive, unusual face and an attractive voice, but she had not yet become the controlled or subtle actress she showed herself to be as early as *The Go-Between* (1970) and as recently as *The Secret Life of Words* (2005). Her chief effects here come from her vivid personality in this tailor-made part. But as an actress her colorings in *Darling* tend only to be

Darling, dir. John Schlesinger, 1965

primary; she is happy or sad, frightened or frisky, all convincingly enough, but the gradations between are not yet within her grasp and seem not even to be in her imagination at this juncture.

Christie's performance can usefully be compared to Dirk Bogarde's as the writer. His technique and sense of complete being continue to mature in *Darling* with all the consistency that the film world permits. Here he underplays with a delicacy and tact, a beautiful suggestiveness, that create this man's infinite privacies, all unspoken. His glances, pauses, and inflections are the result of imagination and empathy at the service of sure craft; and the result is a great deal warmer than such a cold description may suggest. It is an excellent, wide-ranging, finely shaded piece of work. Laurence Harvey, the PR man, glides through his own role like a snake through oil. Nothing that can really be called acting is needed, only a nice, easeful assortment of mannerisms, which Harvey supplies competently.

Raphael's dialogue (for which he won an Oscar for Best Original Screenplay, as did Christie for Best Actress) is almost always bright, brittle, brisk. The sequence in which the girl and the writer fall in love, for instance, is written with understanding and *tendresse*. The Capri sequence with a homosexual photographer, in which the girl plays at living with him like a sister, has the reality of a hopeless, asexual dream in a life harassed by biology. And as against *La dolce vita* (1959), which comparison *Darling* cannot escape, Raphael's symbol of integrity is credible. The old author whom the writer and the young woman visit for a TV interview is an appealing, unselfconscious integer of such integrity, unlike the juvenile conception of the intellectual in Fellini's film.

But there are heavy and uncomfortable elements in this screenplay that Schlesinger chose to film. We can begin with the photographer's statement that life is "a great big steaming mess"—a sentiment more glib than grieving. Then there is the grating moment when, toward the end, the girl suddenly turns out to be Roman Catholic, even though the author has not portrayed her as a Catholic, devout or lapsed. To depict the immoral behavior of a young lady reared in Catholicism (especially when we are privy to her thoughts) no differently at this point in time from that of a girl reared in another religion is a serious fault, and it turns her late Catholicism into a plot device to facilitate her Italian marriage. The last episode, in which the writer takes her to bed on her brief London visit, only to spurn her afterwards, is itself quite incredible. One cannot believe that this man, as drawn, could have been so vindictively cruel, indeed could have physically functioned in bed knowing what he planned to say to the woman. It is the action of an unreconstructed brute or a moral sadist, and since the writer has been shown to be neither, this episode seems like another sorry instance of plot mechanics.

This film thus underscores an ironic contradiction. In an age (continuing well into the first decade of the twenty-first century) concerned with lingering questions of morality, with what people can do to be "saved," the most difficult matter in art is to delineate immorality convincingly. When, as in *A Kind of Loving*, Schlesinger takes us through the initial love and first bedding of the pair, the film rings true (as it does on the visit to the old author or on a lovingly satirical visit to the girl's sister). But the scene, for example, in the empty board room when Christie cavorts on the table, the gambling-as-hell scenes, the Paris orgy—these are all strained. They are not glimpses into Babylon but instead just tired movie naughtiness.

Decadence remains the hardest quality to depict in art, in film art above all, especially when (as in *Darling* and later in Schlesinger's otherwise sentimental *Midnight Cowboy* [1969]) it is equated with promiscuity or homosexuality. By 1965, only what could not be shown in a film might possibly be convincingly decadent, and even then it would not prove that a character was incorrigibly rotten. We knew too much by then of the private lives of many otherwise admirable men and women to believe that some sexual and other practices negated a person's social worth. In short, an age of spiritual starvation, from which this young woman knowingly suffers, cannot be dramatized merely through random fornications—particularly when one remembers that there has been plenty of bed-hopping in religiously replete eras.

Schlesinger's direction in *Darling* ranges from the succinct to the blatant, from the breathtakingly deft to the embarrassingly clumsy. Much of the film moves with stunning cinematic fluency: the way the girl meets the writer, the swift passage (a walk with a priest under an umbrella) where her return to religion is noted, a sequence in which she models for the photographer. These are some random samples of the use of film language to tell much with little and to tell it incisively. But there is also a good deal in the picture that is like the palm-in-the-face shove of a Tony Richardson. (Such in-your-face technique will reach epic proportions ten years later in Schlesinger's grotesque, and grotesquely misconceived, *Day of the Locust*.)

As a charity-bazaar speaker in a posh house mentions helping people irrespective of color, for instance, we get close-ups of turbaned black boy-servants; as this same man speaks about the world's famine, we see a stout, bejeweled lady picking the meat out of her dainty sandwich. As Christie herself reads (quite badly) John of Gaunt's dying speech about England, from Shakespeare's *Richard II*, we are presented with a mocking close-up of a photograph of Queen Elizabeth. The shock cut, that desperation tactic we saw comparatively little of in *A Kind of Loving* and *Billy Liar*, is often used here, and twice in its lowest form: the mask. Once we cut to a scary mask that turns out to be a child playing on a lawn; and a party sequence ends with a close-up of a man putting on a mask, from which we then abruptly cut away. The last shot of *Darling* pans from a newsstand displaying the "Italian" princess's life story to a toothless woman singing the traditional Neapolitan song "Santa Lucia" in London's Piccadilly Circus. Such an image is ugly enough, but what does it signify? Weren't there also toothless street singers in more decorous epochs than this one? Aside from the small fillip out of Cartier-Bresson, then, what use is this as a final comment?

These egregious effects, markedly derivative, are stuck like rhinestones on the film's smooth fabric, and their very flashiness helps—by this, his third film—to define Schlesinger's abilities. He has unusual intelligence, sympathy, and knowledge of acting as well as film technique, but he is also a director without a style, who feels the need to deck out his work with borrowed finery. Again a comparison with *La dolce vita* is fitting. That picture is much hollower than *Darling* and on repeated viewing becomes quite tedious, but there is not a frame in it that could have been made by anyone but Fellini. The sequence of the fake miracle, Anita Ekberg in St. Peter's Square, the final walk through the woods, essentially vacuous as they are, are visually unique and unified in manner—the world as scanned by one man's realistic-become-baroque vision.

The contrary is true of Schlesinger. There is hardly a frame in *Darling*, or *Billy Liar* and *A Kind of Loving* (or any other film of his, for that matter), that could not have been made by another director—Reisz, Richardson, or Lindsay Anderson, let us say. One could hope at this stage for a style to develop in Schlesinger, but one could not have sanguinely expected it. For in his first three full-length films, with all their virtues, there is small indication of a strong personality. That personality continued to diminish in Schlesinger's fourth film, the reductive *Far from the Madding Crowd* (1967)—which, significantly, marked a shift away from the exploration of contemporary mores that had marked his first three features—and on through *Midnight Cowboy* and *Sunday Bloody Sunday* (1971). In this last picture, one might have thought, the openly gay Schlesinger's personal life would find its ideal expression in the story of a homosexual Jewish doctor, a professional woman (and divorcée), and the young male designer with whom they simultaneously conduct a love relationship. But one would have thought wrong.

What artistic personality was left in Schlesinger had, as of the meretricious *Marathon Man* (1976), the forgettable *Falcon and the Snowman* (1985), and the just plain horrible *Pacific Heights* (1990), more or less disappeared. Sadly, the only thing now remaining of the man is contained in Frederic Raphael's 1976 semi-autobiographical volume (and television mini-series), which, as it traces the lives of a group of Cambridge undergraduates in postwar Britain as they move through university and into the wider world, features a most unflattering portrait of a character clearly based on John Schlesinger. The book's title, apt yet ironic: *The Glittering Prizes*.

BIBLIOGRAPHY

Brooker, Nancy J. *John Schlesinger: A Guide to References and Resources*. Boston: G. K. Hall, 1978.

Mann, William J. *Edge of Midnight: The Life of John Schlesinger*. New York: Billboard Books, 2006.

Phillips, Gene D. *John Schlesinger*. Boston: Twayne, 1981.

19

Carl Dreyer's *Day of Wrath* and the Spirit of Tragedy

James Agee was right. One of the attributes of *Day of Wrath* (*Vredens Dag*, 1943) to admire most is connected with tragedy: "its steep, Lutheran kind of probity—that is, its absolute recognition of the responsibility of the individual, regardless of extenuating or compulsive circumstances"(304). Critics speak often of Dreyer's treatment of religious themes and his austere style,[14] but few recognize any tragic intentions on his part.[15] The director himself, however, writes in the foreword to his *Four Screen Plays* that in the films *The Passion of Joan of Arc* (1928), *Vampire* (1932), *Day of Wrath*, and *The Word* (1955)—those that are generally believed to be his best—he "ended up with a dramatic form which . . . has characteristics in common with that of tragedy. This applies particularly to *The Passion of Joan of Arc* and *Day of Wrath*" (7). Dreyer was convinced there was a need for a "tragic poet of the cinema," and he felt that this poet's "first problem [would] be to find, within the cinema's framework, the form and style appropriate to tragedy" (7).

Insofar as that tragedy is concerned, David Bordwell's plot summary of *Day of Wrath* is characteristic of most writing on the film in that it ignores the subject of Absalon's responsibility:

> *Day of Wrath* is the story of how, in seventeenth-century Denmark, Anne falls in love with the son of Absalon, the old pastor whom she has married. A subplot involves Herlof's Marthe, an old woman accused of witchcraft and persecuted by the church elder Laurentius. After Herlof's Marthe is executed, Anne and Martin share a furtive idyll. When Anne tells Absalon of the affair, the old man dies. The

> pastor's elderly mother Merete accuses Anne of witchcraft. When Martin abandons her, Anne finally confesses to having been in Satan's power and is burned as a witch. (117)

Because the pastor Absalon is reticent and because we never see him lust for his wife Anne, it is easy to fail to consider *Day of Wrath* as his tragedy. But Dreyer begins the film with the ferreting out and burning of Herlof's Marthe as a witch precisely so that attention will focus immediately on Absalon and his actions. Absalon seems almost to have forgotten that he pardoned Anne's mother, also accused of being a witch, years before when he was widowed so that he might marry Anne, half his age. But his young wife is no different in function from his first wife: she is his companion and the mistress of his house, not the object of his sexual desire. Anne married Absalon out of obligation; and if she does not love him, she has at least accustomed herself to him.

All is apparently well in Absalon's world, then, at the start of the film. The Herlof's Marthe incident, however, changes matters. It reminds Absalon of the sin he committed to obtain Anne as his wife, and it places him in the position of sinning again, for Marthe asks him to pardon her in the same way that he pardoned Anne's mother. Absalon is thus faced with a tragic choice: spare Marthe and sin again in the eyes of God, or let her go to her death and incur guilt for having spared one witch (for selfish reasons) and not another. He lets Herlof's Marthe go to her death, and she in turn pronounces the curse that he will soon die and prophesies for Anne a fate similar to her own.

Even though Absalon dies and Anne herself will be burned as a witch, *Day of Wrath*—otherwise set during the worst years of the European witch hunts—is not a testimony to the powers of witchcraft. Witchcraft, rather, is something Dreyer contrasts with the piety of Absalon.[16] Witchcraft—setting oneself up as a rival to God—is the gravest sin to Absalon, just as forgiving witchcraft, which he did for Anne's mother, is the gravest sin that he, as a representative of God, can commit. I hesitate to use the term "tragic inevitability" with regard to this film, for it is not simply a tragedy of character. There is too much structural "arranging" going on in it. Absalon to a large extent brings on his own doom, it's true, but there is a sense in which Dreyer makes an example of him for all the world to see and be encouraged by. I stress that Dreyer, not witchcraft or "fate," is making an example of him. Or Dreyer the artist is his own witch-god, which explains the choice of a pastor as tragic figure and of witches as his antagonists: Dreyer wishes to register the artist's power in the universe alongside the forces of evil and the wrath of God.

Let me explain by saying that the view of tragedy I take in this essay is the one first propounded by Bert States in *Irony and Drama: A Poetics*. States writes that

> The idea that the victory inherent in tragedy arrives primarily in the earned nobility of the defeated-victorious hero is actually much overrated as the key to catharsis; the victory is rather in the poet's having framed the definitive fate for his hero-victim. In turning the tables on his hero so *exactly*, getting the all into his one, he shows wherein the imagination is a match for nature in getting her to participate so thoroughly in the fault. This seems the most complete statement that can be made about destructiveness, and when the poet can arrange to make it, as Shakespeare and Sophocles have, he has posed the unanswerable argument against reality in his effort to fortify men against the many forms of disaster. In effect, he has said, "You may destroy me, but I have gone even further. I have conceived the impossible destruction." In other words, the force of tragic catharsis consists in the poet's having conceived a power beyond Power itself; as such, it would seem to be not only a purgation but something of a gorging as well. (50)

Let us not forget, moreover, that Dreyer made *Day of Wrath* in 1943 during the German occupation of Denmark: surely one huge form of disaster or destruction for the Danes. Of the film's immediate historical context, Ole Storm has noted that while

> *Vredens Dag* can hardly be regarded as a Resistance film, . . . it contained unmistakable elements of the irrationality that was characteristic of Nazism: witch-hunting, mass

hypnosis, assertion of power, and the primitive, always latent forces which, in certain conditions, can be exploited by any authority that knows how to license the gratification of blood-lust as an act of justice; whereby a judicial process conducted without witnesses or counsel for the defence culminates in a death sentence passed on the sole basis of a forced confession. (Introduction, *Four Screen Plays*, 19)

The event that clarifies Dreyer's artistic purpose is the entrance of Martin, Absalon's son by his first marriage, into the film. Martin, who has recently graduated from the seminary, is the favorite of his grandmother, Merete, just as her son Absalon was once her favorite. (Merete lives with Absalon and Anne.) Like his father before him, Martin falls in love with Anne and appears to "choose" her over Merete. It all seems a little too pat: father and son love the same woman; the woman prefers the son; disapproving mother-grandmother looks on. In this way Merete is a kind of chorus to events as she disapproves of Anne from the start, and we find ourselves sharing her opinion for all her sternness and stridency. But the deck is stacked in *Day of Wrath* for good reason, even as it is in Euripides' *Hippolytus* (428 B.C.) or Racine's *Phaedra* (1677), to whose love-triangle plot the film is indebted.

To wit: Dreyer wants Absalon to go through the worst possible ordeal before dying; he wants the worst that can happen to him to happen. Absalon the pastor is thus Dreyer's sacrificial lamb. Like his Biblical counterpart, Absalon rebels against his father, God, when he pardons a witch and marries her daughter, and he must be punished for his sin. Furthermore, he will be permitted by Dreyer to utter barely a word of protest throughout his ordeal. This is part of the strategy of outrage: Absalon committed an outrageous act in marrying the young Anne; he sincerely repents his sin of pardoning Anne's mother, but only when he is confronted, outrageously, with the possibility of committing the same sin again; and he dies at the outrageous admission by Anne that she has betrayed him with his own son. Even as he suffers silently the guilt of his original sin of pardoning Anne's mother, so too he suffers silently the revelation of his betrayal: he simply dies.

Carl Dreyer's *Day of Wrath* 317

Day of Wrath, dir. Carl Dreyer, 1943

It was Samuel Johnson, in the Preface to his 1765 edition of *King Lear*, who first complained of the improbability of Lear's proposal to divide his kingdom among his three daughters according to how much each loved him. The same complaint could be made about the staid pastor Absalon's proposing to pardon a witch and marry her young daughter: nothing in Absalon's behavior during the film, and no information Dreyer gives us about him, can account for his going to such extremes to marry so young a woman, especially when one considers the time and place in which he lives. But demands for this kind of believability in a work of art miss the forest for the trees. Like *King Lear*, *Day of Wrath* could be called, in J. Stampfer's term, a "tragedy of penance" (375), in which the enormity of the offending act provokes the enormity of the punishment.

Stampfer makes the important point that *King Lear* is not a tragedy of hubris, like *Oedipus Rex*, but one of penance:

> [The] opening movement [of *King Lear*] leads not to dissolution, exposure, and self-recognition, as in *Oedipus* and *Othello*, but to purgation. And Lear's purgation, by the end of the play's middle movement, is so complete as to be archetypal. By the time he enters prison, he has paid every price and been stripped of everything a man can lose, even his sanity, in payment for folly and pride. As such he activates an even profounder fear than the fear of failure, and that is the fear that whatever penance a man may pay may not be enough once the machinery of destruction has been set loose, because the partner of his covenant may be neither grace nor the balance of law, but malignity, intransigence, or chaos. (375)

Absalon himself repents, but it is too late, and there is no evidence that matters would be different had he repented long before the film begins. Marthe would still have dabbled in witchcraft and she would still have sought sanctuary in Absalon's home, since she herself had hidden Anne's mother and felt that the same favor was due her in return.

Dreyer has Absalon repent only when faced with the possibility of committing the same sin again, and not earlier, not because this is why he is being destroyed in the first place—for sinning monumentally *and living peacefully with that sin*—but because Absalon's late repentance, in Bert States's words, is what "rescues him from perfection in the process of being doomed" (54). That is, Dreyer singled out the pastor for destruction and invented his sin but had to have him repent belatedly to remind us of the seriousness of his transgression. The sin is dim in Absalon's own memory at the beginning of the film and in our minds, as well, for having occurred so long ago and offscreen. (Dreyer keeps it offscreen and in the past, I think, because of its very improbability). Absalon, in other words, had to appear flawed beyond his original sin of pardoning a witch and marrying Anne. And his flaw is his tardiness in repenting, his willingness to tolerate such a flaw in himself but not in his congregation, and least of all in Marthe.

Thus Dreyer makes him appear something less than irreproachable—no small accomplishment in the case of Absalon, who strikes one at first as being absolutely irreproachable. This is important, because the less irreproachable Absalon becomes the easier it is for us to witness, if not finally condone or participate in, his destruction. The destruction of a flawless or completely and quickly repentant man is too easily rationalized as pure accident or pure evil; of a bad man, as poetic justice. Neither is paid much attention. But the destruction of the man in the middle—the good man who has done wrong, yet has neither been perverted by his wrongdoing nor has atoned for it—*this* is more terrible, precisely because it is deserved, yet not deserved, and therefore inexplicable. We pay attention to it.[17]

Ironically, then, even though Absalon chooses God in choosing not to pardon Marthe for her witchcraft and so could be said to be attempting to atone for the sin of pardoning Anne's mother, he still receives the maximum punishment. He chooses God and dies, unforgiven (but still loved) by his mother for having married Anne in the first place, unforgiven by Anne for having robbed her youth, alienated from his son who loves Anne as much as he does. And he is without a fellow minister at his side, as he was at Laurentius's side when the latter died in fulfillment of another of Marthe's curses.

Laurentius's sudden death in itself must not be looked on as a testimony to the powers of witchcraft. Rather, it should be seen as one more punishment inflicted upon Absalon, one more price he has to pay for the folly and pride of coveting a young woman and pardoning her witch-mother in order to get her. He pays the final price in remaining unforgiven by God Himself, Whom one might have expected to show some mercy toward Absalon. That He does not is not an argument against God; it is an argument, using one of God's own as an example, for the fallibility of the human and the inscrutability of the divine. It is an argument that the worst in man—the worst or the flaw in a good man—is combated by the worst in God or simply the universe, and as such it is a form of purgation: this is *the worst that can happen*, and from that we can take comfort. What will happen to us cannot be as bad. Dreyer, finally, has been the engineer of all this, as much to fortify himself against the many forms of disaster, to use Bert States's words, as to assert his own imagination's place as a force in the universe to be reckoned with.

I should like here to return to *King Lear*, about which J. Stampfer further remarks that "there is no mitigation in Lear's death, hence no mitigation in the ending of the play. . . . *King Lear* is Shakespeare's first tragedy in which the tragic hero dies unreconciled and indifferent to society" (366, 371). Lear dies, and there is no one from his family to carry on in his place: with him have died Goneril, Regan, and Cordelia. Absalon dies unredeemed and bewildered, but there is someone from his family to carry on in his place: his son, who turns on Anne and, with his grandmother, accuses her of witchcraft in willing the death of his father. *Day of Wrath* ends with our knowledge that Anne will burn as a witch and with the suggestion that Martin will take over his father's duties as pastor. Martin will occupy the role Absalon filled after the death of his first wife, before he met Anne and pardoned her mother: that of pastor, living with his (grand)mother. Anne's mother has been dead for some time (presumably of natural causes), Absalon is dead, and Anne will die: the sin will thus be completely expiated.

Matters will be returned to a state of grace, then. But we do not *see* them returned to a state of grace. We do not see Anne burn, as we did Marthe, and we do not see Martin become pastor. Dreyer's overriding concern is still with Absalon's destruction, not his society's redemption. Whatever reconciliation we get at the end of the film occurs less in the sense that wrong is righted than in the sense that wrong is *counterpointed*. Absalon yielded to temptation with Anne, whereas Martin ultimately does not do so; and Dreyer juxtaposes the chaos of Absalon's life against the newfound order of Martin's so as to point up the irrevocability of that chaos, as well as the tentativeness of that order.

Dreyer uses this technique of counterpoint again when he intercuts the scene of Absalon returning from the dead Laurentius's house with the one of Martin and Anne in the parsonage, where she wishes Absalon dead. The relationship between these two scenes might seem too obvious, especially when Absalon remarks at one point on the strength of the wind that "It was as if death brushed against my sleeve" (*Four Screen Plays*, 211). But Dreyer is not telling us here that Anne is willing Absalon's death, that even as she wishes his death, he feels it coming. He is portraying Absalon's own sense of his impending doom, of his punishment for his sin. He sees trouble coming, or at least feels very uneasy, outdoors as well as indoors—indeed, he can find no peace anywhere.

Earlier Dreyer had intercut a scene of him at home, full of remorse for having pardoned Anne's mother to marry her daughter, with a scene of Anne and Martin wandering blissfully in the fields at night. She feels no guilt indoors or outdoors for betraying her husband and for wishing him dead. Absalon *can* feel guilt for his sins; Anne cannot. She is, in this way, less the instrument of his doom than its counterpoint. She incarnates evil; he, good gone wrong. Absalon's mother, at the other extreme from Anne, incarnates good, or at least righteousness; while Martin, contrasted with his father in the middle, incorporates good that is tempted but finally abstains.

Even the way in which Anne accepts her witchcraft and her sentence to burn at the stake, after Martin renounces her, stands in direct counterpoint to the way that Absalon receives the revelation of his betrayal and her accusation that he robbed her youth; and this contrast makes the circumstances of Absalon's death clearer. He dies immediately of a heart attack out of guilt and out of shock at the extremity of his punishment. Anne, by contrast, accepts/chooses death-by-burning coolly. She wants to die, not so much because she thinks she has played any part in her husband's death or that this would matter anyway, not so much out of guilt, as to spite Martin, who has betrayed her for his grandmother. She will die out of a spite that is better known as selfishness or self-consumption, whereas Absalon has died for his sins, for his belief in a higher law than the law of self.

Day Of Wrath counterpoints witchcraft with piety, indulgence with abstinence, evil with good. In the process, the film "gorges" itself on Absalon's destruction; but all the while it reassures us that what happens to him cannot happen to us, it warns us that some form of destruction or misfortune lies in wait for everyone. That is its underpinning: Dreyer not only takes out his frustrations absolutely on Absalon, he also is sure to include himself and, by extension, the audience as a potential, if less serious, victim of a malevolent universe. This he does through the character of Martin and the film's visual style. Dreyer is careful not to have Martin succumb in the end to Anne's temptations: he must have a scare but must survive, his virtue, or at least his good intentions, intact, as the character with whom we identify most. Anne herself is too evil, too devious, to identify with; Absalon's mother so good as to be a caricature of goodness, rightness, and caution; and Absalon, of course, is too victimized. Through Martin, Dreyer posits the existence of two separate worlds, the one safe, rational, and certain, the other dangerous, irrational, uncertain; and he shows how simple it is to cross from one world to the next with a single action. Martin rejects Anne at the last minute and remains on the safe side of life.

To the visual style itself of *Day of Wrath*. I said at the start of this essay that many critics have remarked on the austerity and stateliness of Dreyer's style. Paul Schrader, for example, writes that

> the late nineteenth- and early twentieth-century Kammerspiele (literally, chamber plays) were the immediate stylistic precedents for Dreyer's films. . . . In each of Dreyer's films one can detect elements of Kammerspiele: intimate family drama, fixed interior settings, unembellished sets, long takes emphasizing staging, the use of gesture and facial expression to convey psychological states, plain language, and a thoroughgoing sobriety. (114-115)

No one has remarked, however, on how Dreyer contrasts the seeming sureness and reason of this style in *Day of Wrath* with the disorientation and unreason of another style that he puts side by side with it.

Often, for example, Dreyer will shoot a character from one angle and then cut to a shot of the same character from the reverse angle; or he will cut from one character to another, then return to the first at an angle that confuses the viewer as to the place of the characters in the room and their relation to each other. The effect of this is less to suggest that objective reality does not exist, that people and things can be looked at and interpreted in any number of ways, than to give the viewer a sense of the changeability of affairs from moment to moment, a sense of a world in which a permanent state or even complete knowledge of oneself is impossible. In other words, as with his characterization of Martin, so too with his visual style is Dreyer attempting to posit the exisence of two separate worlds: the one orderly, the other unsettled and possibly chaotic.[18] Even as the camera can change worlds from shot to shot, so too can a man change his "world" from one action to the next—except that the camera can go back, can reclaim the orderly after a plunge into disorder. That is not so easy for a man. Martin comes as close as possible to doing it at the end of *Day of Wrath* when he goes from loving Anne and swearing that she is not a witch, to despising her and swearing that she is.

Dreyer himself has written of his camerawork that

> All good films are characterized by a certain rhythmic tension, which is induced partly by the characters' movements as revealed in images . . . For [this] kind of tension, much importance is attached to the lively use of a moving camera, which even in close shots adroitly follows the characters; so that the background constantly shifts as it does when we follow somebody with our eyes. . . . it is of some significance for the adaptation of stage plays that in each act of most plays there is as much action offstage as on, which can yield material for . . . new rhythms. (*Four Screen Plays*, 13-14)

One senses that by "good films" Dreyer means those (like his own masterpieces) that attempt to create tragedy, where the kind of tension he speaks of is essential and underlines another kind, which perhaps constitutes the essence of tragedy: the kind of tension wherein the viewer feels that the outcome of the action is inevitable at the same time as he feels a certain measure of control over his *own* fate, that he himself is not irrevocably doomed. He feels right up to the end, furthermore, that even though the outcome of the action is inevitable, *something* could be done along the way to alter the course of events. (Hence dramatic terms like "turning point" and "moment of final suspense.") Or that alternative values exist somewhere, along with an alternative world. The alternative world is peopled by Martin in *Day of Wrath*, as I have posited. And the chaotic world of Absalon is suggested not only by the cutting but also by the moving camera, which, in following clearly one object or person, turns everything else into a dizzying blur.

Day of Wrath is an adaptation of a play, and Dreyer includes in it offstage action to which he refers in the above quotation—scenes that in the film's source, the historical drama *Anne Pedersdotter* (1908) by the Norwegian playwright Hans Wiers-Jenssen, are only reported by characters. (I want to stress that *Anne Pedersdotter* was an historical drama, one that emphasizes the historical element in its concern with the delusions, superstitions and ignorance that existed in the past; Dreyer transformed the play into a tragedy. See Coiner.) I am thinking specifically of Anne and Martin's meeting in the fields at night and Absalon's return home from the dead Laurentius's house. These outdoor scenes themselves create a rhythmic tension in the film. But the tension here does not derive from the intercutting of outdoor and indoor scenes. It comes from the tilting upward of the camera one moment to the trees above the lovers Anne and Martin, implying that God is judging their sinful actions below; and the leveling of the camera the next moment at the unhappy, fearful, penitent Absalon in the same outdoors to the exclusion of the heavens above, implying that God is not present and will not grant mercy to him. In one instance it seems that the world is inhabited by a just and rational God, in the other that no such God exists. In this way, the outdoor scenes give Dreyer further opportunity to dramatize the two separate worlds he demarcated so tellingly indoors.

I have remarked several times in this essay on the reticence of Absalon: his lack of reflection on, and of exasperation with, what is happening to him compared with Lear. This is the factor that has, up to now, caused critics to look outside his character—namely, to witchcraft and the mysterious—for the key to the film's intentions.[19] I want now only to explain more precisely Absalon's silence, almost his *absence*, since it is so unusual a trait in a character so important and so obviously intelligent. Dreyer makes Absalon silent and passive because *we are not so,* or we think we are not. Absalon's behavior in the face of his misfortune, to us, is one of the worst things that can happen: he does not object (like Lear); he does not run (as Oedipus did from Corinth); he does not suspect or seek counsel (like Othello). We can picture ourselves in all these actions. This is a comfort: we think that we would fight back and perhaps prevail or escape, forgetting momentarily what happened to Lear, Oedipus, and Othello.

Thus, part of the art of *Day of Wrath* is that it beguiles us into thinking we are different, and therefore better off, in a way that Shakespeare and Sophocles do not; then it reminds us, through the character of Martin as well as through its visual style, that we are vulnerable. In other words, it gives us the greatest comfort, and it gives us good caution. If *Day of Wrath* was, as Paul Schrader (127) and Robert Warshow before him (266) believe, one of the first films to attempt to create a "religious system," it succeeds less in the sense that it evokes God than in the sense that it does for us what religion at its best, and art only rarely, do for us: it makes us feel that we are chosen at the same time as it makes us feel we are expendable or incapable.

WORKS CITED

Agee, James. *Agee on Film: Reviews and Comments.* Boston: Beacon Press, 1958.

Bordwell, David. *The Films of Carl-Theodor Dreyer.* Berkeley: University of California Press, 1981.

Coiner, Miles. "Dramaturgy and Theme: A Comparison of *Day of Wrath* and *Anne Pedersdotter.*" Literature/Film Quarterly, 17.2 (1989): 123-128.

Dreyer, Carl Theodor. *Four Screen Plays.* Foreword, Carl Theodor Dreyer. Trans. Oliver Stallybrass. Intro. Ole Storm. Bloomington: Indiana University Press, 1970.

Schrader, Paul. *Transcendental Style in Film: Ozu, Bresson, Dreyer.* Berkeley: University of California Press, 1972.

Stampfer, J. "The Catharsis of *King Lear.*" 1960. In Dean, Leonard, ed. *Shakespeare: Modern Essays in Criticism.* New York: Oxford University Press, 1967.

States, Bert O. *Irony and Drama: A Poetics*. Ithaca, New York: Cornell University Press, 1971.

Warshow, Robert. "*Day of Wrath*: The Enclosed Image." In Warshow's *The Immediate Experience: Movies, Comics, Theatre, and Other Aspects of Popular Culture*. Garden City, New York: Doubleday, 1962.

20

Same Time, Different Children

Mrinal Sen is a quite different character from, say, Andrei Kravchuk—or at least Sen was so in the earlier part of his career, when he could have been described as a utopian visionary of the fervently Marxist kind. Now in his late eighties, Sen has made around thirty feature-length films (together with a number of shorts and documentaries), although few of them have been shown in the United States—and none until the American premiere of *The Case Is Closed* (1982) in 1984. Inarguably, the delay in Sen's U.S. reception has been an ill wind, but it may have blown a little good. That is because, even though his work is distinguished by the attention it pays to the lives of the underprivileged in India ("untouchables," pavement dwellers, servants), most of his films until around 1979 (with *And Quiet Rolls the Dawn*, whose setting and theme resemble those of *The Case Is Closed*) were highly polemical. They were so overtly or urgently political, in fact, that they earned Sen a reputation as India's preeminent activist moviemaker.

I am glad, therefore, that *The Case Is Closed* arrived in the United States first, for it is a watchful, implicative film for the most part, not a blatantly obtrusive, finger-pointing one. Like Sen's later pictures in general (he began his career in 1955, as did Satyajit Ray), and like the best films of the Italian neorealists (whom Marxists once attacked for describing the symptoms of social problems rather than probing their capitalist-generated causes), *The Case Is Closed* thus adopts a subdued tone that trusts the audience to draw its own conclusions from what it has seen—which is one description of humanistic art as opposed to agit-prop, or agitational propaganda. This is not to say Sen's earlier films aren't worth seeing, just that they require the gentler introduction which works like *The Case Is Closed*, *The Kaleidoscope* (1981), and *The Ruins* (1983) can provide.

I saw *The Case Is Closed* again recently and would like to treat it here, not only because this film got very little coverage upon its initial release in the U.S., but also because, like Kravchuk's *The Italian* (2005), it concerns the lot of marginalized children. The story is not told from their point of view, however, as it is in Kravchuk's film, though the children in this instance happen to be first-time performers as well. Not so the adults, who, like those in *The Italian*, are professionals, but, importantly where professionals are concerned, actors with whom this Bengali Indian director has worked on other films in the past. Adapting his screenplay from a story by Ramapada Chowdhury, Sen seems to have wanted to decrease the distance between his two primary adult actors and their roles—between fiction and reality, as it were—by substituting their own first names for the first names that Chowdhury gave to his characters. Moreover, the director includes himself in the equation, for he gives his last name to the family that this man and woman head.

Calcutta during a cold spell in 1981 is the setting. Anjan and Mamata Sen are a modestly comfortable couple with a small, lovable son. Because both parents are busy working and their child needs care, they do what many of their friends do: they engage a boy of eleven or twelve, a country boy from a poor family, to live with them as a servant and babysitter. (The youngster's father turns him over to the couple reluctantly, with great tenderness.) But because the Calcutta winter lasts only two months, the Sens don't buy warmer clothes for their domestic helper; and he is directed to sleep in a damp, unheated cubbyhole under a stairwell. One night, it's so cold that the boy goes to sleep in the kitchen, which is windowless and has a small, coal-fired stove that is still burning. Ignorant of the perils of sleeping in such a space without proper ventilation, he dies of carbon-monoxide poisoning—in a room, furthermore, that is mysteriously locked from the inside.

This is the pivotal event in *The Case Is Closed*, and it happens early. We then follow the effect of the boy's death on the people concerned, and it's like following a laboratory dye as it filters through tissues—staining each one of them differently. No one is criminally to blame for the houseboy's asphyxiation, which was accidental, but different sorts of blame, of guilt, are underscored by it. The film touches, for example, on the economic conditions

The Case Is Closed, dir. Mrinal Sen, 1982

that made it necessary for a peasant father to lease out his son (contrasted with the Sens' pampering of their own young son), and also on the way the police treat the bereaved family more with bureaucratic regulation than human sympathy. Indeed, it is only when the deceased youth's father comes to the Sens' house to collect his son's monthly salary that he receives the shattering news of the boy's death: and not from his employers, but (in an added twinge) from another small boy who has the same job, in the apartment upstairs, as the lad who died and who hovers outside doors and windows, watching and listening—and contemplating what might have been his fate.

But the real focus of *The Case Is Closed* is on Anjan and Mamata, whose initial reaction to what has happened is one of surprise and fear. It had not occurred to them, you see, that their servant's life was uncomfortable or that his living requirements were in any way similar to their own. Their fears increase after the family comes to claim the body, for the police are conducting a postmortem and may, with the urging of the boys' parents, bring charges of negligence against the Sens. Added to their dilemma is the fact that crowds of inquisitive neighbors have got wind of the incident and, seeking news about the "crime," have converged on the couple's residence in footage that has a documentary air about it. Moreover, when the husband finally consults a lawyer, this man quickly exposes the falsity of Anjan's claim that he treated the servant boy just like one of the family.

Under the pressure of their secret guilt, the Sens even curry favor with the father of the deceased, offering to let him spend the night in their home, in a nice bed with a thick mattress and warm quilts. But the grieving man's sentiments prevent him from availing himself of such a luxury, and he says he wants to sleep in the kitchen where his son slept and died. After obtaining the boy's body and taking it to a burning *ghat* for cremation, the hapless father, who is anything but litigious or vindictive, actually goes so far as to *ask permission* from the Sens to return to his native village. So Anjan and Mamata do indeed escape prosecution, but, despite their self-protection tinged with aggressive defense, they have not escaped their own misgivings about the conditions under which they made their young servant live and work. And those growing misgivings give *The Case Is Closed* its quiet, steady momentum until, in the end, the real closing of the case occurs with the uneasy closing of the Sen family circle, or one lone clan, against the world.

Only once does Mrinal Sen let his former polemical self intrude on this understated film: when the dead boy's relatives huddle around a fire in the street, waiting for morning and the chance to claim the body, the flames light up revolutionary graffiti on the wall behind them. Related to this, only a few times does Sen let cinema-consciousness obtrude: he uses several freeze frames in a picture that does not require such italicization, and occasionally he lets the sound of the next scene begin under the current scene—a device that can be subtly used to suggest a continuous or eternal present, but which here, where the agonizing present speaks for itself, is merely distracting. For the most part in *The Case Is Closed*, Sen achieves one sort of filmic purity: we are simply present at an inquiry, with no sense of tortuous manipulation or easy irony through angles, editing, composition, or musical score.

The cinematic style, then, is "no style," or "styleless style," a *via negativa* that doesn't in any way pressure us to admire the director.

To make a film in such a manner requires more experience than one would think—and not just of filmmaking. One further example: the cinematography by K. K. Mahajan, who has also worked with Sen before. Mahajan's palette is controlled to make every unquestionably real object before our eyes—a chair, a table, a bed—look almost (therefore unobtrusively) as if it were a cutout, as if we were watching a realistic morality play unfold (as it would have done during the medieval period) on something less than a realistic stage. The effect is not to make us discount setting and environment in the creation of this drama, in their influence on Anjan and Mamata as well as the dead boy's family. Instead, it is to disattach the central characters of the film from their immediate setting—invisibly, as it were (rather than crudely or forcibly to do so through rack focusing)—in the way only extreme grief, fear, and guilt can subjectively do. The effect of this cinematography is additionally, and ingeniously, to make *The Case Is Closed* linger in our minds or return to our senses, because all during its screening, it has required us—imaginatively, visually, morally, judicially—to complete it, to join the foreground to the background and hence to a higher plane.

The principal actors, guided by Sen of course, heighten our added feeling of espionage (let us call it) on, and involvement with, the confidentiality of their performances. This is a kind of acting that precludes display and is thus easily underrated as mere "behaving," which it decidedly is not. There's a close parallel between the acting here and the look of the film itself: the actor needs skill—enough skill to ignore skill, to concentrate on congruence with character, on permitting us to peep and eavesdrop and participate rather than to project at us. Mamata Shankar (niece of the sitarist Ravi Shankar) and Anjan Dutt have that skill, as do even the two first-time actors who play the servant boys. (Dehapratim Das Gupta plays Hari, the domestic helper in the upstairs apartment, but, in an irony that bespeaks his character's status, the name of the Sens' houseboy has not been available to me, and I don't recall that his character's first or last name was ever used in the film.)

At the time *The Case Is Closed* was made, Mamata Shankar had played in three previous Sen films, while Anjan Dutt played the lead in the picture Sen made just before this one (*The Kaleidoscope*). Shankar is primarily a dancer, which means that, in a compelling paradox, she gives Mamata a consummate, external grace that is belied by her extreme inner torment. Dutt, for his part, has had theater experience (has in fact performed in Europe), which means that he knows how to turn his seemingly continuous presence on screen into a prolonged journey into the interior, just as longer and longer acquaintance with a person in life not only tells us more about him but often alters what we thought we knew about him. In sum, in this film it takes two fine performers from other media—dance and theater—to prove something about the cinema that is rarely paid attention: its superior ability to explore human interiority, the intimacies of the heart and mind, the internal growth or change of a character over time.

Subsequent to my re-screening of *The Case Is Closed*, I made it a point to see *Ten Days in Calcutta: A Portrait of Mrinal Sen* (1984), a documentary by the German director Reinhard Hauff. (Sen and Hauff converse in English.) It's a fascinating portrait of Sen, of a career dedicated to personal, compassionate, concerned filmmaking, of a man working through the years with a small group of colleagues in modest quarters so as to deal cinematically with his world—to put that world on film in a way that he envisions it, without the interference of those who would make only money from the movies. At one point in the documentary, Sen takes Hauff through Calcutta and reveals how this brawling and impoverished, yet vital, city has nourished him. The place and the people come first, in other words, not the fiction and the finance, which is one way of distinguishing the indigenous neorealist cinema of any decade from the global, retro-formalist or fantasist imposture that—ever in the name of "progressive" art, on the one hand, or the "growth" industry of entertainment, on the other—would colonize it.

Since I point out above the implicitly political but not overtly politicized (let alone propagandistic) nature of *The Case Is Closed*, I thought I'd offer a counter-example for the sake of clarification. That film is *Alsino and the Condor* (1982), the first full-length motion picture shot in post-Somoza Nicaragua and the first Central American film to be nominated for an Oscar for Best Foreign-Language Film. It was directed by the Chilean exile Miguel Littin (who was exiled to Mexico shortly after Augusto Pinochet came to power on 11 September 1973 in the violent military coup that ousted the democratically elected socialist president Salvador Allende) and co-adapted by him from the novel *Alsino* (by the Chilean modernist Pedro Prado). I'm particularly concerned to expose this movie because it is often trumpeted as a shining instance of *nuevo cine*, or New Latin American Cinema, which is said to have drawn its own inspiration from Italian cinematic neorealism. Co-produced by the Cubans, *Alsino and the Condor*, however, is little more than a filmic expression of Third-World solidarity—one that (to paraphrase Yeats) instead of making poetry out of its quarrel with itself, makes rhetoric out of its quarrel with others.

The film is related from the point of view of yet another child: in this instance, a twelve-year-old peasant boy who lives in a jungle village in Nicaragua under the brutal Somoza regime (1967-1979)—then at war both with Honduras and the indigenous Sandinistas. While his impoverished country and its rotten buildings crumble all around him, the idealistic Alsino—who lives with his grandmother and plays with Lucia, the little girl next-door—nurtures his dream of flying, literally flying. Naturally, he is awestruck at the sight of helicopters used in the Honduran conflict (promoted by the United States). Soon Alsino is even given a ride in a helicopter by an American military advisor named Frank (Dean Stockwell), but

Alsino and the Condor, dir. Miguel Littin, 1982

this ride, while momentous, does not satisfy the boy's desire to soar freely. He doesn't like the noise or the paraphernalia of technology, and continues instead to envision flying on his own as the condor—the largest flying bird in the Western hemisphere—does.

Late one moonlit night, in the throes of one of his dreams of flight, Alsino escapes out of the tiny farmhouse he shares with his grandmother, climbs to the top of his favorite tree, and, with his arms outstretched, takes off. But instead of flying, the youngster crashes to earth and becomes a physically crumpled wreck, to be known thereafter as "Hunchback." Yet this life-changing injury fails to change Alsino's life (though it does lead to his family's further impoverishment) or his dream, as one might expect: making no attempt to hide the circumstances surrounding his injury, he still wants to fly like a bird. What does change his life, or lead to his disillusionment, is the growing military presence in his village, which has become a base for select operations and which brings with it the things all such military bases tend to bring (including drugs and prostitution).

Alsino's disillusionment comes to a head when he happens one day on government troops in mid-massacre on the spot that once was his favorite place to play. (Earlier, during his wanderings through the Nicaraguan countryside, he had hardly batted an eye as he witnessed the massacre of peasants and the burning of their farms by Somoza's henchmen.) Guerrillas counterattack while the boy watches, and they manage to prevail—though during the fight, Frank's helicopter crashes into the tree that Alsino once loved to climb, and the American is killed. Frank had been warned against befriending children, who were often guerrillas in disguise, and, just so, Alsino decides to join the winning guerrilla band: all of them Sandinistas at war with the corrupt, U.S.-backed Somoza dictatorship controlling Nicaragua. He is welcomed into the outfit as one more freedom fighter, and only then does Alsino's physical regeneration from his handicap take place, as this man-child miraculously straightens out to his full, proud height at the same time as he seems fully to come of age.

If you haven't figured out the unabashedly allegorical nature of the narrative I have just recounted, here it is: Alsino, emblem of the Nicaraguan people, wants political and economic freedom (equated here with flying) of a nationalistic kind, not any foreign and therefore artificial substitute (like the American helicopter). When he tries to get it on his own (by attempting to launch into flight from a tree, by briefly entering the illicit world of drugs-and-prostitution, even by contradictorily selling wild birds whose wings have been crippled to keep them from crawling back into the wild), he fails. But Alsino's dreams finally come true when he commits himself to the collective or communal revolution of the Sandinistas. Not by accident, his metamorphosing into a rebel—which includes his taking the generic name of all the guerrillas, Manuel—and his bodily resurrection occur as death comes to the United States in the form of the demise of the lone military strategist named Frank. How's that for subtlety?

The problem with propaganda of this kind, of course, is that it usually comes full circle to bite you, as it did to Littin in this case when the Sandinista revolution ultimately failed (in 1990). Unsurprisingly, we've had no film on that subject from him, though he continues to work. Born in 1942 in Chile to a Palestinian father and a Greek mother, Littin has made a number of films since *Alsino and the Condor*, among them the documentary *The Road to Rage: Chronicle of the Palestinian People* (2000) and, in 1989, a biographical picture about Augusto Nicolás Calderón Sandino (1895-1934), the Nicaraguan revolutionary whose name was adopted, fifty years after his death, by those who wanted to liberate Nicaragua from the tyranny of Anastasio Somoza but instead created their own brand of police state.

It's true that, as he did not do in *The Road to Rage* and *Sandino*, Littin tries to leaven the politicized dough of *Alsino and the Condor* with bits of magic realism *à la* Gabriel García Márquez (whose nonfiction book *Clandestine in Chile* [1986] had Littin as its subject), but even that ploy was better carried out over three decades earlier by none other than an Italian neorealist, Vittorio De Sica, in *Miracle in Milan* (1950)—as well as being better executed subsequently by Bahman Ghobadi in *Turtles Can Fly* (2004). Littin succeeds more in his casting of Alan Esquivel as Alsino, but here the director relies on another artistic precedent: Truffaut's film *The Wild Child* (1970), whose leading actor (Jean-Pierre Cargol, of Gypsy parentage) Esquivel strongly resembles. Like the wild child—who himself resembles a wild beast in that he neither walks upright, wears clothing, nor has the faculty of speech—Alsino is not beyond feeling but beyond its *expression*, until, in his case, he gets a political education as opposed to the civilizing one received by the *enfant sauvage* of Truffaut's movie.

Lyric Latin populism of this type—at times gaudy and expressionistic, at times gritty and documentary-like—tires me out. Works like this (novels *or* films) want to be all things to all people: coming-of-age story, political allegory, Christian parable, Hispanic folktale (with origins, in *Alsino and the Condor*, in the ancient Greek myth concerning Icarus), childlike fairy tale, and movie melodrama. In the end, however, such fictions add up to nothing for all their calculated maneuverings. "Life is short, art is long," wrote Horace, to which I would add this codicil: "Life distends, art distills." You'll find that distillation process soberly at work during the ninety-five minutes of Mrinal Sen's *The Case Is Closed*. In Miguel Littin's *Alsino and the Condor*, by contrast, for all its seeming brevity (eighty-nine minutes), you'll find only bloat—the kind of bloatedness, moreover, that can only come from self-intoxication.

21

Mind over Medium

I took another look at ten old films recently, films I hadn't seen since they first came out. And I'm sorry I did.

I had seen them for the first time at the Mayfair Theatre, an art-deco house in Miami, Florida, where I grew up (after being transplanted from New York City). And perhaps my once fond memories of the films I'm going to discuss are connected to the place where I first saw them—predictably, a place (1605 Biscayne Boulevard) where only a large mall, the Omni, now stands. The Mayfair was Miami's premiere art-house cinema during the 1960s and 1970s, showing lots of foreign films but also a fair sampling of the so-called New American Cinema. I used to drive there at night, alone, in my Austin-Healey as often as I could during my senior year of high school, as well as during summers and holidays away from college. Much to my parents' dismay, I *liked* seeing movies alone, and I liked driving my sports car downtown (from suburban, at the time even rural, Hialeah) to the theater where I'd see them.

I especially loved those tense moments just before the movie began, the sense of pure promise and incipience they held. Blissfully holding on to the bottom of my seat or the rails of my chair, I would play a little game with time, a game that had several variants, all of them designed to heighten the mystery of beginnings. In its simplest version, the game required that I close my eyes when I sensed the moment approaching for the house to dim. My eyes had to be screwed shut so tightly that I couldn't detect the gradual decrease in illumination as the projectionist brought down the lights; part of the game's object was to bypass that artificially slow transition from light to dark, reality to dream, provided for the sake of less hardy and philosophic souls than myself. No, what I wanted was the exhilaration of the plunge, the leap into a new element. Blocking out the light, I focused my mind instead on the gentle murmur of those spectators who, unlike me, chose to combine moviegoing with companionship. Thus it was only when I heard the general hum fade and conversations suddenly accelerate, scrambling to find some arbitrary point of rest, that I knew the movie had begun. And that was when I would open my eyes, inexplicably gratified to find myself in total darkness.

Mind you, as screening room, the Mayfair itself wasn't all that special. Badly in need of restoration, it had only a tiny foyer with a complimentary coffee pot and no popcorn, (happily) a single screen, and 422 seats. But it *was* located on Biscayne Boulevard, Miami's version of Fifth Avenue; it was an oasis of culture in a city that during this period was a cultural backwater; and the theater's name itself, for a Florida boy, smacked of the exotic—the Anglo-exotic, in this case, since "Mayfair" was a direct reference to the fashionable district of central London built in the early nineteenth century. Moreover, what remained of the Mayfair's art-deco style (the place was built when Miami itself was being built up, in the late 1920s to early 1930s) was just enough to reinforce what I believed, even at the tender age of seventeen: that the movies themselves should always strive to integrate technology and art.

Back then—the 1960s and 1970s—movie theaters still came in many shapes, from the massive picture palaces of the twenties and thirties, with their pipe organs and painted clouds, to dilapidated art houses like the Mayfair and the even rattier second-run theaters that Manny Farber once described as "glorified tattoo parlors." To habitual moviegoers, every theater has its own unique bouquet, some special mix of ambience and programming that wins for it either fondness or contempt. What matters most, however, is that theaters are *places* in a way that living rooms, in their very cosiness and adaptability, are not. Consecrated to a single ritual, at times deliberately modeled on cathedrals, movie theaters emanate a sense of place. And, needless to say, this sense of place has been eroded in recent years as theaters have become homogeneous, modular multiplexes that seem intent on simulating the interior of a television box.

the working class in a white-collar, lower-middle-class position, but the very same story could have featured an upper-class youth. John Braine and Jack Clayton's *Room at the Top* needed its industrial-town setting to show the new social mobility. Karel Reisz and Alan Sillitoe's *Saturday Night and Sunday Morning* needed its lathe-worker hero to show that the new neon-lighted, unionized worker stills feels a kind of Calvinist doom even at higher wage levels. *A Kind of Loving*, however, has no such imperative. It could have been set in Kensington or a garden suburb; its hero could have been an undergraduate collegian or a junior stockbroker.

In sum, the outburst of the Angry Young Men that dates from 1956—in fiction and drama and then film—was welcome and necessary, but a style that is followed for its own sake, as Schlesinger follows that style here, becomes a cliché with astonishing speed. After all, it is just as easy to make bad art about poor people as less poor ones—easier, in a way, because extraneous empathy can be used to mask inferior work. *A Kind of Loving* is certainly not a bad film—it has several solid merits, which I've endeavored to enumerate; still, the gravity that it tries to adduce from its milieu is hollow. There was plenty more to be mined for art in British lower-class life, as the filmmakers Ken Loach, Mike Leigh, and Terence Davies were to reveal, especially during the Thatcherite '80s. But the assumption at this time, the late 1950s and early 1960s, that such life is the only good source of art, or that lesser material can be strengthened with a lower-class setting, turned the youthful, invigorating rebels into the Angry Young Establishment. *A Kind of Loving* is prime evidence not only of such a faulty assumption and the blind alley down which it led, but also of what I described earlier as the neophyte Schlesinger's simultaneous potential for artistic progress and professional stagnation.

Together with Keith Waterhouse and Willis Hall once again, Schlesinger next produced *Billy Liar*. The film is the third metamorphosis of this work, which was originally a 1959 novel by Waterhouse; it was dramatized by him and Hall in 1960 and presented successfully in London (as well as elsewhere). The material is simple: the fantasies of a twenty-year-old provincial clerk that are his refuge from the frustrations to which circumstance and weakness of character have sentenced him. And one of the strengths of this

Walker Percy writes eloquently in *The Moviegoer* (1961) of this dimension of moviegoing, the way in which it anchors one to time and space:

> If I did not talk to the theater owner or ticket seller, I should be lost, cut loose metaphysically speaking. I should be seeing one copy of a film which might be shown anywhere and at any time. There is a danger of slipping clean out of space and time. It is possible to become a ghost and not know whether one is in downtown Loews in Denver or suburban Bijou in Jacksonville. So it was with me. Yet it was here in the Tivoli that I first discovered place and time, tasted it like okra. It was during a rerelease of *Red River* a couple of years ago that I became aware of the first faint stirrings of curiosity about the particular seat I sat in, the lady in the ticket booth. . . . As Montgomery Clift was whipping John Wayne in a fist fight, an absurd scene, I made a mark on my seat arm with my thumbnail. Where, I wondered, will this particular piece of wood be twenty years from now, 543 years from now?

For Percy's moviegoer, the existential hero Binx Bolling, the theater is as important as the movie; perhaps more important, the theater, the physical place as well as its functionaries, provides a solid frame or context that helps combat the tendency of movies to become disembodied and so to disembody the spectator. What movies offered Binx, what the Mayfair offered me, was an experience that fused the Platonic insubstantiality of film's floating images in all their radiant perfection with the okra-like specificity of this room, these chairs, this door, and made of them a single sensation. Body and soul, here and there, reality and imagination: moviegoing enacts the bridging of these contraries as formally and as viscerally as churchgoing once did—perhaps more intensely, because movie theaters carry a greater weight of mortal dross than churches, with their snacks for the stomach, upholstered seats for the buttocks, above all with the way their physicality persists in near-darkness, as corner exits remain faintly visible and walls and ceiling are felt more than seen.

Let me concentrate now not on the place where I saw many old films, but on the ten films themselves. I had remembered the first one, *Elvira Madigan* (and, tellingly, the only European picture in my group of ten), as a beautiful, romantic film from a beautiful, romantic year in my own life: 1967, during which I fell in love (I think) for the very first time. But a film of Beauty—whatever its subject—is a risk forever. And the beauty of Swedish director Bo Widerberg's film did not age well. On re-viewing forty-three years later, *Elvira Madigan* falls short not only through the inevitable tedium—in a sense, the distraction—of the incessantly beautiful, but also because of the very subject on which all that beauty is lavished.

The screenplay, by Widerberg himself, is based on fact. In 1889 a young cavalry lieutenant, Count Sixten Sparre, leaves his wife and children to run off with a circus tightrope dancer named Elvira Madigan. They spend some idyllic weeks in the Swedish summer countryside, hiding out because he is a deserter, as I imagined in 1967 I might be were I called up into the military. A brother officer finds Sixten and tries to recall him to duty and family, without success. The lovers finally run out of money, but rather than return to the world and separate lives, they agree to die. He shoots her and then himself.

Since this story is well known in Sweden, Widerberg's primary job was not one of narration but of fantastification—that is, of satisfying and improving upon previous romantic fantasies, factually based or otherwise, in the minds of his Swedish audience. To this end, he immediately eliminated the element of suspense for *all* audiences by putting a note at the beginning of his film synopsizing the facts of the story. But even without the prefatory note, this is not a movie with much narrative element; it is an exploration of a *state*—of being and feeling—which eventually dissipates. Presumably having chosen the subject precisely for this reason, Widerberg has concentrated on making the texture of that state as voluptuous as possible. His success with that texture is the success—*was* the success, for me, in 1967—and ultimately the failure of *Elvira Madigan*.

To wit, virtually every shot is exquisite. Even the scenes toward the end when the literally starving lovers are scrounging on all fours for mushrooms and herbs, when Elvira gets sick to her stomach,

Elvira Madigan, dir. Bo Widerberg, 1967

are exquisitely photographed. Jörgen Persson's color camerawork has all the golden lights of summer, in noonday fields and golden glades; his interiors are grainy with wood and cool with linen; his lyricism, indoors as well as out, is helped by soft focus and slow motion. Thus flowers float on air, skies are impossibly azure, the fruit and cheese and wine look better than they could ever taste. The faces of the lovers themselves, played by Thommy Berggren and Pia Degermark, are out of Degas, and the hotel cook who befriends the couple has the good-natured, gently lascivious face of all the friends of lovers since lovers needed friends. Like endless slices of delicious cake, then, the shots fall before us, one after the other. But the result is unavoidable: the diet is *too* rich. It cloys. And, from the perspective of 2010, I became overly conscious of the industrious application of beauty—so much so that I wondered whether, somewhere in the Swedish summer of 1889, there wasn't at least one unlovely prospect.

This aesthetic discomfort would probably have arisen in any case, but it is emphasized here for another reason: these two lovers are stupid. (I suspect that Widerberg's justification might be, "But that's the way it really happened." If so, it proves yet again that life is no artist.) What is obvious to the viewer fairly soon (to *this* viewer, more than four decades after the fact!) dawns on these two slowly and surprisingly. What are they going to do when Sixten runs out of money—the little money he has on him? He cannot get a job; there is a brief conversation with a workman to underscore the fact that Sixten doesn't know any trade. And besides, he is a deserter, subject to arrest. Elvira herself makes one attempt to earn money as a dancer, but clearly such an existence—her line of work, and his dependence on it—would be, for him, intolerable. In sum, when Sixten's small purse is empty, their idyll will be done. This seems to surprise the two of them, together with her apparent surprise when she learns that her parents are worried, or his when he learns that his wife is desperately grieved over his departure. What did they expect to happen? How did they expect to live, given the inescapable fact that they are totally shunned by nineteenth-century Swedish society, whose moral code they have outraged?

Now it seems to me that there are two kinds of all-for-love lovers who are tragic: those who make plans to beat the world and who are frustrated (Romeo and Juliet), and those who know they are doomed yet go ahead anyway because they prefer doom to separation (the pair in *Mayerling* [1936, 1968]). But this pair, Elvira and Sixten, have neither any plan nor any sense of what they are getting into. They are just dumb, something that, as a teenager, I guess I could not have been expected to perceive. Their fate has some pathos because they *have* been happy and they do end up dead, but our impatience with them spoils the intended tragic fall. All the breathtaking shots across quiet meadows, the stunning vistas seen through waving grass, in the end seem wasted on these two ninnies.

None of this is the fault of the actors: Berggren and Degermark are subtle and true. Widerberg has handled them as discreetly as he has edited his film surely. Technically, his only lapse is his use of music. He not only plonks down a chunk of the slow, second movement of Mozart's Piano Concerto No. 21 whenever he wants a little more poignancy, he also begins and ends these quotations abruptly. That music was lovely long before Widerberg was born, but, in this instance, the film does not rise to the level of the music; instead, Mozart's music is brought down to the level of *Elvira*

Madigan. Widerberg would have achieved more if he had commissioned the right composer, approved the right score, and mixed his soundtrack gently. In any event, what I had remembered as two lovers' unrealistic, tragic, almost unbearably moving quest for happiness, turned out, in 2010, to be an overblown and sentimental cigarette commercial—and just as dated as one.

I remember leaving the Mayfair after seeing *Elvira Madigan* and overhearing a middle-aged man sneer with contempt at what he called (to his wife) the film's childishness. I didn't know what he was talking about and sneered at *him* for what I believed to be his philistine arrogance. Naturally, the older I get, the wiser that man seems—a man of weathered face, hunched demeanor, and shuffling walk whom I saw only once but, to recast my favorite line from *Citizen Kane* (1941), whom I have thought about ever since, every day of my critical life. He obviously had not been fooled by the film's faux-romanticism, had not been shocked by the "newness" of its depiction of a Sweden that I had never seen, either in person or on film (having not yet discovered Ingmar Bergman). Equally obviously, romantic infatuation of the kind experienced by Sixten and Elvira, and lately by myself, was for him a thing of the past.

If *Elvira Madigan*'s subject was doomed love, the subject of *Carnal Knowledge* (1971) is piratical sex. And while I almost regretted that I had watched *Elvira Madigan* alone, I was very happy *not* to have had female company at my screening of *Carnal Knowledge*; indeed, there were no women present at the Mayfair the evening I saw it, just five or six men of varying ages. This picture had stuck in my mind for years as a clinically sharp casebook, an acid satire, on the American male "dating and scoring" mindset, acquired (by too many men) in adolescence and inflicting curses throughout adult life. The script is by Jules Feiffer, and it's familiar Feiffer territory: the American wars and truces between the sexes, with man cast as the vaginal raider and woman as the castrating bitch. The subtext, of course, is American puritanism plus the latter-day reaction against it (latter-day, here, meaning the late '60s and early '70s). This theme, in text if not subtext, is hardly original, but Feiffer had been working with it for years and, in *Carnal Knowledge*, he took it further as well as deeper. At least that's what I once thought.

The script *is* witty, though less witty than some of Feiffer's other

Carnal Knowledge, dir. Mike Nichols, 1971

writings; and there are patches that may have sounded like satire to my young ears in 1971, but which fall flat for my wizened self today—banally flat. Feiffer tells the story of two friends, Jon and Sandy, from their college days just after World War II up to the present of 1970 (which naturally means middle age for them), in terms of their sex lives or, better, sexual obsessions. And, though I sometimes laughed when I saw *Carnal Knowledge* again, one of my feelings while watching was, "I know all this." (As a bachelor until my mid-40s, I had even experienced a good portion of it.) There's always some pleasure in recognition, to be sure, but very little such pleasure can be found in this film by now because American films have been rendering American sex life realistically for quite some time—ironically, since the very time *Carnal Knowledge* was made. Before this period, American movies rendered American sex life about as realistically as ballet does, and usually less imaginatively.

The problem here is that Feiffer only observes, he doesn't perceive. The characters are like those in his drawings, adroitly and economically sketched but two-dimensional—with two-dimensionality as their apparent reason for being. Each of the figures is stock: a handsome, sexy hero; a less attractive pal whom the hero coaches on how to get a girl (the hero beds her easily, of course, after which he turns her over to his unwitting pal); the nice girl who can't resist the hero but marries the pal; the vacuous but good-hearted show girl with whom the hero gets involved. All four get their tags when they first appear, then just go on displaying them.

And to sledge-hammer matters, there's a slide-photo reprise by Jon near the end, with Sandy as his only audience, of all the girls in his life. Title: "Ballbusters on Parade," an expression that I confess to having grinningly used, as a young man, more times than I'd like to recall.

Through much of my re-viewing of the film, as a result, I sensed a slight invisible nodding—not of drowsiness but of acceptance (which is related to the "recognition" I described earlier), particularly of the final scene, in which the aging hero can now "get it up" only by listening to the trash-talk of a lowly prostitute. And acceptance, or lack of rejection, is an insufficient reaction to purportedly serious work. *Carnal Knowledge* is thus not a drama or even a narrative in any generative sense; it's a chronological series of depositions. Even such a chronology might have had a certain cumulative interest, except that in this case, once we know the premises, we can easily work out the rest for ourselves. There are absolutely no surprises, by which I don't mean plot twists but enrichments, contradictions, puzzlements. Feiffer shows small sense of the paradoxes, even mysteries, which lie beneath a seemingly consistent behavior pattern in an otherwise normal individual.

He's not helped by the cast of *Carnal Knowledge*. Jack Nicholson plays Jonathan Fuerst, who was graduated from Evander Childs High School in the Bronx (not my territory). Jon was evidently conceived as New York Jewish, and Nicholson neither looks nor sounds it. (I missed this in 1971 because, at that juncture in my history, I had insufficient experience of Jews and Judaism.) Because Nicholson is, well, what you could call his old self—the dynamic-defiant-delectable Jack—his inappropriateness for the part is muted but never lost. Art Garfunkel, the Sandy, is not an actor at all; he's a singer-songwriter. Mike Nichols, the director, apparently thought that his personality, which is apt enough, was worth the risk, and he has helped Garfunkel at least not to get in Nicholson's way.

For her part, Ann-Margret—never really the terrible actress she was made out to be at the time, just an actress burdened by terrible parts—has a showy, sure-fire role, and Nichols does his best to whip her up into various frenzies, just as he did with Elizabeth Taylor in *Who's Afraid of Virginia Woolf?* (1966) five years earlier. He had a much harder time, though, with Candice Bergen in a quiet role. Nichols has tried to rid Bergen of her constant strain to *sound* credible; and he has told her something about thought process so that she knows what to do with her eyes (for a change). He has, in short, attempted to shear off Bergen's wooliness. The result may not be a phony performance, but it is not exactly a memorable one, either.

The chief reason the film is not dull, even after almost four decades, is that it was directed by Nichols. Compared with his previous films, the refined camerawork here (by Giuseppe Rotunno) verges on the austere. *Carnal Knowledge* has none of the arty angles of *Who's Afraid of Virginia Woolf?*, little of the cleverish cutting of *The Graduate* (1967), none of the grandiloquence that spotted *Catch-22* (1970). Nichols is simply bearing down in this film, intently; that is, he is concentrating more and more on the frame—the held shot—as a source of power unto itself. Frequently, for example, there is a long take of one person, sometimes in close-up, who is motionless while bustle occurs around him. It's a use of the camera as observer, as *drainer*, rather than as participant—surely not the only way to use the camera but one that implies a growing "stillness" in the director, an unwavering quality that implies a sense of security and seriousness about the decisions he has made. Still, on balance, *Carnal Knowledge* proves—like every other film in Nichols' career—that he has always been a director who essentially looks for things to do, not a director who essentially *has* things he wants to do. This is why, although he is a good craftsman, he has never become a major artist.

The same can be said of Peter Bogdanovich, as any sampling of his filmography will make clear, from *What's Up, Doc?* (1972) and *Saint Jack* (1979) to *Noises Off* (1992) and *The Cat's Meow* (2001). My subject here is Bogdanovich's second film, *The Last Picture Show* (1971), in which he fatefully showed he had progressed happily in most ways (addressing better material and showing even more skill than in his first picture, *Targets* [1968]) except one: the central matter of self, being, style. *The Last Picture Show*, like every Bogdanovich film to follow, revealed that he loved films and knew how to make them (as well as write about them, in books on directors like Welles, Hitchcock, Hawks, and Ford), but it told us nothing about the man himself. Namely, who *is* Peter Bogdanovich? That's a question all really good directors answer about themselves, sooner rather than later. And Bogdanovich's answer has yet to come.

The reason for this, paradoxically, may be that he loves movies so much—other people's movies. For one thing, behind Bogdanovich's choice to make *The Last Picture Show* in elegiac black and white, and behind the gray tonalities of the film, looms the loomable figure of Orson Welles. Along with the adulatory monograph Bogdanovich wrote about Welles in 1961, this picture is surely another homage to him—in this case, to *Touch of Evil* (1958)—particularly in its rendering of a Texas with every gradation of light except sunshine. But it is also an homage to Welles's *The Magnificent Ambersons* (1942), in which the advent of the automobile marked the passing of an era, even as the closing of the town's only movie theater and the advent of television (which was replacing movies as the dream-stuffing of empty lives) mark the passing of a later era in *The Last Picture Show*.

This film's Christmas dance, for example—a sequence that uses country-and-western renditions of such John Ford favorites as "Red River Valley" and "Golden Slippers"—opens with a tracking shot through a doorway copied from the one that initiates the famous ball sequence in *The Magnificent Ambersons*. There are also bows to George Stevens: a long shot of a lonely house (from *Giant* [1956]) and a burial on a hill (from *Shane* [1953]). From a couple of dozen lesser figures, Bogdanovich has even borrowed the Big Object shot: something huge, and preferably tawdry, in the foreground toward which the characters move from far off. He uses it twice—a garbage can, a pair of feet sticking out of a car—which is twice too often. Who *is* Peter Bogdanovich?

I don't know, but I do know that I saw *The Last Picture Show*—a coming-of-age chronicle as much as it is a film about both the final fadeout of the American frontier and the decline of the "Golden Age" of Hollywood moviemaking—when I myself, a compulsive moviegoer, was coming of age. And I liked it then, without reservation or qualification. Critic though I may be now, I wish I liked it more. The script is by Larry McMurtry and Bogdanovich, from the former's novel of the same name. We're in sex-strangulated, power-pent Texas, its alternately sun-baked and frozen landscape as flat as the outlook of most of the inhabitants—especially the young ones.

When, after my junior year of college, I traveled with my best friend through such a Texas—through the whole southwest, on our way to California—I found myself frequently at a crossroads called a town where there was little but wind, asphalt, and thistles, a motel, a gas station, and a diner, together with alien people who pronounced "thing" as "theng." My immediate reaction, as I sought to generalize about what I had seen, was the renewed belief that the unconscious life is not worth living—followed by the reflection that if *I* don't live it, someone else must. And I feel sure that after my hamburger and coffee at one of these crossroads I murmured for the umpteenth time, as I got into the car, "Christ! Imagine living in a place like this!"

The Last Picture Show is about a place like this. It's 1951 in the dying small town of Anarene, and the first thing we see is the local movie house, then the camera pans up the quite unspectacular main street. The very last shot reverses this movement, ending on the movie house, which has shown its last "picture show" (Howard Hawks's *Red River* [1948]) and shut its doors forever. Between those shots, we've seen the hero, Sonny Crawford, move from late adolescence to the beginnings of manhood.

That's the first trouble, and the script itself is framed just as neatly as the film is with those two shots. That is, in order to define the end of a period in the protagonist's life, things are *made* to happen. Toward the close, for instance, not only does an older man (and former cowboy) who has befriended the hero suddenly drop dead, but the boy's long infatuation with the town beauty is exploded by their trick-marriage, his best friend goes off to the Korean War, his affair with an older married woman dissolves, and—as if all that weren't enough—a mute, mentally retarded kid he likes is run over by a truck. Heavy hands are making the calendar turn over during this one-year saga, and, as a result, what for me was once a painful and affecting look at small-town life in the southwestern United States has become a forced and calculated attempt to encapsulate an era (the 1950s) through one young man's sentimental education.

Another big trouble, from today's perspective, is Timothy Bottoms as the hero. There's nothing drastically wrong with him—other than that it takes about twenty minutes to sort him out, in appearance and language, from his best friend (played by Jeff Bridges).

Mind over Medium 349

The Last Picture Show, dir. Peter Bogdanovich, 1971

Bottoms is genuine enough at a time when, in a reaction against studio glitz-and-glamour, genuineness was enough, and was even welcomed by average, unglamorous guys like me; but he's not *good* enough. He never opens anything up to us, never surprises, and is never really touching. The best I could feel about him, in 2010, was that he was never false—which is not enough for a film that's situated squarely in the middle of its protagonist. (Ironically, a number of the actors who surround Bottoms—Ben Johnson as the aging friend, Cloris Leachman as the desperate and doomed adulteress, Ellen Burstyn as a rich man's frustrated wife together with Cybill Shepherd as her spoiled, pretty daughter—are vivid and truthful.)

And Bottoms' performance is a model of what's finally dim about the whole picture. It all seems true enough, but almost every scene reminds us vaguely of something we've seen before and generally seen better. The old cowboy's speech about time passing him by, the chronicles of social snobberies and sexual hang-ups, the bareness of life in the middle of nowhere, the hunger to break out of that life—all these are credible but not illuminated by anything that makes them more than familiar. For long decades, it's true, American films spent most of their time cramming American life into movie molds (often very entertainingly); then, in the late sixties and early seventies many films, like *The Last Picture Show* (as well as *Carnal Knowledge*), began trying to deal with American life as it is and was. But not falsifying, alas, is not enough.

That brings me to *Mean Streets* (1973), which, like *The Last Picture Show* vis-à-vis Bogdanovich, was Martin Scorsese's second—and better—feature film, after the sophomoric *Who's That Knocking at My Door?* in 1967. (Unlike Bogdanovich, however, Scorsese has never really suffered from an identity crisis. In other words, we know who he is from his "personal" or Italian-American films, like this one, *Raging Bull* [1980], and *GoodFellas* [1990], though sometimes—most notably, in *The Age of Innocence* [1993] and *Kundun* [1997]—he has strayed from the self we have come to know.) I remembered *Mean Streets* fondly, in part because it was made in New York's Little Italy, where I spent the first eight years of my life, in part because it seemed to be an intense, integrated work of art with some real flashes of fire, provided largely by the young Robert De Niro in a flash part.

Scorsese himself grew up on Little Italy's mean streets, so you could say that *Mean Streets* is a home movie about his old neighborhood. Such a personal or autobiographical impulse on his part, which would not exactly have been hot news in any other art at the time, was so unusual in American film that it knocked some people sideways—including this eager and impressionable viewer, who instantly recognized all that he simultaneously loved and hated about his own old neighborhood. I mean the sense of extended, nearly suffocating family the film evokes, with its feeling of domestic security, of strength in numbers, tempered by urban menace, ethnic isolation, religious repression, and narrow horizons.

The screenplay, co-authored by Scorsese, centers on two young Italian-Americans, a hood with a conscience and a slightly demented drifter, played by Harvey Keitel and De Niro respectively. The Keitel character, Charlie Cappa, is seen—or is meant to be seen—through a prism of Catholic anguish as his *capo* uncle grooms him for Mafia success, as he writhes through an affair with the drifter's cousin (an epileptic, no less), and as he tries to look after the feckless but violent drifter, who is his best friend. De Niro, gleefully and savagely loony here in the role of "Johnny Boy" (a peculiarly Italian-American designation and the name of at least two of my first cousins), blows up mailboxes and scares people with rooftop sniping, welches on a loan (this leads to the film's set-piece, a poolroom brawl triggered by Johnny in his angry explosion at the usurer), manipulates Charlie's friendship, goes berserk toward the end, and gets Charlie and himself shot, if not killed, in the climactic scene.

I think we're supposed to feel that the plot of this movie is not the point, that *Mean Streets* exists for its graphic milieu and texture. I certainly felt like this when I saw the film upon its initial release, but today it doesn't quite come out that way. So much of the script gets mired in the tropes of gangster melodrama that plottiness in fact intrudes; and, conversely, some scenes limp, so the plottiness itself is undercut. As for texture, the color is garish and flashy in the barroom scenes, as it commits the aesthetic fallacy of trying *too* hard to look like what it's about; but, oddly, Scorsese's cinematographer, Kent Wakeford, abandons this idea elsewhere. And the editing is jumpy, which spells irresoluteness more than it mirrors the "jumpiness," say, of Johnny Boy. In the first church scene, for instance, there's a lot of leaping from long shots to close shots to reverse shots, revealing a lack of vision on the part of the director. Scorsese simply hasn't found the objective correlative in his method (which he *did* find in *Raging Bull*) that would lift banal material beyond itself; instead, he just gropes and stabs and lunges along his lumpy and discursive way.

We get the *Godfather* scenes (recall that Coppola's film was released only a year earlier, in 1972), the stripteaser scenes, the good and the bad slum kids (right out of *Angels with Dirty Faces* [1938]) who are nevertheless pals, the ultimate gunning-down of both. I don't question the truth of this material, even today; I can't, since I experienced some of it directly, as the son of a Sicilian printer and engraver whom the Mafia tried, unsuccessfully, to lure into the lucrative world of counterfeiting, and as the nephew of a couple of mobsters who served time for all the usual "business" reasons. But I do question Scorsese's ability to lift this material out of the movie gutters into which less truthful directors have trampled it. To be sure, honesty of intent like his is rare in any country's films, and, as I pointed out earlier, it had been even rarer in U.S. films until the late 1960s. So when we got an honest film, as *Mean Streets* wants to be—particularly when it was autobiographical in tenor—it overimpressed everybody, me and you and everyone we know. Worst of all, it overimpressed the filmmaker himself, who thought his honesty would see him through his artistic problems. It couldn't, it didn't. Scorsese was out to tell the truth about his origins and his people, *my* people, but he was so insecure as a director-screenwriter that he fell into filmic falsity along the way.

Put another way, he was so intent on telling his particular truth in *Mean Streets* that his intensity often becomes theatrical in the wrong way. Take the Keitel character's religious remorse and spiritual aspiration, which could have been part of the paradox of Mafia Catholicism in general, but which withers instead into a kind of histrionic obtrusion. Charlie Cappa is the only one in the film shown to have religious impulse or doubt (much like Scorsese himself, and much like me, since both of us flirted with the priesthood before devoting ourselves, let us say, to more worldly aspirations). So instead of being generic, Charlie's spiritual longings and questions turn into an idiosyncratic dramatic tag to make Our Hero "sensitive." The way that the protagonist of bad crime novels is the one guy in his gang who won't go to brothels and thus we know he's poetic, that's the way Charlie is the one guy in his gang who goes to church on Sunday.

And the incompleteness of every such inner motion in the film affects it as a whole. To wit, when it's over we want to know what it was all about, in a way we may not have wanted to know when *Mean Streets* was "new." Is the point of the film to tell us what life was like in Little Italy in the early 1970s? A twenty-minute documentary could have done that, and I myself would not have needed to see it. And is that all there was, and is, to life in this particular part of lower Manhattan? Is Scorsese really telling us that everyone there, at the time, was like this, and that there was no escape? If so, to name just one instance, how did Martin Scorsese come out of it? (How would I have done so, for that matter, had my father, for legitimate business reasons, not *taken* me out of it, to another place—completely apart from Sicilian family, immigrant culture, and criminal temptation?) *Mean Streets* gives us no hint, no alternative—no meaning, if you will.

But it does give us Robert De Niro in his so-called breakout role, in which he is wild and strong and true. Yet anyone with any

Mean Streets, dir. Martin Scorsese, 1973

talent at all could have scored as Johnny Boy. The *part* is a success (it always has been); De Niro just happened to be the actor who got it in this instance. (Harvey Keitel has a much less flashy and much more difficult part—not monochromatic like De Niro's, in fact rather scattered in conception—which he works hard to pull together and in which, in general, he succeeds.) In 1973, I couldn't see that the part of Johnny Boy was more important than the actor playing him; De Niro's subsequent work showed it to me, the repetitive, run-of-the-mill stuff (in Scorsese's *Casino* [1995], for one) as well as his imaginative, even transformative acting (in *Raging Bull*, above all).

Something else showed me that the part of Johnny Boy itself is a success, more than Robert De Niro is a success in it: a re-screening of another 1973 film of his, *Bang the Drum Slowly*. In the same year, De Niro thus had some great good luck in casting: a loose, pathetic, obscene quasi-maniac in *Mean Streets*, and a sweet guy doomed to die in *Bang the Drum Slowly*. But the latter role is too quiet to be a success on its own; it requires successful acting, or what I'm going to call interior re-creation, rather than exterior impersonation (which works for Johnny Boy). De Niro plays an amiable, unintelligent catcher in this baseball film, a tobacco-chewer from Georgia with a cornball haircut—and Hodgkin's disease. The actor understood what he wanted to do as the dumb, doomed catcher, and he does it in outline and design, yet De Niro couldn't summon up, from inside, enough of the necessary juices and flavors and seasonings, and the result is that he doesn't fill out the part with sufficient body.

I wasn't so concerned about De Niro's performance when I saw the movie for the first time. I was still a baseball player myself in those days (like De Niro's character, a catcher), in college and then, briefly, in the minor leagues—where I traveled by bus the back roads of Florida, Georgia, and Alabama for the opportunity to play, for a just a little while longer, the game I loved so much. Therefore it was with the baseball-playing in the picture that I was concerned, with *Bang the Drum Slowly* as a *baseball* film. And, in its feeling for the game, this was, and continues to be, the best baseball film I have ever seen—though that's not saying much in a genre known more for sentimentality, melodrama, romance, and comic relief than for baseball. Still, I've seen a lot of other baseball movies through the years (including, at the upper end, *The Natural* [1984], and, at the lower, *The Bad News Bears Go to Japan* [1978]), and none has more of baseball's unique kinetic qualities than *Bang the Drum Slowly*.

The alternation of plateau moments with lightning flashes of action (strike-'em-out, throw-'em-out, or the bang-bang double play), the physical protocol (the careful cap-tugging, bat-weighing, mitt-pounding, and hand-shaking), the superlative grace into which sometimes even clumsy men can blossom (the catcher dancing under a sky-high pop-up behind home plate, his mask tightly in hand; the base-runner sliding under a tag with arms upraised, at the same time as the fielder balletically leaps backwards into the air to avoid the runner's spikes)—John Hancock, the director, understands all this and more. He sees the game whole and renders it whole, with just enough slow motion scattered throughout to serve either as humorous commentary or aesthetic tease.

Something like Bogdanovich in *The Last Picture Show*, Hancock does fall into cliché at the beginning of sequences—pulling back from objects like statues or flags to give us the whole scene—and in

Mind over Medium

Bang the Drum Slowly, dir. John Hancock, 1973

one scene team members are mistakenly wearing road uniforms in their home stadium, but by and large he has done a good job with the atmosphere and action of baseball. And he's greatly helped by the fact that his other leading actor, Michael Moriarty, who plays a major-league pitcher, really has a good throwing motion (in addition to knowing how to use a resin bag correctly)—which is as necessary for his character as a believable quick draw would be for a Western gunslinger.

Formal Matters

But the script, by Mark Harris from his novel of the same name, is just one more variation on the two-pals motif that preceded *Of Mice and Men* (1937) in American writing and has abundantly followed it as well—one pal smart, the other dumb, the two linked by brotherhood as well as a tacit protectorate. And it is this hackneyed aspect of *Bang the Drum Slowly* that stood out for me most when I saw the film again. The novelty here, as against Steinbeck, is that we know from the start that the dumb guy is going to die. His disease is secret from everyone but the Moriarty character (of course) during most of the picture; and the script works the counterpoint between the presence of debilitating disease, or imminent death, and a profession that depends on fine-honed physicality.

Most of the time there's more sentiment than sentimentality in this movie, yet there is an occasional dreadful line, like one that tells us everybody is dying and that's why we should all be nice to

Last Summer, dir. Frank Perry, 1969

one another. With the obeisance to Ring Lardner that every writer about baseball must pay, Harris nonetheless keeps the texture fairly good. The trouble is, there isn't much more to the script *than* the texture, however well orchestrated by Hancock (in his only film of note, incidentally). As in *Mean Streets*, the story simply winds its way to its foreseen end, without much point or theme. The last line is Moriarty's, in response to the fact that team members used to rag the dim catcher before they learned of his illness. He grimly declares, "From now on, I rag nobody." *That's* the point? Pretty puny—and pretty false. What would sport be without ragging, not to speak of American humor in general? What would my trifling baseball career have been without ragging (for reading, of all things, during long stretches on the bench)? What would this *film* be without it?

There's no humor, baseball, or De Niro in *Last Summer*, but I did remember it as a daring movie about adolescence—a kind of serious beach picture made to satisfy the middle-class cultural revolution of the time. I saw it twice in 1969 when I was barely out of my own adolescence, and I touted it to friends, all of whom shared, or would soon share, my admiration (or was it self-congratulation?). The film concerns four young people at a beach resort on Fire Island, Long Island. They are almost the only people in the picture, and the performances of the four (by Barbara Hershey, Richard Thomas, Bruce Davison, and Catherine Burns) remain the best elements in it. But from there on, and from today's vantage point, the compliments get skimpier.

The script by Eleanor Perry (the wife of Frank Perry, *Last Summer*'s director), adapted from Evan Hunter's 1968 novel, is built on a false assumption, which it shares with dozens of novels and stories and films: that, by the very act of choosing adolescence as a subject, it displays special sensitivity, and it invites us to flutter right up there with it onto its assumed poetic plateau. Adolescence was indeed the subject of some genuinely sensitive films made in the same tumultuous decade as *Last Summer*, such as Ermanno Olmi's *Il Posto* (1961), Jiri Menzel's *Closely Watched Trains* (1966), and Jan Troell's *Here's Your Life* (1966). Yet each of these pictures began by treating its adolescents as people, as characters, and then achieved sensitivity as an inevitability of its characters' truth. *Last*

Summer begins by treating its characters as adolescents, who are *therefore* sensitive.

From the start the film has an air of self-conscious, idyllic abstraction, which is heightened by the picturesque isolation of Fire Island's sand and sea and sky. All these produced in me, over forty years later, an immediate foreboding that the four young people were going to act out a poignant allegory—or, better (worse?), a laborious parable. They did. But the moral of the tale is muddied. Does *Last Summer* tell us what happened to the children of a generation of sybaritic parents? (Adults are never mentioned except in terms of ridicule or scorn, as mendacious and corrupt.) Or is the film about the herd instinct and how the security of group violence overcomes finer human instincts? If the former, the case is rigged and the accused don't even get representation. If the latter, *Last Summer* is as profound as those Westerns made some years before it, in which a stranger rode into a town terrorized by a brute and acted out a little pageant about democracy standing up to fascism.

Moreover, *Last Summer*'s would-be profundity isn't helped by some of Frank Perry's direction. When Hershey and the boys dance, for example, we get a shot of them from the ground that would have bored Busby Berkeley. The final shot, by contrast, is from a helicopter zooming up and away from one of the boys on the beach (something I thought "really cool" back in 1969). Troell used a vaguely similar shot at the end of *Here's Your Life* because it showed us the countryside out of which the protagonist had come and which he was now leaving. There, it was a concluding statement of source or origin; with Perry, the shot is an empty aeronautical cliché.

McCabe and Mrs. Miller (1971), for its part, had stuck in my mind for years as a richly textured de-glamorization of Hollywood's image of the Old West. It was helped by the cinematography of Vilmos Zsigmond, who shot the picture in a somewhat misty, less-than-spectacular vein, with lots of smoky interiors. But Zsigmond's fine work here is almost irritating forty years later, like hearing a good orchestra play trash. For *McCabe and Mrs. Miller*, on re-viewing, turns out to be just that: glittery trash, "liberated" but still trash.

Warren Beatty (McCabe) is a supposed gunman—really an ambitious small-timer—who wanders into a Washington State

McCabe and Mrs. Miller, dir. Robert Altman, 1971

mining town, circa 1900, and turns it from a frontier outpost into a booming enterprise, taking over everything in the process, including the brothels. Julie Christie (Mrs. Miller) is a Cockney madam for whom he flips, but who remains cool toward him. Beatty goes through as lot of self-indulgent clowning in the film, as well as through three unexplained stages of bravado, fluster, and bravado, before he's killed in a dumb shoot-out. Christie epitomizes vacuousness in a role, like others of hers at the time, that is launched portentously to nowhere.

The script by the late Robert Altman and Brian McKay, from a 1959 novel by Edmund Naughton, evidently assumes that mere candor and eccentricity will tell us what the West was really like. At this point in his career, Altman had directed *M*A*S*H* (1969), which wandered but was often funny; *Brewster McCloud* (1970), which wandered and was not funny; then *McCabe and Mrs. Miller*, which wanders and is repellent. I thought his camera—or Zsigmond's, under Altman's direction—would never stop zooming in and out, or italicizing the obvious (a whore's cashbox, a floating dead body). Some of the dialogue is literally, and apparently intentionally, inaudible; while the cutting is generally freakish or what would have been termed "freaky" back in the early '70s—I suppose to display editorial freedom. (Further, there is a black barber with a pretty black wife, who somehow manages never to be molested by the drunken, randy miners.)

The thesis of all this seems to be, from my point of view in 2010 in any event, that if you take a corny story, fuzz up the exposition, vitiate the action, use a childishly ironic ending, and put in lots of profanity as well as nudity, you have Marched On with Time. But what *McCabe and Mrs. Miller* really amounts to is a corny story, badly told if sometimes beautifully pictured. There are also several overblown songs by Leonard Cohen, yesterday's hip Oscar Hammerstein, on the soundtrack. They seemed melancholic and plaintive to me back in 1971, when Cohen was all the rage ("a poet *and* a songwriter!"); today, they merely whine and drone.

They Shoot Horses, Don't They? (1969), directed by Sydney Pollack with Jane Fonda and Michael Sarrazin in the leading roles, has also stayed in my mind over the years: in this case as a smart lampoon, via metaphor, of "The American Way." But, four decades later, what this film lacks is any information or revelation about why it was made—except that it wanted to be commended for its forthrightness, its "uncompromised" nature and "downbeat" ending. Yes, in a broad and glib manner, *They Shoot Horses* does lampoon the American way, but that's a pretty big tent into which a lot of people were crawling back in the late sixties without paying any kind of painful admission. Nothing was easier then—or is easier now, for that matter—than free surfing on a wave of national self-excoriation.

Horace McCoy's 1935 novel of the same name deals with a dance marathon in the Hollywood of the Depression years, an

Mind over Medium 361

They Shoot Horses, Don't They?, dir. Sydney Pollack, 1969

event in which couples danced for days in order to win prize money. People paid to watch them struggle, and spectators also offered money for "sprints" when the contestants were particularly tired. The competitors got ten minutes off for rest and food every two hours; and the couple that danced 1,500 hours got $1,500. Tough and even brutal stuff, this, made effective by means of the author's consistently flat tone (as well as some typographical tricks).

Pollack's film (with a script by James Poe and Robert E. Thompson) fiddles with the original viewpoint, for the story is not seen exclusively through the hero's eyes, as it was in the book. It fiddles with the revelation of his dance partner's murder, in an attempt to build up suspense. And it inserts dubious new stuff in addition to omitting important matters. But the movie's basic aesthetic failure is in its texture. Instead of the hyper-naturalistic, black-and-white tone of McCoy's prose, we get the golden glow of color, swirls, and lights—all the apparatus, in other words, of punctured romance instead of the bottom of the pit. And, to make that romance resonate, Pollack and his screenwriters have filled in Fonda's character with action and dialogue that turn her into an aggressive (but nonetheless self-destructive) toughie instead of the hollow tramp she is in the source-fiction.

True, there is still a lot of good 1930s physical detail in *They Shoot Horses*, but that's no problem if you have a big enough budget for research and re-creation. There's some by-now commonplace use of subjective camera, as well. What there is *not*, however, is any artistic reason for this picture to exist. As a cross-section or microcosm of American life, it's ridiculous. As a representative or emblematic phenomenon, the dance marathon is eccentric and badly dated—maybe it was even in 1969. And as intrinsically moving narrative, *They Shoot Horses* is non-existent. Seventy-five years later, McCoy's novel still has some grittiness about it, as if one were being dragged by the ankles over that dance floor, face down. But the visual texture of the movie and the changes in the book's original shape transform what was pretty grim into something grimly pretty—the kind of grim prettiness that, as a young man rarely confronted with the grim but often surrounded by the pretty, I mistook for the real and dirty thing.

It was no doubt Terrence Malick's ability (not shared by Sydney Pollack) to write dialogue, see scenes, and knit a film that so impressed men when I saw *Badlands* for the first time in 1973—long before sensationalist or serial murder had become a kind of running melodrama-cum-detective story on every television "infotainment" program, not to speak of the numerous films to come that would feature homicidal maniacs. Seeing it for the first time since, though, I have severe reservations about the film's concept, as well as Malick's casting of Martin Sheen and Sissy Spacek in the major roles.

Badlands was "inspired" by the story of Charles Starkweather, the nineteen-year-old South Dakota garbage man who, in 1958, went on a killing spree in the Midwest with his fourteen-year-old girlfriend. Ten people were murdered, Starkweather was executed, the girl got life. What fascinated Malick, obviously (and everyone else at the time the film was made, including me), was the cool, almost accidental quality of the story, the smooth and glassy surface with which it covers so much horror, together with the figurative hand-in-hand innocence of the young pair strolling through it. Of that pair, the girl narrates the picture so as to emphasize its reverse-

Badlands, dir. Terrence Malick, 1973

romance, or grim fairy tale: for her rhetoric is straight out of love stories that were published much earlier than the 1950s, and for the most part it is just rhetoric, since she is no more, if no less, interested in sex (or real romantic union) than Charlie.

The story of *Badlands* begins as if it were going to be what it in fact becomes: a tale of two unconventional lovers doomed by convention to trouble. (To make this coupling even more bizarre, more immediately troubling, Malick makes Starkweather twenty-five and his female companion fifteen.) That convention comes right away in the form of the girl's father, who quite naturally warns Charlie off; and, when he finds this young man in the house one day, he goes to call the police. But Starkweather stops him with a bullet—calmly, almost politely. The murderer feels no remorse or panic, while the girl seems only very "interested," like a held spectator. When concern finally sets in, the two set fire to the house and flee.

When they are later discovered by a posse living idyllically but on guard in a forest, Starkweather kills several of its members. Afterwards, he and his girl escape, travel, and leave a trail of slayings behind them. They finish up by driving across the Dakota Badlands in a stolen Cadillac. As capriciously as she first joined Charlie, however, the girl decides not to play the rebel-killer game anymore. Then Starkweather himself sets the stage for his own capture, subsequent to which he is taken away in chains—just as undismayed, reasonable, and conversational as he was at the start.

If my plot summary disappoints, that is because, after thirty-seven years, *Badlands* itself accomplishes very little other than chronicle. And at that it's not much more than the record of an aberrant; unlike *Bonnie and Clyde* (1967), *Badlands* does not use its killer as an epitome of his era (though it might have, given the fact that the real Starkweather resembled James Dean and liked to hear people say as much). Malick thus too easily accepted the aberrant as significant, too easily entertained mindless violence as a self-explanatory semantics, too easily let the mimetic fallacy oppress him. He provides no more than a blank page on which we are to write or draw, but, unfortunately, we don't feel much impulse to write or draw anything.

Such impulse escapes us all the more when we are confronted with the utter non-distinction of Spacek in the role of the girl and the unforceful, poured-on plastic performance of Sheen as Starkweather. Malick drew, and directed, a motiveless protagonist who feels little, but he got the wrong result: *we* feel little about the protagonist, let alone his passive, weirdly impressionable child companion. Underneath all the otherwise quite sophisticated filmmaking in *Badlands*, then (including cinematography, by a three-man team, that perceives landscapes exquisitely without snuggling up smarmily to Mother Nature), there is a somewhat sophomoric acceptance of Nothing as the equivalent of Nothingness—or of infantilism as a synonym for nihilism.

The last film in my group of ten is *Slaughterhouse-Five* (1972), from the 1969 novel by Kurt Vonnegut, which I read when I was in college. I re-read it for this essay and now I understand why I once liked it, and its movie adaptation, so much: it's an example of this much-overrated (and now deceased) author at his best, full of facile wryness, sophomoric rue, and mousetrap adumbrations of cosmic mysteries. Vonnegut's huge success in my college dormitory is now easily explicable: his philosophy could hardly have been more

Slaughterhouse-Five, dir. George Roy Hill, 1972

accessibly ironic, his style more glibly implicative, his humor more nudgingly collusive, his humanism less demanding or more flattering. Like many inferior novelists, Vonnegut films better than he reads; film supplies what he doesn't. But Stephen Geller, the man who adapted Vonnegut's novel in this case, could not supply the fundamental omission at its core: a theme.

The three main stories concern the wartime experience of the hero, Billy Pilgrim (*there's* a modest moniker to give your central character; at least the ominous "Starkweather" was the real killer's own name), during the bombing of Dresden; his postwar upholstered life with a well-upholstered wife; and his dream life (if that's what it is) on the planet Tralfamadore, where a Hollywood starlet is brought to mate with him in a large plastic dome. The war stuff, in book and film, remains as nicely balanced as I had remembered it: German soldiers and American G.I.s (Vonnegut himself had been a prisoner of war in Dresden) alike are victims of power madness. But the suburban stuff, in both, is now a trite cartoon. And the planetary stuff, in either version, today seems like Arthur C. Clarke warmed over, as wise spacefolk look down pityingly on infantile earthlings and try to enlighten them.

Moreover, outside of Vonnegut's cleverness in weaving these three strands together, what was the point of it all? That the war (substitute Vietnam for World War II) was fought only to return to a nefariously materialist society and that Out There people know better? All this cinematic apparatus for that? And the majority of it so banally expressed? Geller, it's true, gives the script a wholeness of form, cohesive and dramatized; Dede Allen, the editor, dexterously braided the three-part narrative; Miroslav Ondricek, the cinematographer, fixed such quintessences as the gravy of suburbia and the gravity of bombed-out Dresden; and George Roy Hill directed with as much compassion and humor as he could muster. But *Slaughterhouse-Five*, in 2010, left me with an unfed feeling. After all the table-setting, and the headwaiter's numerous flourishes, where was the meal? A lot of good makings in this picture, then (excluding the undistinguished cast consisting of Michael Sacks, Sharon Gans, and Valerine Perrine, among others), but very little was made in the end—or very little survived my first, close encounter with this "far-out" piece of fiction.

For me, it's not in itself important that I now think less of these ten films. What disturbs me is that I tampered with my past. It's a problem for anyone, of course—any individual, not just a critic or historian. What I'm talking about is going back, for the non-professional as well as for the professional in his non-professional, basic being, to films that have meant something to him for a considerable time. And one of the reasons that these ten films meant something to *me* is that I saw them when I knew nothing—*nothing*—about the apparatus of filmmaking: how exactly movies were made (let alone financed), how many people were actually present off-camera during the shooting of any one scene, how one of the jobs of the actor is to maintain continuity of character while shooting out of sequence, etc. Rationally, to be sure, I could have deduced all of this (and perhaps did, *after* the film). But emotionally or viscerally, my feeling at the time was that somehow an eye in the sky, or the soil, had simply been present to record what was unfolding before my very eyes. In short, now I am jaded, overexposed, or overeducated. Then

I was virginal, pure, inexperienced, unadulterated—and therefore easily astonished.

I have no fixed time limit, but I'd guess that five years begins to be the danger mark in a film's life. The best films of the past—and I don't have to cite a lot of titles here—are as good as ever when re-seen, often better, often relevant in new ways. I'm talking about the lesser-known pictures that one treasures, that one regards almost as private property. The risks of returning to them are great, and all the more so because you're usually not seeing the original film in its original format (as I was sure to do when I re-saw, at New York's Museum of Modern Art, the ten films in question here). You're seeing it on a television screen, which, even when it is a relatively big one, still makes everything (including the sound) seem smaller or lesser—figuratively as well as literally.

Moreover, unlike DVDs on a television screen, movies make us wait for them, with a corresponding increase in their stature. When they begin, they begin with all the mysterious suddenness and irreversibility of an event. This is true despite the fact that movies can hardly be called events in their own right, as a concert or dramatic performance might; if anything they simulate events, representing them as distant shadows in Plato's cave. And yet movies, even lesser movies like the ones I've treated here—in their theatrical incarnation—possess a quality I'm tempted to call "eventness," embodied in all the ways they force us to enter *their* temporality, to embrace the sense that a given work can be experienced only within a fixed temporal frame. The projector's gears themselves engage the teeth of time; they give form to time's otherness. But by now movies have entered a new dimension of accessibility—that of the ever-available DVD—and in doing so they have passed out of their former dimension, the dimension of time.

Indeed, the DVD-player lulls us with the illusion that time belongs to *us*, that it stands ready to obey our thumb's commands. With the advent of the pause, fast-forward, and rewind buttons, the last vestige of otherness—that of time—has been removed from the experience of film art, and we're left with a medium that responds wholly to *the viewer's* controlling will and momentary desire. However welcome our freedom to whiz past FBI warnings and previews of schlocky action films or romantic chick flicks in our desire to get to the main attraction, that freedom deprives us of one of art's key lessons: that truth and beauty come surrounded by vacancy and boredom, consequently that we must submit ourselves to the one if we desire the other. That is to say, the heightened sense of occasion that moviegoing involves heightens our powers of attention, pulling us out of habitual contexts and framing the experience with margins of tedium: the little rituals of ticket-purchasing, refreshment-buying, seat-finding, then dully waiting for darkness. By the time the movie finally starts, we have been subtly prepared; a kind of inner well of attentiveness has filled up, and as long as the film offers some modest reward for our attention—as my ten "remembered" films once did—we can maintain it at a reasonably intense level.

By contrast, DVD-watching is peculiarly abstracted from time, from aesthetic time, but it is abstracted from place as well. DVDs occupy a kind of hyperspace, like that of computers; their time is entirely synthetic, their relation to space arbitrary. As a result it is more difficult to pay attention to them, to the films themselves, whose quality may then suffer irrespective of their intrinsic quality. One fairly crude illustration of this is the discovery that if we miss some detail—a line of dialogue from *Carnal Knowledge*, a gesture from *Elvira Madigan*, a rapid cut from *Mean Streets*—we can simply rewind and watch again, even pause at a significant frame. (Film students have long made use of such possibilities, usually with the aid of that obsolete device called a movieola; but now they are available to the most casual viewer.) What might seem to encourage closer attention to films, however, in fact hollows it out, because no single moment of attention is experienced as definitive or decisive. We no longer have to strain to catch fleeting nuances of word and image; attention can relax, secure in the knowledge that all may be known in the fullness of time. Each specific viewing, or re-viewing, now takes place in a field of innumerable possible viewings, so that even if we choose to view a particular DVD movie just once, that viewing is subtly altered by the mere possibility of further viewings.

The result is that the slight but palpable sense of urgency which once attended moviegoing, an urgency fed by the unpredictable convergences of interest and opportunity that theatrical programming created, is gone and can never, I think, be recovered. We'll never again be able to think of a particular screening as our only chance to see some enticing or arty (if not obscure) film unlikely to come round a second time. We'll never again think of movies as fugitive visions that must be caught on the fly, as they briefly incarnate themselves here or there, today or tomorrow. They have become, to call up Peter Bogdanovich's movie title, the last picture shows in more ways than one. The 35-millimeter film has thus become an object of nostalgia in its own right, ironically possessed of the very kind of aura that Walter Benjamin once ascribed only to artworks that did *not* exist (as film does) as mechanical reproduction, and that therefore enjoyed spatial singularity or a "unique existence at the place where it happens to be."

Clearly the risk of retrospection, as I have described it, applies to all the arts. But in the cinema it's greater because, in the course of American life (if not that of every country), most of us have watched more films than we have read novels or seen plays, and the films are fused more intimately into fantasy. One of the hidden advantages of the theater is that once a performance is over, it's over: the script, if it's available, is far from identical with the performance we have seen; and any video recording of a theatrical production is an abomination, neither theater nor film but some mysterious hybrid without an artistic life of its own. Peter Brook reportedly once said that he thanks heaven every night that the theater is ephemeral, and I take this to express not only Brook's gratitude that a performance is improvable but also his relief that the performances we have liked cannot be subjected to scrutiny years later. High opinion of past theatrical production is thus forever free from error.

What did I gain from seeing those ten films again? Are my new opinions of them "truer" now? No and yes. They are the truth of my present self, as the former opinions were the truth of my previous self or even selves. As a critic, I would naturally want to be represented by my present views, but this is no more than to say, as I've often said, that all criticism should be dated. If James Agee were alive today, would he let his famous essay on John Huston stand as his current estimate? Would André Bazin, alive today, leave his own little book on Orson Welles unaltered? I doubt it.

Is this an argument for the subjectivity or relativity of all criticism? Of course it is, with these provisos: that, as one grows older, one hopes one's criticism grows wiser; and that criticism's ultimate aim should be, not objective correctness, but objective "correlativeness," by which I mean an extension of T. S. Eliot's use of the term. Just as a work of art creates an objective correlative for a character's condition or an artist's vision, criticism should create an objective correlative for the work of art itself. And that correlative, like all true art, is neither "right" nor "wrong"; it *is*, it exists in a kind of para-reality with, or alongside, the artwork. That reality has its own social, historical, cultural, and political, even technological context. At the same time, it is personal, circumstantial, circumscribed. And, out of that reality, the critic stimulates, provokes, enrages, enlightens, and finally enriches, always knowing that, some day, he will be his own audience.

The critic may not be an artist, then, but he can be said to practice critical artistry, or to set his compass by aesthetic lights: those of form, style, impression, expression; of tension, balance, synecdoche, and organicity. The artist reflects life as well as other art, including the artist's own; the critic reflects art as well as other criticism, including his own. Where the two—art and criticism—meet, well, they meet and meet again: that is the subject of this essay. They live, whole and apart, in eternal, aesthetic time; but they join combustibly in provisional, historic time, only and ever to go their separate ways.

I'm speaking of the *profession* of criticism here, but I am also speaking of the life we all share, which, in our culture, includes a continuous flood of film experience. My past life, like everyone's, has a particularized structure, and films of the past are a prominent part of its particularities. My past is there, familiar and summonable as I need it, with its own hierarchies and clusters and aversions and refreshments. By re-seeing those ten films, my present self is now clearer to my present self, but I have paid a price by disturbing the past, by fiddling with the films of my past.

"We know," wrote Benjamin in *Illuminations*, "that in his work Proust did not describe a life as it actually was, but a life as it was remembered by one who lived it." That was precisely the theme of Fellini's beautiful picture *Amarcord* (1973), which was foolishly criticized by some for not being history or for distorting what must have been the actual events of an adolescent's life. But the film was about what Fellini *needs* of his past, an artist's recognition of memory as a creative force, not as chronicler and analyst. *Amarcord* is what Fellini's memory supplies of his past to his present existence, even as his lungs supply oxygen to his blood.

Film (as *Amarcord* demonstrates) has become a strong and vivid component of memory—memory, the manufacturer and sustainer not so much of realities as of illusions of reality. And film strikes so fiendishly deep and swiftly that the memory, conscious as well as unconscious, of twentieth-to-twenty-first-century human beings must be more heavily trafficked than that of any previous century. All of us are shaped by that trafficking, according to our conditioning, our needs, our desires. For myself, ever since 1954, when my mother took me to see my first picture, films have been barreling through my conscious to my unconscious; but insofar as they remain in my conscious, they get themselves arranged in hierarchies of value and, more important, affection.

Neither I nor anyone else, however, can live on an absolutely simultaneous frontier of the past vis-à-vis the present: there isn't room, or time, for such a frontier. For all of us, there's a line of films, a *sequence*, stretching from the remotest past to the most recent moment, though recentness is not the sole determinant of freshness. (Some older films are far more vivid than some recent ones.) And, on the whole, we have to take a great many of the films in our past on trust, *our* trust in our opinions of them formed at the time we saw them. To tamper with that trust by reexamination—again I'm speaking mainly as an individual, not as a critic—is to wiggle a brick in an otherwise interdependent structure. In any event, I haven't time to re-see every film I've seen in my life and readjust all my opinions; and even if I could, I would, by this ordinance, only have to start all over again immediately.

The above stricture does not reduce to one more replay of Thomas Wolfe's *You Can't Go Home Again* (1940). For one thing, I have always found the Wolfean tag to be false. When I go back to a place where I spent time as a boy or a youth, if the place is more or less still what it was, it's always emotionally very much what it was then—just as beautiful or depressing or exciting or awesome. My issue is really more akin to the old science-fiction formula that we've seen applied in films as superficially different as *It's a Won-*

derful Life (1946) and *Back to the Future* (1985): the modern man who travels by time machine or divine intervention into the past and, by interference there, runs the risk of altering the present that he has just left.

I don't want that danger. So I don't want to see again, say, *The Paper Chase* (1973), with Timothy Bottoms—all the more so because of what I discovered about Bottoms' acting ability upon re-screening *The Last Picture Show*—which had meant so much to me in 1973 as I myself looked ahead to the pressures of law school (where my father wanted me to go) or graduate school (where I went). Nor do I wish to see once more what seemed to me the noblest film I had seen up to then—1971 (which meant that its anti-war stance had something to do with the Vietnam conflict, into which I would soon be drafted)—*Johnny Got His Gun*, also with Timothy Bottoms. I don't want to know what I think of these two films now. I want them to remain what they were, what they *are*, in the fabric of my memory.

Well, I know that this program is impossible in my profession. But at least now I'm more reconciled to the price. I'll have to continue knocking gaps in the past for the sake of furnishing out the present—the critical present as well as my present self—more completely. It's more rational, of course, and more pertinent, to proceed in such a manner. But it still hurts.

WORKS CITED

Agee, James. "Undirectable Director [John Huston]." 1950. In *Agee on Film: Reviews and Comments*. New York: McDowell Obolensky, 1958. 320-331.

Bazin, André. *Orson Welles*. 1972. Trans. Jonathan Rosenbaum. New York: Harper and Row, 1978.

Benjamin, Walter. "The Image of Proust." 1929. In Benjamin's *Illuminations: Essays and Reflections*. Trans. Harry Zohn. New York: Schocken, 1969. 203-217.

_____. "The Work of Art in the Age of Mechanical Reproduction." 1936. In Benjamin's *Illuminations: Essays and Reflections*. Trans. Harry Zohn. New York: Schocken, 1969. 217-251.

Brook, Peter. *The Empty Space*. New York: Simon and Schuster, 1968.

Eliot, T. S. "Hamlet and His Problems." 1919. In Eliot's *The Sacred Wood: Essays on Poetry and Criticism*. London: Methuen, 1920. 95-103.

Harris, Mark. *Bang the Drum Slowly*. New York: Alfred A. Knopf, 1956.

Hunter, Evan. *Last Summer*. New York: Doubleday, 1968.

McCoy, Horace. *They Shoot Horses, Don't They?* New York: Simon & Schuster, 1935.

McMurtry, Larry. *The Last Picture Show*. New York. Dial, 1966.

Naughton, Edmund. *McCabe*. New York: Macmillan, 1959.

Percy, Walker. *The Moviegoer*. New York: Alfred A. Knopf, 1961.

Steinbeck, John. *Of Mice and Men*. New York: Covici-Friede, 1937.

Vonnegut, Kurt. *Slaughterhouse-Five*. New York: Delacorte, 1969.

Wolfe, Thomas. *You Can't Go Home Again*. New York. Harper & Brothers, 1940.

General Bibliography of Related Criticism

Adler, Renata. *A Year in the Dark: Journal of a Film Critic, 1968-1969.* New York: Random House, 1969.

Agate, James. *Around Cinemas.* New York: Arno Press, 1972.

Agee, James. *Agee on Film: Volume 1, Reviews and Comments.* New York: McDowell, 1958.

Anstey, Edgar, ed. *Shots in the Dark.* New York: Garland, 1978.

Arnheim, Rudolf. *Film as Art.* Berkeley: University of California Press, 1957.

Bawer, Bruce. *The Screenplay's the Thing: Movie Criticism, 1986-1990.* Hamden, Connecticut: Archon Books, 1992.

Bazin, André. *Bazin at Work: Major Essays and Reviews from the Forties and Fifties.* Ed. Bert Cardullo. New York: Routledge, 1997.

Braudy, Leo. *The World in a Frame.* Garden City, New York: Doubleday, 1976.

Cardullo, Bert. *Film Chronicle: Critical Dispatches From a Forward Observer, 1987-1992.* New York: Peter Lang, 1994.

_____. *In Search of Cinema: Writings on International Film Art.* Montreal: McGill-Queen's University Press, 2004.

_____. *Screen Writings.* 2 volumes. London: Anthem Press, 2010.

Casty, Alan. *The Dramatic Art of the Film.* New York: Harper & Row, 1971.

Cavell, Stanley. *The World Viewed.* Cambridge, Massachusetts: Harvard University Press, 1971.

Champlin, Charles. *Hollywood's Revolutionary Decade: Charles Champlin Reviews the Movies of the 1970s.* Santa Barbara, California: John Daniel, 1998.

Cooke, Alistair, ed. *Garbo and the Night Watchmen: A Selection of Writings of British and American Film Critics.* London: Jonathan Cape, 1937.

Cozarinsky, Edgardo, ed. *Borges In/And/On Film.* Trans. Gloria Waldman and Ronald Christ. New York: Lumen Books, 1988.

Crisp, Quentin. *How to Go to the Movies*. New York: St. Martin's Press, 1989.

Crist, Judith. *The Private Eye, the Cowboy, and the Very Naked Girl: Movies from Cleo to Clyde*. Chicago: Holt, Rinehart, and Winston, 1968.

Denby, David, ed. *Awake in the Dark: An Anthology of American Film Criticism, 1915 to the Present*. New York: Vintage Books, 1977.

DeNitto, Dennis, and William Herman. *Film and the Critical Eye*. New York: Macmillan, 1975.

Dick, Bernard F. *Anatomy of Film*. 4th ed. New York: St. Martin's Press, 2002.

Durgnat, Raymond. *Films and Feelings*. Cambridge: Massachusetts Institute of Technology Press, 1967.

Ebert, Roger. *Awake in the Dark: The Best of Roger Ebert*. Chicago: University of Chicago Press, 2006.

Ebert, Roger, ed. *Roger Ebert's Book of Film: The Finest Writing from a Century of Film*. New York: W. W. Norton, 1996.

Eidsvik, Charles. *Cineliteracy: Film among the Arts*. New York: Random House, 1978.

Empson, William. *The Book, Film, and Theatre Reviews of William Empson*. Turnbridge Wells, Kent: Foundling Press, 1993.

Farber, Manny. *Negative Space: Manny Farber on the Movies*. Expanded ed. New York: Da Capo, 1998.

Ferguson, Otis. *The Film Criticism of Otis Ferguson*. Ed. Robert Wilson. Philadelphia: Temple University Press, 1971.

Fulford, Robert. *Marshall Delaney at the Movies: The Contemporary World as Seen on Film*. Toronto: Peter Martin Associates, 1974.

Gilliatt, Penelope. *Three-Quarter Face: Reports and Reflections*. New York: Coward, McCann & Geoghegan, 1980.

Greene, Graham. *Graham Greene on Film: Collected Film Criticism, 1935-1940*. Ed. John Russell Taylor. New York: Simon and Schuster, 1972.

Grierson, John. *Grierson on the Movies*. Ed. Forsyth Hardy. Boston: Faber and Faber, 1981.

Haberski, Raymond J., Jr. *It's Only a Movie!: Film and Critics in American Culture*. Lexington: University Press of Kentucky, 2001.

Harrington, John, ed. *Film and/as Literature*. Englewood Cliffs, New Jersey: Prentice-Hall, 1977.

Heinzkill, Richard. *Film Criticism: An Index to Critics' Anthologies*. Metuchen, New Jersey: Scarecrow Press, 1975.

Hoberman, J. *Vulgar Modernism: Writing on Movies and Other Media*. Philadelphia: Temple University Press, 1991.

Hochman, Stanley, ed. *From Quasimodo to Scarlett O'Hara: A National Board of Review Anthology, 1920-1940*. New York: Frederick Ungar, 1982.

Huss, Roy, and Norman Silverstein. *The Film Experience: Elements of Motion Picture Art.* New York: Harper, 1968.

Jones, Kent. *Physical Evidence: Selected Film Criticism.* Middletown, Connecticut: Wesleyan University Press, 2007.

Kael, Pauline. *5001 Nights at the Movies: A Guide from A to Z.* New York: Henry Holt, 1991.

———. *Deeper into Movies.* Boston: Little, Brown, 1973.

———. *For Keeps.* New York: Dutton, 1994.

———. *Going Steady.* Boston: Little, Brown, 1970.

———. *Hooked.* New York: Dutton, 1989.

———. *I Lost It at the Movies.* Boston: Little, Brown, 1965.

———. *Kiss Kiss Bang Bang.* Boston: Little, Brown, 1968.

———. *Movie Love.* New York: Dutton, 1991.

———. *Reeling.* Boston: Little, Brown, 1976.

———. *State of the Art.* New York: Dutton, 1985.

———. *Taking It All In.* New York: Holt, Rinehart, and Winston, 1980.

———. *When the Lights Go Down.* New York: Holt, Rinehart, and Winston, 1980.

Kauffmann, Stanley, ed. *American Film Criticism, From the Beginnings to "Citizen Kane": Reviews of Significant Films at the Time They First Appeared.* New York: Liveright, 1972.

Kauffmann, Stanley. *Before My Eyes.* Harper & Row, 1980.

———. *Distinguishing Features.* Baltimore, Maryland: Johns Hopkins University Press, 1994.

———. *Field of View.* New York: Performing Arts Journal Publications, 1986.

———. *Figures of Light.* New York: Harper & Row, 1971.

———. *Living Images.* New York: Harper & Row, 1975.

———. *Regarding Film.* Baltimore: Johns Hopkins University Press, 2001.

Knight, Arthur. *The Liveliest Art.* New York: Mentor, 1957.

Lane, Anthony. *Nobody's Perfect: Writings from "The New Yorker".* New York: Vintage Books, 2003.

Linden, George W. *Reflections on the Screen.* Belmont, California: Wadsworth, 1970.

Lindgren, Ernest. *The Art of the Film.* London: Allen & Unwin, 1949.

Lopate, Phillip, ed. *American Movie Critics: An Anthology from the Silents until Now.* New York: Library of America, 2006.

Lopate, Phillip. *Totally, Tenderly, Tragically: Essays and Criticism from a Lifelong Love Affair with the Movies.* New York: Anchor Books/Doubleday, 1998.

Lorentz, Pare. *Lorentz on Film: Movies, 1927 to 1941*. New York: Hopkinson and Blake, 1975.

Macdonald, Dwight. *Dwight Macdonald on Movies*. Englewood Cliffs, New Jersey: Prentice-Hall, 1969.

Maio, Kathi. *Popcorn and Sexual Politics: Movie Reviews*. Freedom, California: Crossing Press, 1991.

Mast, Gerald. *Film/Cinema/Movie: A Theory of Experience*. New York: Harper, 1977.

McBride, Joseph, ed. *Persistence of Vision: A Collection of Film Criticism*. Madison: Wisconsin Film Society Press, 1968.

Murray, Edward. *Nine American Film Critics*. New York: Ungar, 1975.

Pechter, William S. *Movies Plus One: Seven Years of Film Reviewing*. New York: Horizon Press, 1982.

Perez, Gilberto. *The Material Ghost: Films and Their Medium*. Baltimore, Maryland: Johns Hopkins University Press, 1998.

Perkins, V. F. *Film as Film*. Baltimore, Maryland: Penguin, 1986.

Powell, Dilys. *The Dilys Powell Film Reader*. Ed. Christopher Cook. New York: Oxford University Press, 1992.

Rafferty, Terrence. *The Thing Happens: Ten Years of Writing About the Movies*. New York: Grove Press, 1993.

Reed, Rex. *Big Screen, Little Screen*. New York: Macmillan, 1971.

Richardson, Robert. *Literature and Film*. Bloomington: Indiana University Press, 1969.

Robinson, W. R., ed. *Man and the Movies*. Baltimore, Maryland: Penguin, 1969.

Romney, Jonathan. *Short Orders: Film Writing*. London: Serpent's Tail, 1997.

Rosenbaum, Jonathan. *Placing Movies: The Practice of Film Criticism*. Berkeley: University of California Press, 1995.

_____. *Moving Places: A Life at the Movies*. New York: Harper & Row, 1980.

Ross, T. J., ed. *Film and the Liberal Arts*. New York: Henry Holt, 1970.

Samuels, Charles Thomas. *Mastering the Film and Other Essays*. Knoxville: University of Tennessee Press, 1977.

Sandburg, Carl. *Carl Sandburg at the Movies; A Poet in the Silent Era, 1920-1927*. Ed. Dale Fethering and Doug Fetherling. Metuchen, New Jersey: Scarecrow Press, 1985.

Sarris, Andrew. *Confessions of a Cultist: On the Cinema, 1955-1969*. New York: Simon and Schuster, 1970.

_____. *The Primal Screen: Essays on Film and Related Subjects*. New York: Simon and Schuster, 1973.

Schickel, Richard. *Matinee Idylls: Reflections on the Movies*. Chicago: Ivan R. Dee, 1999.

_____. *Second Sight: Notes on Some Movies, 1965-1970.* New York: Simon and Schuster, 1972.

_____. *Schickel on Film.* New York: Morrow, 1989.

Sillick, Ardis, and Michael McCormick. *The Critics Were Wrong: Misguided Movie Reviews and Film Criticism Gone Awry.* Secaucus, New Jersey: Carol Publishing Group, 1996.

Simon, John. *John Simon on Film: Criticism, 1982-2001.* New York: Applause Books, 2005.

_____. *Movies into Film: Film Criticism, 1967-1970.* New York: Dial Press, 1971.

_____. *Private Screenings.* New York: Macmillan, 1967.

_____. *Reverse Angle: A Decade of American Films.* New York: C. N. Potter/Crown, 1982.

Sklar, Robert. *Movie-Made America: A Cultural History of American Movies.* New York: Random House, 1975.

Slide, Anthony, ed. *Selected Film Criticism.* Volumes 1-7. Metuchen, New Jersey: Scarecrow Press, 1982-1985.

Sontag, Susan. *Against Interpretation.* New York: Farrar, Straus & Giroux, 1966.

Stephenson, Ralph, and J. R. Debrix. *The Cinema as Art.* Baltimore, Maryland: Penguin, 1965.

Sterritt, David. *Guiltless Pleasures: A David Sterritt Film Reader.* Jackson: University Press of Mississippi, 2005.

Talbot, Daniel, ed. *Film: An Anthology.* Berkeley: University of California Press, 1966.

Truffaut, François. *The Early Film Criticism of François Truffaut.* Trans. Ruth Cassel Hoffman, Sonja Kropp, and Brigitte Formentin-Humbert. Bloomington: Indiana University Press, 1993.

Walker, Alexander. *Double Takes: Notes and Afterthoughts on the Movies, 1956-1976.*
London: Elm Tree Books, 1977.

Warshow, Robert. *The Immediate Experience.* New York: Atheneum, 1970.

Weinberg, Herman G. *Saint Cinema: Writings on Film, 1929-1970.* New York: Dover, 1973.

Wenders, Wim. *Emotion Pictures: Reflections on the Cinema.* Trans. Sean Whiteside and Michael Hofmann. Boston: Faber and Faber, 1989.

Winnington, Richard. *Film Criticism and Caricatures, 1943-1953.* New York: Barnes and Noble Books, 1976.

Wood, Michael. *America at the Movies.* New York: Basic Books, 1975.

Wood, Robin. *Personal Views: Explorations in Film.* Rev. ed. Detroit, Michigan: Wayne State University Press, 2006.

Young, Vernon. *On Film: Unpopular Essays on a Popular Art.* Chicago: Quadrangle Books, 1972.

———. *The Film Criticism of Vernon Young.* Ed. Bert Cardullo. Lanham, Maryland: University Press of America, 1990.

Film Credits

Way Down East, **1920**

Director: D. W. Griffith
Screenplay: Anthony Paul Kelly, elaborated by D. W. Griffith, from the 1897 play by Lottie Blair Parker, Joseph R. Grismer, and William A. Brady
Cinematography: G. W. Bitzer and Hendrik Sartov
Editor: James Smith and Rose Smith
Music: Louis Silvers and William F. Peters (the film was re-released in 1931 with a musical soundtrack)
Art Director: Charles O. Seessel and Clifford Pember
Costume Designer: Lady Duff Gordon and O'Kane Cornwell
Running time: 150 minutes; re-issued at 110 minutes
Format: 35 mm; black and white; silent
Cast: Lillian Gish (Anna Moore), Richard Barthelmess (David Bartlett), Lowell Sherman (Lennox Sanderson), Burt McIntosh (Squire Bartlett), Kate Bruce (Mother Bartlett), Mary Hay (Kate, the Squire's niece), Creighton Hale (The Professor), Emily Fitzroy (Maria Poole, the landlady), Porter Strong (Seth Holcomb), George Neville (The Constable), Edgar Nelson (Hi Holler), Morgan Belmont (Diana Tremont), Josephine Bernard (Mrs. Tremont), Mrs. David Landau (Anna Moore's mother), Viva Ogden (Martha Perkins), Florence Short (the eccentric aunt)

The Little Foxes, **1941**

Director: William Wyler
Screenplay: Lillian Hellman, from her play of the same name (1939)
Cinematography: Gregg Toland
Editor: Daniel Mandell
Music: Meredith Willson
Running time: 115 minutes

Format: 35 mm, black and white

Cast: Bette Davis (Regina Giddens), Herbert Marshall (Horace Giddens), Teresa Wright (Alexandra Giddens), Richard Carlson (David Hewitt), Dan Duryea (Leo Hubbard), Patricia Collinge (Birdie Hubbard), Charles Dingle (Ben Hubbard), Carl Benton Reid (Oscar Hubbard), Jessica Grayson (Addie), John Marriott (Cal), Russell Hicks (William Marshall), Lucien Littlefield (Sam Manders), Virginia Brissac (Mrs. Lucy Hewitt), Terry Nibert (Julia Jordan), Henry "Hot Shot" Thomas (Harold More)

Betrayal, 1983

Director: David Jones
Screenplay: Harold Pinter, based on his play of the same name (1978)
Cinematographer: Mike Fash
Editor: John Bloom
Music: Dominic Muldowney
Production Designer: Eileen Diss
Costume Designer: Jean Muir, Jane Robinson
Running time: 95 minutes
Format: 35mm, color

Cast: Jeremy Irons (Jerry), Ben Kingsley (Robert), Patricia Hodge (Emma), Avril Elgar (Mrs. Banks), Ray Marioni (Waiter), Caspar Norman (Sam), Chloe Billington (Charlotte, age five), Hannah Davies (Charlotte, age nine), Michael König (Ned, age two), Alexander McIntosh (Ned, age five)

Edmond, 2005

Director: Stuart Gordon
Screenplay: David Mamet, based on his play of the same name (1982)
Cinematography: Denis Maloney
Editor: Andy Horvitch
Music: Bobby Johnston
Production Designer: Alan E. Muraoka
Costume Designer: Carol Cutshall
Running time: 82 minutes
Format: 35mm, color

Cast: William H. Macy (Edmond Burke), Julia Stiles (Glenna), Joe Mantegna (Man in Bar), Ling Bai (Peep-Show Girl), Jeffrey Combs (Desk Clerk), Denise Richards (Allegro B-Girl), Mena Suvari (Whore), Dylan Walsh (Interrogator), Russell Hornsby (Shill), Debi Mazar (Atlantic Leisure Club Matron), Rebecca Pidgeon (Edmond's Wife), Lionel Mark Smith

(Pimp), Jack Wallace (Chaplain), Fortune Teller (Frances Bay), Cocktail Waitress (Wendy Thompson), Sharper (Dulé Hill), Pawnshop Owner (George Wendt), Woman on Subway (Patricia Belcher), Preacher (Wren T. Brown), Prisoner (Bokeem Woodbine)

Henry V, 1989

>Director: Kenneth Branagh
>Screenplay: Kenneth Branagh, based on *Henry V* (1599), by William Shakespeare
>Narrator: Derek Jacobi
>Cinematography: Kenneth MacMillan
>Editor: Michael Bradsell
>Music: Patrick Doyle
>Production Designer: Tim Harvey
>Costume Designer: Phyllis Dalton
>Running time: 137 minutes
>Format: 35mm, color
>Cast: Derek Jacobi (Chorus), Kenneth Branagh (Henry V of England), Simon Shepherd (Duke of Gloucester Brother to the King), James Larkin (Duke of Bedford Brother to the King), Brian Blessed (Duke of Exeter, Uncle to the King), Paul Gregory (Westmoreland), Charles Kay (Archbishop of Canterbury), Alec McCowen (Bishop of Ely), Ian Holm (Fluellen, Officer in King Henry's Army), Daniel Webb (Gower, Officer in King Henry's Army), Richard Briers (Bardolph), Geoffrey Hutchings (Nym), Robert Stephens (Pistol), Robbie Coltrane (Sir John Falstaff), Christian Bale (Boy), Judi Dench (Mistress Quickly), Paul Scofield (Charles VI of France), Michael Maloney (Louis, the Dauphin), Harold Innocent (Duke of Burgundy), Richard Clifford (Duke of Orleans), Christopher Ravenscroft (Mountjoy, a French Herald), Emma Thompson (Katharine, Daughter to Charles and Isabel), David Lloyd Meredith (Governor of Harfleur), Nicholas Ferguson (Warwick)

Room at the Top, 1958

>Director: Jack Clayton
>Screenplay: Neil Paterson, from the novel by John Braine (1957)
>Cinematography: Freddie Francis
>Editor: Ralph Kemplen
>Music: Mario Nascimbene
>Art Director: Ralph Brinton
>Running time: 115 minutes

Format: 35mm, in black and white

Cast: Simone Signoret (Alice Aisgill), Laurence Harvey (Joe Lampton), Heather Sears (Susan Brown), Donald Wolfit (Mr. Brown), Donald Houston (Charles Soames), Hermione Baddeley (Elspeth), Allan Cuthbertson (George Aisgill), Raymond Huntley (Mr. Hoylake), John Westbrook (Jack Wales), Ambrosine Phillpotts (Mrs. Brown), Richard Pasco (Teddy), Beatrice Varley (Aunt), Delena Kidd (Eva), Ian Hendry (Cyril), April Olrich (Mavis), Mary Peach (June Samson), Anthony Newlands (Bernard), Avril Elgar (Miss Gilchrist), Thelma Ruby (Miss Breith), Paul Whitsun-Jones (Laughing Man at Bar), Derren Nesbitt (Thug in Fight On Tow Path)

L'Argent, 1983

Director: Robert Bresson
Screenplay: Robert Bresson, from the 1905 novella by Leo Tolstoy
Cinematography: Pasqualino de Santis and Emmanuel Machuel
Editor: Jean-François Naudon
Music: Johann Sebastian Bach
Production Designer: Pierre Guffroy
Running time: 85 minutes
Format: 35mm, in color

Cast: Christian Patey (Yvon Targe), Vincent Risterucci (Lucien), Caroline Lang (Elise), Sylvie Van den Elsen (Gray-Haired Woman), Michel Briguet (Gray-Haired Woman's Father), Béatrice Tabourin (Woman in the Photography Shop), Didier Baussy (Man in the Photography Shop), Marc-Ernest Fourneau (Norbert), Bruno Lapeyre (Martial), Jeanne Aptekman (Yvette), André Cler (Norbert's Father), Claude Cher (Norbert's mother), François-Marie Banier (Yvon's cellmate)

Une Femme douce (*A Gentle Creature*), 1969

Director: Robert Bresson
Screenplay: Robert Bresson (based on "A Gentle Spirit" [1876]), a novella by Fyodor Dostoevsky)
Cinematography: Ghislain Cloquet
Editor: Raymond Lamy
Art director: Pierre Charbonnier
Running time: 88 minutes
Format: 35mm, in color

Cast: Dominique Sanda (She), Guy Frangin (He), Jane Lobré (the maid)

Prisoner of the Mountains, 1996

>Director: Sergei Bodrov
>Screenplay: Boris Giller, Arif Aliyev, Sergei Bodrov, from the story "Prisoner of the Caucasus" (1870), by Leo Tolstoy
>Cinematography: Pavel Lebeshev
>Editor: Alan Baril, Olga Grinshpun, and Vera Kruglova
>Music: Leonid Desyatnikov
>Running time: 99 minutes
>Format: 35mm, in color
>Cast: Oleg Menshikov (Sasha Kostílin), Sergei Bodrov, Jr. (Vania Zhílin), Dzhemal Sikharulidze (Abdul-Murat), Susanna Mekhralieva (Dina), Aleksandr Bureev (Hasan), Valentina Fedotova (Vania's mother), Aleksei Zharkov (Maslov)

The Remains of the Day, 1993

>Director: James Ivory
>Screenplay: Ruth Prawer Jhabvala, Kazuo Ishiguro (novel, 1989)
>Cinematography Tony Pierce-Roberts
>Editor: Andrew Marcus
>Music: Richard Robins
>Production Design: Luciana Arrighi
>Costume Design by Jenny Beavan and John Bright
>Running time 134 minutes
>Format: 35mm, color
>Cast: Anthony Hopkins (Head Butler Mr. James Stevens), Emma Thompson (Housekeeper Miss Sarah 'Sally' Kenton), James Fox (Lord Darlington), Christopher Reeve (Congressman Trent Lewis), Peter Vaughan (William Stevens, "Mr. Stevens senior"), Hugh Grant (Cardinal, Lord Darlington's godson), Paula Jacobs (Mrs. Mortimer), Ben Chaplin (Charlie), Patrick Godfrey (Spencer), Peter Halliday (Canon Tufnell), Emma Lewis (Elsa), Joanna Joseph (Irma), Tim Pigott-Smith (Benn), Lena Headey (Lizzie)

The Dead, 1987

>Director: John Huston
>Screenplay: Tony Huston, James Joyce (original story, 1914)
>Cinematography: Fred Murphy
>Editor: Roberto Silvi
>Music: Alex North

386   Film Credits

   Production Design: Stephen Grimes and Dennis Washington
   Costume Design by Dorothy Jenkins
   Running time: 83 minutes
   Format: 35mm, color
   Cast: Anjelica Huston (Gretta Conroy), Donal McCann (Gabriel Conroy), Cathleen Delany (Aunt Julia Morkan), Helena Carroll (Aunt Kate Morkan), Rachael Dowling (Lily), Ingrid Craigie (Mary Jane), Marie Kean (Mrs. Malins), Donal Donnelly (Theodore Alfred "Freddy" Malins), Frank Patterson (Bartell D'Arcy), Lyda Anderson (Miss Daly), Kate O'Toole (Miss Furlong), Bairbre Dowling (Miss Higgins), Maria McDermottroe (Molly Ivors), Colm Meaney (Mr. Bergin), Dan O'Herlihy (Mr. Browne), Sean McClory (Mr. Grace), Cormac O'Herlihy (Mr. Kerrigan), Maria Hayden (Mrs. O'Callaghan)

Dangerous Liaisons, **1988**

   Director: Stephen Frears
   Screenplay: Christopher Hampton, from his play (1985) and the 1782 novel by Choderlos de Laclos
   Cinematography Philippe Rousselot
   Editor: Mick Audsley
   Music: George Fenton
   Production Design: Stuart Craig
   Costume Design by James Acheson
   Running time: 119 minutes
   Format: 35mm, color
   Cast: Glenn Close (Marquise de Merteuil), John Malkovich (Vicomte de Valmont), Michelle Pfeiffer (Madame de Tourvel), Swoosie Kurtz (Madame de Volanges), Keanu Reeves (Le Chevalier Raphael Danceny), Mildred Natwick (Madame de Rosemonde), Uma Thurman (Cécile de Volanges), Peter Capaldi (Azolan)

Our Hitler, **a.k.a.** *Hitler, A Film from Germany*, **1977**

   Director: Hans-Jürgen Syberberg
   Screenplay: Hans-Jürgen Syberberg
   Cinematography: Dietrich Lohmann
   Editor: Jutta Brandstaedter
   Production Designer: Hans Gailling
   Costume Designer: Barbara Gailling, Brigitte Kuehlenthal
   Running time: 442 minues
   Format: 35mm, in black and white and color

Cast: André Heller (as Himself), Harry Baer (as Himself, Junger Ellerkamp), Heinz Schubert (Zirkusdirektor, Himmler, Himmler-Puppenspieler, Hitler), Peter Kern (Mörder aus "M", Göring-Puppenspieler, Alter Ellerkamp, SS-Mann, Fremdenverkehrsdirektor), Hellmut Lange (Hitlers Kammerdiener, Goebbels-Puppenspieler, SS-Mann), Rainer von Artenfels (Jahrmarkt-Ausrufer, Hitler-Puppenspieler, Junger Goebbels, Schüler des Kosmologen, SS-Mann), Martin Sperr (Himmlers Masseur, Fitzliputzli, Bürgermeister), Peter Moland (Astrologe, Speer-Puppenspieler, SS-Mann), Johannes Buzalski (Hitler als Anstreicher, Eva Braun-Puppenspieler, Mann der Gesellschaft 1923), Alfred Edel (Stimmen der Leute, Mann der Geschichte 1923), Amelie Syberberg (Das kleine Mädchen)

Parsifal, 1983

Director: Hans-Jürgen Syberberg
Screenplay: Richard Wagner (1882)
Cinematography: Igor Luther
Editors: Jutta Brandstaedter, Marianne Fehrenberg
Music: Richard Wagner, from the opera *Parsifal*
Production Designer: Werner Achmann
Costume Designers: Veronicka Dorn, Hella Wolter
Running time: 255 minutes
Format: 35mm, in color
Cast: Armin Jordan (Amfortas), Robert Lloyd (Gurnemanz), Martin Sperr (Titurel), Michael Kutter (Parsifal 1), Edith Clever (Kundry), Reiner Goldberg (Parsifal, voice), Aage Haugland (Klingsor), Karin Krick (Parsifal 2), David Luther (Young Parsifal), Yvonne Minton (Kundry, voice), Wolfgang Schöne (Amfortas, voice)

The Night, 1985

Director: Hans-Jürgen Syberberg
Screenplay: Louis-Ferdinand Céline, Johann Wolfgang Goethe, Martin Heidegger, Heinrich Heine, Friedrich Nietzsche, Novalis, Plato, William Shakespeare, Hans-Jürgen Syberberg, Heinrich von Kleist, Richard Wagner
Cinematography: Xaver Schwarzenberger
Editor: Jutta Brandstaedter
Sound: Lothar Mankewitz
Production Designer: Manfred Dittrich
Running time: 360 minutes
Format: 35mm, in color and black and white
Cast: Edith Clever

The Italian, 2005

Director: Andrei Kravchuk
Screenplay: Andrei Kravchuk and Andrei Romanov
Cinematography: Alexander Burov
Editor: Tamara Lipartiya
Music: Alexander Kneiffel
Production Designer: Vladimir Svetozarov
Costume Designers: Natalia Brabanova and Marina Nikolayeva
Running time: 99 minutes
Format: 35mm, in color
Cast: Kolya Spiridonov (Vanya Solntsev), Maria Kuznetsova (Madam), Nikolai Reutov (Grigori), Yuri Itskov (Headmaster), Denis Moiseenko (Kolyan), Sasha Sirotkin (Sery), Andrei Yelizarov (Timokha), Vladimir Shipov (Vovan), Polina Vorobieva (Natasha), Olga Shuvalova (Irka), Dima Zemlyanko (Anton), Darya Lesnikova (Mukhin's Mother), Rudolf Kuld (Building Guard)

Turtles Can Fly, 2004

Director: Bahman Ghobadi
Screenplay: Bahman Ghobadi
Cinematography: Shahriar Assadi
Editors: Mostafa Kherghehpoosh and Haydeh Safi-Yari
Music: Hossein Alizadeh
Production Designer: Bahman Ghobadi
Running time: 98 minutes
Format: 35mm, in color
Cast: Soran Ebrahim (Satellite), Avaz Latif (Agrin), Saddam Hossein Feysal (Pasheo), Hiresh Feysal Rahman (Henkov), Abdol Rahman Karim (Rega), Ajil Zibari (Shirkooh)

Fateless, 2005

Director: Lajos Koltai
Screenplay: Imre Kertész, from his own novel (1975)
Cinematography: Gyula Pados
Editor: Hajnal Sellö
Music: Ennio Morricone
Production Designer: Tibor Lázár
Costume Designer: Györgyi Szakács
Running time: 140 minutes

Format: 35mm, in color
Cast: Marcell Nagy (György Köves), Béla Dóra (Smoker), Bálint Péntek (Pretty boy), Áron Dimény (Bandi Citrom), Péter Fancsikai (Older Kollmann boy), Zsolt Dér (Rozi), András M. Kecskés (Finn), Dani Szabó (Moskovich), Tibor Mertz (Fodor), Péter Vida (Lénárt), Endre Harkányi (Old Kollmann), Márton Brezina (Younger Kollmann boy)

Woman Is the Future of Man, 2004

Director: Hong Sang-soo
Screenplay: Hong Sang-soo
Cinematography: Hyeon-gu Kim
Editor: Seong-weon Ham
Music: Yong-jin Jeong
Running time: 88 minutes
Format: 35mm, in color
Cast: Yoo Jitae (Munho Lee), Kim Toewoo (Hunjoon Kim), Sung Hyunan (Sunhwa Park)

Battle in Heaven, 2005

Director: Carlos Reygadas
Screenplay: Carlos Reygadas
Cinematography: Diego Martínez Vignatti
Editors: Adoración G. Elipe, Benjamin Mirguet, Carlos Reygadas, and Nicolas Schmerkin
Music: John Tavener
Art Direction: Elsa Ruiz and Daniela Schneider
Running time: 98 minutes
Format: 35mm, in color
Cast: Marcos Hernández (Marcos), Anapola Mushkadiz (Ana), Bertha Ruiz (Marcos' Wife), David Bornstein (Jaime), Rosalinda Ramirez (Viky), El Abuelo (Chief of Police), Brenda Angulo (Madame), El Mago (Preacher), Francisco "El Gato" Martínez (Gas Station Attendant), Diego Martínez Vignatti (Soccer Player), Alejandro Mayar (Police Inspector), Chavo Nava (Neurotic Conductor), Estela Tamariz (Ines)

Day Night Day Night, 2006

Director: Julia Loktev
Screenplay: Julia Loktev
Cinematography: Benoît Debie

Editors: Julia Loktev and Michael Taylor
Production Designer: Kelly McGehee
Costume Designer: Rabiah Troncelliti
Running time: 94 minutes
Format: 35mm, in color
Cast: Luisa Williams (She/Leah Cruz), Josh Phillip Weinstein (Commander), Gareth Saxe (Organizer), Nyambi Nyambi (Organizer), Frank Dattolo (Bombmaker), Annemarie Lawless (Bombmaker's Assistant), Teo Yoo (Driver), Richard Morant (Flirt)

Down in the Valley, 2005

Director: David Jacobson
Screenplay: David Jacobson
Cinematography: Enrique Chediak
Editors: David Jacobson, Lynzee Klingman, and Edward Norton
Music: Peter Salett
Production Designers: Franco-Giacomo Carbone, Michael Atwell, and Robert Greenfield
Costume Designer: Jacqueline West
Running time: 112 minutes
Format: 35mm, in color
Cast: Edward Norton (Harlan), Evan Rachel Wood (Tobe), David Morse (Wade), Rory Culkin (Lonnie), Bruce Dern (Charlie), John Diehl (Steve), Geoffrey Lewis (Sheridan), Elizabeth Peña (Gale), Kat Dennings (April), Hunter Parrish (Kris)

The Proposition, 2005

Director: John Hillcoat
Screenplay: Nick Cave
Cinematography: Benoît Delhomme
Editor: Jon Gregory
Music: Nick Cave and Warren Ellis
Production Designers: Chris Kennedy, Bill Booth, and Marita Mussett
Costume Designer: Margot Wilson
Running time: 104 minutes
Format: 35mm, in color
Cast: Richard Wilson (Mike Burns), Noah Taylor (Brian O'Leary), Jeremy Madrona (Asian Prostitute), Jae Mamuyac (Asian Prostitute), Guy Pearce (Charlie Burns), Mick Roughan (Mad Jack Bradshaw), Shane Watt (John Gordon), Ray Winstone (Captain Stanley), Robert Morgan (Sergeant

Lawrence), David Gulpilil (Jacko), Bryan Probets (Officer Dunn), Oliver Ackland (Patrick Hopkins), Danny Huston (Arthur Burns)

Brokeback Mountain, 2005

>Director: Ang Lee
>Screenplay: Larry McMurtry and Diana Ossana, from the 1997 story by Annie Proulx
>Cinematography: Rodrigo Prieto
>Editors: Geraldine Peroni and Dylan Tichenor
>Music: Gustavo Santaolalla
>Production Designers: Judy Becker, Laura Ballinger, Tracey Baryski
>Costume Designer: Marit Allen
>Running time: 134 minutes
>Format: 35mm, in color

Cast: Heath Ledger (Ennis Del Mar), Jake Gyllenhaal (Jack Twist), Randy Quaid (Joe Aguirre), Valerie Planche (Waitress), David Trimble (Basque), Michelle Williams (Alma), Larry Reese (Jolly Minister), Marty Antonini (Timmy), Anne Hathaway (Lureen Newsome), Scott Michael Campbell (Monroe), Mary Liboiron (Fayette Newsome), Graham Beckel (L. D. Newsome), Jerry Callaghan (Judge), Linda Cardellini (Cassie), Anna Faris (Lashawn Malone), David Harbour (Randall Malone), Will Martin (Carl), Roberta Maxwell (Jack's Mother), Peter McRobbie (John Twist)

Kitchen Stories, 2003

>Director: Bent Hamer
>Screenplay: Jörgen Bergmark and Bent Hamer
>Cinematography: Philip Øgaard
>Editor: Pål Gengenbach
>Music: Hans Mathisen
>Production Designer: Billy Johansson
>Costume Designer: Karen Fabritius Gram
>Running time: 95 minutes
>Format: 35mm, in color

Cast: Joachim Calmeyer (Isak Bjørvik), Tomas Norström (Folke Nilsson), Bjørn Floberg (Grant), Reine Brynolfsson (Malmberg), Sverre Anker Ousdal (Dr. Jack Zac. Benjaminsen), Leif Andrée (Dr. Ljungberg)

Film Credits

Son Frère, 2003

Director: Patrice Chéreau
Screenplay: Patrice Chéreau and Anne-Louise Trividic, from the 2001 novel by Philippe Besson
Cinematography: Eric Gautier
Editor: François Gédigier
Costume Designer: Caroline de Vivaise
Running time: 92 minutes
Format: 35mm, in color
Cast: Bruno Todeschini (Thomas), Eric Caravaca (Luc), Nathalie Boutefeu (Claire), Maurice Garrel (The Old Man), Catherine Ferran (Head Doctor), Antoinette Moya (The Mother), Sylvain Jacques (Vincent), Fred Ulysse (The Father), Robinson Stévenin (Manuel)

Gabrielle, 2005

Director: Patrice Chéreau
Screenplay: Patrice Chéreau and Anne-Louise Trividic, from the 1897 story by Joseph Conrad
Cinematography: Eric Gautier
Editor: François Gédigier
Music: Fabio Vacchi
Production Designer: Olivier Radot
Costume Designer: Caroline de Vivaise
Running time: 90 minutes
Format: 35mm, in black & white and color
Cast: Isabelle Huppert (Gabrielle Hervey), Pascal Greggory (Jean Hervey), Claudia Coli (Yvonne), Thierry Hancisse (The Editor-in-Chief), Chantal Neuwirth (Madeleine), Rinaldo Rocco (The Consul)

Enduring Love, 2004

Director: Roger Mitchell
Screenplay: Joe Penhall, from the 1997 novel by Ian McEwan
Cinematography: Haris Zambarloukos
Editor: Nicolas Gaster
Music: Jeremy Sans
Production Designers: John Paul Kelly and Emma MacDevitt
Costume Designer: Natalie Ward
Running time: 95 minutes
Format: 35mm, in color

Cast: Daniel Craig (Joe), Samantha Morton (Claire), Bill Weston (Grandfather), Jeremy McCurdie (Boy in Balloon), Lee Sheward (John Logan), Rhys Ifans (Jed), Bill Nighy (Robin), Susan Lynch (Rachel), Ben Whishaw (Spud), Justin Salinger (Frank), Helen McCrory (Mrs. Logan), Alexandra Aitken (Natasha), Anna Maxwell Martin (Penny)

Lila Says, 2004

Director: Ziad Doueiri
Screenplay: Ziad Doueiri, Mark Lawrence, and Joelle Touma, from the 1996 novel by Chimo
Cinematography: John Daly
Editor: Tina Baz
Music: Nitin Sawhney
Production Designers: Yves Bernard and Arnaud Le Roch
Costume Designer: Pierre Matard
Running time: 89 minutes
Format: 35mm, in color
Cast: Vahina Giocante (Lila), Mohammed Khouas (Chimo), Karim Ben Haddou (Mouloud), Lotfi Chakri (Bakary), Hamid Dkhissi (Big Jo), Edmonde Franchi (Lila's Aunt), Carmen Lebbos (Chimo's Mother), Ghandi Assad (Sammy), Stéphanie Fatout (Claire Soulier)

My Summer of Love, 2004

Director: Pawel Pawlikowski
Screenplay: Pawel Pawlikowski and Michael Wynne, from the 2001 novel by Helen Cross
Cinematography: Ryszard Lenczewski
Editor: David Charap
Music: Alison Goldfrapp and Will Gregory
Production Designers: John Stevenson and Netty Chapman
Costume Designer: Julian Day
Running time: 86 minutes
Format: 35mm, in color
Cast: Natalie Press (Mona), Emily Blunt (Tamsin), Paddy Considine (Phil), Dean Andrews (Ricky), Michelle Byrne (Ricky's Wife), Paul Antony-Barber (Tamsin's Father), Lynette Edwards (Tamsin's Mother), Kathryn Sumner (Sadie)

Heading South, 2005

    Director: Laurent Cantet
    Screenplay: Laurent Cantet and Robin Campillo, from three stories by Dany Laferrière
    Cinematography: Pierre Milon
    Editor: Robin Campillo
    Music: Elisabeth Joinet
    Production Designer: Frankie Diago
    Costume Designer: Denis Sperdouklis
    Running time: 108 minutes
    Format: 35mm, in color
    Cast: Charlotte Rampling (Ellen), Karen Young (Brenda), Louise Portal (Sue), Ménothy Cesar (Legba), Lys Ambroise (Albert), Jackenson Pierre Olmo Diaz (Eddy), Wilfried Paul (Neptune)

The Bridesmaid, 2004

    Director: Claude Chabrol
    Screenplay: Claude Chabrol and Pierre Leccia, from the 1989 novel by Ruth Rendell
    Cinematography: Eduardo Serra
    Editor: Monique Fardoulis
    Music: Matthieu Chabrol
    Production Designer: Françoise Benoît-Fresco
    Costume Designers: Sandrine Bernard and Mic Cheminal
    Running time: 111 minutes
    Format: 35mm, in color
    Cast: Benoît Magimel (Philippe Tardieu), Laura Smet (Stéphanie "Senta" Bellange), Aurore Clément (Christine), Bernard Le Coq (Gérard Courtois), Solène Bouton (Sophie Tardieu), Anna Mihalcea (Patricia Tardieu), Suzanne Flon (Madame Crespin), Eric Seigne (Jacky), Pierre-François Dumeniaud (Nadeau), Isolde Barth (Rita), Mazen Kiwan (Pablo)

Abouna, 2002

    Director: Mahamat-Saleh Haroun
    Screenplay: Mahamat-Saleh Haroun
    Cinematography: Abraham Haile Biru
    Editor: Sarah Taouss-Matton
    Music: Ali Farka Touré, Diego Moustapha N'garade
    Production Designer: Laurent Cavero

Costume Designer: Hassanie Lazingar
Running time: 84 minutes
Format: 35mm, in color
Cast: Ahidjo Mahamat Moussa (Tahir), Hamza Moctar Aguid (Amine), Zara Haroun (Achta, the Mother), Mounira Khalil (The Mute Girl), Diego Moustapha Ngarade (Uncle Adoum), Koulsy Lamko (The Father), Garba Issa (The Headmaster), Ramada Mahamat (The teacher's wife), Hassan Boulama (Hassan), Hadje Fatime N'Goua (The doctor), Nouraldine Mahamat Alio (Police chief), Christophe N'Garoyal (Factory manager)

Facing Windows, 2003

Director: Ferzan Özpetek
Screenplay: Ferzan Özpetek, Gianni Romoli
Cinematography: Gianfilippo Corticelli
Editor: Patricio Marone
Music: Andrea Guerra
Art Director: Andrea Crisanti
Costume Designer: Katia Dottori
Running time: 106 minutes
Format: 35mm, in color
Cast: Giovanna Mezzogiorno (Giovanna), Massimo Girotti (Simone/Davide Veroli), Raoul Bova (Lorenzo), Filippo Nigro (Filippo), Serra Yilmaz (Eminè), Maria Grazia Bon (Sara), Massimo Poggio (Young Davide), Ivan Bacchi (Simone)

Djomeh, 2000

Director: Hassan Yektapanah
Screenplay: Hassan Yektapanah
Cinematography: Ali Loghmani
Editor: Hassan Yektapanah
Production Designer: Hassan Yektapanah
Running time: 98 minutes
Format: 35mm, in color
Cast: Rashid Akbari (Habib), Mahmoud Behraznia (Agha Mohmoud), Valiollah Beta (The Blind Man), Mahbobeh Khalili (Setareh), Jalil Nazari (Djomeh)

Otomo, 1999

Director: Frieder Schlaich

Film Credits

Screenplay: Klaus Pohl, Frieder Schlaich
Cinematography: Volker Tittel
Editor: Magdolna Rokob
Costume Designer: Henrike Luz
Running time: 85 minutes
Format: 35mm, in color
Cast: Isaach De Bankolé (Otomo), Eva Mattes (Gisela), Hanno Friedrich (Heinz), Barnaby Metschurat (Rolf), Lara Kugler (Simone)

Goodbye, Dragon Inn, 2003

Director: Tsai Ming-liang
Screenplay: Tsai Ming-liang
Cinematography: Pen-jung Liao
Editor: Sheng-Chang Chen
Running time: 82 minutes
Format: 35mm, in color
Cast: Kang-sheng Lee (Hsiao-Kang), Shiang-chyi Chen (Ticket Woman), Kiyonobu Mitamura (Japanese tourist), Tien Miao (Himself), Chun Shih (Himself), Kuei-Mei Yang (Peanut-Eating Woman)

Bad Education, 2004

Director: Pedro Almodóvar
Screenplay: Pedro Almodóvar
Cinematography: José Luis Alcaine
Editor: José Salcedo
Music: Alberto Iglesias
Art Director: Antxón Gómez
Costume Designers: Paco Delgado and Jean-Paul Gaultier
Running time: 106 minutes
Format: 35mm, in color
Cast: Gael García Bernal (Ángel /Juan /Zahara), Fele Martínez (Enrique Goded), Daniel Giménez Cacho (Padre Manolo), Lluís Homar (Sr. Manuel Berenguer), Francisco Maestre (Padre José), Francisco Boira (Ignacio), Juan Fernández (Martín), Nacho Pérez (Ignacio), Raúl García Forneiro (Enrique)

Sex Is Comedy, 2002

Director: Catherine Breillat
Screenplay: Catherine Breillat

Cinematography: Laurent Machuel
Editor: Pascale Chavance
Production Designer: Frédérique Belvaux
Costume Designers: Valérie Guégan and Betty Martins
Running time: 92 minutes
Format: 35mm, in color
Cast: Anne Parillaud (Jeanne), Grégoire Colin (The Actor), Roxane Mesquida (The Actress), Ashley Wanninger (Leo, the first assistant), Dominique Colladant (Willy), Bart Binnema (Director of Photography)

Vengeance Is Mine, 1979

Director: Shohei Imamura
Screenplay: Masaru Baba, from the 1975 novel by Ryuzo Saki
Cinematography: Shinsaku Himeda
Editor: Keiichi Uraoka
Music: Shinichiro Ikebe
Production Designer: Teuyoshi Satani
Running time: 140 minutes
Format: 35mm, in color
Cast: Ken Ogata (Iwao Enokizu), Rentaro Mikumi (Shizuo Enokizu), Chocho Miyako (Kayo Enokizu), Mitsuko Baisho (Kazuko Enokizu), Mayumi Ogawa (Haru Asano), Nijiko Kiyokawa (Hisano Asano)

Last Year at Marienbad (*L'année dernière à Marienbad*), 1961

Director: Alain Resnais
Screenplay: Alain Robbe-Grillet
Cinematography: Sacha Vierny
Editors: Jasmine Chasney, Henri Colpi
Music: Francis Seyrig
Production Designer: Jacques Saulnier
Costume Designer: Bernard Evein
Running time: 93 minutes
Format: 35mm, in black and white
Cast: Delphine Seyrig, Giorgio Albertazzi, Sacha Pitoëff, Françoise Bertin, Luce Garcia-Ville, Héléna Kornel, Françoise Spira, Karin Toche-Mittler, Pierre Barbaud, Wilhelm von Deek, Jean Lanier, Jean Lanier, Gérard Lorin, Davide Montemuri, Gilles Quéant

Film Credits

L'eclisse (Eclipse), 1962

>Director: Michelangelo Antonioni
>Screenplay: Michelangelo Antonioni, Tonino Guerra
>Cinematography: Gianni Di Venanzo
>Editor: Eraldo Da Roma
>Music: Giovanni Fusco
>Production Designer: Piero Poletto
>Costume Designers: Bice Brichetto, Gitt Magrini
>Running time: 126 minutes
>Format: 35mm, in black and white
>Cast: Alain Delon (Piero), Monica Vitti (Vittoria), Francisco Rabal (Riccardo), Lilla Brignone (Vittoria's Mother), and with Louis Seigner, Rosanna Rory, Mirella Ricciardi, and Cyrus Elias

La Règle du jeu (*The Rules of the Game*), 1939

>Director: Jean Renoir
>Screenplay: Jean Renoir, Camille François, and Carl Koch
>Cinematography: Jean Bachelet
>Editor: Marguerite Houlet-Renoir
>Music: Roger Desormières (arranger and conductor)
>Production Desiger: Eugène Lourié
>Costume Designer: Coco Chanel
>Running time: 110 minutes
>Format: 35mm, in black and white
>Cast: Marcel Dalio (Robert de la Chesnaye), Nora Grégor (Christine de la Chesnaye), Roland Toutain (André Jurieu), Jean Renoir (Octave), Mila Parély (Geneviève), Paulette Dubost (Lisette), Gaston Modot (Schmacher), Julien Carette (Marceau), Anne Mayen (Jackie), Pierre Nay (Saint-Aubin), Pierre Magnier (The General), Odette Talazac (Charlotte), Roger Forster (The Homosexual), Richard Francoeur (La Bruyère), Claire Gérard (Madame de la Bruyère), Tony Corteggiani (Berthelin), Nicolas Amato (The South American), Eddie Debray (Corneille), Lisa Elina (The Radio Announcer), André Zwobada (The Engineer), Léon Larive (The Chef), Henri Cartier-Bresson (The English Domestic)

A Kind of Loving, 1962

>Director: John Schlesinger
>Screenplay: Willis Hall and Keith Waterhouse, from the 1960 novel by Stan Barstow

Cinematography: Denys Coop
Editor: Roger Cherrill
Music: Ron Grainer
Art Direction: Ray Simm
Running time: 112 minutes
Format: 35mm, in black and white
Cast: Alan Bates (Victor Arthur "Vic" Brown), Thora Hird (Mrs. Rothwell), Bert Palmer (Mr. Geoffrey Brown), Pat Keen (Christine Harris), James Bolam (Jeff), Jack Smethurst (Conroy), Gwen Nelson (Mrs. Brown), John Ronane (Draughtsman), David Mahlowe (David Harris), Patsy Rowlands (Dorothy), Michael Deacon (Les), Annette Robertson (Phoebe), Fred Ferris (Althorpe), Leonard Rossiter (Whymper), Malcolm Patton (Jim Brown), Harry Markham (Railwayman), Peter Madden (Registrar), June Ritchie (Ingrid Rothwell)

Billy Liar, 1963

Director: John Schlesinger
Screenplay: Willis Hall and Keith Waterhouse, from the 1959 novel by Waterhouse and the 1960 play by Waterhouse and Hall
Cinematography: Denys Coop
Editor: Roger Cherrill
Music: Richard Rodney Bennett
Art Direction: Ray Simm
Running time: 98 minutes
Format: 35mm, in black and white
Cast: Tom Courtenay (William Terrence "Billy" Fisher), Wilfred Pickles (Geoffrey Fisher), Mona Washbourne (Alice Fisher), Ethel Griffies (Florence, Billy's grandmother), Finlay Currie (Duxbury), Gwendolyn Watts (Rita), Helen Fraser (Barbara), Julie Christie (Liz), Leonard Rossiter (Emanuel Shadrack), Rodney Bewes (Arthur Crabtree), George Innes (Stamp), Leslie Randall (Danny Boon), Patrick Barr (Insp. MacDonald), Ernest Clark (Prison Governor), Godfrey Winn (Disc Jockey)

Darling, 1965

Director: John Schlesinger
Screenplay: Fredric Raphael
Cinematography: Ken Higgins
Editor: James Clark
Music: John Dankworth
Art Direction: Ray Simm

Costume Design: Julie Harris
Running time: 128 minutes
Format: 35mm, in black and white
Cast: Laurence Harvey (Miles Brand), Dirk Bogarde (Robert Gold), Julie Christie (Diana Scott), José Luis De Villalonga (Prince Cesare della Romita), Roland Curram (Malcolm), Basil Henson (Alec Prosser-Jones), Helen Lindsay (Felicity Prosser-Jones), Carlo Palmucci (Curzio della Romita), Dante Posani (Gino), Umberto Raho (Palucci), Marika Rivera, (Woman), Alex Scott (Sean Martin), Ernest Walder (Kurt), Brian Wilde (Willett), Pauline Yates (Estelle Gold), Peter Bayliss (Lord Grant), Richard Bidlake (Rupert Crabtree), Trevor Bowen (Tony Bridges), Annette Carell (Billie Castiglione), Jean Claudio (Raoul Maxim), Georgina Cookson (Carlotta Hale), James Cossins (Basildon), Jane Downes (Julie)

Day of Wrath, 1943

Director: Carl Theodor Dreyer
Screenplay: Carl Theodor Dreyer, Poul Knudsen, Paul La Cour, Mogens Skot-Hansen, from Hans Wiers-Jenssens' play *Anne Pedersdotter* (1908)
Cinematographer: Karl Andersson
Editors: Anne Marie Petersen, Edith Schlüssel
Music: Poul Schierbeck
Art Direction: Erik Aaes
Costume Designers: Karl Sandt Jensen, Olga Thomsen
Running time: 97 minutes
Format: 35mm, black and white
Cast: Albert Høeberg (The Bishop), Preben Lerdorff Rye (Martin, Absalon's son from first marriage), Lisbeth Movin (Anne Pedersdotter, Absalon's second wife), Preben Neergaard (Degn), Sigrid Neiiendam (Merete, Absalon's mother)

The Case Is Closed, 1982

Director: Mrinal Sen
Screenplay: Mrinal Sen, from the story by Ramapada Chowdhury
Cinematography: K. K. Mahajan
Editor: Gangadhar Naskar
Music: B. V. Karanth
Art Direction: Nitish Roy
Running time: 95 minutes
Format: 35mm, in color

Cast: Anjan Dutt (Anjan Sen), Mamata Shankar (Mamata Sen), Sreela Majumdar (Sreeja), Indranil Moitra (Pupai), Dehapratim Das Gupta (Hari), Nilotpal Dey (Inspector), Charuprakash Ghosh (Lawyer)

Alsino and the Condor, 1982

Director: Miguel Littin
Screenplay: Isidora Aguirre, Miguel Littin, and Tomás Pérez Turrent, from the novel *Alsino* (1920), by Pedro Prado
Cinematography: Jorge Herrera and Pablo Martinez
Editor: Miriam Talavera
Music: Leo Brouwer
Art Director: Elly Menz
Running time: 89 minutes
Format: 35mm, in color
Cast: Dean Stockwell (Frank), Alan Esquivel (Alsino), Carmen Bunster (Alsino's Grandmother), Alejandro Parodi (The Major), Delia Casanova (Rosaria), Marta Lorena Pérez (Lucia), Reynaldo Miravalles (Don Nazario, the Birdman), Marcelo Gaete (Lucia's Grandfather), Jan Kees De Roy (Dutch Advisor)

Elvira Madigan, 1967

Director: Bo Widerberg
Screenplay: Bo Widerberg, based on the ballad by Johann Lindström Saxon
Cinematography: Jörgen Persson
Editor: Bo Widerberg
Music: Ulf Björlin
Running time: 91 minutes
Format: 35mm, in color
Cast: Pia Degermark (Hedvig "Elvira" Madigan), Thommy Berggren (Lt. Sparre), Lennart Malmer (Kristoffer), Cleo Jensen (Cleo)

Carnal Knowledge, 1971

Director: Mike Nichols
Screenplay: Jules Feiffer
Cinematography: Giuseppe Rotunno
Editor: Sam O'Steen
Production Designer: Richard Sylbert
Costume Designer: Anthea Sylbert

Running time: 98 minutes
Format: 35mm, in color
Cast: Jack Nicholson (Jonathan), Ann-Margret (Bobbie), Art Garfunkel (Sandy), Candice Bergen (Susan), Rita Moreno (Louise), Cynthia O'Neal (Cindy), Carol Kane (Jennifer)

The Last Picture Show, 1971

Director: Peter Bogdanovich
Screenplay: Larry McMurtry and Peter Bogdanovich, from the 1966 novel by Larry McMurtry
Cinematography: Robert Surtees
Editor: Donn Cambern
Music: Bob Wills and his Texas Playboys, Phil Harris, Johnny Standley, and Hank Thompson
Production Designers: Polly Platt and Walter Scott Herndon
Costume Designer: Polly Platt
Running time: 118 minutes
Format: 35mm, in black and white
Cast: Timothy Bottoms (Sonny Crawford), Jeff Bridges (Duane Jackson), Cybill Shepherd (Jacy Farrow), Ben Johnson (Sam the Lion), Cloris Leachman (Ruth Popper), Ellen Burstyn (Lois Farrow), Eileen Brennan (Genevieve), Clu Gulager (Abilene), Sam Bottoms (Billy), Randy Quaid (Lester Marlow)

Mean Streets, 1973

Director: Martin Scorsese
Screenplay: Martin Scorsese and Mardik Martin
Cinematography: Kent Wakeford
Editor: Sidney Levin
Running time: 112 minutes
Format: 35mm, in color
Cast: Robert De Niro (Johnny Boy), Harvey Keitel (Charlie), David Proval (Tony), Amy Robinson (Teresa), Richard Romanus (Michael), Cesare Danova (Giovanni), George Memmoli (Joey), Lenny Scaletta (Jimmy)

Bang the Drum Slowly, 1973

Director: John Hancock
Screenplay: Mark Harris, from his own novel (1956)
Cinematography: Richard Shore

Editor: Richard Marks
Music: Stephen Lawrence
Production Designer: Robert Gundlach
Costume Designer: Domingo A. Rodriguez
Running time: 96 minutes
Format: 35mm, in color
Cast: Robert De Niro (Bruce Pearson), Michael Moriarty (Henry "Author" Wiggin), Vincent Gardenia (Dutch Schnell), Danny Aiello (Horse), Heather MacRae (Holly Wiggin)

Last Summer, 1969

Director: Frank Perry
Screenplay: Eleanor Perry, from a novel by Evan Hunter (1968)
Cinematography: Enrique Bravo and Gerald Hirschfeld
Editor: Sydney Katz
Music: John Simon
Art Direction: Peter Dohanos
Costume Designer: Theoni V. Aldredge
Running time: 95 minutes
Format: 35mm, in color
Cast: Barbara Hershey (Sandy), Richard Thomas (Peter), Bruce Davison (Dan), Catherine Burns (Rhoda), Ernesto Gonzalez (Anibal)

McCabe and Mrs. Miller, 1971

Director: Robert Altman
Screenplay: Robert Altman and Brian McKay, from the 1959 novel by Edmund Naughton
Cinematography: Vilmos Zsigmond
Editor: Lou Lombardo
Music: Leonard Cohen, composer of the songs "The Stranger Song," "Sisters of Mercy," "Winter Lady"
Production Designers: Leon Ericksen, Al Locatelli, and Philip Thomas
Costume Designer: Ilse Richter
Running time: 120 minutes
Format: 35mm, in color
Cast: Warren Beatty (John McCabe), Julie Christie (Constance Miller), Rene Auberjonois (Sheehan), William Devane (the Lawyer), John Schuck (Smalley), Corey Fischer (Mr. Elliot), Bert Remsen (Bart Coyle), Shelley Duvall (Ida Coyle), Keith Carradine (Cowboy), Michael Murphy (Sears)

404   Film Credits

They Shoot Horses, Don't They?, **1969**

Director: Sydney Pollack
Screenplay: James Poe and Robert E. Thompson, from the 1935 novel by Horace McCoy
Cinematography: Philip H. Lathrop
Editor: Fredric Steinkamp
Music: Johnny Green and Albert Woodbury
Production Designer: Harry Horner
Costume Designer: Donfeld
Running time: 120 minutes
Format: 35mm, in color
Cast: Jane Fonda (Gloria Beatty), Michael Sarrazin (Robert Syverton), Susannah York (Alice), Gig Young (Rocky), Red Buttons (Sailor), Bonnie Bedelia (Ruby), Michael Conrad (Rollo), Bruce Dern (James)

Badlands, **1973**

Director: Terrence Malick
Screenplay: Terrence Malick
Cinematography: Tak Fujimoto, Stevan Larner, Brian Probyn
Editor: Robert Estrin
Music: George Tipton
Art Direction: Jack Fisk
Costume Designer: Rosanna Norton
Running time: 95 minutes
Format: 35mm, in color
Cast: Martin Sheen (Kit), Sissy Spacek (Holly), Warren Oates (Father)

Slaughterhouse-Five, **1972**
Director: George Roy Hill
Screenplay: Stephen Geller, from the 1969 novel by Kurt Vonnegut, Jr.
Cinematography: Miroslav Ondricek
Editor: Dede Allen
Music: Glenn Gould
Production Designers: Henry Bumstead, Alexander Golitzen, and George Webb
Running time: 104 minutes
Format: 35mm, in color
Cast: Michael Sacks (Billy Pilgrim), Ron Leibman (Paul Lazzaro), Eugene Roche (Edgar Derby), Sharon Gans (Valencia Merble Pilgrim), Valerie Perrine (Montana Wildhack), Holly Near (Barbara Pilgrim), Perry King (Robert Pilgrim), Kevin Conway (Roland Weary)

Notes

¹ These are the film adaptations, subsequent to Bresson's, of Dostoevsky's novella *A Gentle Spirit*: in 1995, a film version of the novella was made by the Pole Mariusz Treliński as *Łagodna*; in 1989 the Indian director Mani Kaul turned this Dostoevsky story into the film *Nazar*; and in 1998, the Frenchman Raphaël Nadjari did a modern film adaptation of *A Gentle Spirit* set in present-day New York, titled *The Shade*.

² Robert Bresson, *Notes on Cinematography*, trans. Jonathan Griffin (New York: Urizen Books, 1977), 1.

³ Ludmilla Koehler, "Five Minutes Too Late," *Dostovesky Studies*, 6 (1985): 121-122.

⁴ See, for example, Eric Rhode, "Dostoevsky and Bresson," *Sight and Sound*, 39.2 (Spring 1970): 82-83; Jean-Pierre Oudart, "Bresson et la vérité," *Cahiers du cinéma*, no. 216 (October 1969): 53-56; Jacques Chevalier, "*Une Femme douce*," *Image et Son*, no. 232 (November 1969): 120-124; Jonas Mekas, "On Bresson and *Une Femme douce*," *Village Voice*, October 2, 1969, 46; Michel Estève, "Choix des films: *Une Femme douce* de Robert Bresson ou le silence du couple," *Etudes*, October 1969, 406-408; Jean Sémolué, "*Une Femme douce*," *Téléciné*, no. 157 (December 1969): 7-18; Charles Thomas Samuels, "Bresson's Gentleness," in his *Mastering the Film and Other Essays* (Knoxville: University of Tennessee Press, 1977), 161-163; and Lindley Hanlon, "The 'Seen' and the 'Said': Bresson's *Une Femme douce* from the Story *The Gentle Creature* by Fyodor Dostoevsky," 158-172 in Andrew Horton and Joan Magretta, ed., *Modern European Filmmakers and the Art of Adaptation* (New York: Ungar, 1981).

⁵ Victor Erlich, *Russian Formalism: History/Doctrine* (1955; The Hague, Netherlands: Mouton, 1980), 240.

⁶ I am not using "nihilistic" in the twentith-century sense that the world is without meaning or purpose and that existence itself—all action, suffering, and feeling—is ultimately senseless and empty. Rather, I use the term in the sense it was used in Russia beginning in the 1860s, after

its appearance in Ivan Turgenev's novel *Fathers and Sons* (1862), where it is employed to describe the crude scientism espoused by the character Bazarov. In Russia, nihilism became identified with a loosely organized revolutionary movement (ca. 1860-1917) that rejected the authority of the state, church, and family. In his early writing, the anarchist leader Mikhael Bakunin (1814-1876) composed the notorious entreaty still identified with nihilism: "Let us put our trust in the eternal spirit which destroys and annihilates only because it is the unsearchable and eternally creative source of all life—the passion for destruction is also a creative passion!" (*The Reaction in Germany*, 1842). This movement advocated a social arrangement based on rationalism and materialism as the sole source of knowledge and on individual freedom as the highest goal. By rejecting man's spiritual essence in favor of a solely materialistic one, nihilists denounced God and religious authority as antithetical to freedom. The movement eventually deteriorated into an ethos of subversion, destruction, and anarchy, and by the late 1870s, a nihilist was anyone associated with clandestine political groups advocating terrorism and assassination.

⁷ I am, of course, not the first to assert that Bresson invokes mystery or "otherness" in *Une Femme douce*, as in a number of his films. Amédée Ayfre, for instance, has written that the characters in Bresson's films, "even in their most extreme confidences, never fundamentally reveal anything but their mystery—like God himself" ("The Universe of Robert Bresson," trans. Elizabeth Kingsley-Rowe, in Ian Cameron, ed., *The Films of Robert Bresson* [New York: Praeger, 1969], 14-15). See also Paul Schrader, *Transcendental Style in Film: Ozu, Bresson, Dreyer* (Berkeley: University of California Press, 1972). I differ with Ayfre, Schrader, and other critics in my suggestion that Bresson is invoking mystery not for mystery's sake alone, but for the sake of exalting the human, of calling his audience's attention at once to the magisterially divine and the intrinsically worthy in all human beings.

⁸ Bresson, *Notes on Cinematography*, 55.

⁹ The film opened in Paris on July 7, 1939. As a result of the French public's violently negative reaction to *La Règle du jeu*, Renoir re-cut the film. A 113-minute film soon became 100 minutes long; then it became 90 minutes and finally 85. After finally being pulled from distribution, the original negative of *La Règle du jeu* was stored away in a warehouse that was bombed by the Allies in 1942. The shortened version of the film was re-released in 1949 in Great Britain and in 1950 in New York. It wasn't until 1959 that it was restored to nearly its original form by Jean Gaborit and Jacques Durand, who gathered up hundreds of cans of footage and pieced the film together with the help of Renoir. The restored *La Règle du jeu* had its premiere at the Venice Film Festival in 1959.

[10] For a summary of historically-inspired approaches to *La Règle du jeu* since its re-release, see Keith Reader, *"La Règle du jeu": Jean Renoir, 1939* (London: I. B. Tauris, 2010), 88-96. What follows is a further sampling of such approaches:

Renoir's realism allows us to perceive the real tragedy underlying the superficial frivolity of the Colinière society: their spiritual uncertainty has produced a breakdown of the old system of values and of differences that makes for the kind of sacrificial crisis in which violence becomes the inevitable result. . . . The violence will not end until some means is found to stop the erosion of values and the surge of hypocrisy that characterize France of 1939. (T. Jefferson Kline, *Unraveling French Cinema: From "L'Atalante" to "Caché"* [Malden, Mass.: Wiley-Blackwell, 2010], 52.)

What gives the film its edge, what makes the theatrical frivolity so culpable, is the lurking presence of death and war that is present from the moment the film takes us to La Colinière. Gunshots are heard from the neighbouring estate where a cull of rabbits is underway, a cull with sinister echoes for a France bounded by Nazi Germany and a Spain in the final stages of civil war. The gamekeeper, Schumacher, has a Germanic name, and a distinct willingness to use guns against people as well as animals . . . The posture of the dead Jurieu, executed in full flight, visually echoes the slaughter of the fleeing animals and further serves to equate the hunt's savagery with the human slaughter of war. (Martin O'Shaughnessy, *Jean Renoir* [Manchester: Manchester University Press, 2000], 148.)

Raw instincts, physical strength, and willpower . . . combined with the now corrupt and degenerate remains of the old society, are what make for the world of *The Rules of the Game*, a world so clearly on the brink of an abyss. There is little doubt that Renoir's films reflected the increasing bewilderment in 1930s France over the nature of the anticipated next war. (69 in Omer Bartov, "Martyrs' Vengeance: Memory, Trauma, and Fear of War in France, 1918-1940," in Joel Blatt, ed., *The French Defeat of 1940: Reassessments* [1998; London: Berghahn Books, 2006], 54-84.)

'People who commit suicide do not care to do it in front of witnesses,' Renoir . . . wrote in explaining the reaction to *La Règle du jeu*, echoing Carné's charge against audiences who blame cinematic barometers. After being obsessed for so long with male weakness, many in France finally banished anxiety—committed suicide—by relinquishing responsibility and turning their fates over to authoritarian leaders, first the French military and then

Pétain. Temporarily bolstered by the 1939 call to arms, they banished images of weakness, only to experience the return of their self-doubts when the Germans penetrated their Maginot defenses. Perhaps in 1940 they experienced a momentary relief in having their worst fears realized and in surrendering . . . to the seemingly inevitable shadows. However, those films that had barometrically foretold the surrender, like *Quai des brumes* and *Règle du jeu*, had to be banned as humiliating witnesses." (50-51 in Robin Bates, "Audiences on the Verge of a Fascist Breakdown: Male Anxieties and Late 1930s French Film," *Cinema Journal*, 36.3 [Spring 1997], 25-55.)

Now the order of the film would tend to imply that the illegalisms practiced by the aristocracy (most obviously, adultery) amount to a waste of time when the nation would better be readying itself against armed, trigger-happy enemies stationed near the border of Alsace-Lorraine; that the week spent at the château is tantamount to the French Sitzkrieg at the moment when Nazi Germany was about to launch its Blitzkrieg. (103 in Tom Conley, "The Laws of the Game: Jean Renoir, *La Règle du jeu*," in John Denvir, ed., *Legal Reelism: Movies as Legal Texts* [Urbana: University of Illinois Press, 1996], 96-117.)

The Rules of the Game, made on the very eve of World War II, exposes how far the disintegration of French social life had gone. It is a unique historical document, one which dissects the spirit of a people already defeated internally and merely awaiting the end at the hand of an external executioner. (267 in Charles William Brooks, "Jean Renoir's *The Rules of the Game*," *French Historical Studies*, 7.2 [Autumn 1971], 264-283.)

[11] The theatrical origins of *La Règle du jeu* have been widely documented. Here is a sampling of places: Keith Reader,*"La Règle du jeu": Jean Renoir, 1939* (London: I. B. Tauris, 2010), 2; Martin O'Shaugnessy, *Jean Renoir* (Manchester: Manchester University Press, 2000), 146-147; Ronald Bergan, *Jean Renoir: Projections of Paradise* (Woodstock, N.Y.: Overlook Press), 197, 204; Celia Bertin, *Jean Renoir: A Life in Pictures*, trans. Mireille and Leonard Muellner (1986; Baltimore: Johns Hopkins University Press, 1991), 157, 162; Alexander Sesonske, *Jean Renoir: The French Films, 1924-1939* (Cambridge, Mass.: Harvard University Press, 1980), 390-391; Raymond Durgnat, *Jean Renoir* (Berkeley: University of California Press, 1974),192. Gilberto Pérez is worth quoting at length on the subject:

> It may seem surprising that a film so lively and delightful, a comedy of love in society that calls to mind Marivaux and Beaumarchais—and Beaumarchais's musical refashioner, Mozart—

should have met with so hostile a response from the public. But *The Rules of the Game* is a tragedy cast in the form of a comedy. . . . The portrayal of the upper class in *The Rules of the Game* employs the form of classical comedy with an irony grown mordant, devastating, despairing. Tragedy is traditionally the form of singularity, comedy the form of community. *The Rules of the Game* is a tragedy of community. Its fatality resides not in the singular individual, the hero with a tragic flaw—its characters have the flaws of common humanity, the flaws of comedy—but in the order of a society that does violence to nature and human nature, a society that fails to accommodate its individuals into a sustaining community. . . . *The Rules of the Game* enacts the tragedy of a society no longer capable of comedy. (*The Material Ghost: Films and Their Medium* [Baltimore: Johns Hopkins University Press, 2000], 198.)

[12] Renoir's most celebrated stylistic hallmark was just such an ingestion into cinematic syntax of theatrical "place," composition, and—as possible—duration: the combination, that is, of the flow of cinema with the relationships within a frame that are standard practice in the theater. The basis of this style is deep-focus shooting combined with the "sequence shot"—i.e., the shot that contains a sequence of action. In the deep-focus approach, the reliance is on the content of any one shot, rather than on a succession of shots as in montage. The shot is held and people may come in or leave; the camera itself may move (as Renoir's often adroitly does): it's the absence of cutting that makes the difference, the exploitation of different planes of depth within one shot to make the film progress, rather than the addition of new views.

Renoir didn't invent this idea—you can see the conscious, deliberate use of it in Edwin S. Porter's *The Great Train Robbery* (1903) in the scene where the posse captures the bandits—but he used it as a principle, a reaction against the principle of montage that had been dominant since D. W. Griffith (who was quickly followed in this approach by Eisenstein and Pudovkin). To many, the idea of composition in depth was a philosophical position. André Bazin, who *mutatis mutandis* was Aristotle to Renoir's Sophocles, said that such a cinematic style was capable of expressing everything without fragmenting the world, of revealing the hidden meaning in people, places, and things without disturbing the unity natural to them. (Montage, by contrast, relies on joining bits and pieces of film together in rhythmic and pictorial relationships so that an effect is created out of the very way the pieces are joined, an effect additional to the effects of the separate bits unto themselves.)

Renoir's own rationale for his camera style was his belief in the primacy of the actor as focus of cinematic interest and source of inspiration. My view is that Renoir was at least partially motivated by sheer confidence, in himself and in film. He felt that the (still-young) film medium no longer needed to prove its selfhood by relying so heavily on a technique that no other art could employ. The cinema could now be sure enough of itself to translate into its own language a lexicon from another art, the theater. Indeed, Renoir went on to include literal theatrical imagery in his films, from *La Chienne* (adapted from the play by André Mouézy-Eon) in 1931 to his last one, which was actually titled *The Little Theatre of Jean Renoir*. And, in the 1950s, he directed three plays, Shakespeare's *Julius Caesar*, a comedy of his own, and Odets's *The Big Knife*. (The world première of his play *Carola*, directed by Renoir, took place in 1960 at the University of California, Berkeley.)

It is mainly because of his theater-in-film style (though there are other reasons) that Renoir had such an enormous influence on subsequent filmmakers: the Italian neorealists (perhaps above all Luchino Visconti, who had worked as Renoir's assistant on *Toni* [1935] and several other pictures), Orson Welles, Satyajit Ray, and François Truffaut, to name a few outstanding examples.

[13] The argument over Renoir's *oeuvre* frequently takes on such a political dimension. Many of those disappointed by the later films—from 1940 onwards—ascribe his decline (as they see it) to an abdication from political commitment. Indeed, there are those who feel that with his departure for America in 1940 Renoir's career went into a decline from which, despite some fine moments, it never really recovered. For just as many critics, on the other hand, the late films are no less great than the earlier ones, merely different: masterworks of pantheistic humanism produced by a supreme moviemaker mellowing into tranquil, autumnal richness. The love of life, the sense of nature, the texture and density of the earlier pictures remain, but the concern with transient social objectives is transmuted into an all-embracing affirmation, a belief in art as an expression of the ultimate harmony of existence.

Conversely, there are those who have tried to play down or explain away the polemical content of the pre-war pictures, suggesting that *The Crime of Monsieur Lange*, with its popular Front characterizations (Renoir was involved in French Communist Party activities during the mid-1930s), smells altogether too strongly of the poetic realism of Jacques Prévert, or that Renoir, tolerant and obliging as ever, made *The People of France* (1936) mainly to gratify his friends. Ultimately, though, as in the especial case of *La Règle du jeu*, debate over Renoir's "true" political views may be beside the point. If the aspirations of the Popular Front lend an added bite and immediacy to Renoir's films of the period, they hardly account for the consistent richness and vitality of his total output, even less for its curiously pervasive melancholy. Even overtly optimistic pictures such as *M. Lange* and *French Cancan* (1955) are tinged with poignancy, while sadness suffuses the comedy in *La Règle du jeu* as well as *The Elusive Corporal* (1962).

It is this complex of conflicting emotions—of ambiguities, tensions, and uncertainties—underlying all his work that makes the earlier pictures so rewarding on each re-viewing, and which redeems the later ones from triteness. From the innate contradictions within his psyche, then, Renoir created movies that, despite (or even because of) their weaknesses, seem to breathe life. Without a doubt, few other directors have succeeded in conveying so intensely a sense of messy, turbulent, unstructured reality in the cinema. Perhaps this is because of still another paradox or tension in Renoir's aesthetic self: for he was the prime exponent on film of unanism, the poetic movement in early twentieth-century France that reacted against art for art's sake and sought its sources in the lived life around it—yet without returning to pseudo-scientific naturalism and without any attempt at overt "political significance." In fact, one could argue that, had Renoir felt more secure in his political beliefs, his films would have been the worse for it.

[14] See, for example, Jack C. Ellis, *A History of Film* (Englewood Cliffs, New Jersey: Prentice-Hall, 1979), 88-89; Leo Braudy and Morris Dickstein, eds., *Great Film Directors: A Critical Anthology* (New York: Oxford University Press, 1978), 209; Paul Schrader, 114-115; Tom Milne, *The Cinema of Carl Dreyer* (New York: A. S. Barnes, 1971), 12-15; and Ray Carney, *Speaking the Language of Desire: The Films of Carl Dreyer* (New York: Cambridge University Press, 1989), chapter on *Day of Wrath*.

[15] Those that do speak of tragic intentions on Dreyer's part, do so only in passing, like Milne (13), or in vague terms, like Jean-Louis Cornolli as quoted by Mark Nash in *Dreyer* (London: British Film Institute, 1977), 58-59.

[16] David Bordwell seems to support my view here when he writes:

> The film, set during the worst years of the European witch-hunts, relies on a general historical awareness of the Church's persecution of witches.... But what is significant is that at crucial points Dreyer's film refuses to define a position with respect to the historical phenonenon of witchcraft. Gone is most of the paraphernalia of traditional witch-lore: the witch's ability to confound neighbors, the witches' sabbath, etc. Although the apparatus of Church repression is well summarized in Laurentius's interrogation, the film remains silent about the various causes which historians have proposed for the witch-craze (religious strife, the rise of the medical profession, the retention of pagan religious customs). (125-126)

[17] Bert O. States on dramatic flaw is worth quoting at length again. My ideas here and some of my language come from the following:

> What we notice about the great tragic heroes is that their truly dramatic flaws are not such as to worsen their characters in the moral sense, but to make them ambiguously fallible. We would not, therefore, emphasize the fact in Sophocles' version Oedipus' temper hastens his doom, but that it rescues him from perfection in the process of being doomed. . . . Here, perhaps, is the true sense of Aristotle's own idea: to mark the excellent and flawless man for destruction, or conversely the utterly bad man, is to make a statement that is less complete, less *infinite*, than to mark for destruction the median man who simultaneously deserves it (but not quite), yet does not deserve it (but not quite). (53-54)

[18] David Bordwell notes Dreyer's "systematic changes of camera orientation" (124) and the discontinuity that results from such changes, and even documents Dreyer's need to reorient the audience to the action through the use of long shots (121). Yet he concludes the opposite of what I do: that Dreyer is seeking only to produce varied shot patterns for their own sake (121), and that in fact Dreyer is unifying space by separatng it into its component parts, which the audience will then naturally join together (124).

[19] See, for example, Warshow, 265-266; and Braudy and Dickstein, 209.

Index

Abouna, 234-239, 394-395
Abraham Lincoln, 13
Abruzzi, Giorgio, 276
Absurdism, 162, 221
Abu-Assad, Hany, 178
Academy of Motion Picture Arts and Sciences, 13, 96-97, 146, 309, 332
Accident, 24
Acropolis, 132
The Adventures of Dollie, 13
Aeschylus, 132
Les Affaires publiques, 68
After the Rehearsal, 252
The Age of Innocence, 350
Agee, James, 39, 108, 243-244, 313, 369
Agit-prop, 327
Aguid, Hamza Moctar, 239
Airport, 11
Aitken, Harry, 13
Akhadov, Valery, 146
Alexandra, 88
Alice's Restaurant, xiii
Aliyev, Arif, 87
All About Anna, 169
All about My Mother, 250
All My Sons, 243
Allen, Dede, 366
Allende, Salvador, 333

Almodóvar, Pedro, 250-251
Alsino, 333
Alsino and the Condor, 332-336, 401
Altman, Robert, 358-360
Amarcord, 370-371
Amelio, Gianni, 139
American Buffalo, 30, 38
An American Romance, 50
American film, xi-xiii, 157-158
Le amiche: see *The Girlfriends*
Anatomy of Hell, 169, 252
And God Created Woman, 219
And Quiet Rolls the Dawn, 327
Anderson, Lindsay, 49, 252, 312
Angelopoulos, Theo, 173
Angels of the Streets: see *Les Anges du péché*
Angels with Dirty Faces, 351
Les Anges du péché, 63, 65, 68
The Angry Silence, 49
Anne Pedersdotter, 324
Ann-Margret, 345
Antares, 169
Antonioni, Michelangelo, 66, 167, 182, 241, 276-282
Appia, Adolphe, 125-126, 129
The Apple, 139, 151
Aragon, Louis, 163, 168
Aranovich, Semen, 141
L'Argent, 63-68, 83, 384

Aristotle, 10, 12, 409, 412
Armstrong, Louis, 92
Arnheim, Rudolf, 82
Assadi, Shahriar, 153
Atsumi, Kiyoshi, 263
Attal, Yvan, 252
Au hasard, Balthazar, 63, 68
Austen, Jane, 208
Auterism, ix, 23, 87, 192, 195, 229, 251, 252, 259, 263, 265, 267, 285
Avant-gardism, 161-162
L'avventura, 167, 276-277, 279
Ayfre, Amédée, 406

Baba, Masuru, 263
Babenco, Hector, 139
Bach, Johann Sebastian, 77, 131
Back to the Future, 372
The Bad and Happy Lot of Art after World War II, 123
Bad Education, 250-251, 396
The Bad News Bears Go to Japan, 354
Badlands, xiii, 362-364, 404
Baise-moi, 169
Bakunin, Mikhail, 406
Balabanov, Aleksei, 88, 96
The Ballad of Narayama, 265, 267
Ballad of a Soldier, 96
Bang the Drum Slowly, 353-357, 402-403
Bankolé, Isaach de, 247
Banks, Leslie, 46
Bardot, Brigitte, 219
Barstow, Stan, 300
Bates, Alan, 301
Battle in Heaven, 169-177, 182, 389
Bayreuth Festspielhaus, 124, 128-129
Baz, Tina, 217
Bazin, André, 46, 82, 369, 409
Beatty, Warren, 358
Beaumarchais (Pierre-Augustin Caron), 287, 289, 293-294, 408
Beauty and the Beast, 244
Beckerman, Bernard, 6
Beckett, Samuel, 200
Behraznia, Mahmoud, 246
Belle de jour, 171
Bellocchio, Marco, 169, 178
Belushi, John, 185
Benigni, Roberto, 159
Benjamin, 77
Benjamin, Walter, 233, 369-370
Benoît-Lévy, Jean, 140
Bentley, Eric, 4, 124
Beresford, Bruce, 187
Bergen, Candace, 345-346
Berggren, Thommy, 341
Bergman, Ingmar, 129, 201-202, 252, 280-281, 343
Bergmark, Jörgen, 197
Berliner Ensemble, 121
Bernanos, Georges, 63
Bertin, Celia, 286, 288
Bertolucci, Bernardo, 221, 241
Besson, Luc, 253
Besson, Philippe, 202-203
The Best Years of Our Lives, 23
Betrayal, 24-29, 382
Betty Blue, 219
Beyond the Horizon, 11
The Bible, 109
Bicycle Thieves, 139, 239
The Big Knife, 410
Billy Liar, 299, 303-308, 311-312, 399
The Birth of a Nation, 3, 11-14
Biru, Abraham Haile, 238
Black Rain, 267
Blackboards, 150
Bloom, John, 28
Blunt, Emily, 226
Bock, Audie, 259
Bodrov, Sergei, 87-98
Bodrov, Sergei, Jr., 95-96

Body Heat, 218
Boetticher, Budd, 186
Bogarde, Dirk, 309
Bogdanovich, Peter, 346-350, 354, 369
Bonnie and Clyde, xiii, 186-187, 364
Boogie Nights, 38
Boomerang!, 244
Border Street, 159
Bordwell, David, 313, 412
Borgnine, Ernest, 184
Bottoms, Timothy, 348-349, 372
Boudu Saved from Drowning, 286
Brady, William A., 3, 6-7, 9, 11
Braine, John, 49, 51, 57, 303
Branagh, Kenneth, 39-47
Brando, Marlon, 185
Breakheart Pass, 187
Brecht, Bertolt, 121-122, 128, 132, 246
Breillat, Catherine, 169, 252-254
Bresson, Robert, x, 63-85, 176, 405-406
Brewster McCloud, 360
Brezhnev, Leonid, 147
The Bridesmaid, 227-231, 394
Bridges, Jeff, 348
Brinton, Ralph, 57
Brokeback Mountain, 191-196, 391
Bronson, Charles, 187
Brook, Peter, 369
Brother, 88, 96
The Brown Bunny, 169
Brueghel, Pieter, 259
Buchanan Rides Alone, 186
Büchner, Georg, vii, 30
Buffon, Geoges Louis Leclerc, Comte de, 64
Buñuel, Luis, 139, 276
Burns, Catherine, 357
Burnt by the Sun, 96
Burov, Alexander, 141

Burstyn, Ellen, 349
Bury, John, 27
Butch Cassidy and the Sundance Kid, 185
Bye-Bye Africa, 234

Cahiers du cinéma, 285
Calmeyer, Joachim, 201
Cameron, James, 195
Campillo, Robin, 228
Cannes Film Festival, 96, 267
Cantet, Laurent, 227-228
Caravaca, Eric, 203
The Caretaker, 24
Cargol, Jean-Pierre, 335
Carnal Knowledge, 343-346, 350, 368, 401-402
Carné, Marcel, 285, 407
Carola, 410
Cartier-Bresson, Henri, 311
The Case Is Closed, 327-332, 336, 400-401
Casino, 353
Castelo, Joseph, 178
Castle Freak, 36
Cat Ballou, 185
Catch-22, 346
The Cat's Meow, 346
Cave, Nick, 190
Central Station, 146
César, 285
Chabrol, Claude, 229-231
Chamas, Mohammed, 239
Chamber plays: see Kammerspiele
Chamberlain, Neville, 106
Chanel, Coco, 276
The Changeling, 132
Changing Lanes, 208
Chaplin, Charles, 13, 229, 235, 243
The Checkpoint, 88
Chéreau, Patrice, 201-207
La Chienne, 410

416 Index

Children of Divorce, 151
The Children of Heaven, 151
Chimes at Midnight, 44
Chocolat, 247
Chowdhury, Ramapada, 328
Christie, Agatha, 187
Christie, Julie, 305-306, 308, 310-311, 359
A Christmas Mystery, 141
Chronicle of a Summer, 276
Chukhrai, Grigori, 96
Chukhrai, Pavel, 147
The Chumscrubber, 221
Cinderella Man, 226
Cinémathèque française, 68
Citizen Kane, 343
Clair, René, 244, 285
Clandestine in Chile, 335
Clarke, Arthur C., 366
Clayton, Jack, 49-61, 303
Clément, René, 139
Clever, Edith, 123, 128, 131-132, 134
Clift, Montgomery, 339
Cloquet, Ghislain, 82
Close My Eyes, 207
Closely Watched Trains, 357
The Clowns, 252
Cocteau, Jean, 244
Cohen, Leonard, 360
Coiner, Miles, 324
Colin, Grégoire, 252
Colonel Redl, 160
The Color of Paradise, 151
Comedy, 28-29, 31, 38, 40, 68, 112-114, 158, 167, 192, 197, 200, 212, 223, 250, 252-254, 275, 287, 289-290, 295, 354, 408-411
The Comfort of Strangers, 24, 208
Un Condamné à mort s'est échappé, 63, 65

The Confessions of Winifred Wagner, 121, 123-124
Congreve, William, 28
Conrad, Joseph, 204-206
Considine, Paddy, 226
Contempt, 276
The Conversation, xiii
Coop, Denys, 301
Cooper, Gary, 187
Coppola, Francis Ford, 351
Corneille, Pierre, 289
Cornolli, Jean-Louis, 411
The Counterfeit Note, 63, 67
Couperin, François, 293
Courtenay, Tom, 305
The Covered Wagon, 183
Craig, Daniel, 211
Crime and Punishment, 63, 73
The Crime of Monsieur Lange, 410-411
Cross, Helen, 220, 224
Crossfire, 244
Crouching Tiger, Hidden Dragon, 192
Cubism, 274
Cui, César, 88
Currie, Finlay, 306
Currier, Nathaniel, 4
Cuthbertson, Allan, 57

Dagon, 36
Dalio, Marcel, 288
Daly, John, 215, 219
Les Dames du Bois de Boulogne, 63
Dangerous Liaisons, 113-118, 386
Danton's Death, vii
Daou, Vanessa, 219
Dardenne, Jean-Pierre, 68, 145
Dardenne, Luc, 68, 145
Dark Habits, 250
Darling, 299, 307-312, 399-400
Das Gupta, Dehapratim, 331
Davies, Terence, 50, 303

Davis, Bette, 19-24
Davison, Bruce, 357
Day for Night, 252
Day Night Day Night, 178-182, 389-390
The Day of the Locust, 299, 311
The Day a Pig Fell into the Well, 163
Day of Wrath, 313-326, 400, 411-412
The Dead, 108-113, 385-386
The Deadly Companions, 184
Dean, James, 364
Dearden, James, 211
Death by Hanging, 259
Death of a Salesman, 17, 111
De Chirico, Giorgio, 274
Degermark, Pia, 341
Delaney, Shelagh, 49
Delhomme, Benoît, 190-191
Delon, Alain, 277
De Niro, Robert, 350, 352-353, 357
Denis, Claire, 247
De Santis, Pasqualino, 67
De Sica, Vittorio, 243, 335
Devil in the Flesh, 169
Le Diable probablement, 63, 69
Diamond, I. A. L., 272
Diary of a Country Priest: see *Journal d'un curé de campagne*
Diary of a Shinjuku Thief, 259
DiCillo, Tom, 252
Dickens, Charles, vii-viii, 8, 99, 144-145
Diderot, Denis, 63
Dietrich, Marlene, 278
Directors' Guild of America, 13
Djomeh, 244-246, 395
Dmytryk, Edward, 244
Dog Days, 169
La dolce vita, 309, 311
La donna lupo, 169
Dostoevsky, Fyodor, 63, 69-82, 405
Doueiri, Ziad, 150, 214-221

Down in the Valley, 187-189, 196, 390
Doyle, Patrick, 43
Dream Street, 13
The Dreamers, 221
Dreyer, Carl Theodor, 281, 313-326, 411-412
Dubliners, 108
Dulac, Germaine, 73
Durand, Jacques, 406
Dutt, Anjan, 331-332
Duvalier, Jean-Claude ("Baby Doc"), 228
Duvivier, Julien, 285

Early Summer, 258
Eastwood, Clint, 185-186
Easy Rider, xiii, 11
Eat Drink Man Woman, 192
Ebrahim, Soran, 156
Eclipse: see *L'eclisse*
L'eclisse, x, 276-282, 398
Edinburgh Film Festival, 225
Edison, Thomas, 252
Edmond, 29-39, 382-383
The Eel, 260, 267
8½, 99, 252
Eijanaika, 265
Eisenstein, Sergei, vii-viii, 12, 82, 99, 244, 409
Eliot, T. S., 99, 370
The Elusive Corporal, 411
Elvira Madigan, 340-343, 368, 401
Emerson, Ralph Waldo, 178
Endgame, 200
Enduring Love, 197, 208-212, 392-393
Enemies, 213
L'Enfant, 145
The Entertainer, 301
Entomological Chronicles of Japan: see *Insect Woman*
Esquivel, Alan, 335

Eternal Sunshine of the Spotless Mind, 161
Euripides, 316
Europa, Europa, 159
Existentialism, 35, 69, 83, 131, 162, 175, 339
Expressionism, 29-30, 37-38
The Exterminating Angel, 276
Eye for an Eye, 299

Facing Windows, 239-242, 395
Fairbanks, Douglas, 13
Faithful, Marianne, 203
The Falcon and the Snowman, 312
La Fanciulla del West, 187
Fanny, 285
Far from the Madding Crowd, 312
Farber, Manny, 338
Farce, ix, 289, 295
The Farewell, 246
Fargo, 38
Fassbinder, Rainer Werner, 121
Fatal Attraction, 211
Fateless, 159-161, 182, 388-389
Fathers and Sons, 406
Faulkner, Christopher, 287
Feiffer, Jules, 343-345
Fellini, Federico, 99, 252, 309, 311, 370-371
Une Femme douce, 69-82, 384, 405-406
La Femme Nikita, 253
Feydeau, Georges, 289
Feyder, Jacques, 285
Field, Shirley Anne, 302
Filles et Gangsters: see *Pigs and Battleships*
La finestra di fronte: see *Facing Windows*
A Fistful of Dollars, 186
Five Easy Pieces, xiii
The Flavor of Green Tea over Rice, 258

Flynn, Errol, 96
Fonda, Henry, 23
Fonda, Jane, 196, 360
Fonda, Peter, 196
A Fool and A Girl, 12
For a Few Dollars More, 186
Forbes, Bryan, 49
Forbidden Games, 139
Ford, Aleksander, 159
Ford, John, 186, 244, 346-347
Formalism, ix, 74, 332
Fowles, John, 24
Francis, Freddie, 56-57
Frangin, Guy, 75
Frears, Stephen, 113-118
Freedom Is Paradise, 88
Freeman, Morgan, 186
Freeze. Die. Come to Life., 139
French Cancan, 411
The French Lieutenant's Woman, 24
Freud, Sigmund, 124, 128, 223
From Beyond, 36
From Here to Eternity, 213
From Morn to Midnight, 30-31, 33, 35
The Fugitive, 244

Gaborit, Jean, 406
Gabrielle, 204-207, 212, 392
Gagarin, Yuri, 148
Gallo, Vincent, 169
Gans, Sharon, 366
Garfunkel, Art, 345
Gautier, Eric, 203, 206
Gédigier, François, 203
Geller, Stephen, 365-366
Genèse, 63
Genêt, Jean, 34
A Gentle Creature: see *Une Femme douce*
A Gentle Spirit: see *Une Femme douce*

Germany, Year Zero, 139, 150
Germi, Pietro, 241
Gesamtkunstwerk (total work of art), 123
Ghobadi, Bahman, 150-156, 335
Ghost Dog, 247
Giant, 347
Gill, André, 127
Giller, Boris, 87
Giocante, Vahina, 219
The Girl of the Golden West: see *La Fanciulla del West*
The Girlfriends, 279
Girotti, Massimo, 241-242
Gish, Lillian, 278
Giulia, 169
Glengarry Glen Ross, 29-30
The Glittering Prizes, 312
The Go-Between, 24, 100, 308
"God Sees the Truth, But Waits," 95
Godard, Jean-Luc, 68, 257, 276, 278-279
The Godfather, 351
Goethe, Johann Wolfgang von, 75, 131-132
Gogol, Nikolai, 69
Goin' South, 185
Goldberg, Reiner, 127
Golden Age (Japanese), 259
Gondry, Michel, 161-162
The Good, the Bad, and the Ugly, 186
Good Morning, Night, 178
Goodbye Dragon Inn, 248-250, 396
GoodFellas, 350
Gordon, Stuart, 32, 36-37
Gorky, Maxim, 132
The Gospel of John, 158
The Graduate, xiii, 346
Grainer, Ron, 301
La Grande illusion, 286, 288, 294
Grant, Hugh, 212

Granville-Barker, Harley, 39
Gray, Simon, 28
Great Expectations, 244
The Great Train Robbery, 183, 409
Green, Guy, 49
The Greenhouse, 146
Greggory, Pascal, 206-207
Griffies, Ethel, 306
Griffith, D. W., vii-viii, xi, 3-15, 82, 122, 278, 409
Grismer, Joseph R., 3, 6-7, 9, 11
Grotowski, Jerzy, 132
Guardami, 169
Guess Who's Coming to Dinner, 220
The Gunfighter, 183, 187
Gyllenhaal, Jake, 195

Hackett, James K., 12
La Haine, 214
Half Moon, 152
Hall, Peter, 27
Hall, Willis, 300-301, 303, 306
Hamer, Bent, 197-201
Hamlet, 31, 46, 60, 77, 132, 201
Hammerstein, Oscar, 360
Hampton, Christopher, 113-118
Hancock, John, 353-357
Handke, Peter, 132
Hang 'Em High, 186
Haroun, Mahamat-Saleh, 234-239, 242
Harris, Mark, 356-357
Hartley, L. P., 24
Harvey, Anthony, 207
Harvey, Laurence, 309
Hatred: see *La Haine*
Hauff, Reinhard, 332
Haugland, Aage, 128
Hawks, Howard, 346, 348
Heading South, 227-228, 394
The Heat of the Day, 100
Heavenly Creatures, 221

Heidegger, Martin, 131
Heine, Heinrich, 131
Hellman, Lillian, 4, 19-42
Henry: Portrait of a Serial Killer, 267
Henry IV, Part 1, 41-43
Henry IV, Part 2, 41-42
Henry V, 39-47, 383
Henry VI, 42
Hepburn, Katharine, 219
Here's Your Life, 357-358
Hernández, Marcos, 177
Herrmann, Bernard, 208
Hershey, Barbara, 357
Herzen, Alexander, 69
Herzog, Werner, 247
Hidari, Sachiko, 261
High Noon, 183
Hill, George Roy, 364-366
Hillcoat, John, 189-192
Hippolytus, 316
Hird, Thora, 302
The Hired Hand, xiii, 196
Hirohito, Emperor, 259
Hiroshima, mon amour, 271
Historical epic, ix
Hitchcock, Alfred, 175, 346
Hitler, A Film from Germany: see *Our Hitler*
Hitler, Adolf, 100, 104, 106, 121-124, 159, 287
Holden, William, 184
Hölderlin, Friedrich, 131
Holland, Agnieszka, 159
Hollywood, xi-xii, 14, 69, 157, 169, 177, 188, 213, 220, 226, 234, 239, 243-244, 246, 286, 347, 358, 360, 365
The Holy Girl, 221
The Homecoming, 24
Hong, Sang-soo, 161-168, 170
Honky Tonk Freeway, 299
Horace, 336

Horwitz, Andy, 37
House of Fools, 88
House of Games, 4, 37-38
Hugo, Victor, 69
Hulk, 192
Hunter, Evan, 357
Huppert, Isabelle, 206-207
Hurt, John, 190
Hussein, Saddam, 152-153, 156
Huston, Anjelica, 112
Huston, John, 108-113, 369
Hyeon-gu, Kim, 168

I Stand Alone, 169
I Wanted to See Angels, 88-89
Ibsen, Henrik, 10, 124, 132, 204, 243
The Ice Storm, 192
Ichikawa, Jun, 161-162
The Idiot, 63, 73
The Idiots, 169
Ifans, Rhys, 212
Imamura, Shohei, 257-269
In America, 226
In the Cut, 169
In the Realm of the Senses, 169
In Search of Unreturned Soldiers, 262
Ince, Thomas, 13
Insect Woman, 260-261
Intimacy, 169, 201
Intolerance, 3, 12-13, 122
Irony and Drama: A Poetics, 315
Ishiguro, Kazuo, 100-108
Isn't Life Wonderful?, 13
It All Started Here, 139
The Italian, 139-150, 328, 388
It's a Wonderful Life, 371-372
Itskov, Yuri, 142
Ivan the Terrible, 244
Ivashev, Vladimir, 96
Ives, James Merritt, 4
Ivory, James, 100-108

Jacobi, Derek, 46
Jackson, Peter, 221
Jacobson, David, 187-189
Jacubowska, Wanda, 159
La Jalousie, 271
Janni, Joseph, 307
Jansenism, 74
Japón, 170, 173, 176
The Jar,
Jarmusch, Jim, 235, 247
Jellicoe, Ann, 18
Jezebel, 22-23
Jhabvala, Ruth Prawer, 100-101, 104
Johnny Got His Gun, 372
Johnson, Ben, 349
Johnson, Samuel, 317
Johnston, Bobby, 37
Jones, David, 27-28
Jones, Henry Arthur, 204
Jones, James, 213
Jonson, Ben
Jordan, Armin, 128
Journal d'un curé de campagne, 63, 80-81
Joyce, James, 64, 99, 108-113, 275
The Judge and the Assassin, 206
Judith of Bethulia, 13
Julius Caesar, 410
July, Miranda, 161-162, 221

Kabale und Liebe, 132
Kael, Pauline, xii
Kafka, Franz, 220, 273
Kaiser, Georg, 30
The Kaleidoscope, 327, 331
Kammerspiele, 322
Kanevsky, Vitali, 139
Karayuki-san: The Making of a Prostitute, 262
Karina, Anna, 278-279
Karl May, 121

Karlovy Vary Film Festival, 96
Kassovitz, Matthieu, 214
Kataev, Valentin, 147, 149
Kauffmann, Stanley, 82
Kaul, Mani, 405
Kawashima, Yuzo, 258
Kazan, Elia, 50, 244
Keen, Pat, 302
Keitel, Harvey, 350, 352-353
Kelly, Anthony Paul, 6
Kemp, Philip, 286, 288
Kertész, Imre, 159-160
Khalil, Mounira, 239
Khotinenko, Vladimir, 88
Khouas, Mohammed, 219
Kiarostami, Abbas, 150, 173, 244-245
The Kid, 235
Kim, Ki-duk, 161-162
Kim, Toewoo, 168
A Kind of Loving, 299-304, 307, 310-312, 398-399
King Lear, 317-318, 320, 324-325
Kinoshita, Keisuke, 259, 267
Kitchen Stories, 197-201, 212, 391
Kleist, Heinrich von, 64, 131
The Knack, 18
Kneiffel, Alexander, 146
Koltai, Lajos, 160-161
Kolya, 96, 146
Konchalovsky, Andrei, 88
Kopple, Barbara, 50
Korczak, 159
Kraevsky, A. A., 69
Krapp's Last Tape, 200
Kravchuk, Andrei, 139-150, 327-328
Kruger, Franz, 150
Kuld, Rudolf, 145
Kundun, 350
Kurosawa, Akira, 186
Kuznetsova, Maria, 142

Laada, 236
Laclos, Choderlos de, 113-118
The Lady without Camelias, 279
Laferrière, Dany, 228
Łagodna, 405
Lakeboat, 37
Lancelot du Lac, 63
Landru, 229
Landscape, 25
Lanzmann, Claude, 158-159
Lanzoni, Rémi Fournier, 286
Lardner, Ring, 357
Last Days, 161
The Last Picture Show, 346-350, 354, 372, 402
Last Resort, 220-221, 226
The Last Stage, 159
Last Summer, 356-358, 403
Last Year at Marienbad, 271-276, 281-282, 397
Latif, Avaz, 156
Lawrence, D. H., 224, 299
Leachman, Cloris, 349
Lean, David, 244
Lebeshev, Pavel, 89
Leccia, Pierre, 230
Ledger, Heath, 195
Lee, Ang, 192-196
The Left-Handed Gun, 187
The Left-Handed Woman, 132
Leigh, Janet, 277
Leigh, Mike, 50, 221, 303
Lenczewski, Ryszard, 221, 223
Leone, Sergio, 186-187
Lermontov, Mikhail, 69, 88
Lesnikova, Darya, 143
Lesage, Alain-René, 69
Lester, Richard, 18
Les Liaisons dangereuses: see *Dangerous Liaisons*
Liebestod, 133
Lieh, Lo, 187

Life Is Beautiful, 159
Life Is Ours: see *La Vie est à nous*
The Lighthouse, 88
Lila Says, 214-221, 226-227, 393
Littin, Miguel, 332-336
Little Big Man, 184, 187
The Little Foxes, 4, 19-24, 381-382
The Little Theatre of Jean Renoir, 410
The Little Train Robbery, 183, 185
Living in Oblivion, 252
Lloyd, Robert, 128
Loach, Ken, 50, 221, 303
Loghmani, Ali, 245
Loktev, Julia, 179-181
The Loneliness of the Long Distance Runner, 49, 305
Look Back in Anger, 49, 300
"The Love Song of J. Alfred Prufrock," 99
Lovecraft, H. P., 36
Ludwig II: Requiem for a Virgin King, 121, 128
Lulu, 201
Lynen, Robert, 239

Mac, 50
MacDonald, Dwight, xii
Machuel, Emmanuel, 67
MacLeish, Archibald, 274
Macmillan, Kenneth, 43-44
Macy, William H., 37-38
Madame Bovary, 206
Magimel, Benoît, 231
The Magnificent Ambersons, 347
The Magnificent Seven, 186
Mahajan, K. K., 331
Makhmalbaf, Samira, 139, 150
Malick, Terrence, 362-364
Malle, Louis, 68
Maloney, Denis, 37
Malory, Sir Thomas, 63
Malraux, André, 244

Index   423

The Maltese Falcon, 113
Mamet, David, 4, 29-39
Man About Town, 244
A Man Escaped: see *Un Condamné à mort s'est échappé*
A Man Vanishes, 259
Mann, Thomas, 124
Man's Hope, 244
Marathon Man, 312
Marius, 285
Marivaux, Pierre Carlet de Chamberlain, 287, 289, 408
Marooned in Iraq, 152
Márquez, Gabriel García, 335
The Marquise of O., 132
The Marriage of Figaro, 293
Marshall, Herbert, 19-24
Martel, Lucretia, 221
Marvin, Arthur, 13
Marx, Karl, 127
M*A*S*H, 360
Massari, Lea, 277
Mast, Gerald, 288
Matador, 250
La Maternelle, 140
Matewan, 50
Matisse, Henri, 11
Maugham, Robin, 24
Mayerling, 342
McCabe *and Mrs. Miller*, 185, 358-360, 403
McCann, Donal, 111-113
McCay, Brian, 359
McCoy, Horace, 360-362
McCrea, Joel, 184
McCutcheon, Wallace, 13
McEwan, Ian, 24, 208, 211
McMurtry, Larry, 192, 347
McNaughton, John, 267
Me and You and Everyone We Know, 161, 221
Mean Streets, 350-353, 357, 368, 402

Meet Pamela, 252
Mekhralieva, Susanna, 95
Melodrama, 3-15, 51, 54, 56, 60, 146, 178, 187, 217, 336, 351, 354, 362
Menshikov, Oleg, 96
Menzel, Jiri
Mephisto, 160
Mesquida, Roxane, 252
Messiaen, Olivier, 83
Metropolitan Opera (New York), 129
Meyerbeer, Giacomo, 131
Michell, Roger, 208-212
Middleton, Thomas, 132
Midnight Cowboy, xiii, 310, 312
Mifune, Toshiro, 187
Mikhalkov, Nikita, 96
Miles, Vera, 277
Mill, John Stuart, 69
Miller, Arthur, 243
Milne, Tom, 411
Minton, Yvonne, 128
Miracle in Milan, 335
The Miracle of the Bells, 243
The Mirror, 151
The Missouri Breaks, 185
Mizoguchi, Kenji, 259
Moby Dick, 109
Modernism, 82, 250, 277, 281, 333
Mohammed-Khani, Aida, 239
Moiseenko, Denis, 142
Molière (Jean-Baptiste Poquelin), 289
Moment of Impact, 179
Monsieur Verdoux, 229, 243
Monte Walsh, 184
Moriarty, Michael, 355-357
Moro, Aldo, 178
Morricone, Ennio, 186
Morton, Samantha, 212
Mosley, Nicholas, 24

The Mother, 208, 211
Mouchette, 63, 65, 68
Mouézy-Eon, André, 410
Moussa, Ahidjo Mahamat, 239
The Moviegoer, 339
Mozart, Wolfgang Amadeus, 129, 293-294, 342, 408
Much Ado about Nothing, 46
Munich, 178
Munk, Andrzej, 159
Murder on the Orient Express, 187
Muriel, 276
Murphy, Fred, 111
Museum of Modern Art (New York), 367
Mushkadiz, Anapola, 177
Music and the Art of the Theatre, 126
Musical comedy, ix
The Muslim, 88
Musset, Alfred de, 287, 289
My Last Move, 121
My Summer of Love, 220-227, 393
My Wife Is an Actress, 252

Nadjari, Raphaël, 405
Nagy, Marcel, 161
Nair, Mira, 139
Naruse, Mikio, 259
The Nation, 243
National Theatre (London), 25
The Natural, 354
Naturalism, 4, 30, 38, 50, 68-69, 182, 221, 267, 275, 302, 361, 411
Naughton, Edmund, 359
Nazar, 405
Nazari, Jalil, 246
New American Cinema, 337
New Cinema (British), 49
New German Cinema, 121
New Latin American Cinema, 333
New Novelists (France), 271
New Wave (French), 49, 68, 257, 285

New Wave (Japanese), 257-259
The Next Best Thing, 299
N'Garade, Diego Mustapha, 238
Nichols, Mike, 18, 343-346
Nicholson, Jack, 185, 345
Nietzsche, Friedrich, 35, 124, 127, 131, 223, 230
The Night (Syberberg), 122-123, 129-134, 387
Night and Fog, 158
Night and Fog in Japan, 259
Night on Earth, 247
Nihilism, 405-406
9 Songs, 169
No Man's Land, 24-25, 28
Nobody Knows, 155
Noises Off, 346
Non-Professionals, 88
Norma Rae, 50
Norström, Tomas, 201
North, Alex, 111
Northern Lights, 50
Norton, Edward, 189
Nostalgia, 68
Notes on Cinematography (Bresson), 82
La Notte (*The Night*, Antonioni), 276-278
Notting Hill, 208, 212
Novalis (Georg Philipp Friedrich Freiherr von Hardenberg), 131
Nuevo cine: see New Latin American Cinema

O Lucky Man, 252
Odd Man Out, 244
Odets, Clifford, 50, 299, 410
Oedipus Rex, 318, 325, 412
Øgaard, Philip, 197
Of Mice and Men, 356
Ogata, Ken, 265
Özpetek, Ferzan, 239-242

Old Times, 24-25
Oleanna, 37
Oliver Twist, 144
Olivier, Laurence, 39-46
Olmi, Ermanno, 357
Los Olvidados, 139
On the Occasion of Remembering the Turning Gate, 163
On the Waterfront, 50
Once Upon a Time in the West, 187
Ondricek, Miroslav, 366
O'Neill, Eugene, 11
The Oresteia, 132
Osborne, John, 49, 299
Oshima, Nagisa, 169, 257-259
Ossana, Diana, 192
Othello, 318, 325
Otomo, 246-247, 395-396
Ouédraogo, Idrissa, 235-236
Our Father: see *Abouna*
Our Hitler, 386-387, 121-124, 128, 130-131
Ozu, Yasujiro, 64, 258-259

Pacific Heights, 312
Pados, Gyula, 161
Pagnol, Marcel, 285
Palmer, Bert, 302
The Paper Chase, 372
Paradise Now, 178
Parker, Lottie Blair, 3, 6-7, 9, 11
Parillaud, Anne, 253
Paris Belongs to Us, 276
Parsifal, 123-134, 387
Pasolini, Pier Paolo, 241
The Passenger, 159
The Passion of the Christ, 158
The Passion of Joan of Arc, 313
Paterson, Neil, 51, 56
Pawlikowski, Pawel, 220-226
Pearce, Guy, 190
Peckinpah, Sam, 184, 190

Peer Gynt, 132, 201
Penhall, Joe, 208
Penn, Arthur, 187
The People of France, 410
Percy, Walker, 339
Perez, Gilberto, 408
Perrine, Valerie, 366
Perry, Eleanor, 357
Perry, Frank, 356-358
Persona, 202
Persson, Jörgen, 341
Persuasion, 208
"Persuasion," 211
Pétain, Philippe, 408
Phaedra, 201, 316
Phillpotts, Ambrosine, 57
Piaf, Edith, 223
The Pianist, 159
The Piano Teacher, 206, 231
Picasso, Pablo, 11, 274
Pickford, Mary, 13
Pickles, Wilfred, 306
Pickpocket, 63, 65, 68
Pierce-Roberts, Tony, 108
Pigs and Battleships, 260-261
Pinero, Arthur, 204
Pinochet, Augusto, 332
Pinter, Harold, 24-29, 100, 102, 208
Pippa Passes, 13
Pirandello, Luigi, 237, 251
Pixote, 139
Plato, 339, 367
Plato Cave Memory, 123
The Playwright as Thinker, 124
Poe, James, 361
Pohl, Klaus, 246
Poil de Carotte, 239
Polanski, Roman, 144, 159
Polax, 169
Poliakoff, Stephen, 207
Pollack, Sidney, 360-362
The Pornographers, 259-260, 262

Porter, Edwin S., 12, 409
Post, Ted, 186
Il Posto, 357
Powell, Michael, 225
The Power of Kangwon Province, 163
Prado, Pedro, 333
Press, Natalie, 226
Pretty Persuasion, 221
Prévert, Jacques, 410
Prieto, Rodrigo, 191
"Prisoner of the Caucasus," 87-98
Prisoner of the Mountains, 87-98, 385
Le Procès de Jeanne d'Arc, 63, 65
The Profound Desire of the Gods, 259, 261-262
The Proposition, 189-192, 196, 390-391
Proulx, Annie, 192, 194
Proust, Marcel, 25, 370
The Proust Screenplay, 25, 100
Psycho, 277
Puccini, Giacomo, 187
Pudovkin, Vsevolod, 409
Purcell, Henry, 77
Pushkin, Alexander, 69, 88

Quatre nuits d'un rêveur, 63
Queen Margot, 201

Racine, Jean, 316
Raging Bull, 350-351, 353
Rahman, Hiresh Feysal, 156
The Rain People, xiii
Rameau, Jean-Philippe, 293
Rampling, Charlotte, 228
Raphael (Raffaello Sanzio da Urbino), 67
Raphael, Frederic, 307, 309, 312
Rashomon, 163
Ray, Satyajit, 327, 410
Realism, 9, 12, 18-19, 27, 29, 37, 49, 51, 65, 68, 126, 139, 141, 146-147, 150-151, 167, 170, 176, 181-183, 221, 225, 249-250, 273, 275, 282, 300, 306, 312, 327, 331-333, 335, 344, 407, 410
Re-Animator, 36
The Red Badge of Courage, 108-109
Red Desert, 278-279
Red River, 339, 348
Red Sun, 187
Reed, Carol, 244
Reed, Donna, 213
La Règle du jeu, x, 285-297, 398, 406-411
Reisz, Karel, 49, 303, 312
The Remains of the Day, 100-108, 385
A Remembrance of Things Past, 25
Rendell, Ruth, 230
Renoir, Jean, 285-297, 406-411
Rescued from an Eagle's Nest, 12
Resnais, Alain, x, 158, 271-276, 279, 281-282
"The Return," 204
Reutov, Nikolai, 145
Reygadas, Carlos, 169-177
Richard II, 311
Richard III, 41-42
Richard's Things, 207
Richardson, Tony, 49, 301, 305, 311-312
Richter, Sviatoslav, 131
Ride the High Country, 183
Ride with the Devil, 192
Ring of the Nibelung, 124
Ritchie, June, 301-302
Ritt, Martin, 50
Rivette, Jacques, 257, 276
The Road to Rage: Chronicle of the Palestinian People: 335
Robbe-Grillet, Alain, 271-276
Rogozhkin, Alexander, 88
Rohmer, Éric, 132, 257-258
Roma, 252

Romance, ix, 31, 73, 102,105, 107, 184, 189, 192, 215, 217, 220, 224-225, 354, 361, 363
Romance, 169
Romanov, Andrei, 141, 146, 149
Romeo and Juliet, 17, 342
Romoli, Gianni, 239
Room at the Top, 49-61, 300, 303, 383-384
Rosebiani, Jano, 155
Rosetta, 68
Rossellini, Roberto, 150, 241
Rothko, Mark, 83
Rotunno, Giuseppe, 346
Rouch, Jean, 276
Rousseau, Jean-Jacques, 113
Rowley, William, 132
The Ruins, 327
Ruiz, Bertha, 177
The Rules of the Game: see *La Règle du jeu*
The Russian Ark, 142

Saakyan, Mariya, 88
Sacks, Michael, 366
Sade, Donatien Alphonse François, Marquis de, 113, 117
Saint Jack, 346
St. Petersburg Institute of Film and Television, 141
Saint-Saëns, Camille, 223
Saki, Ryuzo, 262-263
Salaam Bombay!, 139
Saleem, Hiner, 155
Samba Traoré, 236
Sams, Jeremy, 208
San Francisco, 13
Sanda, Dominique, 75
Sandino, 335
Sandino, Augusto Nicolás Calderón, 335
Santosh, Sivan, 178

Sarrazin, Michael, 360
Sarris, Andrew, xii
Satie, Erik, 11
Saturday Night and Sunday Morning, 49, 300-303
Sawhney, Nitin, 219
La Scala, 126
Schaubühne (West Berlin), 132
Schiller, Friedrich, 131-132
Schindler's List, 159, 161
Schlaich, Frieder, 246-247
Schlesinger, John, 299-312
Schoenberg, Arnold, 82
Schöne, Wolfgang, 128
Schrader, Paul, 68, 322, 325, 406
Schwarzenberger, Xaver, 130-131
Scorsese, Martin, 350-353
Scott, Randolph, 184
The Search, 243
"The Secret Life of Walter Mitty," 306
The Secret Life of Words, 308
Sen, Mrinal, 327-332, 336
Sennett, Mack, 13
Sense and Sensibility, 192, 195
Sesonke, Alexander, 287
The Servant, 24
The Seven Samurai, 186-187
Sex Is Comedy, 252-254, 396-397
Seyrig, Delphine, 276, 281
The Shade, 405
Shakespeare, William, 10, 39-47, 60, 69, 289, 315, 320, 325, 410
Shane, 347
Shankar, Mamata, 331-332
Shankar, Ravi, 331
Shaw, Bernard, 124-125
Sheen, Martin, 96, 362, 364
Shepherd, Cybill, 349
Sheridan, Richard Brinsley, 28
Shiang-chyi, Chen, 248
Shinoda, Masahiro, 257-258

Shoah, 158
Shoeshine, 139, 243
Shuvalova, Olga, 144
La signora senza camelie: see *The Lady without Camelias*
Silence, 25
Sillitoe, Alan, 49, 303, 305
Simon, John, 82
Singer, Isaac Bashevis, 213
Slaughterhouse-Five, 364-366, 404
Smet, Laura, 231
Sochi Kinotavr Film Festival, 96
Sokurov, Alexander, 88, 141-142
Soldier Blue, 184
Somoza, Anastasia, 332-335
The Son, 68, 145
The Son of the Regiment, 147
Son Frère, 201-204, 212, 392
Sophocles, 315, 325, 409, 412
La souriante Madame Beudet, 73
Spacek, Sissy, 362, 364
Spanglish, 220
Spielberg, Steven, 159, 178
Spiridonov, Kolya, 140
Stagecoach, 183
Staiola, Enzo, 239
Stampfer, J., 318, 320
States, Bert, 315, 318, 320, 412
Steinbeck, John, 356
Sternberg, Josef von, 278
Stevens, George, 347
Stockwell, Dean, 333
Stolen Children, 139
Stolen Desire, 261
Stone, Oliver, 178
Stoppard, Tom, 28
Storey, David, 49
Storm, Ole, 315
The Stranger, 187
Stranger than Paradise, 235
Strauss, Botho, 132
Stravinsky, Igor, 11

A Streetcar Named Desire, 111
The Struggle, 13
Sturges, John, 186
Summer Trip to the Seaside, 141
The Sun Legend of the Tokugawa Era, 258
Sunday Bloody Sunday, 312
Sung, Hyunan, 168
Surrealism, 68, 163, 273-274
Sverák, Jan, 96
"The Swan," 223
Syberberg, Hans-Jürgen, 121-136

A Tale of Cinema, 163
Tales from a Southern Isle: see *The Profound Desire of the Gods*
Tannhäuser, 124
Targets, 346
Tarkovsky, Andrei, 68
A Taste of Honey, 49, 300-301
Tate, Allen, 110
Taurus, 143
Tavener, John, 175
Tavernier, Bernard, 139
Taxi Driver, 187, 189
Taylor, Elizabeth, 345
The Tempest, 131
Ten Days in Calcutta: A Portrait of Mrinal Sen, 332
Tender Mercies, 187
The Terrorist, 178-179
Tessier, Max, 260
Thatcher, Margaret, 303
They Shoot Horses, Don't They?, 360-362, 404
The Thief, 147
This Man Must Die, 229
This Sporting Life, 49
Thomas, Richard, 357
Thompson, Emma, 195, 219
Thompson, Robert E., 361
Thoreau, Henry David, 302

Index   429

Three Evenings: see *Trois Soirées*
3-Iron, 161
Thurber, James, 306
A Time for Drunken Horses, 152
Time Out, 227-228
Titanic, 195
To Live in Peace, 244
Todeschini, Bruno, 203
Tokyo Story, 258
Toland, Gregg, 21-22
Tolstoy, Leo, 63-69, 87-98
Toni, 410
Tony Takitani, 161
Tora-san (or *Otoko wa Tsurai yo!*), 263
Torquato Tasso, 132
Toscanini, Arturo, 126
Touch of Evil, 347
Touré, Ali Farka, 238
Touré, Drissa, 236
A Town of Love and Hope, 259
Tragedy, ix, 3, 18-19, 39, 53-56, 59-60, 113, 124, 163, 194-195, 217, 224, 246, 290, 295, 313-325, 407, 409, 411-412
Tragicomedy, 105, 221, 235
Transcendentalism, 68, 74
Treliński, Mariusz, 405
The Trial of Joan of Arc: see *Le Procès de Jeanne d'Arc*
Tristan and Isolde, 126
Trividic, Anne-Louise, 202, 204
Troell, Jan, 357-358
Trois Soirées, 202, 204, 206
Truffaut, François, 68, 252, 257, 285, 335-336, 410
Tsai, Ming-liang, 248-250
Turgenev, Ivan, 406
Turner, Kathleen, 218
Turner, Ted, 113
Turtles Can Fly, 150-156, 335, 388
Twilight of the Gods, 133

Ulysses, 99, 275
Under the Volcano, 109, 111
Unforgiven, 185-186
Unholy Desire, 260
Updike, John, 178

Vacchi, Fabio, 207
Vampire, 313
Van Cleef, Lee, 187
Van Dyke, Woody, 13
Van Gogh, Vincent, 64
Van Zant, Gus, 161-162
Vengeance Is Mine, x, 257-269, 397
Venice Film Festival, 406
The Verdict, 29
Vermeer, Johannes, 181
La Vie est à nous, 287-288
Vignatti, Diego Martínez, 177
Vigo, Jean, 243, 285
Virgin Stripped Bare by Her Bachelors, 163
Visconti, Luigi, 241, 410
Vitti, Monica, 276-277, 279-281
Vivre sa vie, 276
Vonnegut, Kurt, 364-366
Le Voyeur, 271
Vredens Dag: see *Day of Wrath*

Wag the Dog, 38
Wagner, Richard, 121, 123-128, 131, 133-134
Waiting for Godot, 200
Wajda, Andrzej, 159
Wakeford, Kent, 351
Walton, William, 43
Wanda, xiii
The War Within, 178
Warshow, Robert, 157, 183, 325
Washbourne, Mona, 306
Waterhole No. 3, 185
Waterhouse, Keith, 300-301, 303, 306

Way Down East, xi, 3-15, 381
Wayne, John, 339
Weber, Anton, 82
The Wedding Banquet, 192, 196
Welles, Orson, 44, 68, 346-347, 369, 410
The Well-Tempered Clavier, 131
Wenders, Wim, 247
Wesker, Arnold, 49
West Beirut, 150, 214, 217-218, 220, 239
Westbrook, John, 57
Westerns, ix, 121, 183-196, 355, 358
What's Up, Doc?, 346
What Time Is It There?, 248
Where Is the Friend's House?, 151
The White Balloon, 151, 239
Who's Afraid of Virginia Woolf?, 18, 345-346
Who's That Knocking at My Door?, 350
Widerberg, Bo, 340-343
Wiers-Jenssen, Hans, 324
The Wild Bunch, xiii, 184, 186
The Wild Child, 335-336
Wilde, Oscar, x
Wilder, Billy, 272
Will Penny, 184
Williams, Luisa, 179, 181
The Wind Will Carry Us, 150
Winstone, Ray, 190
Winterbottom, Michael, 169
Wise Blood, 109

Wolfe, Thomas, 371
Woman Is the Future of Man, 161-168, 182, 389
Wood, Robin, 288
The Word, 313
World Trade Center, 178
Woyzeck, 30, 33
Wozzeck, 201
Wyler, William, 19-24
Wynne, Michael, 220, 224

Yaaba, 235
Yamada, Yoji, 263
Yanks, 299
Yeats, W. B., 39
Yektapanah, Hassan, 244-246
Yojimbo, 186
Yong-jin, Jeong, 167
Yoo, Jitae, 168
Yoshida, Yoshishige, 257-258
You Can't Go Home Again, 371
Young, Vernon, 82

Zambarloukos, Harris, 212
Zampa, Luigi, 244
Zavattini, Cesare, 141
Zeffirelli, Franco, 17
Zegen, 262, 265
Zemlyanko, Dima, 143
Zero for Conduct, 243
Zola, Emile, 275, 299
Zsigmond, Vilmos, 358, 360

DATE DUE

Demco, Inc. 38-293